Software Test Design

Write comprehensive test plans to uncover critical bugs in web, desktop, and mobile apps

Simon Amey

BIRMINGHAM—MUMBAI

Software Test Design

Group Product Manager: Gebin George
Publishing Product Manager: Kunal Sawant
Content Development Editor: Rosal Colaco
Technical Editor: Pradeep Sahu
Copy Editor: Safis Editing
Project Manager: Prajakta Naik
Project Coordinator: Manisha Singh
Proofreader: Safis Editing
Indexer: Manju Arasan
Production Designer: Ponraj Dhandapani
Business Development Executive: Kriti Sharma
Marketing Coordinator: Sonakshi Bubbar

First published: November 2022

Production reference:1111122

Published by Packt Publishing Ltd.
Livery Place
35 Livery Street
Birmingham
B3 2PB, UK.

ISBN 978-1-80461-256-9

www.packt.com

To my wife, Daniela. You are my rock and my inspiration; thank you for so much support for so long. And to my kids, Dominic and Hannah, who fill our lives with joy. I love you all!

– Simon Amey

Contributors

About the author

Simon Amey has worked in the high-tech industry for over 20 years, in roles as diverse as software engineer, product manager, project manager, support engineer, and operations manager. However, most of his time has been spent breaking other people's code as a tester and test manager.

He has worked in organizations as small as 30 people and as large as some of the biggest tech companies in the world; he has seen companies go out of business and worked at those successfully acquired for their technology. All that experience has given him a deep insight into the development process. In particular, he knows the problems caused by inadequate testing and how to solve them.

I want to thank the people who have been close to me and supported me, especially my wife, Daniela, and my parents.

A huge thanks to all the amazing engineers I have worked with over the years. It's been a pleasure building great products and learning together with you.

About the reviewer

Craig Risi is a software architect who has spent the past 18 years focusing on software testing, automation, and providing software quality for several global organizations. He possesses a passion for software design and, more importantly, software quality and designing systems that can achieve this in a technically diverse and constantly evolving tech world.

Craig is also the writer of the book *Quality by Design* and writes regular articles on his blog sites and various other tech sites around the world.

When not playing with software, he can often be found speaking at conferences, writing, designing board games, or running long distances for no apparent reason.

Table of Contents

3

How to Run Successful Specification Reviews   63

4

Test Types, Cases, and Environments   77

Part 2 – Functional Testing

5

Black-Box Functional Testing   103

6

White-Box Functional Testing
145

7

Testing of Error Cases
181

8

User Experience Testing — 207

9

Security Testing   249

10

Maintainability   275

Part 3 – Non-Functional Testing

11

Destructive Testing   307

12

Load Testing   325

13

Stress Testing   355

Conclusion   375

Appendix – Example Feature Specification   379

Index   387

Other Books You May Enjoy   400

Preface

This book will show you how to comprehensively test new software features, whether implemented on web pages, a desktop, or mobile applications. It covers everything from generating in-depth specifications to detailed black- and white-box testing, handling error cases and user experience considerations, to areas sometimes missed off test plans such as maintainability and operating under failure conditions.

The same bugs and defects crop up repeatedly in software development, so this book has a huge range of tests to run and scenarios to check to help you achieve great test coverage. They're illustrated by dozens of example issues I've encountered during my decades in the software industry. While it's never possible to guarantee a product is bug-free, the recommendations here give you the best chance of catching defects.

Who this book is for

Many different people can perform testing during a development cycle. In addition to dedicated testers, developers should always try their code, and product owners, support engineers, and technical writers can also provide more or less formal feedback.

This book is for anyone involved in software testing, regardless of their official job title. Everyone can use the suggestions here to increase test coverage and improve the quality of the features you release.

Testing has a lovely learning curve. You can start with manual testing on easy-to-use public interfaces that have been well polished and documented. From there, you can go deeper into the system, checking logs and metrics and using internal interfaces. Testers with the right skill set can improve code directly by performing code reviews and writing unit tests. This book describes all these approaches to improve your testing, whether you're a novice or an expert tester.

Is this book for Agile or waterfall projects? Both!

This book does not discuss different development models such as **Agile** or **waterfall**. Whichever you are using, you will need to design a comprehensive test plan to exercise new features and discover their defects.

However, there will be significant timing differences depending on the method you're using. Waterfall projects may extend over many months, with weeks allocated to the different areas of testing described here. In contrast, Agile projects rapidly cycle through the different types of testing, doing a little of each in cycle after cycle.

Despite their differences, both project types, and the many real-world hybrids used in practice, require a thorough test plan covering the many different aspects of system behavior. Whatever project type you work on, this book can help you write better test plans.

Is this book for manual or automated testing? Both!

This book has many proposals for *what* you should test. It does not cover *how* those tests should be run. The aim, after applying this book to your feature, is to produce a comprehensive test plan with steps to detect many defect types.

How you run that test plan is up to you. Some areas must be done manually – **exploratory testing**, for instance, involves a tester getting their hands on a feature to investigate how it behaves in an unstructured way. Only once you have learned how it works can you write the feature specification and do systematic testing, either manual or automated. **User experience testing** is also best started with a genuine user present. Conversely, **load testing** requires automation to reach the required load levels and cannot be done by hand.

In between much of the functional testing, security, error cases, and even some user experience testing can be automated. Where possible, that is a vital stage in the testing process to free up testers' time for future test designs. That is especially true when following a **Continuous Integration/Continuous Deployment** (**CI/CD**) pipeline, in which changes are pushed to live systems within minutes. There, you must automate tests and carefully choose which to run on each change.

This book does not discuss how to perform manual testing, automate tests, or what tools you should use. Those are subjects for other books in the Packt catalog. Here, we will describe what tests you should run and how you should design your test plan.

Types of testing

There are several levels of testing, but this book focuses on just one – **system testing**. This is the hardest part of testing because it covers the whole system working together, end to end. Because it is so difficult, it requires the thought and planning described here. That does not mean it is the only kind of testing. You should supplement all the system testing here with testing at other levels since they each have different strengths.

At the lowest level is **unit testing**, also known as **component testing**, where scripts exercise individual functions or modules. This form of testing is often performed by developers, as they know what to expect from their code and are best placed to write test harnesses to drive it. Unit tests can thoroughly test individual actions, but they can't find issues that arise when functions are used together.

To find those issues, you need **integration testing**. This approach involves running entire modules isolated from the rest of the system, such as user interfaces or databases. At this stage, the testing becomes much more complex. Because far more can go wrong, it allows you to find another class of issues. While both *function A* and *function B* may work well on their own, incorrect assumptions or implementations might mean they do not work together. Integration testing finds that class of bugs. It can be carried out by either developers or dedicated testers, although it requires a significant amount of automation and is unsuitable for manual testing. Using modules or clients independently of the rest of the system needs test harnesses to stand in for areas that are not being run.

Beyond integration testing is **system testing**, the focus of this book. Once the whole system is working together, with all modules integrated with the others, then the final class of bugs is revealed. These issues only occur when running the full system in a realistic environment, such as loading and problems between modules. On the plus side, system testing can find all the realistic bugs that will affect users. On the downside, it is difficult to translate from system behavior down to the individual functions that are failing, and systems can be complex to test fully. This book aims to give techniques and ideas to successfully navigate that challenge.

The naming convention used here follows the **International Software Testing Qualification Board** (**ISTQB**) syllabus, which refers to component, integration, and system testing. There is some overlap with the topics covered there, although this book takes a far more hands-on, practical approach rather than focusing on the theory. By selecting the most useful pieces of the ISTQB syllabus, and expanding their practical aspects, this book will show you how to thoroughly test software features.

Test process

There are many important topics that this book can't address. This book is only about writing excellent test plans to find a wide variety of issues in your application. It does not cover test teams or anything associated with test processes.

Test prioritization is not covered in detail here. The aim is to give you a large bank of ideas and test scenarios, from which you can decide their relative priority for your application. Judging risk and the likelihood and impact of issues will depend on your circumstances. It's up to you to apply these ideas.

This book also doesn't cover team organization. How many testers do you need in your company? How should they be arranged to work with the product owner and developers? How much time should they devote to the different forms of testing? It also doesn't cover managing communication, such as how bugs should be raised and their life cycle, but it will tell you how to find those bugs.

Finally, this book doesn't describe the release process, including how test results should be evaluated, internal usage and beta programs, and how to sign off and perform releases. Again, that depends on your product and industry. Even if you don't decide to run all the tests here, you can deliberately choose which ones you exclude so that you have the best possible idea of the risks you are taking.

The aim, by the end of this book, is that you should be able to quickly prepare a comprehensive test plan, rapidly covering many different areas of testing relevant to your product and its features. Often in software development, the factor limiting your speed is identifying what you should do, so by understanding the main types of testing and common failures, you can develop tests faster.

That lets you find more issues earlier in the development cycle, save time, speed up projects, and give your customers a better user experience.

With that said, we can now see the areas this book covers in detail.

What this book covers

Part 1, Preparing to Test, covers the necessary steps before you can start writing the test plan.

Chapter 1, Making the Most of Exploratory Testing, describes how best to perform exploratory testing and when you should do it. The main goal of exploratory testing is not to find bugs but to understand a feature better in order to improve the feature specification and test plans. It also finds any blocking issues that may delay future testing.

Chapter 2, Writing Great Feature Specifications, shows how to write comprehensive and useful feature specifications. This document will be the basis for all subsequent testing, so it needs to cover all the questions that could arise. That requires input from multiple groups, so this document always needs a thorough review.

That specification review is covered in *Chapter 3, How to Run Successful Specification Reviews,* in which you check the specification with the developers and product owners. The developers should highlight any special cases or conditions they had to add code for, while the product owner makes decisions that could affect the user experience and the scope of the changes. Successfully running that review to get what testers need from it is your responsibility.

Armed with the specification and the experience of exploratory testing, you can start designing the test plan. *Part 2, Functional Testing,* of this book explains the many different types of functional testing, in which your product responds to different inputs.

Chapter 4, Test Types, Cases, and Environments, examines how best to write test cases and where you should run them. It shows how unit, integration, and system tests can work together and where they fit in the release cycle.

Chapter 5, Black-Box Functional Testing, is the most familiar area of testing, and the first one people think of. When you use the feature, does it work correctly and achieve its stated goals? Even within this type of testing, there are many ideas and suggestions for how to find common weaknesses and issues.

Chapter 6, White-Box Functional Testing, is informed by a knowledge of the underlying code and its architecture. Understanding how the code works lets you add another important set of tests.

Chapter 7, Testing of Error Cases, is devoted to invalid inputs or situations and how the application handles them. This is a large area of testing because the number of invalid inputs often massively outweighs the possible valid inputs. In addition, error cases are more likely to have defects because less time is spent thinking through their consequences than happy path scenarios.

Chapter 8, User Experience Testing, covers the unique set of considerations to ensure your application is easy to use. This is far more subjective than other areas of testing and may require judgments on, for instance, which command name is clearest, or which function will be used most and should be accessed most easily. It's vital to get those questions right to give your users the best experience.

Chapter 9, Security Testing, lists common security vulnerabilities that should routinely be checked by your test plans, as well as different attacks you can craft to ensure the appropriate protections are in place.

Chapter 10, Maintainability, considers your application's logging, event generation, and monitoring. If there is an issue, how easy will it be to diagnose and fix? This can be of lower importance to businesses, since it is not directly customer-facing, but is of high importance to the test team and other internal users who spend large amounts of time chasing down issues.

Those chapters conclude the functional areas of testing, where you perform a certain action and check a certain outcome. If the application under test has passed all these tests, then it will work for users under normal circumstances. *Part 3, Non-Functional Testing*, considers abnormal circumstances such as high load and system failures.

Chapter 11, Destructive Testsing, considers scenarios in which different parts of the system are deliberately disabled or degraded to ensure that the rest of the system behaves gracefully and can recover from issues.

Chapter 12, Load Testing, checks the behavior when your application runs at its maximum performance. While it may be able to perform individual actions correctly, is it reliable when they're repeated many times? These tests also check that your application continues to perform well, even when some subsystems are placed under load.

Finally, *Chapter 13, Stress Testing*, describes tests that deliberately load the system beyond its capabilities – for example, if too many entities are configured or if the system is taken beyond its loading limits. As with destructive testing, the correct behavior is to fail gracefully and recover once the stress condition is lifted.

The *Appendix* contains an example test plan that puts these ideas into practice for an example feature – users signing up to a web page.

Applying this guide gives you the best chance of finding defects in your software. However, despite all the suggestions here, in my experience, you find the most interesting bugs when you go off the test plan. Trying out ideas for yourself or following up on something odd that you spot is a great way to think up test cases no one else has considered. Observation and curiosity are vital throughout testing, so always keep your eyes open.

The suggestions here aren't a recipe to be followed but instead a guide from which you can create your own test plans. Testing is like fishing. You can't guarantee what you'll find, and there'll be plenty of smaller catches among the big issues that you're really seeking. However, by looking in the most promising places and using the best techniques, you give yourself the greatest chance of success. Happy bug hunting!

Download the color images

We also provide a PDF file that has color images of the screenshots and diagrams used in this book. You can download it here: https://packt.link/W0Uic.

Conventions used

There are a number of text conventions used throughout this book.

`Code in text`: Indicates code words in text, database table names, folder names, filenames, file extensions, pathnames, dummy URLs, user input, and Twitter handles. Here is an example: "For instance, to test whether a textbox can handle inputs including spaces, we may use the string `one two`."

A block of code is set as follows:

```
create_user(permission)
{
    user = create_user()
    if(permission == ADMIN)
    {
        make_admin(user)
    }
    return user
}
```

Bold: Indicates a new term, an important word, or words that you see onscreen. For instance, words in menus or dialog boxes appear in **bold**. Here is an example: "That limit should be apparent before users try to use it – the **Add user** button should be grayed out with a note saying why, for instance, instead of letting users click the button."

> **Tip or Important note**
> Appear like this.

Get in touch

Feedback from our readers is always welcome.

General feedback: If you have questions about any aspect of this book, email us at `customercare@packtpub.com` and mention the book title in the subject of your message.

Errata: Although we have taken every care to ensure the accuracy of our content, mistakes do happen. If you have found a mistake in this book, we would be grateful if you would report this to us. Please visit `www.packtpub.com/support/errata` and fill in the form.

Any errata related to this book can be found at `https://github.com/PacktPublishing/Software-Test-Design`.

Piracy: If you come across any illegal copies of our works in any form on the internet, we would be grateful if you would provide us with the location address or website name. Please contact us at `copyright@packt.com` with a link to the material.

If you are interested in becoming an author: If there is a topic that you have expertise in and you are interested in either writing or contributing to a book, please visit `authors.packtpub.com`.

Share Your Thoughts

Once you've read *Software Test Design*, we'd love to hear your thoughts! Scan the QR code below to go straight to the Amazon review page for this book and share your feedback.

`https://packt.link/r/1-804-61256-1`

Your review is important to us and the tech community and will help us make sure we're delivering excellent quality content.

Download a free PDF copy of this book

Thanks for purchasing this book!

Do you like to read on the go but are unable to carry your print books everywhere?

Is your eBook purchase not compatible with the device of your choice?

Don't worry, now with every Packt book you get a DRM-free PDF version of that book at no cost.

Read anywhere, any place, on any device. Search, copy, and paste code from your favorite technical books directly into your application.

The perks don't stop there, you can get exclusive access to discounts, newsletters, and great free content in your inbox daily

Follow these simple steps to get the benefits:

1. Scan the QR code or visit the link below

https://packt.link/free-ebook/9781804612569

2. Submit your proof of purchase

3. That's it! We'll send your free PDF and other benefits to your email directly

Part 1 – Preparing to Test

Before we begin testing, we need a detailed description of the desired behavior. This information comes from three main sources: exploratory testing to examine the currently implemented functionality; written specification documents, which generally need to be improved by the test team; and formal, detailed discussions with the product owner and development team. This part examines each of those sources of information and looks at different types of tests and how to use them to the best effect. Together those details fully prepare you to begin testing.

This part comprises the following chapters:

- *Chapter 1, Making the Most of Exploratory Testing*
- *Chapter 2, Writing Great Feature Specifications*
- *Chapter 3, How to Run Successful Specification Reviews*
- *Chapter 4, Test Types, Cases, and Environments*

1
Making the Most of Exploratory Testing

"Begin at the beginning," the King said, very gravely, "and go on till you come to the end: then stop."

- Lewis Carroll, Alice in Wonderland

This chapter introduces **exploratory testing**: manually trying out a new feature to get rapid feedback on its behavior. We'll describe exploratory testing in detail, consider its strengths and weaknesses, and when you should perform it in a project.

We'll look at the prerequisites you need to begin exploratory testing and the approaches you should take. This testing can be a miniature version of the complete test plan, taking a customer's point of view, and using your naivety about how the feature works to identify confusing areas.

Exploratory testing should be used as part of a larger test strategy but can be run in isolation when time is short. We'll finish by looking at what you should check when performing this testing, and the importance of curiosity, both here and throughout the testing process.

In this chapter, we will cover the following topics:

- What is exploratory testing?
- Advantages, disadvantages, and alternatives
- Understanding when testing should begin
- Understanding the test activities
- The spiral model of test improvement
- Performing the first test
- Mapping out new features

- Using your naivety while testing
- Running complete exploratory testing
- Using exploratory testing by necessity
- Checking exploratory test results
- Using curiosity in testing

What is exploratory testing?

Exploratory testing is a vital tool in your armory. It involves you using a new feature in an ad hoc, unstructured way to quickly find issues and understand its workings. It is typically used early in the test cycle to achieve three main goals: to let you understand the feature you are testing, to discover any tools or knowledge you need, and to find blocking bugs that may delay the testing later on.

In exploratory testing, the test design, implementation, and interpretation are conducted simultaneously. This is also known as **ad hoc testing**, which has been frowned upon due to its unstructured format. However, it is a valuable stage in a project if deployed alongside other testing techniques. In a large project, it can be used early on to help plan more comprehensive tests, or if deadlines are tight, exploratory testing might be the only testing there's time for.

In an ideal cycle, the team will plan both the feature and its testing at the start of development. In that case, exploratory testing enhances the test plans that already exist. In other development teams, testers are involved later in the project and may only plan the testing in earnest once the first version is already running. In both cases, exploratory testing is a necessary step for you to see a new feature working in practice so that you can write detailed test plans with the exact behavior in mind.

Exploratory testing must be performed manually so that you can get your hands on the new feature and see what inputs and outputs are available. Other parts of testing can be run manually or with automation, but exploratory testing must be manual because the main aim isn't to find bugs but to understand the feature. Based on that understanding, you can plan further testing.

Not everyone can perform exploratory testing. In particular, it needs input from someone other than the developer who worked on the code. The developer should ensure the feature is working for them, but exploratory testing shows whether it can work in another environment for another engineer. That is the second goal of exploratory testing: to find issues significant enough to block further tests.

If the new feature doesn't run in the test environment, if a page throws an error, or parts of the functionality aren't available, that will block testing of those whole areas. Exploratory testing can quickly find those issues so that they can be fixed early in the development cycle and not cause delays later on.

First, we'll consider the advantages and disadvantages of exploratory testing, along with alternative approaches that perform similar roles.

Advantages, disadvantages, and alternatives

Exploratory testing has distinct strengths and weaknesses. It is an important part of the testing cycle, but only if combined with other forms of testing to mitigate its shortcomings. Throughout this book, we'll see how the advantages of different forms of testing complement each other and why you need a mixture of different approaches to get great coverage of a feature. Here are a few of the advantages and disadvantages of exploratory testing:

Advantages	Disadvantages
Quick to perform	Difficult to reproduce issues
Easy to see bugs	Should only be carried out by experienced testers
No prerequisites other than the code itself	Difficult to measure coverage
	Tests will be repeated later
	Poor coverage of non-functional tests

Table 1.1 – Advantages and disadvantages of exploratory testing

Exploratory testing is quick and easy. So long as you have the running code, you don't need any other prerequisites, such as documentation or testing tools. That said, there should be user stories or other guidance material that you can work from to enable the feature and improve the effectiveness of your testing. Finding bugs is simple because you are watching the product as you use it; you don't need to check a monitoring console or automated test output for errors. You can see what the system was doing at the time because you were using it yourself.

On the downside, it can be difficult to reproduce issues. Unlike an automated test that precisely performs a documented set of actions, if you were just *clicking around* when something strange happened, it may not be obvious what you did to trigger the problem. I once found a bug because I rearranged the windows on my screen partway through testing – changing the size of the browser window caused the issue. It took me some time to realize that had caused the problem, instead of all the actions I had taken in the application itself.

To make it easier to find the cause of bugs, you can record your session, either simply on video, within the application, or in the web browser that you are using for your tests. That takes a little time to set up and review but can be very helpful when trying to reproduce issues.

While exploratory testing doesn't need many prerequisites, it helps to have a description of the feature so that you know any areas of functionality that aren't obvious from its interface.

Another requirement is that it should be carried out by an experienced tester. Because exploratory testing is not reviewed or planned, its success depends on the skill of the individual carrying it out. A tester with experience will know the areas that are likely to cause bugs and can try tests that have failed in the past. They will also know what to check to find issues. A junior tester will not reach the same level of coverage.

The skills involved in exploratory testing – the curiosity and alertness it requires – are required throughout the test process, even when running more formalized test plans. Whether or not you are officially performing exploratory testing, you should always approach manual tests with this same mindset.

The coverage provided by exploratory tests is also difficult to measure. How much of a feature have you tested with exploratory testing? In practice, you will need to perform all these tests again as part of a more rigorous test plan, so you will repeat anything you do during exploratory testing. For this reason, you should limit how long you spend on these tests. They provide valuable feedback, but only so long as you are learning from it. Comprehensive testing starts later in the process.

To measure what coverage you have achieved, you can have a debrief to talk through the testing you've done with the product owner and developer. They can also suggest other cases to try. See *Chapter 3, How to Run Successful Specification Reviews*, to learn more about reviewing the specification and the scenarios that should be tested.

The final weakness of exploratory testing is that it does not cover non-functional tests. Here, you are just checking whether the feature works at all, not that it can achieve high loads, work in many environments, or recover from failure conditions. All those tests will come later but are not a priority at this stage.

The alternatives to exploratory testing include detailed specifications and preparing user stories and UI mockups, although, in practice, exploratory testing complements all those tasks. A sufficiently detailed specification should give enough detail that you can write the test plan from it directly. However, in practice, it is much easier to finish the details of the specification when you can use the code for exploratory testing. The same is true of user stories. They are very useful for defining and refining the core functionality but don't usually cover error cases. Those can also be easier to find in real usage. User interface mockups are also massively helpful to define how a feature will look and its options, but it is still valuable to try those for real when they are available.

It may seem strange to begin the discussion of testing with exploratory testing, which can only begin once an initial version of the feature is complete. The following section describes the place of exploratory testing in the development life cycle and shows that while it might not be the first testing task that you start, it is the first you can finish.

Understanding when testing should begin

There is no clear line between development and testing, even when testing is a dedicated role within a company. It might seem obvious that first, you design your intended product, then you build it, and then you test it, as shown in the following diagram:

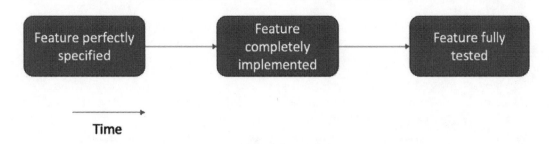

Figure 1.1 – An idealized waterfall model

This is known as the **waterfall model** of development. It has the advantage of having a clear point where testing should begin – that is, when the development team hands over the code. However, while such strict and simple handovers might work for bridges and houses, software development has more complexity – it has to handle many different inputs, and has the opportunity to be far more flexible.

In **Agile** approaches to software development, development cycles have multiple interacting feedback loops that contribute to the final product. As a tester, you begin your work at some point within those cycles. While testing could wait until the developers are perfectly happy with their product, in practice, this adds too much delay. Getting testers involved early in a project has many advantages:

- Helps the testers understand the feature
- Gives testers time to prepare tools or datasets that they need
- Lets testers provide feedback on the design process
- Lets testers begin testing earlier (than usual), even if only in a limited way

This is a part of **shift-left** testing to involve testers early in projects, which is a worthy goal but is challenging as there is no clear place to start. There is no day when a task is complete and testing should begin. Instead, testers need to gradually start testing based on the available specifications and code.

Another challenge for early testing is to integrate with other methods of verification. The developers will (hopefully) perform manual checks on their code and write unit tests for individual functions. This will already produce bugs and suggestions that feed back into the code implementation and the feature specification, as shown in the following diagram:

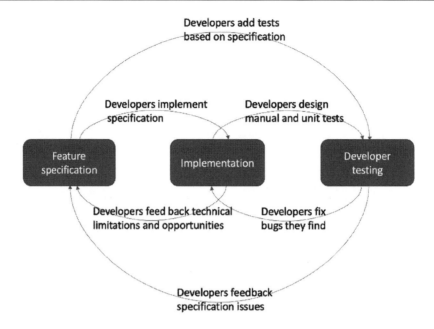

Figure 1.2 – Interactions and feedback in an Agile development model

In an Agile model, the specification still guides the implementation and suggests tests for developers and testers to run. But now, there can be far more feedback – the specification can change based on technical limitations and possibilities, then the developers will fix their bugs, and some developer tests may uncover changes needed in the specification.

While the waterfall model had a specific flow in time – in *Figure 1.1*, from left to right – in an Agile model, there is a constant back and forth between the different tasks. They are performed almost simultaneously. The specification is still a necessary first step to state what the developer should implement, but after that, the phases largely overlap. In **test-driven development** (**TDD**), for example, the testing will come before the implementation.

Notice that system testing performed by a separate test function isn't included in this diagram yet. The only testing described there is performed by the developers themselves, which is an important ingredient in the testing mix. The system testing described in this book extends and completes the testing started by the developers.

Crucially, in an Agile project, this flow won't happen to an entire feature in one go. Instead, the feature is broken down into multiple parts, each of which might be developed in parallel by different team members:

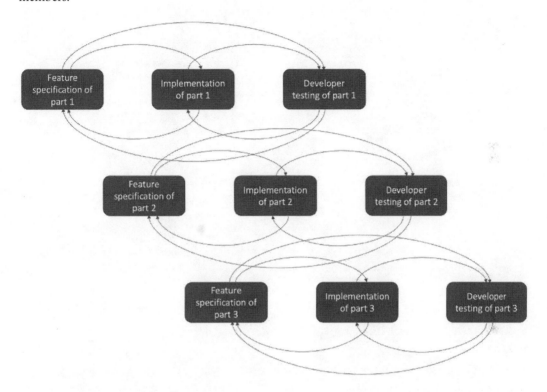

Figure 1.3 – Different parts of a feature developed in parallel within an Agile model

Instead of a feature being fully specified and fully implemented, as shown in the waterfall model in *Figure 1.1*, Agile recommends splitting tasks into the smallest possible functional units so that work can proceed on each unit in parallel. In this model, all those interactions happen simultaneously for different parts of the project as they are implemented and developers start their testing. This parallel working, with the opportunity for feedback at multiple levels, give Agile projects great flexibility.

The situation becomes even more complicated than this, of course, since the lessons you learn while implementing **part 2** of a feature can feed back into **part 1**, whether from its specification, implementation, or initial testing, as shown in the following diagram:

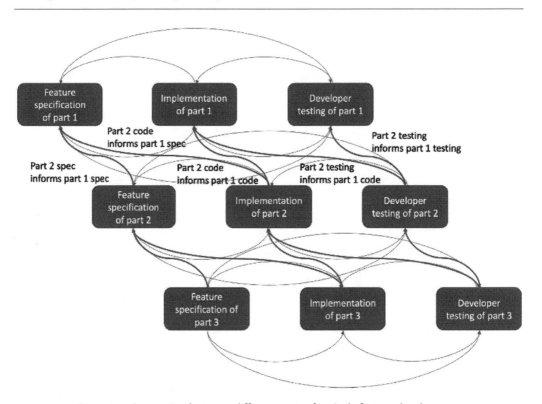

Figure 1.4 – Interaction between different parts of an Agile feature development

While writing the specification for **part 2**, you may identify changes you need in the specification for **part 1**. Likewise, the implementation or developer testing of **part 2** might need a specification change. The implementation and developer testing of **part 1** might also benefit from insights learned while implementing **part 2** so that there is constant feedback between those development tasks.

There are several lines of interaction not drawn in *Figure 1.4*. The developer testing also feeds back into the specification, and the work in **part 3** of the feature feeds back into the tasks in **part 1**, and so on. I left those lines off the preceding diagram for sanity's sake.

Where, in that mess of interactions, should system testing start? Where should it fit into this development flow overall? At any time, any part of the feature will be partially specified, partially implemented, and partially covered by development tests.

Unlike the waterfall model, there is no clear starting point where system tests should begin. However, there is a place where system tests can fit into this development cycle, which we can see if we simplify the diagram by considering a single feature. System testing should build from the developer testing while being guided and providing feedback to all previous stages, as shown in the following diagram:

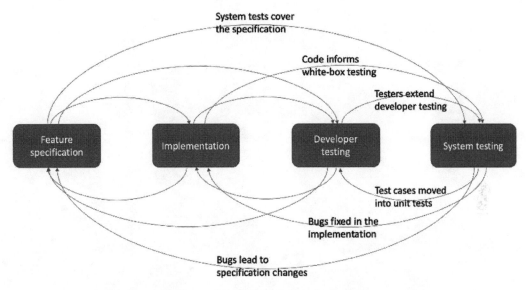

Figure 1.5 – System testing as part of an Agile development model

Considering a single feature, the system test design can begin as soon as the specification has been started. Once there are requirements, you can develop the tests to check them. Once the implementation has begun, you can design tests using white-box techniques (see *Chapter 6, White-Box Functional Testing*) to ensure you have checked every code path. And the system tests should extend and complement the testing the developers perform.

The system testing should also provide feedback on the other tasks in the development cycle. Most obviously, bugs found in system testing need to be fixed in the implementation. Some bugs will lead to specification changes, especially clarifications or descriptions of complex situations that weren't initially described. System tests also interact with the developer testing. They should avoid overlap but cover the gaps in unit tests, and some tests identified at the system test level might be best implemented as unit tests and should be moved there.

Remember, the preceding diagram doesn't show the tasks in a timely order. Just because system testing appears on the right doesn't mean it is performed last. Like the implementation and developer testing, it can start as soon as the first parts of the feature specification are ready. You can design tests against those specifications before any work by the developers starts and you can provide feedback on that specification.

Finally, we can put all this together, showing the interactions as multiple parts of a feature are developed and tested simultaneously:

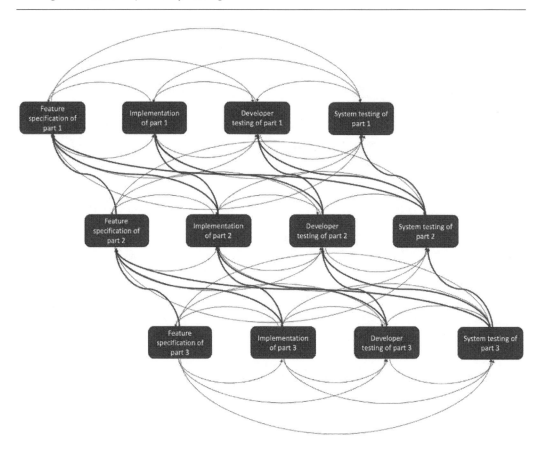

Figure 1.6 – Interaction between different parts of a feature under development, including system testing

As the preceding diagram shows, there is a lot to manage, even at this high level of detail. This book will show how to write great feature specifications (see *Chapter 2, Writing Great Feature Specifications*, and *Chapter 3, How to Run Successful Specification Reviews*) and how to build on the developer's implementation and testing (*Chapter 6, White-Box Functional Testing*). In addition, you need to consider the details of the system tests themselves, which will be covered in the remainder of this book.

Next, we'll consider the main tasks involved in system testing and where to begin.

Understanding the test activities

When performing system testing, there are four main activities. Each of them interacts and feeds into all the others, as shown in the following diagram:

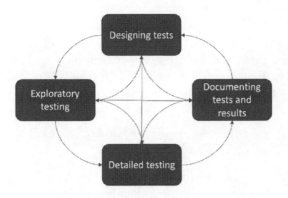

Figure 1.7 – The main test activities and their interactions

Test design includes all the information gathering and preparation activities performed before you begin testing, excluding exploratory testing, which is significant enough to have its own category. Test design means reviewing all the available information for this feature to plan your testing. The written materials you base your testing on are collectively known as the **test basis** and may include documents such as the following:

- User stories
- Specifications
- User interface designs
- Technical design documents
- Competitive research

These documents help show the new behavior, although you will need to add extra details yourself. This will be described further in *Chapter 2, Writing Great Feature Specifications*. Even the written information is insufficient and needs to be augmented with practical experience of the feature, which comes from exploratory testing.

Exploratory testing is an oddity. Technically, it is part of the test design since its main focus is gathering information to inform future testing. However, it occurs relatively late in the process, when there is code ready to be tested, and unlike the rest of the test design, it involves testing and potentially finding bugs. Because of this dual role, it gets its own category.

With the information from the test basis and exploratory testing, you can document the feature specification and the test plan based on it. This should exhaustively describe a feature's behavior, covering all possible eventualities.

> **Important note**
> The detailed testing then methodically runs the entire test plan. That may involve manual testing or writing and running automated tests. This book does not describe *how* to run your tests; other titles in the Packt library have excellent descriptions of those possibilities. This book focuses on the test design to show *what* tests you should run.

The final step is further documentation, this time of your test results. This includes all the bugs you need to raise and describing the tests that have passed.

These are the main activities a tester performs. There are other important jobs around planning, including allocating personnel and resources, estimating timescales, and scheduling work. Those are not shown in the preceding diagram and are out of scope for this book because they primarily require skills in project management. They must also be in place to run a successful test project, but here, I am concentrating on the details of what testing is required so that you can plan these activities as accurately as possible.

Each of those four test activities feeds back into the others. Designing tests is necessary before they can be documented and run, but the test results also show where more tests are needed. Some test planning is essential for exploratory testing, but exploratory testing also shows which tests need to be designed and executed for complete coverage. Documenting the feature specification should start before exploratory testing so that you know what changes to expect. However, it can only be finished once exploratory testing is complete, to answer any questions that arise.

Where in those interrelated activities should we begin? As you can see from the title of this chapter, I believe exploratory testing is a good place to start. There will be specifications and planning before that, but exploratory testing is the first test task you can finish. With that in place, you can aim to complete the specification, the test plan design, and the detailed testing itself. Because of that unique attribute, we will start with it here.

For each part of the feature, testing should move between those different test activities and feed back to the other design tasks of writing specifications, implementing, and developer testing described previously. How do these tasks fit together, and how do they progress toward the goal of releasing a well-specified and tested feature? The following section describes the ordered flow of activities and their progression.

The spiral model of test improvement

Developing tests from the initial specification into detailed, completed test plans can be thought of as a spiral looping through four repeated stages. Of course, it is more complex in practice, and there is extensive back and forth between the different stages. This simplification illustrates the main milestones required to generate a test plan and the main flow between them. It is similar to **Barry Boehm's spiral model** of software development. However, this model only considers the development of the test plan, rather than the entire software development cycle, and doesn't spiral outwards but instead inwards toward test perfection:

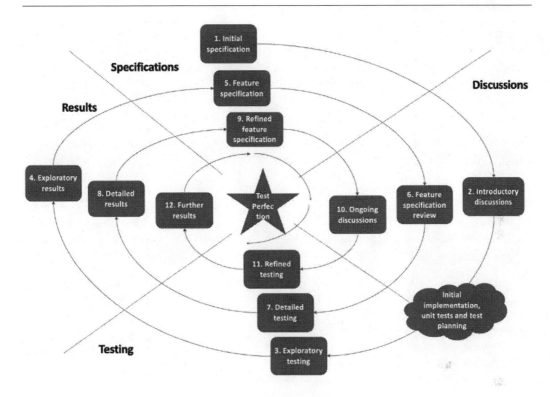

Figure 1.8 – The spiral model of test development

The four stages you go through when iterating a test plan are as follows:

- **Preparing specifications and plans**
- **Discussions and review**
- **Performing testing**
- **Analyzing and feeding back the result**

Software development begins with an initial specification from the product owner, which is a vital start but needs several iterations before it is complete. The product owner then introduces and discusses that feature. Based on that initial specification, the development team can prepare an initial implementation, and you can generate ideas for exploratory testing.

Once an initial implementation is complete, you can start improving the specification, the test plan, and the code itself. This begins with **Exploratory testing**, which is step **3** in the preceding diagram. By trying the code for real, you will understand it better and prepare further tests, as described in this chapter. While there are several essential steps beforehand, the process of improving the code begins with exploratory testing.

Armed with the exploratory test results in step **4**, you can then write a feature specification, as shown in step **5** in the preceding diagram. This will be covered in more detail in *Chapter 2, Writing Great Feature Specifications*. This specification then needs a review – a formal discussion to step through its details to improve them. That review is step **6** and is described in *Chapter 3, How to Run Successful Specification Reviews*.

When that review is complete, you can perform detailed testing of the feature. That one small box – step **7** in the preceding diagram – is the subject of most of this book and is covered in *Chapter 4* to *Chapter 13*.

Preparing the test plan isn't the end, however. Based on the detailed testing results, you can refine the specification, discuss it, and perform further targeted testing. That may be to verify the bugs you raised, for example, or to expand the test plan in areas with clusters of bugs. The results of the testing should inform future test tasks. That feedback improves the testing in this and subsequent cycles, asymptotically trending toward, though never quite reaching, test perfection.

Behind this spiral, the code is also going through cycles of improved documentation and quality as its functions are checked and its bugs are fixed.

The preceding diagram shows how both the theoretical descriptions of the feature from the specification and other parts of the test basis must be combined with practical results from testing the code itself to give comprehensive test coverage. Relying only on the documentation means you miss out on the chance to react to issues with the code. Testing without documentation relies on your assumptions of what the code should do instead of its intended behavior.

By looping through this cycle, you can thoroughly get to know the features you are working on and test them to a high quality. While it is just a point on a cycle, we begin that process with a description of exploratory testing, starting with the first important question: is this feature ready to test yet?

Identifying if a feature is ready for testing

It is very easy to waste time testing a feature that is not ready. There is no point in raising a bug when the developers already know they haven't implemented that function yet. On the other hand, testing should start as early as possible to quickly flag up issues while the code is still fresh in the developers' minds.

The way to reconcile those conflicting aims is through communication. Testing should start as early as possible, but the developers should be clear about what is testable and what is not working yet. If you are working from a detailed, numbered specification (see *Chapter 2, Writing Great Feature Specifications*), then they can specify which build fulfills which requirements. It may be that even the developers don't know if a particular function is working yet – for instance, if they believe a new function will *just work* but haven't tried it for themselves. There's no need to spend a lot of time gathering that information, so long as the developers are clear that they are unsure about the behavior so that you can try it out.

Also, look out for testing code that is rapidly changing or is subject to extensive architectural alterations. If the code you test today will be rewritten tomorrow, you have wasted your time. While it's good to start testing as soon as possible, that doesn't mean as soon as there's working code. That code has to be stable and part of the proposed release. Unit tests written by the developer can indicate that code is stable enough to be worth testing; but if that code isn't ready yet, find something else to do with your time.

> **Real-world example – The magical disappearing interface**
>
> I was once part of a test team for a new hardware project that would perform video conferencing. There would be two products – one that would handle the media processing and another that would handle the calls and user interface, with a detailed API between the two. The test team was very organized and started testing early in the development cycle, implementing a suite of tests on the API between the two products.
>
> Then, the architecture changed. For simplicity, the two products would be combined, and we would always sell them together. The API wouldn't be exposed to customers and would be substantially changed to work internally instead. All our testing had been a waste of time.

It sounds obvious that you shouldn't start testing too early. However, in the middle of a project, it can be hard to notice that a product isn't ready – the developers are busy coding, and you are testing and finding serious bugs. But look out for repeated testing in the same area, significant architectural changes, and confusion over which parts of a feature have been implemented and which are still under development. That shows you need better communication with the development team on which areas of code they have finished, and which are genuinely ready for testing.

When the development team has finalized the architecture and completed the initial implementation, then you should start testing. Getting a new feature working for the first time is a challenge, though, so the next section describes how to make that process as smooth as possible.

Performing the first test

A major milestone in a project is being able to test at all. Getting a feature working for the first time means that all the code is in place and working in the test environment. It has been successfully moved from the development system and works elsewhere, be that in a full test environment, a test harness, your local machine, or a containerized environment (see *Chapter 5, Black-Box Functional Testing*, for a discussion of test systems). Getting the feature running opens up a vast array of possible tests.

For instance, if you are testing the signup page of a website, does that page load and accept input? If so, then there are many follow-on test types you can perform. If not, let the developer know that you can't even start yet.

Carrying out that first test requires many development tasks to be completed. Another easy way to waste time is by testing a feature that hasn't been enabled yet. You can also solve this with better communication with the development team.

The specification will say what a feature should do (see *Chapter 2, Writing Great Feature Specifications*), but testers need another level of detail, which is how the feature is configured. Before testing begins, ensure you understand the following:

- What the minimum version requirements for all relevant parts of the system are
- What the necessary configuration is
- How to check that a feature is working

Version requirements are clear enough – you have to be running the version with the new code before you can test. However, sometimes, it is far from obvious which parts of a system are dependent on each other. Or, while the feature is implemented on the *5.3 branch*, is it in *build 5.3.8* or *5.3.9*? A feature may be delivered piecemeal, in which case, exactly which functionality is in each build?

For your very first test, only try the most basic functionality. Does the new screen load, are API calls accepted, or is the new option available? Be clear on which versions you need before spending your time on the first case. Which feature flag do you need to enable for this feature? Which setting needs to be updated, and which file is that in? Again, the challenge is to get all the necessary details from the development team to avoid wasting time looking for them.

If you have all the requirements in place but have found several blocking issues, check with the development team that this feature is ready for testing. The developer should have done enough testing on their system to be confident that it will work for others, but that isn't always the case. If there are repeated problems, get the developer to recheck their code.

Finally, how can you tell if the feature is working? Sometimes, features are obviously customer visible – is the new web page present, or does the new option appear? Sometimes, however, it's hard to tell if the new feature is enabled, especially during code refactoring or subtle performance changes. Which log lines should you look out for? What statistics will indicate this change is being used?

Those details won't be in the feature specification; again, this is an extra level of detail that the test team requires to check on the behavior or even the existence of a feature in a particular build of code.

From a project point of view, getting the first test running is on the critical path. Being able to start testing delays everything else, so make sure you complete that early. Don't spend ages getting everything in place, for instance, finishing six other projects so that a large team of testers is ready to descend on a feature… only to find that it's not working, and you can't test it at all. Check the feature early to make sure the functionality is basically in place, and quickly bounce it back to the developer if they need to make any changes. Once that first test has passed, you can leave it for a while until you can test it properly. But make sure it's ready first.

Once you have the feature happily running, then the real work begins. Where to start with exploratory testing will be described in the next section.

Mapping out new features

To start exploratory testing, you need three things: to be confident that the code is stable enough to test, to be running the required versions, and to have the correct configuration in place. Once they are ready, exploratory testing can begin.

It's important to keep in mind the purpose of exploratory testing. This is not detailed testing with results you will rely on in the future. Everything you do during exploratory testing is likely to be repeated later in a more formal round of testing, so exploratory tests should be limited in time and not take too long. It is easy to waste time duplicating effort between this and later test rounds. You should only test until you have met the three goals of exploratory testing:

1. To learn about the feature to plan further testing.
2. To identify the tools and knowledge you need to perform further testing.
3. To uncover bugs that block further testing.

Firstly, and most importantly, you can learn about the feature to prepare the feature specification. In an ideal world, you would prepare the feature specification in advance, and the implementation would match it exactly. However, during development, there are often changes; for instance, some functions might be postponed for later releases. Sometimes, later discussions and changes don't make it to the specification, especially about the user interface. Product specifications often don't detail error cases, security, and loading behavior. Exploratory testing is your chance to see what changes were completed and which weren't in this release, which parts of the feature were dropped, and any that were added.

Good exploratory testing will check every screen, read every field, enter details in every input, and press every button at least once. Don't aim to cover all possible input values or perform exhaustive testing on the functionality; just see as much as possible. Some examples of areas you should aim to cover are as follows:

- Loading every page/screen
- Entering details into every input
- Using every function
- Transitioning through every state (dialing, ringing, on-call, hanging up, for example, or signing up, awaiting verification, verified, logged in, and so on)
- Checking user-visible outputs
- Checking internal state (via logs, database contents, and more)

By touring the feature, you can find out how it works for real and bring the specification to life. It is much easier to find issues and think through consequences when you have a working feature in front of you than for the developers and product owners who could only imagine what it looked like. Make the most of that advantage.

It may be that some aspects of the feature cannot be used, for instance, if it is an API and you need to implement a client to drive it, or if you need to generate specific datasets before you can use them. This is the second aim of exploratory testing: to discover what you are missing to perform detailed testing in practice. Again, hopefully, this was clear from the initial feature specification and test planning. However, exploratory testing is a vital check that those plans can be used for real and to find any alterations you need to make.

By the end of this testing, you should know all the configuration options relevant to this feature and their effects. That will be vital to map out the dependent and independent variables for comprehensive functional testing. For instance, tracking a user's age may just be for information and not change any behavior of this feature or product. It is written to the database and only read to simply be displayed back to the user. In that case, it is independent of other aspects of the feature. Or it may be that certain options or behaviors only appear for users of certain ages. Then, you will need to check each combination of age and those features to ensure correct behavior in each case. This is your chance to see those interactions.

The third aim of exploratory testing is to find any major issues that will block further testing. In the same way that getting to test number one is on the critical path for releasing a feature, so are any bugs so serious that they block entire sections of the test plan. For instance, if a page doesn't load at all, you can't test any of the inputs or outputs on it, or if an application crashes early in its use, you cannot try scenarios after that. Exploratory testing is your chance to quickly check that everything is testable and ready to go. You can raise issues with the development team while preparing comprehensive tests rather than delaying the project when you are ready.

By the end of exploratory testing, the aim is to be able to conduct more thorough testing later. You should come away with detailed knowledge of the interface, all inputs and outputs that were implemented in this version, the configuration options, and the basic functionality. What's missing are the details and interactions, which we will discuss in *Chapter 5, Black-Box Functional Testing*.

Exploratory testing is a quick, fun way to get to know a new feature, which doesn't require the rigor of the full test plans you will design later. The challenge at this early stage is that you know very little about the product, but you can use that to your advantage, as described in the next section.

Using your naivety while testing

Exploratory testing is an ideal opportunity for feedback about the usability of a feature. When you start testing, you may be the first person to see this feature who wasn't part of its design. To begin with, that lack of experience is a strength. Your task, as a tester, is to notice and explore possibilities, avoiding the prejudgment and expectations that come from greater experience in this area.

Later, it is important to understand the design and implementation of the code. The technique of **white-box testing**, described in *Chapter 6, White-Box Functional Testing*, requires you to check all code paths and try each special case using knowledge of the system. However, at the outset, this lack of knowledge is important to discover surprising or unexpected results, especially for user-facing interfaces and functionality. Anything that surprises you may also surprise your customers, so look out for anything that wasn't obvious.

Keep track of anything you had trouble finding, any text you had to read twice, and anything that caught you by surprise while using the feature. That is all vital feedback for user experience design. Don't assume it's your fault if you didn't understand something on first use – it may be the designer's fault for not making it clearer. Some topics are inherently complex and require background knowledge before users will understand; however, any users of your product will probably have background knowledge of its existing functionality or other products within this domain. A well-designed interface should be able to build on that knowledge intuitively. If that's not the case, then that's a defect too. See *Chapter 8, User Experience Testing*, to learn more about **usability testing**.

The world of user experience has no firm answers, and just because something wasn't obvious to you doesn't mean that it will be for anyone else. Unlike other parts of testing, where there should be a clear answer as to whether the product meets the specification, user experience is much more subjective. It is worth raising any points you find challenging to gather others' opinions. If enough people agree that something is confusing, it is a good argument to change it. You have to highlight those issues to start that discussion and decide on improvements.

Armed with this naïve approach, open to possibilities, and examining each one, you should aim to touch all the major functions of your new feature. From there, you can complete a miniature version of new feature testing, using all the different types of testing available. They are described in more detail in all the subsequent chapters of this book, but this is your chance to perform a cut-down version of different types of testing quickly and early in the project, as we'll learn in the next section.

Running complete exploratory testing

Exploratory testing is a smaller version of all the following testing, pulling out a few of the most important tests from each section. It is introductory testing, which means it briefly covers many areas in the same way that this chapter has introduced this book. Exploratory testing should cover the following aspects:

- Black-box functional testing
- White-box functional testing
- Error cases
- User experience testing
- Security testing

- Tests for maintainability

- Non-functional testing

With less time available for exploratory testing than in the complete test plan, you should prioritize these aspects carefully.

As we've seen already, exploratory testing starts with black-box functional testing, using no knowledge of the underlying implementation, and concentrating only on the working cases. This should form the majority of the work you do here.

While there are advantages to naivety about how a feature is implemented, even during exploratory testing, it is helpful to know some details of its architecture and design. If one minor aspect of the feature requires a large section of code, then you should test that aspect far more than its use might suggest. If there's more code required for its implementation, then there is more to go wrong and a higher chance of defects. So, even while exploring, it's essential to do some white-box testing, informed by knowledge of the feature's design. This should come after black-box testing so that you can make the most of your lack of assumptions about its behavior first.

You can also start trying error cases during exploratory testing, for instance, by deliberately leaving fields blank, entering invalid information, or attempting to trigger errors. This shouldn't be the focus – making sure the feature works comes first. But even this early, you can probe the behavior with incorrect inputs.

As described previously, exploratory testing is a great time for finding usability issues when a feature is new to you before you learn how it works, inside and out. Feedback on usability should be a key deliverable from all exploratory testing.

You can also test security during the exploratory phase. Again, you need to prioritize these tests – the most obvious attacks can be quick to run **SQL injection** and **scripting attacks** or attempting to access information without the necessary permissions. Are the required certificates in place, and is the traffic encrypted? See *Chapter 9, Security Testing*, for more details on how to run those kinds of tests. Major deficiencies such as those can be easily spotted and raised early. Security shouldn't be a focus for exploratory testing compared to functional and usability testing, but this is where it can start.

Exploratory testing can also start to examine the maintainability of the code. How useful are the logs? Do they record the application's actions? Are the relevant events generated? What monitoring is in place for this service? Early in the project, in the first version of the code, the answer might be as simple as noting that events are not ready yet, or the gaps within them. This is the time to start writing the list of those requirements. Maintainability can be low on the priority list for a project, so it's important to note the requirements early.

Exploratory testing does not typically cover non-functional testing since that often requires scripts and tools to exercise, which takes longer than the available time. However, if you have tools prepared from previous testing and this feature is sufficiently similar that you can quickly modify them, you can run initial **performance** and **reliability testing** (see *Chapter 12, Load Testing*, for more details). Again, this isn't a priority compared to the usability and functional testing elements.

As you go through these types of testing, note down ideas and areas that you should cover in the complete test plan. Exploratory testing is a time to try out some ideas, but also to identify what you want to spend more time on later. You won't be able to cover everything initially, so record what you have missed so that you can return to it.

This is also your chance to uncover trends within the bugs. Defects aren't randomly scattered through a product; they are grouped. So, check what parts of this feature or product are particularly suffering from issues. Adapt your test plans to add extra detail in those areas, to find further problems. This lets your testing be reactive to the feature, to give the best chance of finding bugs. See *Chapter 5, Black-Box Functional Testing*, for more on reactive testing.

By the end of this testing, you should have a very good idea of how this feature works and have ensured it doesn't have any major issues. Usually, that will prepare you for more detailed testing to follow, but sometimes, it is all that is possible, as the next section explains.

Using exploratory testing by necessity

While normally used at the start of testing large features, exploratory testing is also vital when you don't have time for anything else. As we've seen, exploratory testing combines test design, execution, and interpretation into a single step and is highly efficient at the cost of having less planning and documentation. In the hands of an experienced tester, it can provide broad coverage quickly and rapidly gain confidence in a change.

This is useful toward the end of a project when there are minor changes to fix critical bugs. You need to check those changes, but you must also perform **regression testing** to ensure that no other errors have been introduced. Regression testing involves carrying out tests on existing functionality to make sure it still works and hasn't been broken. Exploratory testing mainly focuses on new behavior, but it can also check your product's main functions.

> **Real-world example – Fixing XML**
>
> At the end of a long, **waterfall development cycle** that lasted over 6 months, we were almost ready to release a new version of our product. We found one last blocking bug that required a new build, so the development team made that change and provided us with the release candidate code. Unfortunately, they hadn't only fixed the blocking bug. While in that area, the developer had noticed that our XML formatting was wrong and had taken the opportunity to fix it.
>
> The developer was right. The formatting was incorrect, but he hadn't realized that the system that read that data relied on that incorrectness. By *fixing* the formatting, the other system could no longer read the message. That critical bug was introduced at the end of the release cycle, but we quickly found it through exploratory testing. It delayed the whole project since everything had to stop to wait for the fix, but it didn't take long to roll back the change.

When pressed for time, exploratory testing is the fastest way to get broad coverage of a change. You can rapidly gain confidence that a feature is working but beware of overconfidence if these are the only tests you have run. There can still be blocking issues even after exploratory testing has passed. Non-functional tests are often poorly covered by exploratory testing: does the feature work on all web browsers and operating system versions? Does it work with a high load? Does it handle poor network conditions? Even if the feature works well in one tester's environment, real-world situations may hit problems.

So, be aware that exploratory testing is not comprehensive. Rather than putting more effort into this form of testing, use it to plan out exhausting test plans that will be documented and automated. Even when you have more time, you should always limit how long you spend on this form of testing.

Checking exploratory test results

While the input of exploratory testing is often clear – use all the new features, choose all the new options – checking its behavior may be obscure. If parts of the user interface haven't been implemented yet, there may be no visible changes. The only available output might be database fields or log lines showing that the internal state has changed. If there are user-visible changes, they might be incidental – for instance, a changing interface that indicates that another change has occurred.

Sometimes, complete testing is impossible until some other change has been made. One part of the system is ready, but another part that uses it is not, for example. In that case, you can check whether the new functionality is ready and that it hasn't broken any existing behavior, but full system testing will have to wait until all the elements can be used together. If so, you can complete some testing, and leave a task to complete it when the code is ready.

Early in the project, there may not be much documentation, or the specifications might not go into sufficient detail to describe the database implementation and logging output. Either way, you need to have a conversation with the developer to check what exact changes you expect to see in this code version. Only armed with that information can you be confident that not only are you exercising all the variables but that they also have their intended effect.

As well as the outputs the development team suggests, keep your eyes open for anything else that is strange or unusual. Be curious, both in the tests you run and in the checks you make. Curiosity is vital throughout testing, but especially in exploratory testing, as covered in the next section.

Using curiosity in testing

The approach to take throughout exploratory testing is that of maximum curiosity. Constantly ask yourself, "*I wonder what happens if I do that?*" All the questions you can think of are valuable while testing; testers are there to ask the right questions.

All testing requires that same curiosity, but you can see it most clearly in exploratory testing, where there is no test plan, and you only have your curiosity to work from.

All curiosity is not equal, however, and exploratory testing is an area that benefits massively from experience. With only a limited time, you must aim directly for the weak spots in your system to avoid wasting time testing mature code that has already been well covered in previous cycles or with **automated testing**.

One area of potential weakness is the new change that hasn't had any test coverage before. But what existing features should you combine with these new ones to find problems? This is where your experience comes into play. What are the weaknesses of your system? Where have bugs been seen before?

The **International Software Testing Qualifications Board** (**ISTQB**) is an organization dedicated to improving the software testing practice, which runs certification schemes for practitioners. They note that bugs are not evenly spread throughout code but tend to cluster in certain areas.

Examples of classic areas for problems that affect many systems are as follows:

- Running on low specification machines with limited memory or CPU
- Running on low-resolution screens or small window sizes
- Behavior after the upgrade when you transition to using the new feature
- Problems around boundaries and edge conditions
- Problems with times and time zones
- Problems with text inputs (blank, too long, Unicode characters, SQL injection, and more)
- Backup and restore
- Behavior under poor network conditions

In addition to the preceding problems, track all the weaknesses that affect your particular application or web page. Create a document that lists the areas of weakness that you've hit in the past, and keep it updated as you discover new issues.

This technique is known as **error guessing**, as described in the ISTQB syllabus. It stresses that the tester's experience is needed to anticipate where the errors might fall. Often, you find the best bugs when you go off the test plan. This is the corollary to the ISTQB testing principle about the **weedkiller paradox** – the more you test in one particular way, the fewer bugs you find, analogous to using a weedkiller that gradually kills fewer weeds. Only those less affected by it thrive. Tests that you have run many times before are unlikely to find an issue this time around, and in addition, the idea behind them may be well known to the development and test teams, so the developers will remember to handle that case. You're more likely to find bugs with new ideas for tests and in new combinations of functionality that haven't been previously considered.

Because of the dependence on experience for exploratory testing, it is best carried out by senior testers. Junior testers can cover other parts of the testing process, such as implementing test plans designed by others or regression testing. For exploratory testing, make sure experienced team members lead the way. If you are a test manager, you can make that decision; if you are a tester who has been given the task, let others know if there is someone more suitable. Experience can be domain-specific, of course. While you may be highly experienced in one area, perhaps someone else is better placed to do exploratory testing for this particular feature.

Experience is also important when it comes to choosing what to check. While some errors are visible on the user interface, others may be subtle, such as warnings in the logs or database fields being written incorrectly. As well as using your curiosity when deciding what to do, ensure you scour the system for issues and items you can check.

Curiosity is vital throughout the test process, not just during exploratory testing. There is no hard divide between ad hoc testing and that which follows a plan. Instead, it's a spectrum. While exploratory testing has little structure, lists of likely weaknesses such as the preceding one can also help to guide it. So, even exploratory testing can have some documentation.

Functional testing can be descriptive – for example, a test such as "*Upload a .jpeg image*," which means that each tester will choose a different image to use. That reduces the reproducibility of the test while broadening coverage. Alternatively, tests can be prescriptive, describing exactly what to do; for example, "*Upload image test1.jpeg*." Even within these tests, the environment can change, the state of the system may be different, or you might run tasks in an unusual order. Always look out for new ways to test and new things to try.

Testing is an arms race of creativity, with testers trying to find new ways to break products and developers inadvertently adding new problems and issues. This is the fun and the skill of testing, so go crazy and enjoy yourself! When testing a new feature, you are the first to do something no one has done before. You are the vanguard of the army, charging into battle; you are the pioneer heading into an unknown land. So, use your experience, prepare for surprises, and keep your eyes open for the unexpected.

Summary

This chapter described exploratory testing – when it should be carried out and by whom. We saw where exploratory testing fits into the development cycle, and that it is a powerful tool to find issues soon after code has first been implemented because it is quick and requires little planning. However, it needs a senior engineer to do it well, is not widely reviewed, and doesn't produce extensive documentation. It can be hard to judge the coverage that exploratory testing provides, and non-functional tests may receive little coverage. That leaves the risk of issues in real-world usage even after exploratory testing has passed. The aim of exploratory testing should be to understand the feature better so that you can prepare comprehensive test plans later.

This chapter has shown when to start exploratory testing, not beginning too early when the code is still in flux, and the steps to get the first test running successfully. We've seen the importance of curiosity and naivety at the start of the test process, both in choosing what to test and checking the outcomes. Finally, we learned how to map out a feature, ready to perform a miniature version of the complete test process.

The next chapter takes the experience from exploratory testing and applies it to writing a detailed feature specification that will guide all the subsequent testing.

2

Writing Great Feature Specifications

"How can I know what I think till I see what I say?"

– Attributed to Graham Wallas, E. M. Forster, and W. H. Auden, et al.

In the previous chapter, we saw the importance of exploratory testing to map out a feature. With that experience, you're now ready to prepare a first draft of the feature specification. This is a vital document that will guide all future testing. It is also known as the **Software Requirements Specification (SRS)**, but here, I will refer to it as the feature specification.

Writing a clear and precise feature specification gives you the best chance of releasing a feature quickly and successfully. Without a detailed specification, you risk surprises throughout the feature's development, even after it has gone live.

In an ideal project, the feature would be comprehensively specified before any work by the development and test teams begins. The product owners should clearly state what they want from the feature; then, the development and test teams can refine it so that everyone is clear about what they will deliver. If that is not the case, push for it in your organization. Again, early planning prevents later surprises.

But even if a feature has a great initial specification, it is worth revisiting it after the initial design. Due to timing or technical issues, the implementation may have deviated from the plan, the plan may have changed, or exploratory testing may have identified behavior that needs to be specified. This chapter will show you what to aim for in a feature specification, whether it's part of that initial plan or after exploratory testing.

You'll see how to write requirements to cover the external functionality but not the implementation in clear, independent, testable statements. You'll learn the ideal format of the document to make it easy to reference and to ensure it covers the core concepts. This chapter will then describe how to write requirements that cover all the different testing areas and how to write a test plan based on those requirements.

In this chapter, we will cover the following topics:

- Advantages, disadvantages, and alternatives to feature specifications
- Improving the handover from the product owner
- Understanding the requirements format
- Requirement priority
- Improving requirement statements
- Improving requirement content
- Completing the specification
- The first draft of a feature specification
- Turning a specification into a test plan
- Countering arguments against specifications

First, we will consider the advantages and disadvantages of functional specifications and alternative forms of documentation that perform similar roles.

Advantages, disadvantages, and alternatives to feature specifications

Precisely describing your features has many advantages, but specifications can be neglected due to the time they take to write. The onus can fall on testers to prepare these specifications since they need to know how the product will work in practice. If no one else has written a description by the time the feature reaches you, it may be up to you to prepare it. Despite its downsides, preparing a feature specification is well worthwhile, as described in the following table:

Advantages	Disadvantages
Early chance to find bugs in the requirements	Takes time to prepare
Avoids surprises for developers and testers	No immediate payback
Saves time by avoiding misunderstandings	
Great source of information for development, test, support, and documentation teams	

Explicitly writing out the feature specification is a chance to catch bugs early in the development cycle. If your team is organized and the specifications are written upfront, you can head off issues before they are even coded. More often, in my experience, the detailed specification is prepared during or after coding, at which point you'll need to spend time fixing any problems you find.

Some of my proudest moments as a tester have been when I've highlighted issues at the specification stage. I didn't click a button or run a single test. A well-placed question was enough to send the feature back to the drawing board, as these simplified exchanges show:

- Product Owner: "This new feature will let administrators disable users instead of just deleting them."

- Me (Tester): "Okay. External integrations are a kind of user, so can we disable them too?"

- Product Owner: "We'll need to think about that…"

The following example shows an alternative:

- Lead Developer: "This feature will read external meetings into our service's calendar so that we can display them all together."

- Me (Tester): "What happens if a user reads in an external meeting, then adds it to our service's calendar too?"

- Lead Developer: "That would be a problem, yes…"

While it's a shame that the feature will take more time to develop, it's vastly quicker than discovering those issues later in the process. That's always the way with testing: it'd be faster not to find any bugs at all, but given that there are bugs, it's always better to find them today rather than tomorrow.

A specification also lets you avoid surprises later in the project. It's slow and costly for the product owner to spot an enhancement they need during **beta testing** when the feature is already implemented. Imagining exactly how a feature will look and behave is very difficult, so it's very easy for mistakes and misunderstandings to creep in. There's no simple way to solve that but thinking through the behavior and explicitly describing it gives you the best chance.

The specification also saves time by avoiding misunderstandings. Testing can go very quickly when the tests are passing but for that, you need to be clear on the product's behavior. As soon as a test goes wrong, testers need to stop to investigate, double-check their config, and be sure of their results before checking the results with the development team. If you expect one behavior but see another, you will have to investigate that discrepancy, such as a bug. You can save that investigation time if you know what to expect, thanks to precise requirements.

The specification also lets other teams understand what a feature will do. When a customer has a specific question about how your product works or the documentation team need to write up a description, they can read the specification. It's a massive help to speed up others' work and empowers them to find answers for themselves without checking the product behavior or asking for help.

All those benefits accrue over time. The problem with writing feature specifications is the effort they take upfront. They take thought from the test and development teams, as well as the product owner when they have many other tasks to keep the project moving. It takes their time, but they are mainly the source of information, and it doesn't directly help them. Because of that, it can fall to the test team to drive the process of getting specifications created. In my experience, everyone is happy to help and appreciates them when they are done, but it takes a push to make it happen. If specifications aren't written in your organization, then it's up to you to make that change. All the testing described in this book relies on detailed knowledge of how the product should behave. This is a necessary step for releasing quality code.

Alternatives to feature specifications

There are many alternatives to having a feature specification that are worth describing. Whatever its form, you need some documentation telling you how the feature should behave. This cannot be the code itself because the whole point is to test that against some independent measure. In the ISTQB, the source of your tests is known as the test basis, a deliberately vague term whose only requirement is that it forms a base from which to design your test plans. This section considers some related documents, as well as possibilities for that basis, aside from a feature specification:

- **Business Requirement Document (BRD)**
- Technical specifications
- User stories
- Implicit specifications
- User interface mockups
- Diagrams
- Test plans

You can use some of these methods to complement a specification, such as UI mockups, while others could be a replacement. This section considers each of those document types in more detail.

Business Requirement Document

Before you write a feature specification, there needs to be a BRD. This lays out the commercial case for developing this feature or product. The size of this document will vary in size, roughly correlating with the size of the development effort required.

The BRD does not contain details of the product behavior, so it isn't suitable for writing tests. It will contain the business need for the change by analyzing competitors' products, the likely commercial returns, the scope of the change, and potential risks the project will face. It will identify stakeholders and list the user stories that this change will satisfy.

I assume the product owner has done all this before the project begins, so I won't consider it here. The product owner should have taken those business requirements and worked with the development leads to propose a solution they intend to implement. That solution is documented in the feature specification.

Technical specifications

As we shall see, the feature specification should say *what* the product will do, but not *how* it should do it. Those implementation details can be recorded in a technical specification, which describes how the product or feature works. This might include descriptions of the following:

- Functions and classes that need to be written
- Modules and how they will interact
- Database design
- Program flow
- Internal APIs

While internal APIs should be part of the technical specification, public APIs are testable and should be recorded in the feature specification instead.

The technical specification can be helpful when designing white-box tests (see *Chapter 6, White-Box Functional Testing*), and you need to know the workings of the code. However, like the BRD, technical specifications aren't an alternative to the feature specification but provide different details. These documents work together to describe the change, but the functional requirements are most valuable to you, the tester.

User stories

User stories are a great way to work out the problems your users are facing and how to solve them. For example, "*As an e-commerce business owner, I want to see my bank account balance to check that recent transfers have cleared.*"

User stories should always state who has the need and a persona with a brief history to understand why they have this need. There should be a specific problem they want to solve – for instance, knowing their bank balance – and each user story should tie into a larger goal. Why do they have this need? That will let you judge how important it is and how well different solutions might work.

User stories describe a problem, not a solution. In the preceding example, there are many ways the balance of a bank account could be shown: in a title bar, in an overview list, or on the details page for that account, for instance. The user story only states the customer's needs; another layer of detail is needed to say how that need will be met. That layer of detail is the feature specification, which states what the product should do.

For instance, this is not a good user story because it contains too much detail: *"As an e-commerce business owner, I want to see my bank account balance on the top left of the Accounts Overview page."*

User stories are a powerful tool for determining the requirements, but for this book, I assume they have already been decided. As a tester, you need a detailed description of the product's behavior, so you need a specification rather than the user stories that helped generate it.

Implicit specifications

The most successful onboarding of a new tester I ever achieved was by using implicit specifications. He found 10 genuine bugs in his first 2 days in a product still under development. I've never seen anyone get up to speed and be so productive so quickly. While he did turn out to be a great engineer, using implicit specifications made that success possible.

The trick was saying that our new product had to do everything our old product did, but on new and more powerful hardware. He could use all the menus and functions of the old product and see what was still missing or behaved differently on the new product. Having that detailed information at his fingertips made finding bugs vastly easier.

The problem with implicit specifications is that you rarely have anything to compare against. Unless you are running a project to reimplement a feature or product, for instance, using a new software framework or hardware platform, you won't have anything to implicitly specify your requirements. Most features are unique, providing a function that has never been done before or never done in that way, so there is nothing to compare with.

Look out for the opportunity to use implicit specifications. Use them when you can, but unfortunately, you cannot rely on them being available. For most features, you need to explicitly state the requirements yourself.

User interface mockups

A picture says a thousand words, as they say. You should use UI mockups to specify how user-facing sections of your product will look, in addition to written feature specifications. The color and position of UI elements are best shown in a picture instead of an extended description. A single picture is what both the developers and testers need to work from.

Of course, a picture doesn't give all the details. Should an element be of a fixed width from the edge or a percentage of the distance across the screen? A single screenshot won't illustrate that. The precise color of UI elements needs to be documented, as well as shown. And most importantly, the behavior should be described. What are valid inputs? What is the effect of the buttons and links? What are the outputs? All of these need to be captured in the specification.

So, a UI mockup does not remove the need for a feature specification but is a vital addition for user-facing changes.

Diagrams

As with UI mocks up, diagrams are a great addition to a feature specification. I love having visual representations of information to make it clearer. This might show the code architecture, the information flow, user journeys through a feature, or anything else associated with your product. It all helps stakeholders understand the feature better to see any issues or changes they want to make.

They are particularly useful when detailing APIs and data flows within an application to give a clear and instantly understandable view of the behavior that might be difficult to discern from a paragraph of text.

However, a diagram isn't a replacement for the specification. As well as being shown, you should also write about each step of your information flows or user journeys so that the implementation and test plans can cover them. Specifications serve as valuable checklists for developers and testers, so they should be a complete list of the behavior. Diagrams help illustrate that but shouldn't be used as a replacement.

Test plans

Rather than putting your effort into writing and reviewing a feature specification, why not write the test plan directly? For testing, the test plan is the outcome we need to work from, so why add the extra complexity of a feature specification? After writing the specification, you will need an additional step to generate the test plan from it, so writing the test plan directly avoids that step.

I recommend writing a feature specification because it is accessible and valuable to more teams. Test plans are not very readable and are intended only for testers. On the other hand, product owners can use the specification to ensure the feature will work as expected. Developers can use it as a checklist to ensure they have implemented all the necessary functionality. The documentation team can use the specification to understand the feature and describe it in the help section. The support team can use it to look up the details of product behavior when they get questions from customers. That's in addition to you being able to use it for your test plan.

As well as being beneficial to the whole development team, specifications provide a useful intermediate step to help you think through the test plan. Some requirements may need a single test to cover them, but others may require several. For instance, you need to try a whole range of values in text input fields (see *Chapter 5, Black-Box Functional Testing*). Having a specification lets you know if you have covered everything by dividing it into clear sections.

So, while a test plan is a final goal we're working toward, writing a specification is the best way to get there. See the *Turning a specification into a test plan* section later in this chapter for more details on generating the test plan.

Round-up of feature specification alternatives

You can use many other documents and sources of information to guide your test plan, but a single feature specification is the most important. With that as a guide, you can flush out any issues and describe all the behavior precisely. Diagrams, UI mockups, and other visual aids are helpful but should always be in addition to the feature specification. Implicit specifications can likewise be a great source of detailed product behavior but should complement the specification, not replace it.

The next section describes how to prepare your specification, starting with improving the handover from the product owner.

Improving the handover from the product owner

I have seen features handed to the test team with nothing more than a name and a few notes tracking the required code changes. I was supposed to pick the testing up with no details about the feature's function, appearance, or implementation. If you're in that state, then have a word with the product owner and developers. Throwing features over the fence to test in that way is massively counter-productive; the communication needs to be much better.

> **A note on naming**
>
> I refer to the person who prioritizes the features and describes their functionality as the product owner. They go by different names in different organizations, such as product managers or project managers, so you'll have to translate it for your situation. The important point is that this is the person who advocates for the customer's needs, prioritizes features, and decides their behavior. That may be an individual or an entire team, depending on the size of your company. Whoever that is in your organization, that's whom I'm referring to here.

Most of the time, the situation for me was much better, and the product owner did provide a feature specification of new features. However, those specifications rarely had sufficient details for complete testing. Encourage your product owner to provide all the information they can, but always be ready to add to it.

After the product owner's draft, you should follow the same philosophy, adding as much description as possible while knowing that your draft is not the final article. The drafts are just that – drafts – until the product owner, the development team, and the test team have sat down together to review them (see *Chapter 3, How to Run Successful Specification Reviews*). Until then, there will always be gaps. Your job is to get the specification sufficiently detailed – to identify all the requirements you can – that the review meeting can provide the remaining answers.

To illustrate this, we will consider the example of some requirements written for us by a product owner for a new feature they want to add to a website – the ability to sign in. For *version 1*, signing in won't allow any extra functionality, and users will just register to enable other functions in the future. The feature is a simple username and password combination with no **Two-Factor Authentication** (**2FA**) or temporary code. Here is the initial specification that they provide:

Login feature specification – draft 1

Users can log into the `example.com` website
By default, when upgrading to a version that supports logging in, logging in is disabled
Users enter their email address and will be sent an email to verify it is valid
When users click a link in the verification email, they will be sent to a page to choose a password
When users have entered a password, they can log in

This seems simple enough and covers the functionality. You can see what this feature is supposed to do, especially since I've chosen an example that we've all used dozens of times for dozens of different services. You've been a user, and there's a good chance your company has a signup page of some kind in its product too.

If you received this level of detail from your product owner, you'd probably be grateful for it, but I'm about to massively expand it to produce a comprehensive document covering all testing aspects. It is already pretty good – it's a list of specific and testable statements, which, as we'll see, is just what we need.

One exception is the first requirement, which is an umbrella statement describing the feature overall. It is too vague to be tested on its own because logging in involves a whole sequence of steps. Having an umbrella requirement like that is acceptable for readability, but only if it is followed by specific statements describing how the product will meet the general requirement.

Notice that I just referred to *the first requirement*. You'll discuss these statements, refer to them, and link them to tasks and bugs, so the first thing to change in this example is to make that referencing easier, as shown in the next section.

Understanding the requirements format

I don't care how you format the feature specification document. Feel free to have an overview and an introduction, state the scope and the stakeholders, or add versioning tracking every change. If you find those useful for the time they take to prepare, add that information. If not, don't.

Many tools let you track requirements more flexibly than having a single *document*. They have features such as reusing requirements between projects and mapping requirements onto the test cases that cover them. While I'll refer to the specification as a *document* here, I recommend that you use these tools since they give you greater control to move requirements around and tie them into your development team's processes.

If you're stuck with wiki pages or shared documents until you persuade everyone to change, a few formatting rules will make everyone's lives easier. The other improvements listed here apply to the text itself, and should be used with whatever tracking system you are using.

Numbering

The requirements in `Login feature specification - draft 1` are in a bullet point list, which makes them easy to read and separates different statements. If you're presented with a paragraph of text as a specification, your first job is to turn it into a list of statements instead.

Then, whatever requirement tracking tool you are using, make sure you uniquely number all your requirements. The previous example uses bullet points, which don't identify the different statements. That's no good and needs changing. As with many of the suggestions here, this is a minor point but makes everyone's lives easier:

Login feature specification – draft 2

Section 1 – Main functionality	
1.1	Users can log into the `example.com` website
1.2	By default, when upgrading to a version that supports logging in, logging in is disabled
1.3	Users enter their email address and will be sent an email to verify it is valid
1.4	When users click a link in the verification email, they will be sent to a page to choose a password
1.5	When users have entered a password, they can log in

This description lets everyone refer to the requirements easily. You can read requirement *1.2* to see if you have tested it and raised bugs against it. I have heard objections to numbering the requirements because the statements aren't ordered, and numbering artificially imposes an order. In the preceding case, there is an ordering at the moment – users will work through them chronologically as they sign up – but even without that, it's important to be able to refer to the requirements easily. Even if the statements jump from topic to topic, with no connection from one line to the next, give them numbers so that you can reference them.

Now that we have a numbered list of statements, we can group them into relevant sections to make them easier to write and read.

Sections

The specification needs to be split into different sections to track the different aspects of the feature. Currently, our entire specification is only five lines long, but as we expand it, we will need to group requirements. For instance, we will need a section about how we enable the feature, which deserves a section on its own.

Dividing the specification into sections helps keep the document clear for everyone to read and means renumbering has less effect. The specification is a living document and should be improved by developers, testers, and product owners throughout the development cycle, so you may need to renumber requirements as you go along. To fully reference a requirement, you not only need to state which number it is but also which version of the specification it is from. Edits and changes should be encouraged, even if they require renumbering requirements. Usually, mentioning the version number of the specification is unnecessary, but changing requirements can cause confusion, so that is the way to resolve ambiguities.

This isn't necessary when you only have a few requirements, but if you have a section with dozens of requirements, always split them up to make it clearer.

Now that the requirements are easy to reference and read, we need to consider their relative importance and responsibility for tracking each requirement's priority.

Requirement priority

All requirements are not equal, and the product owner should assign a priority to each one. That will let the development team know their relative importance so that they can make informed choices when they have to make inevitable tradeoffs.

I won't describe that process here; instead, I focus on what you need for testing. Once the priorities have been decided and the technical limitations and opportunities have been explored, you need a final description of what will be shipped in this release. As a tester, your job is to make the specification binary – whether a requirement is included or not. Product owners and developers work in the gray areas of deadlines and feature estimates, so it's your job to make the outcome black and white.

Feature prioritization and estimation are skills in their own right, but they are beyond the scope of this book. Here, I will concentrate on describing the features that made the cut by being clear on the behavior of this release. We will do that by looking at the style you should write requirements in and some common pitfalls to avoid.

Improving requirement statements

There is an art to writing requirement statements. It's easy to write vague or useless requirements, so you need to be strict and follow a particular style. Specifically, your requirements should have the following properties:

- Specific
- Measurable
- Agreed
- Realistic
- Complete
- Consistent
- Independent
- No implementation details

This section will examine each of those qualities in turn. The first four come from the **SMART** acronym for management objectives and are a great guide to writing goals in general. The **T** in SMART stands for **timed**, and that's one aspect that these requirements don't need to cover. Project planning is a skill that is beyond the scope of this book, but it isn't necessary for the functional requirements. It only records what the product should do, not when. Let's compare two requirements to illustrate the qualities that requirements need to have:

A. Reading the database tables should be fast enough

B. The **User Details** page fully loads within 3 seconds

I hope you can already see which one is superior, and here, we'll describe exactly why.

Specific

First, requirements need to be specific. Which screen do they apply to? Under what conditions? Both of the preceding requirements imply they *always* apply, but there are many different conditions. Requirement *A* is very vague. Which database table does it mean? All of them? And how fast is fast enough? It's a poor requirement and needs improving. Requirement *B* is better because it refers to a specific page and a specific time. Even then, there are many different values the **User Details** page might show, so you'll need to pick a worst-case scenario to gain confidence that it will always load within the time limit.

Look out for the word *all* or *every* in requirements, which can be a tester's nightmare. Consider the following requirements:

> C. Every event is rendered correctly in the reporting screen

> D. All API calls correctly return error messages

For requirement *C*, does anyone have a list of all the events? And how is a tester supposed to generate them all? Even worse, for requirement *D*, the tester needs to generate every error for every API call. There are a lot of possible errors!

Keep the requirements specific. Requirement *B* refers to a single screen, which you can turn into a single test case within a more extensive test plan. It's clear where the requirement starts and stops, what it refers to, and what it leaves out. If you want to make a blanket statement such as *C* or *D*, be aware that you need to turn the word *all* into a list of testable cases.

Watch out for comparative requirements, for example, being *better* than a competitor. Better in what way? Again, that lacks specificity, and your requirements need greater clarity.

However, your requirements needing to be specific presents a problem. What if you don't know what the behavior should be? If you ask detailed questions, possibly no one has worked out what should happen in those scenarios. Is it better to write down potentially incorrect requirements or leave out those sections? I propose always making your assumptions explicit, even if they may be wrong. It's much easier to correct a precise statement than improve a vague one or add in a requirement that wasn't specified before.

Be precisely wrong rather than vaguely right

Let's return to our example feature specification:

Login feature specification – draft 2

Section 1 – main functionality	
1.1	Users can log into the `example.com` website
1.2	By default, when upgrading to a version that supports logging in, logging in is disabled
1.3	Users enter their email address and will be sent an email to verify it is valid
1.4	When users click a link in the verification email, they will be sent to a page to choose a password
1.5	When users have entered a password, they can log in

Requirement *1.2* states that login in is disabled after the upgrade. This implies there is a feature flag to control that configuration, and feature flags can be turned both on and off. So, what happens if we enable the feature, users sign in, and then we find a critical bug and have to turn it off again? The specification doesn't say, so we need to document and test it.

This presents a problem because we don't know what the behavior is if we disable the feature flag. This is another area where product owners are sometimes remiss. While they are very keen on turning a feature on, they may not specify what happens if it is turned off.

You could add a requirement to say, *The login function can be disabled via a config option*. This might be true but isn't useful. What exactly happens? Are current users logged out? Are the login details of everyone who's signed up saved? Hopefully, they aren't all deleted and are ready to be used again when the feature is re-enabled in the future. However, there aren't any requirements about that at present, so who knows what the development team has implemented. They may not have thought through that case themselves and may not know the behavior without checking.

If you find yourself unsure of the behavior, don't write a vague statement that fudges the issue. All the requirements in the specification need to be, as the name suggests, specific. Only then are they testable, and the statements you add should be no exception.

In this case, if you're not sure what the behavior is, make it up. Invent the behavior out of thin air. What do you assume should happen? Testers constantly test against their assumptions about what a feature should do, so make those assumptions explicit.

If you add a requirement that you are unsure of, note that it needs to be reviewed. That means it will be discussed in the specification review meeting, as described in *Chapter 3, How to Run Successful Specification Reviews*. In effect, these statements are questions, but instead, they propose a specific, testable behavior. That lets other stakeholders disagree. Importantly, there's no escaping the question – the system will do something, so it must be specified.

You could ask the other stakeholders these questions as you go along, but there are likely to be many of them. For now, note that this needs checking, but fill the specification document with the detail it needs.

Isn't that a terrible way to work, you may ask, to write down statements that aren't correct and which you have made up? No. It turns out it's much easier to fix requirements that are precisely wrong than those that are vaguely right. By being specific, you can highlight issues and decide what the behavior should be in consultation with other teams.

Here is our specification with those details added in. You can see the complete version of the feature specification in *Appendix, Example Feature Specification*. In this section, we can see that `Section 1 - enabling login` is now how to enable login, with the other requirements following in `Section 2 - main functionality`:

Login feature specification – draft 3

Section 1 – Enabling login	
1.1	Users can log into the `example.com` website
1.2	By default, when upgrading to a version that supports logging in, logging in is disabled
1.3	Logging in can be enabled via a configuration option
1.4	Logging in can be disabled via a configuration option
1.5	When logging in is disabled, the login button disappears from the web page
1.6	When logging in is disabled, all user details are saved
1.7	When logging in is re-enabled, users who had previously signed up can log in again
Section 2 – Main functionality	
	(*Section 2 requirements continue here*)

Requirement *1.7* is the important one. If you enable the feature, sign up, disable the feature, then re-enable the feature again, you can still log in. You don't lose any user details when you disable the feature. Has the development team implemented it that way? Is that what the product management team wants? These are questions for the specification review. By adding a clear, specific statement, you can now precisely decide what the feature should do.

Measurable

As well as being specific, each requirement should be measurable:

> A. Reading the database tables should be fast enough
>
> B. The **User Details** page fully loads within 3 seconds

Requirement *A* is too vague. What counts as *fast enough*? What is a pass, and what is a failure for that case? Watch out for words such as *sufficient*, *large*, or *quick*, which describe a measurable number without actually giving the number to measure against. Requirement *B* says that 3 seconds is the acceptable limit. That's great: you can test against it and get a clear pass or fail result.

It isn't easy or obvious how to make those decisions. What should count as fast enough, or what capacity is large enough? These are decisions for the product owner, and it's part of what makes that role so challenging. Feel free to give your opinions to help them decide, but in the end, it is up to them.

Requirement *A* is also too detailed to be easily measurable. It refers to the speed of database reads, which you'll need tools or logs to check. Sometimes, code is being refactored, and you can only measure low-level changes like those but, wherever possible, relate requirements to user-visible changes. Requirement *B* is better because it refers to the whole page loading. It's no good database reads being quick if some other bottleneck slows the page loading. Requirement *B* is also easier for testers and test tools to check.

Agreed

All the requirements need to be agreed upon by both the product owner and the development team. It's no good for the product owner to state that a page should load within 3 seconds if the developers know that that will never happen in practice. Conversely, the developers aren't allowed to sneak in caveats and exceptions they haven't been able to deliver without explicit signoff from the product owner. *Chapter 3, How to Run Successful Specification Reviews*, covers this in more detail.

Realistic

After being agreed upon, the requirements need to be realistic. Maybe the product owners and developers would both like to implement some functionality but, given the time and the team available, it's highly unlikely to happen. The specification needs to describe exactly what you'll deliver in this project. You can update it in each cycle as you add functionality, and you can have a *future* section where you list the plans of features you will add later. However, you need a realistic description of the current implementation to test against.

Complete

The requirement document needs to be complete. That is the real trick of requirements and finding all the subtleties and interactions is the skill of writing a great specification. That will depend on the specifics of your feature, of course, but the main categories are described later in the *Completing the specification* section.

Independent

Each requirement should be independent of the others. It should be possible to pick a requirement, read it in isolation, and check that the product fulfills it. The aim is that they can fail individually, that any of them could fail independently of the others. So long as each describes an atomic unit of functionality, they can be developed and tested separately.

This means that the requirements will be somewhat repetitive, but that is a small price to pay for making them clear. Consider the following requirements:

A. The **User Details** page fully loads within 3 seconds

B. It displays the username, email address, and profile picture

Requirement *B* only makes sense if you read it along with requirement *A*. Instead, make sure that each requirement is a statement on its own:

A. The **User Details** page fully loads within 3 seconds

B. The **User Details** page displays the username, email address, and profile picture

This means extra writing but helps avoid any possible ambiguities. Ambiguities lead to misunderstandings, which lead to bugs, which lead to late surprises, project delays, and unhappy customers. This is your chance to stamp them out, even if it makes your document sounds like a 5-year-old wrote it: *The house is big. The house is strong. The house is made of red bricks.* Such writing isn't elegant, but it is very clear, and that's what you need for your requirements.

Keeping requirements independent isn't always possible. Even in our simple example, the later stage depends on the earlier ones. `Section 2 - main functionality` of our specification states this:

Section 2 – Main functionality	
2.1	Users can log into the `example.com` website
2.2	By default, when upgrading to a version that supports logging in, logging in is disabled
2.3	Users enter their email address and will be sent an email to verify it is valid

If you don't receive your login email, for instance, you can't set up a password. In that case, you can still make the dependencies as loose as possible – the requirement to send a login email doesn't depend on setting up the password, so the dependency is only in one direction. While each requirement needs the previous one to succeed, most describe separate steps. One exception is this requirement:

2.3	Users enter their email address and will be sent an email to verify it is valid

It seems innocuous enough but needs improving. Both the step to enter your email address and send emails have many different conditions to consider, so this needs to be split up and expanded:

2.3	Users enter the email address they want to sign up with
2.4	An email is sent to the entered email address with a link to verify their authenticity

This way, you can track a failure on the text box for entering address information separately from failures in the mechanism to send emails. Watch out for the word *and* in your requirements because it probably indicates a statement that needs splitting up.

If you have a list, add that in as a sub-requirement. Consider this hypothetical section later in the specification. Here, we have the following:

10.1	The **User Details** page displays the username, email address, and profile picture

Instead of writing that, we can write this:

10.1 (revised)	The **User Details** page displays the following details:
	A. Username
	B. Email address
	C. Profile picture

This keeps each requirement entirely separate, and you can reference any fields that aren't available. If the username and email address are present but the profile picture is missing, the system doesn't fulfill requirement *10.1 (revised) C*, for instance.

Consistent

The requirements also need to be consistent with each other. This is obvious to say but harder to achieve in practice, depending on the size of your specification.

Real-world example – The duplicated requirement

I once had the task of responding to **Requests For Quotations** (**RFQs**) for large projects. Telecom network providers would produce vast specifications of systems they wanted to buy. Different hardware vendors would propose their products and say how many of those requirements their system could meet. We were one of those vendors, trying to make our product match up to the thousands of requirements in the RFQs.

Having spent a week preparing and refining our answers for one RFQ, I noticed that *requirement 371* was the same as *824* (I don't remember the actual numbers!) Worse, the requirements were in different contexts. In one, we had said we were partially compliant, but in the other, we'd claimed to be fully compliant. Claiming too much for the product meant urgent feature requests and emergency projects to deliver functionality. Once we had responded, we were contractually obliged to provide everything we'd promised, so we had to be incredibly careful what we said.

In specifications with tens of requirements rather than hundreds, spotting inconsistencies is much easier. Still, look out for general requirements overlapping with specific ones:

11.1	The **User Details** page fully loads within 3 seconds

Then, later in the same specification, you may have the following:

11.17	All user pages load within 2 seconds

The **User Details** page has a laxer specification, so the product may not meet the more general requirement if you just test that.

Implementation-free

Finally, the requirements shouldn't contain any implementation details. The users don't care what database technology you choose or the web framework you are using; they don't care about the code modules or functions involved. The specification is a **black box** because it only describes the result.

The feature specification should only state *what* the behavior is, not *how* it will be implemented. That is up to the development team. Sometimes, there is a clear route to achieving the functionality you want, which the product owners have in mind, and maybe that is the best solution. Product owners should also know at least one way to achieve what they want, to be confident they're not asking for something impossible or at least incredibly costly to implement. However, it is the development team's responsibility to decide how to implement a feature. They have complete discretion to achieve these requirements in whatever way they like. They will think it through, considering technologies and options that product owners don't need to worry about.

The specification document should reflect that. If you find any implementation details appearing, remove them. This document should be silent on how functionality is achieved; it should only list what is necessary. This applies both to technical details to deliver the feature and user interface decisions, which are best left to the **user experience (UX)** team.

For instance, take a look at the following requirement:

12.1	The user state is read out of the `user_details` table

Don't mention database tables in the specification. The development team will choose where the data should be stored. The important point is, what user-visible effect does having the user state cause?

12.2	A table shows the values for each product over the last 12 months

Maybe the user experience team wants to have a diagram or a chart instead of a table. The only requirement is that the information is available, not how it should be shown:

12.3	The system sends a message to initiate a recording of the session

Maybe there's one message, or maybe the API involves several. The requirements shouldn't prejudge the messages the application sends. If you find yourself writing requirements like this, stop and think about how you can rephrase them as a behavior rather than implementation details. For instance, take a look at the following requirements:

12.1 (revised)	The user state is displayed on the **User Details** page, including the following information: • Name • Email
12.2 (revised)	The **Product History** page displays the values for each product over the last 12 months
12.3 (revised)	The system can initiate a recording of the session

The changes are subtle but important. These requirements are much better because they say exactly what the system should do but don't mention any user interfaces, APIs, databases, or other implementation details that will make that possible.

However, some implementation details are important, not least where the option is to turn this feature on, for example. You should add these as notes to the requirements. They are not requirements in themselves, but they are necessary to document for the test team:

Login feature specification – draft 4

Req no.	Requirement	Notes
Section 1 – Enabling login		
1.1	Users can log into the `example.com` website	
1.2	By default, when upgrading to a version that supports logging in, logging in is disabled	
1.3	Logging in can be enabled via a configuration option	Set the `enable_login` option to `True` in the `login_configuration.conf` file

This version separates the implementation from the functional requirements. The implementation can change without affecting the requirement to have a configuration option available somewhere.

Round-up of requirement statement improvements

There's a lot to remember when writing specifications. These meta-requirements for the requirement statements mean there are many ways to go wrong. Instead of trying to remember all these rules, it's best to practice lots, then edit them to make sure they meet all the criteria:

- Specific
- Measurable

- Agreed

- Realistic

- Complete

- Consistent

- Independent

- No implementation details

In practice, you develop a style that makes it easier to see when you've strayed into describing implementation or become too vague. To help, you can start by writing clear statements about the feature's basic functionality before adding more detail. The following section describes those first, obvious requirements and the actual content of your feature specification.

Improving requirement content

Now that we've seen how to format the requirements and the best style to write them in, we can consider what they should say. The rest of this book describes the different aspects of testing you should consider and capture within the specification, while this section covers the general principles you should apply to the content of the requirements.

Keep it obvious, cover everything

The first requirements to track are the most obvious ones: the main functionality of this new feature. The product owner should cover these requirements, but even here, there can be gaps. There is an art to identifying your assumptions and saying them out loud. Never be shy about being obvious – every so often, something that was *obvious* to you will be the source of disagreement and confusion. You can only resolve that confusion by asking precise questions, starting with the easy ones.

Real-world example – The vote counter

I once worked on a large project for a national mobile phone network. We provided the network hardware for SMS, text message, delivery, and value-added services. One of these was a system for voting by text message to provide the service you regularly see on television programs. The specification document was vast, stating the connections and inputs to other networks, the rate of SMSs arriving we had to sustain, the different events we could host simultaneously, and the output statistics we had to support.

Looking through the document, I realized one requirement was missing. The system went straight from describing all the inputs and messages arriving to describing all the outputs and how they would be displayed. However, there was no requirement to actually count the votes. In that case, the requirement was so obvious that it didn't cause problems. Of course, our system supported that. Other projects with missing requirements aren't so lucky.

So, start simple and cover everything. Don't be shy about stating the obvious before moving on to the more detailed requirements.

Version requirements

The specification needs to list all the prerequisites for this feature to work. This detail is difficult for product owners to add – they may know what they want, but it is up to the development team which version they implement it in. For testing, that is the first piece of information you need. Which versions have this new feature, and how do we turn it on?

If you have performed exploratory testing (see *Chapter 1*, *Making the Most of Exploratory Testing*), you already have this information and can add it. However, ideally, the specification document comes first to tell you what you need:

Login feature specification – draft 5

Req no.	Requirement	Notes
Section 1 – enabling login		
1.1	In *version 5.7.1* and later, users can log into the `example.com` website	
1.2	By default, when upgrading to a version that supports logging in, logging in is disabled	
1.3	Logging in can be enabled via a configuration option in *version 5.7.1* and later	Set the `enable_login` option to `True` in the `login_configuration.conf` file

Adding the version number to the umbrella requirement shows that all the subsequent requirements rely on that version. An alternative is including the version in the description of the entire document. You can say this is the feature specification for *version 5.7.1*, then list the behavior.

Including the version is a gray area because it is an implementation detail and, as shown in the previous section, the feature specification generally shouldn't describe the implementation. However, the product version also determines the user-facing behavior of the system, so it is valid to include it as a requirement. It's essential since it decides whether the feature will work at all.

Describing configuration

What about settings? While this feature is present in *version 5.7.1*, it is turned off by default. You also need to change a setting to make this behavior appear, so you must add that to the specification. This is another vital detail for the test team that the product owner may miss.

Having feature flags and options to enable new functionality is hugely beneficial. It lets you separate rolling out new code from changing its behavior (see *Chapter 10, Maintainability*). Feature flags mean you can get important bug fixes and other improvements out to your customers without being dependent on new features working. They mean you can disable problematic features without requiring a downgrade that might reintroduce old bugs and remove other new features. If your development team isn't using this method already, I highly recommend it.

Your specification needs to record all the settings associated with this feature, starting with those that enable it. That is why this requirement is so important:

1.2	By default, when upgrading to a version that supports logging in, logging in is disabled	

We now know that to see this new feature and start testing, we need *version 5.7.1*, and we need to have enabled it. That's great, but how do we turn it on? As we saw, there is a big difference between documenting implementation and behavior in feature specifications. While you should record that detail, it is a note, not a requirement itself.

So far, the improvements to the initial test plan have been around its presentation – the numbering and sections, the wording, and how to divide up requirements. The following section concentrates on the content – what requirements should cover. As with exploratory testing, this will be a miniature tour of the remainder of this book.

Completing the specification

To make the specification complete, we need to tour all the different areas of testing once more:

- Functional tests
- User experience tests
- Security tests
- Error case testing
- Maintainability
- Non-functional tests – performance and load requirements

This time, you need to think them through in detail to capture all the product's behavior. Later chapters describe these more thoroughly, but here, we will examine how they relate to the feature specification, ready to be fleshed out later. First, we will cover the functional requirements that describe the main use cases.

Functional test requirements

The feature specification needs to describe all the feature's designed behavior, starting with the happy-path cases of the functionality it is supposed to provide. State machines are an excellent way to step through the different points on a user's journey, tracking the various stages. At each one, list what should happen based on all their possible actions and all the outputs that they should see.

In our example of a signup feature, a user first sees the screen to enter their email address. This has a text field, so there are many possible inputs. Those will be considered in more detail in the next section, as will the restrictions on email addresses. But what happens if that email address is already in use? What happens if that email address has been entered but not verified yet? You need to identify all the possible system states to choose which tests you need to run in each. Here, we have up to five:

1. A new email address.

2. An email address that has been entered by not verified.

3. An email address that has been verified but that doesn't have a password set up.

4. A verified email address with a password but that has never logged in.

5. An email address that has been used to log in at least once.

Possibly states 4 and 5 are equivalent from the database's point of view. Only by identifying those states can you work with the developers on the necessary tests. For the feature specification, all these different states need statements describing the behavior:

Req no.	Requirement	Notes
Section 4 – sign up		
4.1	If the user signs up with a new email address that has never been used before, then an email is sent to that address to verify the account	
4.2	If the user signs up with an email address that has been entered but not verified, then another email is sent to the address to be verified	
4.3	When a user signs up, no feedback should be given to the requester as to whether the email already exists	This avoids leaking information about any email addresses already in use on the system
4.4	If the user signs up with an email address that has been verified but doesn't have a password set up, then another email is sent to the user with a new link to the password page	
4.5	If the user signs up with a verified email address with a password set, then they are sent another email with a link to the page to reset their password	

Note that requirement 4.5 covers both states 4 and 5. The behavior doesn't differ depending on whether the user has logged in, so we don't need to spend time trying both cases.

Designing the functional test part of the specification involves carefully stepping through all possible situations the code could encounter and its inputs. For each, ask what could happen and record the planned behavior. It sounds so easy! Of course, it is not in practice and will require your skill to do well. After the happy-path cases, you can move straight to documenting what should happen with invalid data.

Error cases

What happens when things go wrong? Again, this is an area that can be overlooked by product owners, in my experience. They mainly concentrate on the behavior they want to have rather than what should happen when things go wrong. This area also requires lots of input from the user experience team, and you may need more text to cover failures than for the working cases since there are more of them.

Failures should be graceful, and errors should guide users, where possible, to resolve their issues. In our example, we have to cover users entering invalid email addresses or mismatched passwords, email delivery failing, or users clicking out-of-date links.

More severe internal failures are considered as part of non-functional testing. Otherwise, this section follows the same principles as that of the rest of functional testing – identifying the different states and specifying what should happen when things go wrong in each one. See *Chapter 7, Testing of Error Cases*, for more details.

User experience specification

One area the requirements in our preceding example did not cover was the user experience. We stated that the user should be able to log on, but not how that screen should look. If you are in a company of any size, a dedicated user experience team should decide this. They will specify the font, placement, colors, and exact text of all the user-visible elements. These should be produced in a tool for quickly mocking up user interfaces, and there are many to choose from. The UX team should then share those mockups with the test team to compare against the actual implementation. This is one of the more accessible areas of testing, similar to playing spot the difference. Does the implementation match the request?

The other important aspect of user experience is the location and flow of user tasks. Maybe there should be a button to change your password, but if it is buried in four layers of menus, then no user is likely to find it. That is also a bug, although a problem with the specification rather than the implementation.

As well as the ideal cases, the user experience section should list the full range of systems your application or web page supports. You need to list all the operating systems and web browsers your product supports, the lowest screen resolution, and the maximum. Those must all be specified, ready to become part of the test plan.

Security test requirements

Security considerations will also be covered in more detail later, including covering the cases of authentication and authorization, and the triad of **Confidentiality**, **Integrity**, and data **Availability** (**CIA**). In our login example, security testing should describe timeouts on email links and logins, the generation of secure keys, and rate limits on password attempts and form submissions.

Notice the preceding requirement:

2.3	Users enter the email address they want to sign up with

You fill in the signup form with anyone's email in the world, which will fire off an email that could be used maliciously to annoy someone you dislike if they use this service. While that's not so different from emailing them from any other account, this time, it'll have your company's name on the spam messages. To block that, there should at least be a limit on how often you email to one account.

In this example, users choose passwords, so you must specify the complexity requirements you will enforce. You also need to check that those passwords are stored securely. On one website that shall remain nameless, when I requested a password reminder, they emailed my current password to me. Passwords should be stored hashed so that even those with access to the database cannot read them.

This applies to all passwords and PINs, not just those protecting user accounts. In a company I worked for, the main passwords were hashed, but users could assign passwords or PINs to protect recordings. They were stored in plain text, so we could see what people had chosen. Wherever there is a password, it must be unreadable, even to the development team. It's your job to check that.

Security requirements are often an anomaly because they effectively limit the behavior of features rather than stating available functionality. The specification needs to capture all those restrictions and protections.

Maintainability

This section is always close to my heart, even if it is not always a priority in projects. How easy will this be to debug? Specifications rarely go down to the level of what logging the system will provide, but that is necessary to work with the feature long-term. Are the log lines understandable? There should be a clear line recording each user interaction, including the contents of the messages. If a user with a particular email address had trouble signing up, you have to be able to search for that email address to find the actions associated with it. Are errors and warnings usefully logged, and can you easily aggregate and view them? Again, add those requirements to the specification because no one else may.

The specification also needs a dedicated section to record the events and instrumentation. How will you measure how well this code is performing, how much your users are using it, and in what ways? While not part of the main functionality, this is vital information for your company, and it needs to be specified along with the feature itself.

None of these requirements help your customers when they first start using your new product, but it will make your life a lot easier, in the long run, to specify the behavior you need while everyone is thinking about this feature.

Non-functional tests

As Rex Black notes in his book, *Advanced Software Testing*, non-functional areas of software testing tend to be underspecified, so they may need particular attention from you.

What's the maximum number of users that can sign up for the service? When I have asked this, I sometimes got blank looks. There is often no limit in the code – it is only limited by the memory and disk space of the system it's running on. If user records take a few bytes of data each, on a system with gigabytes of storage, that will be huge. In that situation, the solution is to pick an arbitrary limit and test up to that. Verify that the system works successfully with up to a million users, for instance. That gives you confidence for the foreseeable future, and everyone knows when you are approaching the dangerous ground of untested behavior. Most importantly, as a tester, you have an actionable test and either pass or fail.

Often, with non-functional tests, the pass criterion isn't as simple as a behavior. Maybe the system can support a million users, but at that size, it takes over an hour to send out emails to verify people's addresses. It works, but far too slowly. All functionality is assumed to work within a specific time, so make that explicit in the specification: *All the pages load within 3 seconds*, for instance. Then, you know what time to set as a time out in automated tests, and if responses get slow when the system is in use, you know precisely what a pass or a fail is.

What rate of signups can your web page support? Excessive usage is a good problem to have, but it's still a problem. If your next marketing video goes viral and suddenly you are inundated with eager users, you don't want their first impression of your fantastic company to be a signup page that doesn't load. As with other load limits, it's possible that product management hasn't thought of this number, and the development team doesn't know what the system can support in practice. So, again, choose a limit and test to that. This form of testing is vital as you, the tester, determine the system's performance. See *Part 3*, *Non-Functional Testing*, of this book for more details.

Documentation

Finally, the specification needs to describe what documentation is provided for the customer. Are there tooltips or help boxes, manuals, or instructional videos? Ideally, a product's user interface is clear enough that little guidance is required, but it's always useful to provide help if people need it.

This is technically a subsection of the user-interface testing but can be worthwhile pulling out into its own section within a specification to ensure it is considered in detail. As with the rest of the user interface, ideally, the documentation needs to be specified by a dedicated user experience team who will finalize its wording and format.

When they provide those details to you, the testing just involves working through the interface to ensure all the planned fields have been implemented correctly. While testing the presence of help files is black and white, the content of the help will benefit from feedback and suggestions. If there is anything you struggle to understand or have to read twice, report that back to the UX team. If others face similar difficulties, that area should be changed.

Feature flags are useful for rolling out features but can make documenting interfaces harder. Often, feature flags control menu systems or other visible elements, removing them altogether when the feature is disabled. As well as making sure the configuration is correct for your testing, the documentation team needs to ensure all screenshots and videos show the correct features.

The documentation needs to be reviewed regularly. Even a tiny change on a single page might render many screenshots and videos out of date. It can be hard to tell where changes need to be made, so the documentation team will need to record which pages appear in which screenshots so that they know when to update them.

Round-up of specification sections

This section contained brief notes about the different areas and what you will need to specify and test. They all need more detail, which will be added later in this book, and you need to apply them to your particular products and features. When testing a feature, your main task is to work out what it should do and the questions to ask about its interactions, so if you complete this section thoroughly, your testing is well on the way. The following section describes taking this specification, refining it, reviewing it, and using it as a basis for future testing.

The first draft of a feature specification

Remember the five requirements we received from the product owner? While they seemed to describe the feature well enough, they are nowhere near sufficient to cover all the previous considerations. Remember, this is for three new pages – login, signup, and password reset – that provide no additional functionality. After considering all the aspects of the feature described previously, we can complete a draft of the specification. This is included in *Appendix, Example Feature Specification*, which shows a good first draft for a feature specification. Note how the requirements are independent, implementation agnostic, and specific.

This book aims to help you quickly produce specifications like this for the features you are testing. The same considerations crop up repeatedly in different forms, so it's a case of learning them and applying them to your system while watching out for special cases.

Even after expanding the requirements to 10 times their initial size, you're not finished. There are still many gaps in this feature specification that need to be reviewed and corrected by the developers and product owners. Remember all those times you chose to be precisely wrong rather than vaguely right? You need to get an agreement for them. You need to check all those performance numbers you plucked out of the air. By choosing those options yourself, you speed up the process and have the best chance to have a clear, helpful conversation in the feature specification review. Preparing the specification as you see it is only the first step. The next chapter covers the review in more detail, but here, we will skip straight to the stage after – that is, producing a test plan from the requirements.

Turning a specification into a test plan

This book is about designing great system test plans; however, I propose that those test plans are secondary. They are an outcome of having a great feature specification.

You only need to put in the effort once to design and create a comprehensive document describing the feature. You could put that effort into creating the test plan directly, then get that reviewed by the various stakeholders. However, as we saw in the *Advantages, disadvantages, and alternatives to feature specifications* section, a feature specification is more valuable to many different teams. The product management team can read a specification and agree that they want those requirements. The documentation team can use it to describe and document behavior and the support team can read it to check on details to answer customer questions. The development team can use it to track the progress of their implementation, and, of course, the test team can use it to prepare the test plan. Because of that, I recommend that the document you spend the time on is the feature specification, although it leaves you an extra step to produce a test plan from it.

The relationship between the test plan and the feature specification should be straightforward. So long as you have precise, declarative, independent statements in your specification, each can become one or more tests in your test plan. Let's look back on the main functionality section of our specification:

Login feature specification – draft 5

Req no.	Requirement	Notes
Section 2 – Main functionality		
2.1	Users can log into the `example.com` website	
2.2	By default, when upgrading to a version that supports logging in, logging in is disabled	
2.3	Users enter their email address and will be sent an email to verify it is valid	

Requirement *2.1* is an umbrella requirement fulfilled by the statements that follow it, so you don't need to test it separately. Requirement *2.2* is testable – when you first upgrade, there should be no change in functionality. Requirement *2.3* lets users enter their email addresses. That is a text box that needs many tests to verify, which will be described in *Chapter 5, Black-Box Functional Testing*. From the previous *Error cases* section, we had the requirement that the application should reject invalid email addresses with a suitable error message. Email addresses can be incorrect in many ways, however, so those all need to have test cases added. That one requirement needs many test cases to cover it completely.

Other parts of the specification also require unpacking, and most of the rest of this book will be devoted to describing common patterns of requirements and the tests you need to run to check them.

While feature specifications have many benefits, it can be hard to convince a development team to fully embrace them. The following section considers some arguments against feature specifications, and how to counter them.

Countering arguments against specifications

I've encountered various reactions to specification documents over my years in the software industry. Usually, people's reactions are positive, or at least hopeful. Most people would love to have a clear description of the feature under development, but between changing priorities and a lack of time, specifications can be challenging to produce in practice. Other people are more actively negative and argue for spending valuable project time elsewhere. As you can tell, I am firmly in favor of specifications, so here are some anti-specifications arguments and some counterarguments against them.

"This feature is too small to be specified"

Sometimes, a feature is so small that it hardly seems worth writing a specification for it. If a feature is obvious and everyone seems to know what it does, why spend the time writing that down? Some changes are so small that there seems to be nowhere for surprises to hide.

To counter that, consider the many different areas of testing listed previously. Have all the error cases been thought through? Have its maximum load limits been specified and tested? What events and logging does it generate? What documentation changes does it need? Even the simplest change can render multiple screenshots and videos out of date, as we mentioned previously. And even seemingly simple changes can hide issues.

Real-world example – The two tick boxes

There was once a minor feature request at a company where I worked to expose two tick boxes on our customer-facing portal. These controls were already present in our internal tools, but we got so many requests to change them from customers that the support burden was significant enough to justify a little development time to make them public. Two tick boxes – what could go wrong?

Two binary options produce four possible states in total, and it turned out that one of those four states was invalid. Our internal system detected that arrangement and blocked it, but the public-facing pages used an API that bypassed that check. Should we have used a dropdown instead of two independent options when only three states were valid? Absolutely! But we had not.

Such a minor change received a cursory test to check that both options worked, and they did, individually. But we didn't write a specification and didn't methodically step through the four possible choices. After all, they already worked internally, didn't they? We released the broken code so our customers were the first to find that the invalid configuration didn't work, and I learned that even the smallest features can hide critical bugs.

On the plus side, small changes in functionality only require a small specification. It doesn't take a significant investment of time to write a specification for a minor modification, so it scales in proportion to the project. Even small features can hide surprises, so it's always worth spending time upfront finding all the details you can.

"We don't know that behavior"

While you are busy as a tester asking difficult questions, other team members have the even more challenging job of answering them. Another argument against a specification is that no one knows what the current desired behavior is, with the implication that it isn't worth the time to find out.

This objection comes in two different versions:

- The first one is temporary – we don't know that *yet*. As with exploratory testing, it's possible to begin the specification too early when the feature is still in flux. The product owner may still need to make decisions, or different design options may result in different outcomes. If that is genuinely the case, keep talking to people and wait for the feature to be ready. Just make sure it's not a stalling tactic; you will need that specification sooner or later.

- The second version of this objection is that some questions can't be answered. This is generally around non-functional specifications or interoperability. Does the application work on old browsers and operating systems? What is its maximum throughput? Questions like those can become tasks for you, the tester, to answer. If you pick them up as a task or track them as unanswered questions, they are no objection to getting the rest of the feature fully specified.

"We don't have time to write a specification"

The most common argument against writing a specification is that there isn't sufficient time. Yes, they're important; yes, they're a good investment of time; but the deadline is looming, and if the choice is between delivering the product and writing about it, you should choose to deliver it.

This is another area where you can help. Do as much as you can on the specification yourself. It may not feel like part of your job. Ideally, the specification would be an input into the test team: you would be given a feature and a description of what it should do, ready to test one against another. However, in practice, since you need the specification, it's sometimes up to you to produce it. While it will also need time from the development team and product owner to review, you can do the heavy lifting by writing it out. All they have to do is agree, and that is far quicker.

That is why I have spent so long in a book about testing talking about how best to write requirements. Clarity of thought is vital both for specifications and testing, and being able to clearly describe the feature and ask questions about it. The real reason was practical: testers need to know how to write specifications because it will often fall to you to get it done.

This book aims to let you write better test plans faster. If you are better at designing specifications, it takes less time and is less of a drain on the project. By reading this book, you will learn about the important considerations so that you can rapidly think through how they affect each feature. Producing a specification faster is the best argument against anyone who says they take too long.

Summary

In this chapter, you learned how to turn a short, basic description of a feature into a comprehensive feature specification. That is one small step away from the test plan you need to guide all your testing.

You've seen the strengths and weaknesses of a specification and the other types of documents in a project. Many of those complement the feature specification, but none fully replace it, and it's the feature specification you need to base your test plan on.

We've covered the journey of a specification, from the initial handover from the product owner to how to structure the document in terms of numbering and sections, then the vital guidelines to writing requirement statements. They need to be specific, measurable, agreed, realistic, complete, consistent, independent, and contain no implementation details.

There's a lot to remember, but once you've mastered the style, it's simple enough to work through the many areas of a feature that you need to specify. They mirror the chapters of this book, from functional, security, and usability testing to non-functional tests and documentation.

Finally, we looked at how the specification relates to the test plan and countered some arguments against writing specifications. As you have seen, even seemingly small and straightforward features can hide blocking bugs.

Your specification is just a first draft, despite all your work turning the brief requirements from the product owner into a comprehensive description. It will still have many holes until you review it with the product owner and the development team to answer the many uncertainties and fill in all the areas that you haven't realized that you've missed. How to run that review successfully is the topic of the next chapter.

3

How to Run Successful Specification Reviews

"He who knows only his own side of the case knows little of that."

- John Stuart Mill, On Liberty

In the previous chapter, you learned how to develop an excellent feature specification from a short description given by a product owner. However, even with all those details added, your test plan is incomplete. So far, the only inputs into the test plan have been that initial draft and your exploratory testing and ideas. You also have to hear from the developers to understand their choices, the configuration options they added, and the areas they are worried about. From the product owner, you need clarification on any unspecified user-facing questions. The specification review meeting is the place to gather that information.

This chapter will show you how to run a successful review meeting. As with the functional specification, this may be carried out by someone else, but if it isn't, it's up to you, as a tester, to ensure this is in place. You need a specification to test from, and you need everyone to agree to it. This chapter describes how to get that done.

We'll cover the following topics in this chapter:

- Why do we need a specification review?
- Advantages, disadvantages, and alternatives of specification review meetings
- Inviting the right people
- Scheduling the meeting
- Running the meeting
- Fixing incorrect requirements
- Opening the black box

- Setting a good tone for the meeting
- Prioritizing requirement testing
- Review meeting checklist

We'll describe how to structure the meeting and set the tone, and what questions to ask to draw out important points. Finally, you'll learn how to prioritize the testing and run through a checklist to ensure your review is complete.

Why do we need a specification review?

The goal of the specification review meeting is to agree on all the requirements for this feature. By the end of the meeting, you should know exactly what the feature specification should say, even if it's not fully written up yet. Armed with that agreement, the test and development teams know exactly what they should deliver.

The specification review requires getting the right people to the meeting and giving them sufficient time to prepare. They may or may not take advantage of that time, but it's important to offer it.

Of course, you can have many other discussions during the feature development aside from the review meeting. Keep communicating before and after review; this meeting isn't a replacement for that. However, the review meeting serves as a final, systematic check that the specification is complete and ready to go.

In my experience, developers are only too happy to have a tester checking that their feature has been implemented well. No subject is off limits at this stage of the project because you are still planning out the testing you will carry out. After the feature review, finding gaps in the test plan becomes less positive since there is always the question of why these issues weren't discovered earlier. A successful review meeting avoids those surprises later.

First, we will consider the advantages and disadvantages of a review meeting and some alternatives.

Advantages, disadvantages, and alternatives of specification review meetings

The key advantages of the specification review stem from the communication between the key stakeholders. Its main disadvantage, as with writing the specification itself, is the time it takes. It's your job, as a tester, to convince the project team that the investment of time is worth making. Here are its advantages and disadvantages:

Advantages	Disadvantages
Gets all the key stakeholders together	Takes the time of senior team members
Structured discussions are made based on the test plan	Difficult to set the right tone
Chance for rapid discussion and decisions	Requires a detailed specification to be useful
Chance to uncover problematic scenarios	

Table 3.1 – Advantages and disadvantages of specification review meetings

Advantages of specification review meetings

Getting all the key stakeholders together for a detailed discussion of a feature is a massive boost to a project. This should be relatively late in the development cycle when the first implementation is already running, and you have performed exploratory testing. You've had a chance to get your hands on the feature, and you've drafted the specification. Now, you can examine the feature in detail and check for any gaps or omissions in its design.

The specification provides a detailed structure for examining all the minutiae of the feature. Having written the specification, you should be well acquainted with the feature's workings but you'll still have questions about different areas. This is your chance to ask those questions and solicit for any *unknown unknowns* – the questions you didn't know you should have asked.

Having asked those questions, you can rapidly uncover any problems. Sometimes, there are bugs in the specification or scenarios that haven't been considered yet. For other cases, you can quickly discuss and decide how the feature should behave. A well-run review provides detailed, swift, and decisive answers.

Disadvantages of specification review meetings

The disadvantage of the test plan review is that it requires time and thought from senior members of the project, who tend to be very busy. I believe this meeting is worth their time and will more than repay that investment, but some team members might need persuading.

Another difficulty is setting the right tone. Often, testers come into a project relatively late and have spent far less time thinking about a feature than the product owner and developer, who might have been working on it for days or weeks. You'll have many questions to ask, which can be embarrassing. You need a thick skin and confidence in your abilities to keep questioning until you have the answers you need.

Conversely, some developers might see such questions as a threat, so they need to be asked respectfully. It can be a tricky line to tread, asking for senior developers' time for the review and then checking their work. Staying polite, positive, and impersonal will help smooth the way.

As well as the investment of time, the specification review meeting requires a specification to review. If you haven't put in the time to write that document, you can't get the benefits of the review to draw out further details.

Alternatives to specification review meetings

The ISTQB has a lot to say about meetings: the different kinds you can have and the attendees who should be there. You can review the user interface, the technical implementation, or the functional behavior of a feature. Here, we will only consider their usefulness for reviewing functional specifications because the test plan is based primarily on that. The ISTQB lists four types of review:

- **Informal reviews**: Informal reviews have no specified agenda or intended outcomes but are unstructured discussions about the products and their workings. Like exploratory testing, their unstructured nature means their usefulness will depend greatly on the individuals taking part, and senior team members are likely to achieve more with them. There is no requirement for informal reviews to be documented, but they can be; photographs of whiteboard diagrams can be used to produce more official documentation later, for instance. These ad hoc discussions about crucial points are an important way to exchange information, especially if you need to know an answer before further testing. They are quick and don't consume many resources, although their usefulness will vary.

- **Walkthroughs**: Walkthroughs are more formal. They are led by the author, either of the code, the design, the specification, or whatever is under review. Their structure is variable, and they can be more or less formal, depending on how you would like to run it, but they all have the same goal: to examine a particular project asset. They tend to be open-ended, so you can quickly cover easy, obvious sections and have deeper discussions on any areas of contention or confusion. They help other team members understand more and are a chance for a reviewer to find defects.

- **Technical reviews**: Technical reviews include multiple different tasks. There will be discussions, some of which involve evaluating alternatives and choosing between them. You may solve technical issues and, most notably for testing, identify defects at the specification level, such as missing or contradictory requirements. While the specification document provides a structure to the review, the format is very flexible and can be whatever you need.

- **Inspections**: The final form of review listed by the ISTQB is an inspection. This is a formal acceptance of a change and might be used for code reviews, for instance, before developers merge changes into a product. Peers often conduct inspections, and they include a documented discussion and a pass-or-fail outcome. It's mainly used to find defects as a check alongside the testing.

The review I propose here is what the ISTQB calls a technical review. It's a structured discussion of a particular document, which in our case is the functional specification, which acts as a checklist to work through. It requires a draft of that document as an input and will produce a reviewed version as an output. Reviewers need to attend, both those working on the feature and possibly senior members of the team as well. For the test manager, this is the most important meeting to attend. You get to see a complete description of the feature, participate in discussions around the problematic areas, and see the testing that needs to be done.

The different strengths and weaknesses of these reviews mean they are beneficial at different times. Informal reviews help the team understand the feature and answer specific questions, and walk-throughs can be an extended version of that, especially to introduce newcomers to a planned feature and give an overview. Inspections are especially valuable for code reviews between developers. But for testers, I recommend a technical review of the feature specification as the key meeting. It provides the structure and flexibility to thoroughly examine a new feature, so long as the right members of the team are present. The following section considers the necessary guest list for a successful specification review.

Inviting the right people

The most important part of the specification review is inviting the right people to the meeting. If you get that wrong, nothing else you can do will make the meeting a success. So long as you have the right people and a detailed specification to work from, you are ready to begin. So, who should you invite?

While there are many roles necessary to make the specification review a success, three people are critical: the product owner, the lead developer, and the lead tester. Optionally, the senior developer, user experience team, and project manager can also attend:

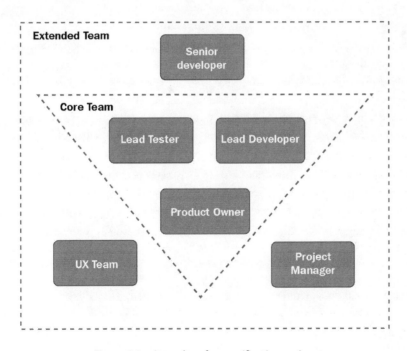

Figure 3.1 – Attendees for specification reviews

The ISTQB suggests six different roles for specification reviews. Personally, as a test team leader, I was usually all of those, performing multiple different roles simultaneously, so I don't consider them necessary. However, it's worth describing the meeting roles, especially if they will fall to you. As described previously, ideally, you will be presented with a detailed, reviewed specification to base your testing on. However, since that may not be the case, you need to know how to do these tasks and do them well:

- **Leader** (arranging the review meeting): Being the meeting leader means ensuring that the specification review happens by finding availability and sending out invitations to all the stakeholders.

- **Manager** (allocating resources to testing): The manager performs the vital task of assigning the resources. If the project doesn't have the time or equipment to succeed, there's no point in planning out the testing. Since this book doesn't cover project management or prioritizing tasks, I will assume you have the resources and can concentrate on planning out the tests.

- **Author** (you, the person who wrote the specification under review): The author of the specification should attend to present their work. Again, here, I assume that is you. Even if you didn't write the feature specification, as the tester, you need to be thoroughly familiar with everything it says. Writing it yourself is an excellent way to ensure that.

- **Scribe/recorder** (documenting the outcome of the meeting): The scribe plays a vital role. If you don't write down the results of the discussions, then points will be missed when you look back. Ideally, the scribe should present their notes during the meeting so that everyone can see what notes they are writing. That way, the minutes aren't just the scribe's recollection of discussions and decisions; everyone can see what they agreed on. If you can delegate or find a volunteer for this, I highly recommend it. Let someone else write notes so that you can concentrate on facilitating the discussion.

- **Facilitator/mediator** (resolving conflicts): The facilitator plays the important role of drawing out questions, shutting down side-discussions, summarizing conclusions, and keeping the meeting moving forward to ideally finish on time. This is a skill in itself and worthy of its own book, so here, I will just note that it is necessary. Specification review meetings have a great structure – you step through the requirements, line by line, so that they have a clear start and end. The review is also documented by default because if no one says anything, then the specification is correct as it stands. Sometimes, the challenge is to make people speak up; other times, you'll need to take a discussion offline to make progress elsewhere. This will be your main task during the meeting if no one takes on that role.

- **Reviewers** (providing technical input).

All these roles provide the structure of the meeting. The content will come from the reviewers. The ISTQB notes that there need to be reviewers, but not who they should be, so that role requires additional detail.

There should be a minimum of three people in the specification review:

- The **product owner**, who describes what the customer requires and makes any customer-facing decisions
- The **lead developer**, who describes the implementation, including any limitations or special cases that need to be tested
- The **lead tester**, to ask about error cases, feature interactions, and feature details

The product owner has to be present to advocate for the customer and give the underlying rationale for this change. They should approve any decisions with customer-visible effects. The lead developer can describe the implementation and any scenarios for which they had to write code to ensure the specification covers them. They can also explain how they handled error cases or the current behavior of the code in different situations. And finally, the lead tester must be present. You can ask questions about the feature and present the current specification you are planning to test.

In addition to those three, several other people may be necessary:

- The **project manager**, to prioritize tasks and decide the scope of changes
- The **user experience team**, to propose any changes that are needed to the user interface
- The **senior developer**, who will oversee the development of this feature
- The **senior tester**, who will oversee the testing of this feature

Discussions in the specification review will often cover features you would like to add but haven't had time for yet. The product owner will decide what is necessary to ship this feature, and a project manager may support them in planning out that work and when it can be delivered. The project manager can also guide the project if it looks like it will take too much time or too many resources.

The user experience team should be present for any feature with significant user-visible changes. Those can be the most contentious areas, so the UX team should attend to provide their opinions and approve any changes you need to make.

Finally, there should be senior developers and testers present to make sure the junior members of the team are performing well. This meeting is a key handover: it describes the detailed behavior of the feature, how it has been implemented, and how it will be tested. If a junior engineer has worked on this feature, then plan to invite the senior engineer they have been working with, to help answer any questions or make decisions. A software architect should also be involved if the scope of the work is large. For any managers who haven't been closely involved in this feature, and only come to one meeting to learn details, it should be this one.

While it's great to have more opinions, aim to keep meetings as small as possible to avoid wasting people's time and encourage questions and discussions. Having a large group can discourage people from speaking up, but always ensure the key people are present. Otherwise, you will just have to arrange another meeting to get their input too. The trick is to require just one meeting, and the best way to schedule that is described in the next section.

Scheduling the meeting

You should send around the feature specification a few days before the meeting to give everyone a chance to review it and submit comments in advance. If there is a critical misunderstanding – an area of functionality not covered or described incorrectly – it can be flagged up without wasting people's time in the meeting. It works well to have both a written and spoken review. The reviewers can take their time and think through their comments, and then you can rapidly discuss them and reach decisions.

You may need to have multiple test plan reviews. If you have planned out the feature before it has been implemented, there should be a review before implementation begins. After it has been implemented, there should also be a review to catch any necessary changes. Often, not all functionality will be delivered in the first version, so this is the chance to describe the exact behavior in this version and what will be added in the future.

For large features, it may be necessary to break the review up. These meetings require concentration and discussion, but it can be easy for reviewers to switch off, fail to pay attention to requirements, and fail to raise objections. For this reason, you should aim to keep specification reviews to under an hour. If a specification needs more than that, split it into different meetings. These should be close together so that reviewers remember the detail of what they discussed, but with breaks so that everyone is refreshed. This helps them listen carefully and think through the consequences of every requirement statement.

While you might schedule the meeting for an hour, everyone will appreciate it being shorter than that! Keeping the meeting on track and moving forward successfully is the skill of running the meeting well, as described in the next section.

Running the meeting

The meeting format is simple enough – step through the feature specification, read each requirement to see if there are any disagreements, and sign it off. Was it the behavior the product owner wants? Has the developer implemented it (or have they agreed to implement it)? This is a form of **static testing** – testing without running the code. This lets team members step through design documents, technical specifications, or, in this case, functional specifications to look for errors or issues. This contrasts with **dynamic testing**, where you run the code to see how it behaves in practice. Only this chapter, *Chapter 2, Writing Great Feature Specifications*, and parts of *Chapter 6, White-Box Functional Testing* cover static testing; the remainder of this book focuses on different types of dynamic testing.

With a large specification that you are already familiar with, you may find it tempting to breeze through the requirements quickly. Don't. Take your time, read each requirement slowly, and make sure that everyone has heard and understood them. While you have given everyone time to prepare and read the specification, be ready for anyone who has turned up without doing their homework. If this is the first time they are seeing these requirements, read them slowly enough that they can keep up.

Remember that you are looking for objections. Questions are good! Disagreements are good. You might hope that your specification is perfect, and you might be eager to get to the end of the meeting, but take your time and solicit as much feedback as possible. In church, when the priest asks if anyone has any objections to marriage, no one wants to find any. In this case, you want objections. You want to have as much discussion as possible as early as possible, to air any worries anyone has, and to work through them. You are actively seeking communication.

The worst thing that can happen in a specification review is that you miss a requirement and test against an incorrect or incomplete specification. This is your chance for people to raise any concerns they have. Maybe there's a vague worry they haven't been able to articulate yet. This meeting should be a safe, supportive environment for them to ask their confused question, even if they don't fully understand what they're asking. For a detailed explanation, refer to the *Setting a good tone for the meeting* section.

If you read through the specification and everyone sits in silence, don't congratulate yourself on having written a perfect document. More likely, they haven't read it or aren't listening and adequately considering it. There is always more to add, so if everyone is sitting in silence, ask them direct questions (or say something outlandish!) to ensure they're paying attention.

Alternatively, your document may generate too much discussion. As with all meetings, you need to ensure you don't go down rabbit holes. If there is a particularly contentious area, you'll need to continue the discussion in a separate meeting. Leave it to one side, and continue with the other requirements, which don't depend on that decision. If you disagree about something fundamental, which impacts the entire feature, you need to get that agreed upon first. However, hopefully, those decisions are made long before the specification review.

For contentious issues, always summarize them at the end of the discussion. It's possible that some people still won't be happy with the outcome, but you need to let everyone know what you are planning to do. It's no good if people come away with different understandings at the end of the meeting. That's why it's so useful for the scribe to present the notes they're taking as they go along, so everyone can see what's been decided. That is usually simple enough, but it's vital for controversial decisions.

These conversations are necessary to decide on any behavior you weren't sure of when writing the feature specification, as described in the next section.

Fixing incorrect requirements

You have to get feedback on any requirements you weren't sure of. For any load limits you plan to measure and any failure modes that could be handled differently, you have to ask for confirmation explicitly. As a tester, you need an answer to those questions, but you might not be best placed to make those decisions. The user experience team and product owner will have a better idea, so ask them the specific questions you need.

As previously noted, reviewers may object to choosing a limit for system metrics. They may say there's no point stating that the system can only support 1 million users, for instance, when in all likelihood it could do many times that number successfully, or conversely, it might not get anywhere near that number in reality. While there may be no difference between 1 million and 10 million users for the development team, there is a large difference in what you have to test and support, so you need to agree on that number.

These are likely to be areas the reviewers haven't considered before, which will generate some discussion. Except for when it affects testing, it's best to let the subject matter experts decide those points. Your contribution to the process was asking the question and recording the answer. The same applies to learning about feature behavior, as shown in the next section.

Opening the black box

The most valuable part of the specification review is quizzing the developers on the extra work they had to do. Which special cases did they have to write additional code for? Explicitly ask that question because it may not be evident from either the product owner requests or your exploratory testing what work has been necessary.

You can invite the developers to present the architecture to discuss how the different sections work together and how this feature was implemented. This loses the naivety that was helpful during exploratory testing but, at this stage, it's much more important to be an expert in the workings of the feature.

Understanding the architecture helps explain which variables are independent of each other and can be tested individually and which you should expand out to test the entire matrix of possibilities. It also helps show areas of the test plan that need to be covered in detail and which can be checked with a single test. This will be examined more in *Chapter 6, White-Box Functional Testing*.

The developers can also let you know about the areas where they have the most concerns. What do they want to see tested? Are there any far-reaching changes they've made that they haven't been able to check? Listen carefully to that and include those concerns in the test plan. Conversely, a developer being overly confident in an area is necessary but insufficient to suggest its quality. Be wary of those areas too.

Paying attention to the confidence of individual team members and the overall tone of the meeting is important enough to need explanation and is covered next.

Setting a good tone for the meeting

So far, this review sounds like it's being conducted by polite robots, dispassionately discussing the best way to approach a feature. The team members will already have a lot invested in it, and conflicting characters might cause issues, so your specification review meeting should have a friendly and supportive tone. This is vital to drawing out discussions and resolving them successfully. If you are running this meeting, it is your job to set the meeting's tone.

Why should a technical book about testing have a section on being nice to people? Aren't SQL injections, database performance, boundary value analysis, and other things more important? While I will cover those areas, testing involves a lot of communication, both to understand features and to report issues. I promise it will only be this once, but, especially during the specification review, personal interactions can be the difference between a successful feature release and a failure. It's worth explicitly describing the tone you should set in a review meeting.

> **Real-world example – A failure to communicate**
>
> Early in my career, I worked on a feature with a senior developer. He was a big character around the office. Bombastic, you might say. Though I knew vastly less than him, I thought there was a problem in one section of the code he'd worked on, so I pointed out that he might want to rethink that area.
>
> He replied that he was perfectly happy with that section of code, and we left it at that. Later, the code was released, and the behavior I'd flagged was indeed a bug we had to fix urgently. He asked why I hadn't told him about that problem. I thought I had, but I'd failed to get my point across, and the product had suffered as a result.

Specification reviews challenge the developers and product managers to see whether they have thought through this feature well. Any contradictions or gaps you find are errors they made. As a tester, you're a professional at pointing out other people's mistakes. Software development is such a complex field that fixing it is a full-time job and an entire industry. Despite your experience at finding bugs, perhaps the product owner doesn't take kindly to you rewriting their specification, or the developers are happy with the error handling they've already implemented and are disinclined to revisit that code.

All the techniques you use when raising bugs apply here, too: be specific, respectful, and impersonal. If in doubt, phrase concerns as questions rather than statements. "*Is this wrong?*" rather than "*This is wrong.*" Press your case if you don't get a satisfactory answer; keep asking questions until you're sure you understand. You need the confidence to be able to ask *stupid* questions, to start at the beginning, but make sure you fully understand the feature and how it works.

Asking questions is the best way to understand a feature. Officially known as the **Socratic method**, you can query what the behavior should be in different scenarios or how certain aspects were implemented. As a disinterested observer, you can spur the conversation to find the details you need. Arguing for specific points is good too, but the fundamental goal of the review meeting is clarity. How exactly will this feature behave? If you can specify that, then the meeting was a success.

There can also be tensions within the test team. Writing a long, detailed specification means someone has some long, detailed testing in their future. It can help if the person writing the specification is different from the person who will eventually perform the testing. It can be easier to sign up to work if someone else will carry it out. It worked well when I, as the team manager, wrote specifications for my team members to test, though team members could take turns preparing the specifications for one another. The disadvantage is that you need to hand over the task from one team member to another, but that cost can be worth it.

Having drawn out all the issues and documented the changes you need, you can then start to plan out how to approach your testing. That too needs to be reviewed by these stakeholders.

Prioritizing requirement testing

Describing how to plan and track testing tasks is beyond the scope of this book, but the specification review meeting is an excellent opportunity to prioritize the testing. All parts of the feature specification are not equal; some will be well understood and covered by the developer's testing and used by product owners, while others will be risky and/or rely solely on the test team. As described previously, the developers can indicate which areas they are most worried about. If it's possible to disable some parts of the feature, the product owners can tell which areas are the most important to test and release first.

Some areas of the test plan are easy to test, such as customer-facing interfaces. Others are backend systems that may require specialist knowledge or areas that need scripting or test tools to exercise. Those areas that will take the longest to set up should ideally be started first. If you have multiple people working on a project, someone can start with those while another team member starts testing the riskiest areas.

With those details in place, you need a final check to make sure everything is ready before the meeting is over.

Review meeting checklist

The goal of the review meeting is to agree on all the requirements in the feature specification so that detailed testing is possible and the development team knows exactly what to deliver. To achieve that, before you let everyone go at the end of the meeting, make sure you have covered all the following points:

- Has the team agreed to all the requirements in the feature specification?

- What questions are outstanding? Who will answer them, and who will check they've been answered?

- Have you asked the developers for any code paths they had to add to cover special cases?

- Are there any configuration options that aren't listed in the specification?

- Has the team agreed to all the cases where you proposed a requirement or behavior? (That includes any requirements you wrote aiming to be precisely wrong rather than vaguely right.)

- Have you prioritized different areas of the specification? Which sections should you test first?

If all that is in place, you are ready to write up your notes, issue one last version of the feature specification with all the changes included, and begin testing in earnest.

Summary

In this chapter, you learned how to run a successful feature specification review. We looked at the advantages and disadvantages of a meeting dedicated to reviewing the specification and some alternatives. No other meeting gives the same coverage and flexibility as a specification review, making it the best way to finalize and agree on feature specifications.

To run a successful review, you need to invite the right people, including the product owner, lead developer, tester, and user experience designer, for any customer-facing features. System architects, senior developers, and testers may also come along, especially if junior engineers have developed this feature. The project manager can also attend to check on scope changes and their effect on timescales. They should be invited with sufficient time to read the specification and prepare. In the meeting, step through each requirement, either agreeing on it or debating what changes it needs. Keep the tone open and friendly to solicit all possible comments and objections.

One key piece of feedback is knowledge of how the feature works internally. We'll revisit this in *Chapter 6, White-Box Functional Testing*, but here, you can get the first description of how a feature's implementation affects its visible function.

Finally, at the end of the review, you can run through a checklist to ensure that everything has been covered and plan out the priorities for which test tasks to approach first.

The functional specification review is such a vital part of the process that it deserves a dedicated meeting and a dedicated discussion. Whenever I have tried to skip this step, either because a feature appeared small and obvious or due to other work impacting the project, I have always regretted it. You can gain some of the same benefits from informal conversations, but there is no substitute for systematically working through every one of the requirements. Recommend that senior members of the team attend this meeting. If they only attend one meeting associated with the feature, make it this one, because it includes all the details of how the feature will work and it forms the basis of future testing.

With the feature specification written and reviewed, you can begin to plan the testing phase. This is the topic of the next chapter and the next section.

4

Test Types, Cases, and Environments

A tourist asks a local, "Which way is it to Dublin?"

The local answers, "Well, if I were going to Dublin, I wouldn't start from here."

– An old joke

Before we can start detailed considerations of test cases and plans, we must be clear about what each test case should include and evaluate the different approaches to writing them. Should they explicitly prescribe every action to take or merely describe the intended test, leaving individual testers to implement the details?

You have to choose your test environment. You could test on developer's machines, where new code has been written seconds before, on your live running instance available to your users, or in various locations in between, such as dedicated test areas. Using VMs and containers, as well as defining infrastructure as code, lets you create consistent environments. Choosing the right one is vital to building a successful, reproducible test process and making sure you start your testing from the right place.

Your testing must also have the conflicting strengths of being systematic and rigorous, carefully trying each possibility, while simultaneously being driven by imagination and curiosity and guided by feedback on previous errors. The specification is your guide and you need to thoroughly test it, but also improve it as you go along. We'll explore how to achieve those conflicting aims simultaneously.

We'll cover the following topics in this chapter:

- Understanding different levels of testing
- Defining test cases
- Prescriptive and descriptive test steps
- Evaluating different test environments

- Setting the correct version, configuration, and environment

- Performing systematic testing

- Testing in the release cycle

- Using curiosity and feedback

In this book, we refer to **system tests**, which test the whole production system working together. Unit tests should also be written to cover individual functions, and **integration tests** are needed to drive separate modules or services. These are generally easier to write because the system under test is simpler. You should definitely use those tests too, and they are discussed more in *Chapter 6, White-Box Functional Testing*. However, there is a class of issues that only appears during system tests, and since your customers run the entire system together, these are the most realistic and complete tests you can perform. The following section describes these types of tests in more detail and considers their strengths and weaknesses.

Understanding different levels of testing

Consider the following simplified architecture of an example system as shown in *Figure 4.1*. It has two user-facing inputs: a web interface and an API, labeled **A** and **B** on the left-hand side of the diagram, respectively. Those requests are processed by **Module 1**, which has several functions, before being passed over an internal API, labeled **C**, to **Module 2**. **Module 2** also comprises several functions. It communicates with **Module 3** using a backend API, labeled **D**. **Module 2** also has two external, read-only interfaces: a web report, labeled **E**, and automated emails, labeled **F**:

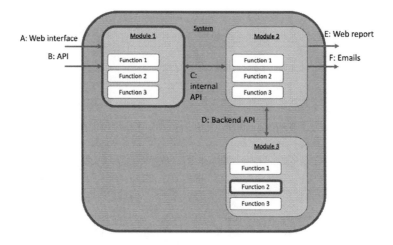

Figure 4.1 – Diagram of an example system, showing unit, integration, and system tests

Unit tests are the lowest test level, breaking the code into the smallest testable entities. That means trying individual functions and classes to ensure they correctly respond to inputs. As shown in the diagram, that would mean testing **Function 2** of **Module 3** independent of the rest of the system to ensure it functions correctly in isolation. The same could be done to any of the individual subsystems shown in the diagram.

Integration testing isolates a particular module. As highlighted in *Figure 4.1*, to test **Module 1**, you need to control its three interfaces, **A**, **B**, and **C**. The web interface and the API are public-facing and are likely to be well-documented and understood. The output of **Module 1** is the internal API, **C**. To test that, you would need to be able to mimic the behavior of **Module 2** by building a **stub** or a **mock** program.

Stubs are simple pieces of code that return fixed values – for example, always indicating success. They are stateless and hardcoded and are therefore closely coupled with the tests that use them. They're most helpful for checking the state of the system under test.

Mocks are more complex. They are configurable via some interface and have a broader range of behavior, making them less closely coupled to the tests that use them. They check the communication with the system under test and the interface between them.

In our example, we would need a stub or a mock on interface **C** to ensure that **Module 1** sends the right messages. Then, we can completely ignore the behavior of **Module 2** and **Module 3**; they don't even need to be running. This is especially useful in a big project to decouple the requirements. If you have a new feature and the change is finished in **Module 1** but not in **Module 2**, you can't system-test it entirely yet. However, by adding it to the mock program on interface **C**, you can still perform integration testing on **Module 1** in isolation.

Finally, you can perform **system testing** around the system as a whole. Then, you can ignore internal interfaces **C** and **D** and only test the inputs on interfaces **A** and **B** and the outputs on interfaces **E** and **F**. Your tests should only focus on those interfaces, although the tests can be informed by the contents of interfaces **C** and **D** when you design white-box tests (see *Chapter 6, White-Box Functional Testing*).

System testing is closely related to **end-to-end testing**, which also tests the external interfaces of a product. End-to-end testing is a subset of system testing, specifically focusing on the flow through the different states of your product and the data integrity during each state. How to consider your system's state machine is described in *Chapter 6, White-Box Functional Testing*. System testing is broader and encompasses usability, maintainability, load testing, and the other subjects of subsequent chapters, so I will discuss end-to-end tests as part of system testing.

The next section illustrates the different types of testing with a worked example.

Test level examples

To illustrate these levels of testing, let's consider the example of creating a new user within the system shown in *Figure 4.1*.

At the lowest level, unit tests should focus only on a single function in a single module of the code – in this case, the function that creates the user. So the test would call that function and assert that the user is present in the database with all columns set to their correct default values.

This test needs the code and database to be running but doesn't depend on the **user interface** (**UI**) or any internal APIs. Even within this limited test, note that you need to check every column to ensure it is correctly populated – don't just check for the presence of the user. Even with a small and seemingly simple test, it is possible to leave gaps.

The intermediate level is integration testing – for example, internal APIs between different modules within the code. An example test would send an internal API message to the database to create a new user. Check that the user is available with its data correctly populated.

This API message should be identical to the one that the frontend system sends to the database. Aim to mimic the real usage as closely as possible, which means updating the test if the frontend behavior changes. You'll need to keep these tests up to date or risk missing bugs, as they behave differently to the live system.

When the user is created, check its result at the same level by sending another command with the same API. This ensures you are testing a single interface, but checks the whole module's performance, including the database, processing, and transmission of data. If you check the database directly, for instance, as in the previous unit test, you will miss bugs on the internal API.

Finally, the system tests use the entire system in a realistic way. An example test would create a user and ensure all their information is visible on their profile screen.

This test requires the UI and all the internal steps. It relies on the UI working, as well as its connection to the backend and the database. The check is performed at the same level again by reading the UI to verify the entire application. The system test is the most complex and has the most dependencies; it is also the slowest to run. However, it provides the most complete testing. If that passes, the internal interfaces must be working.

The unit test example covered a back end function, but you should also have unit tests for the frontend, of course. For instance, check that user screens are identical after each code change that is supposed to leave them untouched.

These are unit, integration, and system-level tests. The majority of this book will describe system tests, as they are the most complex and have many possible variations, but next, we consider how the different levels of tests should work together.

Test ordering

In this book, I have described exploratory testing being run first, along with specifying the feature. In practice, unit tests are likely to be written by the developer first during the initial implementation. Recall the testing spiral from *Chapter 1, Making the Most of Exploratory Testing*; the first round of unit testing is completed along with the initial implementation.

Here, I imagine a tester picking up the code for testing after that initial implementation, or possibly working with the developer to review and consult on their work. At that stage, you will need to explore and thoroughly specify the feature – then, you can check on any tests that are already present before expanding them and designing more.

How many tests you should aim to have at each level is considered in the next section.

The testing pyramid

The testing pyramid was described by Mike Cohn in his book *Succeeding with Agile*. While I have tweaked the details of his description, the overall philosophy is very useful. Cohn proposed that unit tests form the base of the pyramid, with *service tests* above that and *UI tests* at the peak. Here, we will translate those into *integration tests* and *system tests,* respectively, to apply the same ideas:

* Write many small, isolated tests covering limited functionality (unit tests)
* The more functionality tests check, the fewer of them you should have (integration and system tests)

It's important to have tests at multiple levels. The analysis of advantages and disadvantages in the next section doesn't conclude that one type is superior, but rather that you need all kinds of tests to mitigate the weaknesses of the others.

The test pyramid, following the terms used here, looks like this:

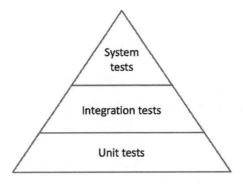

Figure 4.2 – The testing pyramid in terms of unit, integration, and system tests

The key strengths of **unit tests** are how small and fast they are to execute. Because each test is so limited, you will need lots of them, but that's fine because they are quick to write and run.

At the next level are **integration tests**. These cover a wide range of functionality but are still limited to one area of the system. You should aim to have fewer of those since they are harder to write, run, and maintain.

Finally, at the top level are the **system tests**. These are the slowest to run and the hardest to maintain, but provide invaluable coverage of the entire system working together. There may be fewer of them, but they give you the most confidence that your product will work in practice. Due to their scope and complexity, this book focuses on system tests.

The following sections describe the strengths and weaknesses of each kind of test in more detail.

Advantages and disadvantages of unit tests

Now that we've seen how the different types of tests work, we can consider their strengths and weaknesses. First, let's refer to unit tests. Because they check such small pieces of code, the number of variables and possible outcomes is also small. This simplicity is their main strength, as shown in this table:

Advantages	Disadvantages
Simple	More code to change during refactoring
Reliable	Require developer time
Easy for the developer to write	Hard for anyone else to write
Don't require a full system	Ill-suited to UI tests
Increase code documentation	Risk being unrealistic
Find problems early	Limits to what they can cover
Fast to run	
Easier to maintain	
Easier to debug	

Table 4.1 – Advantages and disadvantages of unit tests

Unit tests tend to be small and reliable, testing a particular function with a known and limited set of inputs and outputs. They are tightly coupled to the code, making them easy to write for the developer associated with that feature but harder for anyone else. Because the tests are limited, they don't require a whole system to run nor do they require stubs or mock interfaces; this makes them quicker and simpler to set up than integration tests. By showing how the code behaves, they help to increase the documentation, and as they are written at the same time as the feature, they find problems early in the release cycle.

Because they are small functions only running part of the code, unit tests are usually faster than integration or system tests, which can require frameworks or applications to run. Because they each test a very specific function, they have very few dependencies, making them more reliable. Crucially, that makes them easier to debug and maintain, which is the major ongoing cost of automated tests.

On the downside, unit tests are closely coupled with the code they test. If that code is refactored, you will also have to refactor the unit tests, which isn't the case for integration and system-level tests, which only interact with the interfaces to the system. Since developers usually write unit tests, these cost the developer time and can't easily be handed over to the test team. However, if the test team can be trained to write these tests, it is useful for them and the project. Unit tests are also poorly suited to graphical outputs such as UIs and are the least realistic test type considered here. You can show that a function behaves correctly with some inputs, but it may never receive those inputs in the running system. Conversely, it may receive inputs that the unit tests don't cover. It can be hard to make unit tests cover realistic scenarios, which is easier with other forms of testing.

In summary, unit tests are a quick and reliable way to find bugs early. They will improve the quality of your code and should be a part of your test strategy. However, they will never be complete, so you should augment them with integration and system tests.

Advantages and disadvantages of integration tests

Integration tests are more realistic than unit tests because they test an entire module or service. With many functions working together, you can test their interactions without requiring the whole system to be running. The strengths and weaknesses of this approach are as follows:

Advantages	Disadvantages
Can decouple sections of large projects	It takes time to set up stubs and mocks
Match testing to functional units	Risk being unrealistic
Match testing to organizational units	Take developer time
Failures are isolated	More complicated than unit tests
Simpler than system tests	Limited coverage
Agnostic to implementation	
Don't require a full system	

Table 4.2 – Advantages and disadvantages of integration tests

Integration tests help decouple different parts of projects. If one team has completed the work in their module, you can test that in isolation and gain confidence, even if other necessary work elsewhere isn't complete yet. You need further system testing when both sections are finished, but testing can start before that. Integration tests match up with the functional units of the code, making it easier to identify who is responsible for any issues you find. If a single team owns that module, that team needs to fix the problems you encounter there. The failures are quicker to diagnose because they come from a single module, making them easier to debug than system tests where multiple modules work together.

Unlike unit tests, integration tests are agnostic to the implementation. You can refactor the code completely, but as long as the behavior on the module's interfaces is unchanged, the tests will keep passing without being updated. Integration tests also don't require a complete system, making them cheaper and less resource-intensive.

The disadvantage of not running on the whole system is that you must substitute stubs or mock programs on the interfaces to other parts of the system. Those take time to write, have to be set up and maintained, and need to be kept up to date to accurately reflect the behavior of the other modules. That takes development time, and stubs can be unrealistic even then. This might invalidate the testing, which is always a risk with integration tests.

An integration test could fail because a specific module returns an invalid response to a particular input. However, if it never receives that input in the actual system, the bug would never be triggered. Integration tests can find such an issue, which should be fixed in case a future code change reveals it. However, that isn't a realistic bug, so it's a false-positive result. System testing avoids such false-positives by only performing realistic testing.

Integration tests are far more complicated than unit tests to run and debug, but even with that extra complexity, there are still classes of issues they can't find, such as issues between modules. Two modules may work individually and pass their respective integration tests, but they can still fail when they run together. For instance, if one module counts users including disabled users while another counts users excluding disabled users, their respective totals and behaviors won't match. You can only find that class of bug with system testing.

Integration testing can be helpful in systems that are difficult to set up and test as a whole. Still, they take effort to run and maintain while lacking the simplicity of unit tests and the comprehensive coverage of system tests.

Advantages and disadvantages of system tests

System tests are the only tests capable of finding all classes of realistic bugs. For all their disadvantages, that fact makes them indispensable. The following table shows their overall strengths and weakness:

Advantages	Disadvantages
Most realistic	Most complicated
Easiest to set up	Difficult to diagnose issues
Can be performed by any user	Issues have to be assigned to the right team
Agnostic to implementation	Require all components to be available
The only way to find certain issues	Slowest to run
	Least reliable

Table 4.3 – Advantages and disadvantages of system tests

System tests are the most complicated to run. Considering all possible system states and inputs, the potential test matrix becomes impossibly large for an application of any size. You always have to choose and prioritize which tests you will perform. As well as being complicated to run, issues are challenging to diagnose, as they could come from any part of the system. The root cause of a problem may be far from the visible symptom. That needs to be investigated and understood before issues can be assigned to the right team, which can add confusion and delays that don't affect unit and integration tests. System tests also require all components to be available. You can't carry out system tests on a new feature that spans different modules until all the modules have code ready to test, making it the last form of testing you can run.

System tests are usually the slowest to run, requiring a complete system with messages traversing every stage. If you add shortcuts or mock interfaces, you'll lose the realism that makes system tests so useful, so there is a limit to how fast they can be executed. Because they use a whole system, they have the most dependencies, which makes them the least reliable form of testing. A failure in any part of the system can result in an error, making it the hardest to maintain.

Despite those disadvantages, system testing is the most realistic. System tests can accurately represent real behavior if you use comparable hardware and data to that of your live product. System tests don't require developers to write dedicated tests or stub programs. Testing can start with a tester pretending to be a new user and stepping through the initial setup. While creating realistic load levels or comparable data is simplest with system tests, generating realistic load levels can be challenging. However, that is ultimately down to the limitations of your setup; system tests can perform those checks if the tools are available.

Because they involve using your product for real, any user can perform system tests, from developers and testers to product owners and from the documentation team to companies for external testing. As with integration tests, they are agnostic to the implementation. The development team can completely refactor the code, but the same tests will pass if the interfaces are unchanged. Most crucially, there are some bugs that only system testing can find. Due to that unique completeness, system tests must form a part of your test strategy, despite their complexities and difficulties. Because of that completeness, system testing is the form of testing I focus on here to show you how to resolve its challenges and mitigate its weaknesses.

Before running our first systematic test case, we need to be clear about what a test case is, which is described in the next section.

Defining test cases

You will be running many test cases as part of your testing, so it's important to be clear about exactly what they entail. Each test comprises four elements:

- Prerequisites

- Setup

- Procedure

- Result

First, you must set up the necessary prerequisites: are you running the correct services with the correct version and configuration? It's obvious, but it's easy to miss a critical step and waste test time. The upcoming *Setting the correct version, configuration, and environment* section describes testing prerequisites in more detail. Those only need to be prepared once for a whole series of tests.

For each test, you need to make sure the setup is correct. Do you need a user or a particular set of data, or is the requirement explicitly to start without any information? Consider the initial state you need for your test and make it explicit. The trick is to make your assumptions clear. There are an infinite number of variables that you could specify; you need to pick the variables relevant to this test. While some are obvious, others might not be. Do users need to clear their cookies, uninstall a program, or clear registry entries before a test? What state might be left behind by previous tests that could confound your tests?

> **Real-world example – Too many upgrades**
>
> We tested many development builds during a waterfall development cycle, finding and fixing scores of bugs. We finally released it on our live system, only for the upgrade to immediately fail. We couldn't upgrade it at all and had to roll back. We'd never seen that problem in any of our tests, but every live upgrade failed. What had gone wrong?
>
> The live system jumped from the last build on our previous branch, *5.0.17*, to the final build on our new branch, *5.1.23*. However, it hadn't gone through all the intermediate steps of *5.1.1*, *5.1.2*, *5.1.3*, and so on. One of our database migrations was faulty and would only work if performed in stages. We had gradually upgraded all our test systems between those builds, but the live system hadn't been. We needed a new blocking test to perform the upgrade precisely as it would apply to live customers. We required an explicit prerequisite not to go through intermediate builds.

With the procedure and setup clearly described, you can perform the planned tests, and this book describes many possible test procedures for common design patterns. Finally, you need to document the result. As with the setup, there are many different states you can check. The skill in designing the tests is carefully choosing the checks you will perform. Those considerations are discussed in the upcoming *Determining what to check* section.

You need to document each part of the test case, so you need a test management system to track them. As well as having explicit steps for each test, you also need to be able to reference them. Every test should have an ID that links to the requirements it covers and the bugs it reveals. That lets you track which tests were most useful.

Each test should follow these six principles:

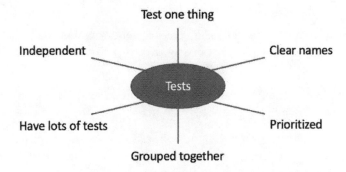

Figure 4.3 - Principles when writing test cases

- **Be independent of other tests**: Ideally, each test would pass or fail on its own. That way, where there is a failure, there is a clear indicator, rather than many tests failing all at once. In practice, this is hard to achieve and many tests depend on previous tests passing. In that case, make tests as linear as possible, so it's obvious that nothing beyond a certain step worked. Again, that makes investigation much easier.

- **Each test should check one thing**: In addition to being independent of others, each test should have one purpose and check only one piece of functionality, as far as possible. Then, you know the cause of the failure and can easily debug it.

- **Don't be afraid of having many tests**: A corollary to each test checking only one thing is that you may need a lot of them. Again, that is fine. Lay them out clearly.

- **Group your tests together**: With lots of tests to manage, ensure they are divided up into different sections and folders so you know where to find them and where new ones should be added.

- **Give tests clear names**: When looking down a list of failures, make it easy to see what went wrong by including clear names. This may mean you need long names and that's fine.

- **Prioritize test cases**: Plan to have lots of test cases, but not for them all to be equal. If they start taking too long to run, focus on the happy path tests and areas of known weakness where you've found bugs before.

Following these principles also makes test statistics more meaningful. How many tests have you run and how many are left to do? Is the pass rate rising or falling? You need graphs and charts to see the status of your testing at a glance. That comes from accurate reporting of the test cases and their results. If you aren't documenting that already, set up a system to track your next round of testing.

Once your documentation process is in place, you can consider the content of the tests, starting with the level of detail they should contain.

Prescriptive and descriptive test steps

When writing manual tests, you can choose how precise your descriptions are. Either you can specify exactly what to do and how to do it, or you can only say what to do, leaving the details for each tester to decide.

For instance, a descriptive test might say: "On the user settings page, upload an avatar `.jpeg` image between 100 KB and 5 MB in size."

Note that while there are instructions on what to do, the tester can use any image they like that matches those criteria. In contrast, a prescriptive test might say exactly which file to use: "On the user settings page, upload `/fixtures/image1.jpeg` as an avatar image."

Here, `image1.jpeg` is a suitable image within that size range. If you are testing a text input, you can specify the exact strings to try or just describe what contents they should have.

Prescriptive tests are also known as *low-level* test cases, with complete detail on what to do and how to do it. **Descriptive tests** are also known as *high-level* cases, stating the goal of the test but leaving out implementation details. Both approaches have different strengths, but overall, there is a benefit to not being overly prescriptive in your test cases.

The advantages and disadvantages of prescriptive test cases are as follows:

Advantages	Disadvantages
Quicker for manual testers to perform	It takes more time and effort to design them
The test is more likely to be run correctly	Limit creativity
Even junior team members can run tests correctly	May make the testing role dull for testers
Easily automatable	Limit test coverage
Easier to describe the required outcomes	

Table 4.4 – Advantages and disadvantages of prescriptive tests

If the test plan describes an exact input, that is quicker for manual testers since they don't need to decide what text to use, for instance, or find a suitable .jpeg image. They are also more likely to perform the test correctly since there is less choice about what they are doing. That means they are easier for junior testers to run because they can see exactly what to do. Prescriptive tests are easy to automate since there is one exact step to take, and means there is a single expected outcome for both automated systems and manual testers to check. Because of that, automated tests are almost always prescriptive.

However, writing a prescriptive test case takes more time and effort because you need to work out precisely the steps to take. That limits the tester's creativity; they don't get to choose what to do, discouraging their curiosity and exploration. That makes the role of a tester less interesting, making it harder to find and retain the best team members. Worst of all, though, is that prescriptive tests limit the test coverage you achieve. If you run the same test repeatedly, it will catch regressions in that area, but it will never uncover a new issue.

By allowing testers to use different files in upload, for instance, you add variety that is more likely to discover possible issues and is more like customer behavior. Maybe a new format or option, such as higher resolution files, has gained popularity. Using a single file is fixed in time. If you are still running that same test five years later, you will never try new formats, but by using a new file each time, you have the chance to find that change. If every tester uploads a different image in their tests, you have tested a wider range of inputs. Ideally, you could think this through in advance and review and update tests to use any new options or formats that appear. However, allowing testers some leeway gives them a chance to catch such changes.

Descriptive tests, in contrast, don't specify the exact method to follow, allowing testers to make choices for themselves. The strengths and weaknesses of descriptive test cases are as follows:

Advantages	Disadvantages
Provide more varied testing	Less reproducible
Keep up to date with changes	Require more experienced staff
Help to avoid the pesticide paradox	May be performed incorrectly
Quicker to define	
Use the tester's experience	

Table 4.5 – The advantages and disadvantages of descriptive test cases

As noted, descriptive tests provide more varied testing and keep up to date with changes in how your users use your product. Varying inputs also help avoid what the ISTQB syllabus calls the *pesticide paradox*. One of its seven software testing principles is that tests are less and less likely to find issues if you keep running the same ones. That's analogous to using the same pesticide, which gradually becomes less effective, as only pests with resistance to that chemical will remain. In the software domain, that is because the code in that area becomes more mature and stable; it may have fewer changes after its initial implementation. Running the same code, in the same way, will keep passing. You need a more varied approach to find issues and altering the inputs is an excellent way to achieve that.

Because you don't have to specify the exact steps to take, descriptive tests are quicker to write, making the most of a tester's experience. If a tester can think up interesting new cases to try, they can perform them as part of that test run.

On the downside, descriptive test cases are less reproducible. If you see a problem with one particular file, for instance, you may not know what about that file caused the test to fail. Your bug reports need to include the details of your choices because those details aren't included in the test plan.

Descriptive tests need more experience to run, both to try out interesting new cases and ensure they are run correctly. Their vagueness increases the chance of mistakes. For instance, a tester might choose a file that doesn't meet the test criteria and so does not test the particular case they were meant to exercise. Testers will need more training and monitoring to make sure they understand precisely what they should be doing.

This isn't an area where compromise works well, so don't have a mixture of prescriptive and descriptive tests. Pick one approach and stick to it. Mixing tests means that testers will be surprised by a lack of information in the descriptive sections and may not be ready to add the extra detail themselves.

Overall, the superior test coverage provided by descriptive tests is more important. If a tester needs help, you can suggest what they should do, or a test plan could have examples of scenarios to run in case testers are unsure. Ideally, they should not use the old examples, however, but use their own system in their own way to find new bugs. You always find the best bugs when you stray from the test plan.

This discussion of prescriptive and descriptive tests applies to manual testers running a written test plan. For automated testing, you have to specify the file, or set of files, that the automated system will use. If you are writing test cases to be carried out manually, you can let the tester decide, but when running automated tests, you have to choose the dataset it will use. The automated tests then repeat that example on every test run, so it suffers from the disadvantages of prescriptive testing. To mitigate that, you could have a bank of different options that the tests choose between each time, but the possibilities are all specified as part of the auto-test system.

The data you use for automated tests should be regularly reviewed and updated to avoid the pesticide paradox and give you the chance to find new issues. To simplify that, ensure that there is a clear separation between your tests and their data, so you can easily check their values and add new entries.

With the test cases defined and documented, we can start to put the prerequisites in place, the first of which is the test environment. There are several options for that, as described in the next section.

Evaluating different test environments

For system testing, you need a test environment. Unit testing and some integration testing can be carried out on individual modules and components, but to perform system testing, you need a system to test, as the name suggests. That cannot be development machines where the developers may be making constant changes and it cannot be the live environment, by which time it's too late to prevent the damage bugs cause. You need a test environment between the development and live installations to perform your testing. If you don't have one, setting that up is your first task before you can do any testing.

The test environment could be a blank installation that you spin up as needed, picking up the latest code. Alternatively, you could have a staging area or beta environment that constantly runs. Both approaches have different benefits, considered next.

Using temporary test environments

This table shows the advantages and disadvantages of temporary test environments:

Advantages	Disadvantages
Guaranteed to be running the latest code	All users need to be able to create the environment
Always start from a known state	Need configuring for non-standard tests
No ongoing maintenance	No real historical usage
No ongoing running costs	
Easy to test multiple changes in parallel	

Table 4.6 – Advantages and disadvantages of temporary testing environments

With temporary testing environments, you always start from a known state and are guaranteed to be running the latest code. This is great for development when you can try out a new change compared to the old behavior, and that means there are no ongoing maintenance or running costs when the system isn't in use. Best of all, many different users can create environments, so they can all make many changes simultaneously. That makes this arrangement necessary for development. Testers can also test changes in isolation when they are new and more likely to have issues. When they have passed that initial testing, then changes can be combined.

On the downside, all the users need to be able to create that environment; there isn't one sitting there ready to be used. That is easier for developers who are more used to the tools and spend most of their time working on the system. For users who only use the test system as a part of their job, such as product owners or the support or documentation teams, setting up a new environment can be more of a challenge, depending on how simple and reliable that process is. Ideally, use infrastructure as code to specify and create the environment in the same way every time it is needed. There should be as few steps as possible for users so that it is quicker and easier with fewer places where it could go wrong.

Because the system is always newly created, you'll need to configure any non-standard settings you need for your testing and it doesn't have any real historical usage. You can simulate this by generating test data, but it may not reveal genuine issues.

Using permanent staging areas

In contrast, staging areas run constantly, bringing different strengths and weaknesses. This table lists their advantages and disadvantages:

Advantages	Disadvantages
Quick to use for short tests	Require upgrades
Easier to monitor	Require maintenance
Can find issues due to running long term	Can contain bad data from development builds
Accumulate historical data	Issues affect many users simultaneously

Table 4.7 – Advantages and disadvantages of a permanent testing environment

Staging areas are great for short tests. They run continually, so you can quickly go to the feature you need and try out your test case. That's useful for product owners trying out new features or testers answering a quick question. You can set up monitoring that matches the live system on the staging area to report errors or system issues. Staging errors make it easier to spot the problems that appear over time, such as memory leaks or excessive disk usage. They also naturally accumulate historical data, such as the configuration created on old versions that have been migrated. This means you get some background testing for free, although it's hard to judge its extent and coverage.

On the downside, staging areas require upgrades and maintenance. You can automate upgrades, but breakages need to be investigated and triaged and that can be a difficult and unpopular task among the team. Staging areas can also generate spurious errors due to bad data written by the development code. If an early version wrote incorrect data, you have to find and fix the code that went wrong and remove or correct the erroneous data. These can create subtle problems and I've seen issues appear over a year after the initial bug. For instance, a new version of code might add additional checks that reject invalid data, whereas before, there were no visible symptoms. A temporary test environment with new data for each installation avoids those uninteresting problems.

And finally, because many users share staging environments, any outages cause problems for many people. You can't perform destructive tests (see *Chapter 11, Destructive Testing*) without giving a warning and potentially disrupting other people.

Temporary testing environments and staging areas are helpful for different tasks and I believe you always need both. Temporary environments are useful for developers to work on and staging areas are useful for more realistic testing or quick tests, such as those performed by product owners. Testers sit between those two, so you can choose where is best to base your testing.

Once you have selected your test environment and successfully run it, you need to ensure you are on the correct version with the correct configuration, as described next.

Setting the correct version, configuration, and environment

One of the biggest wastes of time when testing is using the wrong version or configuration. Testing can go quickly when everything is working as planned. As soon as something goes wrong, you must stop and investigate, which should be reserved for genuine bugs. Anything you can fix yourself, you should do first.

Before it can run the correct version, your product must have proper versioning. If your development team lets you test whatever code happens to be in the repository, that is the first thing that has to change. The test team needs to use a stable, numbered build. That isn't required for exploratory testing and lower-level tests, such as component and integration tests, which can run on every build and use nothing more than a build number. However, by the time you come to run the comprehensive functional tests, you need to know which version of code you were running.

Within fully **Continuous Integration/Continuous Delivery** (**CI/CD**) deployments, where every change is tested and pushed live, versioning becomes much more fluid, but even there, you can specify individual builds or tag particular builds to run tests on. That tag might be as singular as "nightly build 1,432," but by the time you have put effort into designing and running system tests, using the whole system together, getting build numbers from the development team is a hard requirement.

These builds should be available every day or so during a project to ensure that changes are being picked up regularly, but not so often that the system under test is constantly changing. For system tests, builds being produced more than once a day is too often. Similarly, if you're only getting one build per week, that allows too much time to be wasted between introducing defects and them being tested and discovered. A build every day or so keeps everything moving. If upgrades push new code to the test environment automatically, then all the better.

Development team processes vary massively, usually as a function of team size. Possibly, you work in a large multinational, and the thought of not having regular, numbered builds would instantly lead to chaos. Alternatively, you are possibly working as a small, independent software developer with legacy systems, where the idea of having CI is a distant dream. The only requirement is that once you have a test team large enough, specialized enough, and with enough time to be reading this book, you need numbered builds to run against.

Given that you have numbered builds, updated every few days, and an environment on which to run them, you can prepare the system to be tested. Which versions do you need to enable this feature? These details should be tracked in the feature specification. There will often be an obvious machine you must upgrade, but are there any others you need?

Any complex system is likely to have multiple independent builds with different build numbers, so as well as the obvious version you intend to test, you need to know all its dependencies. What other systems do you need to upgrade to use the feature successfully? The developer responsible should provide a complete list, so make sure that you have everything in place. These details aren't part of the main feature specification but should be part of the notes describing the implementation.

Next, you must check that the configuration has enabled the new feature. While the developers have made it possible to turn it on, is it actually enabled? Again, this is an easy way to waste time. Ensure that all the requirements are documented in the feature specification and then check and enable them in your test environment before you begin.

Using feature flags is a great way to control the testing and rollout of features. They let you turn a feature on for a subset of users or only in certain situations. While useful, they add another setting you have to check as a tester. If you're wondering why you don't see your new feature working, check the feature flags first.

When you have all the correct versions running, with all the necessary dependencies and configuration enabled, systematic testing can begin.

Performing systematic testing

The first step for functional testing is to systematically work through the feature specification, expanding each requirement into all the test cases required to cover it. When well-written, with sufficient detail, and each independent of the others, many requirements should need only a single test case to cover them. However, some, especially around error cases or freeform inputs such as textboxes, will require many tests to check all the possible valid and invalid cases.

The feature specification is vital here since it describes all the core functionality. By carefully writing and reviewing the specification, the test plan becomes a secondary document that is easy to prepare. Make sure you use the specification to guide the testing. This section concentrates on the happy path cases and the working routes that exercise the entire feature without hitting errors. Other sections will build on this by adding invalid cases, the performance under load, or the logging that should be written to track the system's actions. All those other forms of testing rely on the feature working, so you have to run these tests first to find any issues that block subsequent testing.

There may be tests you want to run but don't yet have the tools to carry out – maybe you need a tool to receive and parse emails or generate large amounts of load. If that's the case, add them to the test plan anyway. Make sure they aren't forgotten. Even if you have to skip them for now and raise them as longer-term test tasks, write the tests you want to perform. While someone performs the test plan, others should set those systems up. Within a test team, some members should constantly be working on improving the tools and environment, while others perform the testing of new features.

The functional specification should describe this feature's effects on all the system's interfaces. As shown in *Figure 4.1*, defining the interfaces is key to system testing. Those might be web interfaces, APIs, apps, emails, instant messages, **Simple Network Management Protocol (SNMP)**, **SSH File Transfer Protocol (SFTP)**, or many others. On hardware products, interfaces can include screens and serial interfaces. Ensure you have an explicit list of all your product's interfaces that you can consider in your testing. As you start systematic testing, check each of those interfaces and the tests you will run on each of them.

Once you have listed your interfaces, you can consider each variable within them. That might be a field in an API, data entered by the user, different responses from third parties, or different states your system can be in. For each variable, consider all possible values it can take and how you can group them. That is described in more detail in the *Understanding equivalence partitioning* section.

All variables and relevant values should be explicitly listed in the functional specification, but designing your test plan is the last chance to find any you have missed. Once you can see the space of possible inputs and states, you can then determine which are significantly different and require individual tests. That is described in more detail in the *Mapping dependent and independent variables* section.

Track which tests cover each requirement from the functional specification. A test tracking system will give you tools to make those references to see whether there are any requirements you haven't covered. If a requirement needs multiple tests, it's harder to spot, and you need to check that you have them all, so pay particular attention to those.

The next section considers when tests should be run as part of your release cycle.

Testing in the release cycle

You need to choose when you will run these different tests within your release cycle. You can select a subset of your automated tests to run against every product change as part of a CI/CD pipeline, separate from new feature testing. These CI/CD tests are vital checks to avoid bugs and issues from running live, especially if they are set to block the release process. However, these tests have strict requirements:

- **Speed**: They must run fast enough that they don't overly delay releases
- **Reliability**: They must work consistently and only fail when there is a real issue
- **Coverage**: They must cover all critical aspects of your product

There is a natural trade-off between speed and coverage: the more you test, the slower it goes, so you need to carefully judge the tests to include. These tests also need to be highly reliable, as they are run so often and can delay releases. Unit tests are ideal here as they have fewer dependencies, but you also need a few system tests to ensure the overall application still works.

CI/CD tests are just one place in the release cycle you might run tests, however. Test plans can be categorized into four levels, as shown here:

Figure 4.4 - Subsets of test cases

The base layer is **Comprehensive new feature tests**, covering anything and everything you can imagine. This book is concerned with that block of tests, which expands as you add new features to your product. Some of these tests might only be run once when a new feature is added. For instance, if you have a country dropdown with 200 options, you might try them all but only once. If Albania works, there's no reason to suspect that Armenia won't, but you would want to try it before it goes live for the first time

At the next level are **Regression tests**. These are almost as extensive as the comprehensive tests but only include tests you do want to run when this feature is modified. While there are no code changes, you don't need to run all these tests.

At the next level are **Manual/Nightly tests**. These have a time limit – for instance, 12 hours for an overnight run – so they need to be carefully prioritized. They find issues that might affect live users and would be minor outages, but cover cases that are too time-consuming to include in the CI/CD tests.

Finally, **CI/CD tests** quickly cover the critical functions of your program, providing confidence after every code change.

These levels, along with examples, are summarized in this table:

Level	When it is run	Example test
Comprehensive tests	Once, when a new feature is added	Test that users can be created with every possible country setting
Regression tests	Any time that feature is changed	Test that users can be created with all localized languages and a selection of others
Manual/nightly tests	Nightly or on-demand	Test that all pages are localized for each language
CI/CD tests	After every code change	Test that one screen is localized for each language

Table 4.8 – Examples of different test plan levels

The design of testing within a cycle and the prioritization of tests is beyond the scope of this book. Here, we focus on writing comprehensive tests covering many eventualities. With a large library of tests for your system, you can choose which to promote to the shorter test runs.

However, you can only promote tests to CI/CD testing from your library if you have an extensive test library to start with, so that is what this book aims to describe. In the next section, we consider the importance of curiosity and imagination when designing your test plan.

Using curiosity and feedback

Stepping through the test cases that the feature specification suggests may sound like a dull, robotic task, but expanding them into detailed test cases requires curiosity and investigation. As described later, it's impossible to consider every possible combination of inputs, so you must constantly pick and choose which particular options you will try. It's also always possible to extend tests – once you're in a given state, you can vary conditions and perform checks that the specification and test plan don't mention.

Throughout the entire test design and execution, maintain the inventiveness and curiosity you needed during the exploratory tests. Constantly be on the lookout for other interactions, other things to try, and other things to check. Once you are running manual tests or coding automated tests, you are spending longer examining this feature's behavior, with more information, than anyone else in the project. Make the most of these advantages to think everything through in more depth and find conditions that hadn't been previously considered.

Recall the feedback diagrams from *Chapter 1*, *Making the Most of Exploratory Testing*. You are reviewing the specification as well as the implementation. Does this feature make sense as implemented? Is there a simpler way to achieve the same aims? Are any interactions surprising or unclear? Despite all the work you put into the specification, it is never too late to identify improvements and even fundamental changes. As a tester, you are the harbinger of bad news, so lean into that and never shy away from suggesting changes, no matter their size.

While the feature specification and test plan should be as comprehensive as possible, you find the best bugs when you go beyond the test plan. Use the tests as a guide, but it's only when trying situations that haven't been considered before that you find the biggest problems. In *Chapter 1*, *Making the Most of Exploratory Testing*, I mentioned stepping through a test plan on a particular web page, then being interrupted and making the window smaller. The test plan worked fine but shrinking the browser window triggered a bug. Look out for edge cases of this kind so they can become test steps in your future test plans. The *Testing variable types* section lists common, general variables and cases to get you started. Still, you should expand these based on your situation and your product's particular behavior and weaknesses.

The test plan is a living document and should not be considered fixed. Look out for areas that regularly uncover errors and expand your testing in those areas. The results of exploratory testing and early parts of the system testing should feed back into the rest of the test plan to guide later testing. Bugs aren't evenly distributed throughout your system; they cluster in certain areas and around particular functions. Find those areas and add as much detail as possible there. Feedback is vital to uncover further bugs in those areas.

If necessary, explicitly schedule a time to consider the bugs you've found so far and how to expand the test plan before you sign it off. That can remind you to add this feedback. If you write a test plan and then simply follow it from beginning to end, you've missed the chance to improve. Iterate and learn as you go.

Testing needs to combine the rigor of carefully stepping through every case with the freedom and randomness of curiosity and exploration. A good tester will be able to call on both these contradictory skills. Your test plan is just the starting point, ready to grow and evolve based on the bugs it finds. It should be a great, detailed document, but also one you're not afraid to constantly change and improve.

Summary

In this chapter, you have learned about the different levels of testing and their respective strengths and weaknesses. Unit tests are simple and quick to write but require detailed knowledge of the code and cannot find classes of bugs that only appear when the whole system works together. System tests are the only way to find that class of bug, but they are harder to write, which is why this book focuses on them.

We looked at what a test case should include – its prerequisites, setup, procedure, and result. These are obvious enough to list, but it takes discipline to document them all consistently. You will save valuable time by being clear about what a test requires and what results you should see, so make sure they are a part of your test plans.

Prescriptive tests define precisely what steps you should run, but it can be more powerful to use descriptive tests, which allow variations within given parameters. Those tests should be run on a carefully chosen environment, not live or on the developer's machines, but a temporary or permanent environment dedicated to testing.

We saw that you should always explicitly ensure that the environment and versions are correct since using the wrong settings is the easiest way to waste time while testing. While running the tests, you also need to aim for the conflicting goals of being both rigorous and systematic while also being curious and responding to feedback. Only by embodying both these roles can you perform top-class testing.

With these considerations in place, we can turn to the details of the tests themselves, starting as a user with little system knowledge checking the main platform functionality: black-box testing, which is covered in the next chapter.

What we learned from Part 1, Preparing to Test

Part 1, Preparing to Test, has covered the necessary preparation for testing. In an ideal world, every feature would have a detailed written description of exactly what it does. In that case, you could skip *Part 1, Preparing to Test*, entirely and jump straight to *Part 2, Functional Testing*, where we consider how to test features.

However, in my experience, the test team isn't always provided with feature specifications, and those that exist aren't in sufficient detail. It's almost always up to testers to ask further questions and fill in the gaps in the description. We saw three important stages to achieve that.

Using exploratory testing you map out a feature's behavior, considering the many approaches described in this book: functional testing, error handling, usability, security, maintainability, and non-functional testing. Exploratory testing also lets you quickly find issues that would block more detailed tests.

Next, you write a feature specification to list the detailed functionality. Those specifications have a particular style – independent, testable statements that describe the behavior but not the implementation.

You cannot write the specification alone, however. You always require input from at least the product owner and lead developer. An official review meeting should step through every requirement in turn to uncover any objections or concerns. With those included, you have an excellent document on which to base your testing.

Finally, *Part 1, Preparing to Test*, discussed the different levels of testing and types of test cases. We evaluated different test environments and saw the importance of curiosity throughout the test process.

Turning your specification into test cases requires you to consider many other possible scenarios, which forms the skill of testing. *Part 2, Functional Testing*, shows how to design thorough functional test plans quickly and successfully.

Part 2 – Functional Testing

Once you have gathered detailed information about the new feature from exploratory testing, feature specifications, and test plan reviews, testing can begin in earnest. The first tests to write and perform are those assuming no knowledge of the system – black-box testing – in which the tester naively attempts to use the feature like a new user. That is followed by white-box testing, which is informed by knowledge of the underlying code to ensure that all code paths have been checked.

As well as the working cases, testing always needs to consider the error cases, invalid inputs, and internal failures, followed by user experience testing. Even though a feature may work, it may be difficult for users to learn or use. It's a tester's job to highlight those weaknesses, which have a different set of considerations. The feature must be tested for security weaknesses, and you need to check the logs and event metrics. With all that testing complete you can be confident of a secure, easy-to-use, and robust feature, but there are still loading and system failures to consider, which are covered in *Part 3, Non-Functional Testing*.

This part comprises the following chapters:

- *Chapter 5, Black-Box Functional Testing*
- *Chapter 6, White-Box Functional Testing*
- *Chapter 7, Testing of Error Cases*
- *Chapter 8, User Experience Testing*
- *Chapter 9, Security Testing*
- *Chapter 10, Maintainability*

Black-Box Functional Testing

"Suppose everyone had a box with something in it: we call it a "beetle." No one can look into anyone else's box, and everyone says he knows what a beetle is only by looking at his beetle…

The thing in the box has no place in the language-game at all; not even as a something: for the box might even be empty. No, one can 'divide through' by the thing in the box; it cancels out, whatever it is."

- Ludwig Wittgenstein, Philosophical Investigations

Black-box functional testing is what most people imagine when they think of software testing. Of all the chapters in this book, this one will likely be most familiar to you. If you've done any software testing, it will have started here.

Black-box testing covers the happy-path scenarios—the working cases that show the feature behaving as it should under normal conditions. Since this is only one chapter in a much larger book, you can see testing comprises more than that, but the main functionality is where your testing should start. Without the basic functionality in place and working, there's no point continuing onto the finer points of testing. If a user can't even enter their password, you can't test how secure it is; if emails fail to send, you can't test whether it can handle a thousand in a minute, and so forth. This chapter describes how to test those first cases in detail.

We'll cover the following topics in this chapter:

- How to enable new features
- Different types of testing: API-based, CRUD testing, and negative testing
- Identifying worst-case scenarios
- Equivalence partitioning and boundary value analysis
- How to test different variable types
- Uncovering hidden defects

- Optimizing error guessing

- Determining what checks to perform

- Precision versus brittleness in automated tests

- Comparing bugs and features

As we have seen, system testing breaks down into multiple approaches, such as usability, security, maintainability. Here we consider black-box testing, starting with its strengths and weaknesses.

Advantages and disadvantages of black-box testing

The different forms of testing have neatly interlocking advantages and disadvantages. Therefore, unlike in *Part 1, Preparing to Test*, I won't consider alternatives to each kind of testing. Each one is suited to finding a distinctive class of bugs but suffers from particular weaknesses. Only by combining them can you mitigate those shortcomings and achieve comprehensive test coverage.

The advantages and disadvantages of black-box testing are as follows:

Advantages	Disadvantages
Realistic	May not cover all the code
Covers the main functionality	Does not cover error cases
Takes a user's point of view	Difficult to debug
No need to learn implementation details	Repeats previous tests

Table 5.1 – Advantages and disadvantages of black-box testing

The advantages of black-box testing are that it is realistic, performing actions your users will take themselves. In other testing areas, we will cover rarer cases: errors and system failures, security attacks, and loading, among others. Those are essential cases, but you are unlikely to hit them on any given day. On the other hand, black-box testing covers the main use cases and the parts of your product that must work well. These tests take the user's point of view, with no allowance for the code or system architecture. This means you are most likely to hit the issues that will affect real customers.

These tests are also relatively easy to run. You don't need to know a programming language or understand the code; you don't need to learn techniques for security testing, nor have tools to generate excessive load like other testing areas. That means a wide variety of users can carry it out; this part of system testing could be performed by product owners or a documentation team, or it could be outsourced to an external team.

Despite its ease and realism, black box testing is unlikely to cover all possible code paths because it doesn't consider the implementation. That requires white-box testing, described in the next chapter. While you might try error cases as part of black-box testing, they aren't tried systematically here. Because black-box testing tests the whole system, it is difficult to diagnose the root cause of issues and debug them. Bugs also need to be triaged, which adds delays. And due to covering common cases, these tests are likely duplicates of exploratory testing or testing the developer performed. However, it is still necessary to step through them systematically and thoroughly to ensure you haven't missed anything.

As we will see, the disadvantages of the different types of testing aren't reasons not to carry them out. Instead, they show it's necessary to perform varied testing. You can mitigate their weaknesses by augmenting tests from one area with those from another. For instance, you can explicitly list error cases (see *Chapter 7, Testing of Error Cases*) to ensure they are covered separately from the primary use case testing. For complete coverage, you need to consider all these different types of testing.

The following sections consider specific examples of test patterns that repeatedly appear in applications. Firstly, we explain what to test when enabling a new feature.

Enabling new features

How do you enable new functionality? Some features are simple and stateless, such as a new command in an API, a new button, or a new interface for existing functionality. The current system can continue without these features, and enabling them has little effect on the rest of the system. Stateless features are simple, and you can just enable them and begin testing.

Other features are more complex and stateful, such as database migrations or new forms of data storage. Some require several steps, such as enabling a new system, migrating users onto it, then disabling the old system. Breaking changes on interfaces need all downstream systems to be ready for the change. This section considers the complexities around enabling and disabling such stateful features.

Stateful features might be enabled with a feature flag or be available immediately after an upgrade. For this discussion, these two methods are equivalent: all you need is a way to enable the feature by turning the flag on or upgrading and a way to disable the feature by disabling the flag or downgrading.

The first pair of tests cases are the following:

- Check entities that can be created with the feature enabled
- Check entities that were created on the old system, then have the feature enabled for them

These will follow different code paths and may reveal different bugs. Your tests need to try both. For each case, you must ensure that the new functionality works and check for regressions in other areas.

For complex upgrades, you will also need to consider dependencies and ordering. Which parts of the system need to be upgraded before the feature can be enabled? Are there any interacting features?

If those upgrades occur over time, there is a matrix of upgrade states the system can be in, and you need to test them all, as seen in the following table:

Module A	Module B	Feature flag	State
Downgraded	Downgraded	Disabled	1. Initial state
Upgraded	Downgraded	Disabled	2. First dependency ready
Upgraded	Upgraded	Disabled	3. Upgrades complete
Upgraded	Upgraded	Enabled	4. Feature fully enabled

Table 5.2 – The states of a gradual upgrade process

Simple features only have states 1 and 4, with a feature that is on and off. For more complex upgrades, you need to enumerate all the intermediate arrangements to check that the system works in each of them.

Are there any special considerations during an upgrade? For large, risky changes, it is worth implementing a way to gradually move to the new system but keep the existing one in use for some percentage of users. That lets you identify any test escapes without requiring a downgrade of the entire system, but this means there are more states to test.

Consider the following possible problems:

- Is the upgrade instantaneous, or do any parts of the system need to be restarted to take effect?

- Is there a significant load placed on the system when the feature is first enabled, for instance, data downloads or processing?

- Does the upgrade replace old functionality or does it add new functionality to exist alongside it? Do the current methods still work correctly in its presence?

- How are users routed to the new versus the old system? Are those controls working correctly?

  - For instance, if 10% of users are assigned to the new method, you will need to check a sample of users to see that that figure is applied.

Finally, for complex changes, you need to consider the case of a feature being enabled, disabled, and re-enabled. Again, this is easy for stateless features: a button vanishes on the UI, an API call starts returning 404, and so forth. More complex, stateful features require dedicated code paths to handle the feature being disabled, such as database migrations or alternative processing.

To give a concrete example, consider adding friend connections to the users in your database. Previously, you had users who could sign up and use your product, but now they can look up other people on your system and add them as friends. You enable the feature for some users but then discover a critical bug and have to disable it. What happens to the connections users made while the feature was enabled?

Those code paths require dedicated tests, such as the following examples:

- Can the feature be successfully disabled?
- What happens if you enable a feature, create new entities (for example, friend connections), then disable it?
  - What happens to those entities?
  - Does the system go back to its initial state?
- What happens if you create entities with a new feature, disable it, then re-enable it?
  - Are those entities available again?
  - If your system performs processing over time, how does it handle the gap when it was disabled?

Enumerate any limitations or invalid operations. Possibly it isn't worth the development time to fully support disabling a feature, so when a feature is disabled, new users will lose any new entities they had created. If the product owner is happy with that behavior, you can test to ensure it works correctly, but be sure to identify and describe that case upfront so it isn't a surprise later.

In my experience, fundamental and far-reaching features often suffer these delays and require multiple attempts to enable them. Unfortunately, that means they are most likely to interact with new features. When you re-enable a feature, you might not want to run its entire test plan again, but just verify the changes and fixes you made since last time. However, you also need to consider any other new features added since the previous test run. Re-enabling a significant feature isn't as simple as trying the same thing twice; you are aiming for a moving target. Carefully examine not just the feature but also its interactions.

Finally, always check that you can downgrade your system again. This operation should rarely be necessary. Most upgrades will succeed, and of those that fail, you can generally issue a rapid patch rather than having to roll back. However, every so often, an issue is so large that the change will take too long, and you need to get back onto working code as soon as possible. In that case, you have to be confident that downgrading will work. This is a stressful time when people will ask how such a critical bug was written and missed by testing. Those questions have to wait until later.

> **Tip**
> Make sure that downgrading is part of your test plan, as well as simply disabling the feature. After upgrading to broken code, the last thing you need is to discover you are stuck because the database migration fails on a downgrade. Always check that you have a way back and that your disaster recovery plan will work.

Turning on features can be as simple as performing an upgrade or enabling an option, but for large, complex changes, the upgrade itself can require a test plan. Work through the different states your system can be in, considering upgrades, creating entities, and downgrades.

The next sections consider the main methods used in black-box testing, from testing APIs and interactions with storage, to negative testing and worse-case scenarios. We start with **API testing**.

Performing API testing

Verifying an API is one of my favorite types of testing. The coding you need is generally straightforward and accessible, requiring a few complex tools and a little setup. Best of all, APIs usually have detailed and exhaustive documentation, either created directly from the source code or as part of customer-facing documents.

Using that documentation as your **test basis**, API testing involves stepping through each message and field and systematically trying different values. See the *Testing variable types* section for the important equivalence partitions for common data types. You can choose what level of coverage you need to reach, varying from a single check that fields are accepted to exhaustive testing of valid and invalid inputs.

APIs can vary greatly. Hideous binary, tag-length-value, or fixed-width protocols have to be completely specified in advance and need to be decoded before they become human-readable. If you are using a text-based SOAP or REST-based protocol with labeled text fields, count yourself lucky. But all types of API require significant checks with the same style of tests.

Example API command

Consider a simple API command to create a new user with the following fields:

Field Name	Type	Required?	Parameters
UserName	string	Yes	Minimum length: 1 Maximum length: 256
Age	integer	No	
Country	string	No	ISO 3166 3 letter code

Table 5.3 – An example API command to create a user

For simplicity, we will ignore whatever authentication mechanism is in place to restrict access to valid users. This request will generate either a success or failure response. If the API request to create a user is a success, it will return a user ID, which can be used in future API calls, for instance, to update or delete that user:

Field Name	Type	Notes
UserID	integer	Used to reference a user in future API commands

Table 5.4 – An example API response to create a user

If the request fails, there are a limited number of error responses:

Error Name	Code	Notes
InvalidInput	400	There was an error in the request message
UserLimitReached	405	The system already has the maximum number of users configured
InternalError	500	A problem on the server meant the request could not be fulfilled

Table 5.5 – An example of API error responses to creating a user

There would be other API commands in the same format to query, edit, and delete that user. Other entities in this example system would follow the same pattern, but this example is sufficient to illustrate the key tests to run. In an HTTP-based API, commands to create and edit entities will typically use POST commands, while those retrieving data will use GET commands, so check they are implemented correctly and the alternative is rejected.

Next, check whether the API supports missing out fields. The age and country fields are supposed to be optional, so is the command successful if they are absent, and are the correct defaults set in that case? Conversely, is the message rejected if the required UserName field is missing?

Given the fields are present, test their values. What if the UserName field is too short or too long, the age is out of range, or the country code is invalid? Those cases should generate error responses with code 400, otherwise, it is a bug. Those rejections should also write a warning log line. It shouldn't be an error because this is an expected failure. For more on that, see *Chapter 10, Maintainability*.

You then need to test the other cases. These are considered more in *Chapter 7, Testing of Error Cases*, but the key is to systematically cause each error case. Here, that means reaching the maximum number of users or triggering an internal error, for instance, by blocking the database from writing the new user details.

For the successful case, check whether you receive a user ID. Can that ID be used in subsequent commands? When checking API calls, don't rely on a successful return code; instead, independently verify the change with a subsequent check, as described in the next section.

Checking API commands

You can check the results of API calls in three main ways:

- **Examining the return value of the API call**: Examining the return value of an API call is necessary but not sufficient to measure its success. A success result may only indicate that the application accepted an API call and began processing it, not that it was completed.

- **Performing an API call to check the outcome**: Because checking return values is insufficient, you should always check the outcome of API commands independently with at least one other API call. For instance, if you sent a command to create a user, follow up with a request to list users to ensure your entry is included.

- **Performing a check on a different interface to check the outcome**: Even better, check whether your new value is available via a different interface, for instance, on a web page or other graphical interface. To continue the previous example, after creating a user via the API, check that that user is visible on user lists presented on a web interface. That shows that the new data has been successfully written and can be translated to other outputs. Conversely, you can use APIs to check that data is correctly added via other interfaces for a more robust check.

Within API testing, you will also need to consider the system's internal state (see *Chapter 6, White-Box Functional Testing*) and possible error cases (see *Chapter 7, Testing of Error Cases*). Those are described in more detail in the following chapters but look for common sequences such as creating, updating, and deleting entities. That pattern of data entry and retrieval is common to many systems. In the next section, we move on from APIs to consider storage commands. Those can be triggered by APIs or other interfaces and have their own set of test requirements.

Performing CRUD testing

The four fundamental data operations of stateful computing systems are as follows:

1. **Create**
2. **Read**
3. **Update**
4. **Delete**

These apply to any system with data storage, whether in a document or relational databases, text or binary files, or some other method. In all those cases, it is possible to create new records or write new data and then read it back for display or processing. You can update information that has already been written and, finally, delete it. Those operations apply to many systems, so you can use them to guide your testing.

The relative frequencies of those operations will depend on your system. Typical systems, however, will perform reads most of all, followed by updates, creations, and deletions. An HR database, for instance, will list users any time someone looks at the users page. A staff member might have their details updated occasionally after their creation, and while there are a positive number of user entries, creations will outnumber deletions. So, in terms of frequency, you can expect the order to be *Read, Update, Create, Delete*. Check whether your system is an exception. For instance, version control software tracks all history and often adds records but seldom updates or deletes them. There are other exceptions, so check the frequencies on your system.

Luckily, the riskiness of those operations is almost the reverse of their usual frequency: *Delete, Update, Create, Read*.

Testing deletion operations

Deletes are most dangerous because you remove data. You need to be sure that you have removed only the correct data and removed it completely. The rest of the system must be aware of the deletion so it doesn't attempt to access the missing records.

> **Real-world example – The dangers of deletion**
>
> In one company I worked at, we provided a messaging service where we stored the complete history on private servers that we ran. Messages were immutable – we had no easy way to delete them, and any customer requests to do so needed development time.
>
> As a new feature, in one release, we added messages in meetings. Users could then easily message each other for the duration of a conference, after which messages weren't available. The feature worked well in testing, and all its functionality in meetings was good. The problems came after conferences ended.
>
> For the first time, messages were deleted, not explicitly, but after meetings, and we had a series of crashes as the code tried to access non-existent entities. Sending more messages was fine; deleting them was far harder.

Trying to reference null pointers or invalid objects is a common cause of crashes in lower-level languages such as **C**, which lack memory management. In your test plan, focus on deletion operations and what happens afterward. Consider the following cases:

- Rapid deletion and creation of entities:

    - Is there a race condition around deletion?

    - Is it impossible for other parts of the system to access deleted data?

    - Is there a narrow window when it is still available?

- Accessing stale entities:

    - For instance, open a list of entities in two browser windows

    - On one, delete an entity, then attempt to reference it from the other

    - Is a reasonable error message displayed?

- Accessing related entities:

    - After deleting an entity, check all related operations

    - Can it be accessed anywhere?

    - Do any parts of the system still have a reference to it?

- Recreating entities:

    - After deleting an entity, recreate it in the same place

    - Make a new entity as similar as possible

    - If data can be stored in different locations, move data from location A to B, then back from location B to location A

All those tests are designed to check the completeness and robustness of delete operations. Backups and restores also test deletions, described further in *Chapter 11, Destructive Testing*. This is a rich source of bugs, so cover it thoroughly in your test plans.

Testing update operations

The update command is the next most risky operation, because it also affects existing information. While it isn't as destructive as a delete command, it is still an unrecoverable operation if you alter the wrong data.

> **Real-world example – Where's the WHERE?**
>
> This example is a cliché, but I've seen it happen for real. In one video conferencing company I worked at, we hit an issue on our live system that required a change to the live database. A senior engineer needed to manually update one customer's conference number with an SQL command, requiring a WHERE statement to specify the number to change.
>
> The engineer missed the WHERE clause. Instead of changing a single conference number, he set every conference number in the cloud to the same value. Calls failed around the world as the routing went wrong. To his credit, the engineer kept his cool and had it fixed within minutes. We implemented stricter checks on any live database updates from then on, even from senior engineers.

That is an example of an operational issue rather than a bug found in testing, but the same principles apply. Either updating the wrong entries or updating the right entries to the wrong values instantly causes bugs. Watch out for complex data types and translations because they are most likely to go wrong; these include the following examples:

- Dates

- Times

- Currencies

- Entities with many subcategories

- Entities with complex data transformations

These are considered in more detail later. The most important class to identify is your system's intricacies, so you can concentrate your testing there.

> **Real-world example – Updating subcategories**
>
> At one company I worked at, there were six subcategories of users, such as system administrators, external integrations, and our normal users. That complexity was a breeding ground for bugs.
>
> For instance, different system modules counted different subcategories, so the total number of users varied depending on which module you used. When we added new features, such as the ability to disable users, we had to consider the effect on all six subcategories. If the developer missed one, there was unexpected behavior and issues.

Testing creation operations

Creation is the next safest operation since it leaves existing data intact. The worst possible outcome with a creation command should be for it to fail and leave the system in the same state. It's easy to test for those failures.

Creation can cause broader disruption if it allows you to add duplicate entities. For example, setting up a new machine with a duplicate IP address will disrupt routing to the previous machine that had been working. Your system should flag up and block the creation of duplicate entities wherever possible, and you should raise that as a bug if that's not the case.

Another subtle bug around creation is for new entities to be created incorrectly, missing certain pieces of data or configuration. This will need careful checking to ensure that new entities are fully functional and not just present. You need to write those checks into test plans and auto-test systems.

Testing read operations

Finally, read operations are safest since they neither change existing data nor add to it. The bugs around read operations are user-facing: are all data values shown correctly? What about long values, numbers with rounding, emojis, and so on? These are considered in more detail in the *Testing variable types* section.

CRUD testing is a fundamental part of checking your system's data storage. Here I can only list general considerations; you will need to examine your system in detail to understand its complexities and where bugs are likely to be found. When performing updates and deletions, you need to check for not only incorrectly changing the data you wanted to modify but also changing data that should have been left untouched. That is **negative testing**, considered next.

Performing negative testing

Testing changes always come in two parts: was the entity changed correctly, and was everything else left unchanged? That second aspect can sometimes be overlooked, so ensure you include it in your testing. For every positive test case you write, consider the equivalent negative case; here is an example:

- If one user is deleted, are other users still available?
- Does a user have the access they should and are they barred from areas they shouldn't have access to?
- Is the configuration updated correctly, and are the other configuration options unchanged?

We already saw the catastrophic example of the missed WHERE clause. The positive test for that change passed – the faulty customer did have their conference number updated. The only problem was that all the other numbers in the cloud were changed simultaneously. This is a problem when it's unclear how widely the configuration is used. A setting might be local to one part of the system but is actually shared in many other contexts. The larger and more complex a system is, the more likely this is to be the case.

A popular bug-tracking tool demonstrates this issue. It has several layers of indirection, with fields, field configurations, and field configuration schemes, among others. Each is highly configurable and can be shared between different projects. You need to carefully check each level to see how widely it is used. Otherwise, making a change will have unexpected consequences for other users.

> **Real-world example – Fight Club branding**
>
> In one company I worked for, we could apply branding to our conferences by overlaying text on the screen. The feature wasn't used very much, and the configuration was fiddly. One customer was behind on payment, and we wanted to inform their meeting participants. I tested the feature to ensure it still worked on the live cloud by branding my organization's conferences. Given the context, you can see where this is going.
>
> Unfortunately, my branding configuration wasn't unique, and I simply inherited the global configuration. When I set branding to apply to my organization, it affected all unbranded live customers too. Anyone who started a conference just then saw my test phrase across the bottom of their screen: *Brought to you by Tyler Durden.*
>
> To my shame, I thought the test was working just fine until I got a panicked call from a member of our sales team doing a demo for a customer. I'd checked that my change had been successful but not that everything else had been left unchanged.

While positive tests are easy to see, negative cases can be harder to identify. When you make a change, an infinite number of things should be left unaltered, and you will never know whether you've caught them all. You will have to judge what areas are likely to change and, therefore, what you should check for each update you make.

Because it's hard to describe negative test cases, you will have to carefully check what interactions exist in your system. They may be as obvious as shared configuration between different modules, or the connections may be more subtle. You will need to map out the connections for your product.

As well as simple, individual changes, you should work out the most complex operations possible on your system. The following section describes how to identify worst-case scenarios. If they work, any simpler operations should also be successful.

Identifying worse-case scenarios

To maximize the efficiency of your testing, identify the worst-case scenarios and just test them. If they work, then all simpler cases should be successful as well. Many tests will be a subset of complex tests, so it's fastest just to perform the complex ones. For example, if your users can have multiple copies of many different relationships, add multiple instances of every kind of relationship. If that works, then having just one relationship should work, as well as having multiple copies of just one type because those are simpler cases.

One exception is with newly written code, where you can expect to find issues. Then, if you test the worst-case scenario, you're likely to hit a problem and possibly several simultaneously. In that case, it's faster to gradually build up to the most complex configuration. Then you can isolate and debug issues as they arise, and you know which step triggered them. However, once each aspect of the test has passed individually, it's quickest to combine them.

The hardest part is identifying the most complex configuration for your system, so consider the following guides:

- Add the maximum number of configurable entities to your system
- Add all possible types of configurable entities to your system
- Fill the entity's history with one of each possible event
- With the most complex configuration and history in place, perform each system action:

  - Upgrade
  - Migration to an alternative system/location
  - Conversion between types
  - Backup and restore
  - Deletion

- Perform as many actions simultaneously as possible

If your most complex configuration can survive the most complex system operations, you should be well-placed for simpler commands. However, every so often, complicated cases are not a superset of simpler cases, so watch out for those, as they will need separate tests. I learned that the hard way.

Real-world example – Load testing prototypes

One of the most annoying bugs I ever shipped was by concentrating on worst-case scenarios and missing a simpler case. We were working on a new hardware product that implemented the functionality of our previous platform but with an entirely new architecture and chipset. That meant we had a mature product with years of feature development to test, but anything could be broken. To make matters worse, we only had three prototype units to test on.

We hammered those units, running lots of functional testing, as well as worst-case load and stress tests, putting them through their paces for months, and fixing many bugs before release. We finally shipped, and… they suffered crashes almost immediately. What had I missed?

It turned out that one test we hadn't done was to leave them alone. Real customers used the units far less than we had, leaving them idle for days at a time. In that case, a buffer wasn't flushed, so it overran, causing a crash. Doing nothing with the unit was one test that hadn't been in our plan.

Sometimes there is no single worst case. If two configurations are mutually exclusive, you will need two different cases to cover those. Interactions between conditions are also difficult to judge and write tests for. You rapidly hit combinatorial explosions of possible test cases if you try to cover every combination. Where possible, do everything at once; where that's not possible, you will have to judge their relative importance.

Identifying worst-case scenarios is essential for designing your test plans, so consider them for each new feature. Next, we consider grouping variables based on their characteristics. The following section describes how best to do that using equivalence partitioning.

Understanding equivalence partitioning

It is impossible to test every possible input into your system, so we have to group them into categories demonstrating the behavior of a whole class of inputs. You are undoubtedly already doing that within your test plans, and its official name is **equivalence partitioning**. By considering it in the abstract, you can learn how to identify possible test cases quickly and completely.

For instance, to test whether a textbox can handle inputs including spaces, we could use the string "one two". This string is an example of all possible strings that include a space between words. They are all equivalent, so we have partitioned them together, and that example is our single test to check the whole group. The following example strings test other partitions:

Partition	Example test
Strings including spaces	"hello world"
Strings including accented characters	"Élan"
Strings including capital letters	"Hello"
Strings with special characters	";:!@£$%îèà{[('")}]"

Table 5.6 – Examples of equivalence partitions for strings

A classic example of tests performed with equivalence partitioning is tax rates. For instance, a 0% rate is applied up to £12,000, 20% up to £40,000, and 40% above that. In this case, the partitions are clearly stated in the requirements, and you should choose one value to test within the 0%, 20%, and 40% tax ranges for a total of three tests to cover all three valid partitions.

Those aren't the only test cases you need, of course. You are probably already worried about invalid partitions, considered in *Chapter 7, Testing of Error Cases*, and the boundaries between different partitions described in the upcoming *Using boundary value analysis* section. Performing equivalence partition tests does not cover every condition, but it identifies cases you should include.

The tax rate example listed the possible partitions in the specification, but usually, you won't be lucky enough to get partition boundaries explicitly laid out, and you'll have to identify them for yourself. Other examples of partitions are included in the following list:

- Different system states:

  - For example, users who are already members, users registered but without a password, and new users who have not logged in

- Different options enabled
- Valid and invalid inputs
- Functionally different numeric values:
  - Over 18 versus under 18
  - Orders expensive enough to get free shipping
- Different input data types:
  - Currencies, time zones, languages, and so on

As you can see, there are many possible partitions across many different variables. You will need to analyze your system to find the partitions relevant to you.

Once you have identified the different equivalent partitions, you must write test cases to exercise each one. As with identifying worst-case scenarios, you can often combine testing partitions to reduce the number of test cases. For instance, you could try this string:

```
Hello ;:!@£$%îèà{[('")}]
```

If that one works, you have tested accented characters, some special characters, capital letters, and strings with a space simultaneously. Such combinations reduce the total number of tests.

On the downside, if that string fails, you don't know which aspect caused the failure. When the chance of tests failing is higher, for instance, in new code, it is worth separating the different test conditions, even though it means running more individual tests. Likewise, combining cases can save time with automated testing, but debugging is easier if the conditions are separate. However, if you are stuck running regression tests manually, they are both slow and likely to pass. In that case, combining test conditions can speed up the process.

Look out for partitions due to the implementation that are invisible to the user. For instance, integers may be encoded in 2 bytes up to 65,535 and 4 bytes above that value. Those are two different partitions, and although the requirements do not distinguish between them, the implementation does. This will be considered in more detail in *Chapter 6, White-Box Functional Testing*.

By applying the principle of equivalence partitioning, we can generate test cases for common inputs, such as strings and files, but you also need to consider the boundaries between partitions. This is covered by **boundary value analysis**.

Using boundary value analysis

Within a partition, not all values are equally important. Bugs are much more likely on the boundaries of partitions where off-by-one errors may be present, for instance, if *greater-than-or-equals* is used instead of *equals*. The idea is simple enough: when there is a boundary, you need to test the values just lower and higher to ensure the divide is in the right place.

As with equivalence partitions, boundaries might be explicitly listed within the specifications or they may be implicit aspects of how a feature was implemented. Examples of explicit boundaries are:

- **Tax rates**: The values up to X thousand are taxed at one rate, and values from X to Y thousand are taxed at another

- **Ages**: Users below 13 are banned, users between 13 and 18 get a child account, and users over 18 get an adult account

- **Passwords**: The length of passwords must be over eight characters

Examples of implicit boundaries will depend on your product's implementation details, but look out for values and lists that are implemented in one way up to a certain point, then differently for other values. For instance, integers of different sizes might be stored differently. The implementation will attempt to hide those details, but issues may be present.

The values for integer boundaries are simple enough—for the previous password example, for instance, you need to test that the application rejects passwords with seven characters and accepts passwords that are eight characters long.

For non-integer numeric values, the value *just above* the boundary needs to take precision into account. If your first £10,000 is tax-free, you need to test what happens at £10,000.01, one penny above that. Given that you can't claim 20% on a penny, what happens to the rounding? That, too, is part of the boundary analysis. If the feature specification isn't precise about the behavior, whether it should be rounded up or down, for instance, then you need to add it in.

The age example also has non-integer values. At 12 years and 364 days old, users are rejected; you need to test that value, as well as 13 years and 0 days old. Is age measured any more finely than days? Hopefully not! But that, too, needs to be explicitly stated in the specification.

Boundary value analysis can be two-value, as described previously, or three-value, also known as **full boundary analysis**. For that, you test the values one lower, equal to, and one above the boundary. So, for the eight-character password, you would try seven-, eight-, and nine-character passwords. Personally, I can't see a nine-character password failing if an eight-character password was accepted correctly. However, three-value boundary analysis is part of testing theory, so I would be remiss if I neglected to mention it.

As well as the boundaries between values, you also need to check how values will interact with each other, as described in the following section.

Mapping dependent and independent variables

Glaring bugs that happen under a wide range of circumstances are easy to find, even with exploratory testing. If the **Logout** button never works, you will see that the first time you log out. However, if it usually works but only fails on a certain web browser, a certain browser version, or only after you have changed the browser window size, you might not find the issue. If you don't test those situations, the **Logout** button will work in your test. Bugs that only occur under certain circumstances, are much harder to find: you can do X, and you can do Y, but you can't do X and Y together.

Bugs that depend on multiple variables are challenging to find because the test plan you need is huge. First, you have to identify the variables affecting your system. Some essential variables will have far-reaching effects, such as the operating system you're running on or the web browser you are using. Those are common, but also consider variables for your system that fundamentally alter its behavior. Maybe you can use it with users logged in or not or as a paid rather than a free user. There may be different interfaces, such as an application, web page, API, or a white label versus an own-brand offering. You will need to examine your system to discover the important variables for you.

Some variables are independent and only need to be tested once. For a simple function, such as inviting a new user by their email address, you could have one test with emails with capital letters to ensure they are correctly accepted. A second test could try a shared email domain, such as `outlook.com`, versus a company email domain, such as `microsoft.com`, which is reserved for Microsoft employees. Some applications behave differently in those cases, although initially, we'll assume there is no difference between them.

If those two variables are independent of one another, then we only need to invite two email addresses to cover those cases:

	Email capitalization	**Email domain**
Test case 1	All lowercase	Company domain
Test case 2	Including capital (uppercase) letters	Shared domain

Table 5.7 – A test plan with independent variables

However, suppose your application considers company email addresses far more valuable than shared ones. Your application is effectively split in two—it checks the type of email address early in the processing and gives a completely different experience if the email address belongs to a company. Then the email domain would massively change the application's behavior, and many other variables would depend on it, including whether it correctly handled capitalized email addresses. Now, these are dependent variables, so you have to try every combination of them:

	Email capitalization	Email domain
Test case 1	All lowercase	Company domain
Test case 2	Including capital letters	Company domain
Test case 3	All lowercase	Shared domain
Test case 4	Including capital letters	Shared domain

Table 5.8 – A test plan with dependent variables

This presents you with a problem. With dependent variables, the length of the test plan has doubled. Dependent variables have a multiplicative effect on the amount of testing you have to do, and the greater the number of options, the larger that effect is. You face a combinatorial explosion of possibilities. What happens if company domains are fine on **Windows** and **macOS** but fail on **iOS**, with long strings, on full moons, or by the last light of Durin's Day?

Tests can become as obscure as you want, which shows that no test plan can ever be complete. This demonstrates why exhaustive testing is impossible, as one of the ISTQB principles states. However, testing some combinations is achievable, and how deep should you go, and which combinations are important?

This is where the skill of testing begins, and here I can only give guidance and heuristics. Identifying which variables interact can be challenging to predict in advance and will depend on the details of the system you are testing. I can only advise you to identify the different variables and consider each pair carefully. These interactions are perfect places for bugs to hide, and it is the tester's skill to find and test those interactions. Still, systematically laying out the variables as previously shown and considering them gives you the best chance to identify potential issues.

Aim to identify orthogonal, independent variables, which do not interact and can be considered separately. They are valuable because they do not expand the matrices of possible cases. Conversely, identify the dependent variables and possible interactions that can be a poly-dimensional array. If you have five variables that all interact, then it's a five-dimensional array with potentially scores of tests, depending on how many values each variable can take. Automation can help you step through all cases systematically, so long as you can spend the time to do so. Even if you choose not to cover every case, it's important to have identified them all, so you know what you are not testing.

In my time as a tester, there has been a whole class of test escapes caused by failing to test combinations of variables. I got close enough that we tried A and B but didn't try A and B together. I kicked myself every time we found a combination I had missed. If I identified this variable and that variable, why hadn't I tried them together?

> **Real-world example – Swimming through the sky**
>
> My favorite example of two dependent variables didn't come from my work but from a bug I hit in an old Spyro the Dragon game. At one point, you had to chase a thief around a pre-defined course. When you caught him, you were transported to talk to a character who thanked you for your efforts.
>
> The problem was that part of that course was underwater. If you caught the thief while you were swimming, you were transported out of the water, but the game thought you were still swimming. Since you could swim up as well as down, you could swim through the sky and reach everywhere in the level.
>
> Catching the thief outside the water worked and swimming normally worked, but catching the thief while swimming revealed a fun bug.

You can't test everything, so there will always be gaps. The best you can do is apply your knowledge of the most likely areas to break and learn from any combinations you miss. A helpful tool to map out dependent variables is **decision tables**, which are explained in the following section.

Using decision tables

To capture complex interactions between dependent variables and system behavior, it can be helpful to write out the possibilities in a table. This provides a basis for writing test cases and ensures that all conditions are covered. By expanding out the variables in a systematic way, you confirm you haven't missed any combinations.

Consider a web application with basic or advanced support depending on the operating system and web browser it runs on. The advanced mode isn't a replacement for the basic mode; some users may choose the basic mode even though the advanced mode is available.

The specification states the following:

- **Chrome** supports basic and advanced modes on Windows and macOS
- **Edge** supports only basic mode on macOS
- **Safari** only supports basic mode and only on macOS
- **Edge** supports basic and advanced modes on Windows

Do those requirements cover all possible cases? They do, although that isn't immediately obvious. We can make those conditions clearer by writing them out, which also shows us how many tests we need in total:

OS	Browser	App mode	Is it supported?
Windows	Chrome	Basic	Yes
Windows	Chrome	Advanced	Yes
Windows	Edge	Basic	Yes
Windows	Edge	Advanced	Yes
Windows	Safari	Basic	No
Windows	Safari	Advanced	No
Mac	Chrome	Basic	Yes
Mac	Chrome	Advanced	Yes
Mac	Edge	Basic	Yes
Mac	Edge	Advanced	No
Mac	Safari	Basic	Yes
Mac	Safari	Advanced	No

Table 5.9 – A decision table for application support on different operating systems and web browsers

We have two operating systems, three web browsers, and two application modes totaling 2 x 3 x 2 = 12 cases. Even though some arrangements are unsupported, you also need to test those to ensure they fail in a controlled way. Writing out the entire table takes a little time but has the advantage of explicitly listing every test case.

To avoid redundancy, you can collapse lines that don't depend on a variable. For instance, in the first two lines of the preceding table, Chrome on Windows supports both basic and advanced app modes:

OS	Browser	App mode	Is it supported?
Windows	Chrome	Basic	Yes
Windows	Chrome	Advanced	Yes

Table 5.10 – An excerpt of an expanded decision table

We can rewrite that to show that Chrome on Windows is supported regardless of the app mode:

OS	Browser	App mode	Supported?
Windows	Chrome	–	Supported

Table 5.11 – An excerpt of a collapsed decision table

Removing all redundancy from the preceding table gives the following collapsed decision table:

OS	Browser	App mode	Supported?
–	Chrome	–	Supported
–	Edge	Basic	Supported
Windows	Safari	–	Unsupported
Windows	Edge	Advanced	Supported
Mac	Edge	Advanced	Unsupported
Mac	Safari	Basic	Supported
Mac	Safari	Advanced	Unsupported

Table 5.12 – A collapsed decision table for application support

Note that the first line indicates that both operating systems support Chrome in both app modes. Four lines have collapsed down to one. Start with one column first and collapse it down as far as possible before moving on; otherwise, you can end up with overlaps.

While the collapsed decision table is neater, it no longer shows the explicit tests you need to run, so the expanded decision table can be both simpler to write and more useful in practice.

Boundary value analysis and equivalence partitioning complement decision tables. Equivalence partitioning identifies the variables and their different values, and then you can determine which are dependent and independent of each other. Decision tables expand the complete list of possible test cases, and you can then, if necessary, identify the boundaries between them by performing boundary value analysis.

Where multiple variables interact, it can be helpful to display the dependencies visually. Cause and effect graphs are one way to achieve that, as described next.

Using cause-effect graphing

In the preceding example, application support depended on which operating system and web browser you were using. This can be visually presented in a **cause-and-effect graph**, which lets you visually display relationships between different variables and specific outcomes. These use standard logic operators of **AND**, **OR**, and **NOT**. The following diagram displays an AND relationship:

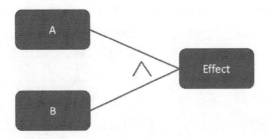

Figure 5.1 – AND relationship between two variables and an effect

These diagrams use traditional symbols representing the logical operators:

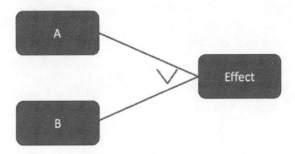

Figure 5.2 – OR relationship between two variables and an effect

The AND and OR operators can take two or more inputs and have their usual truth table outputs. The following diagram displays a NOT relationship:

Figure 5.3 – NOT relationship between variable A and an effect

Using this technique, you can map complex relationships between inputs and outputs to see their effects more clearly. You can create maps of arbitrary complexity, including operators with more than two inputs, multiple causes, intermediate states, and multiple effects. The following diagram shows such a combination:

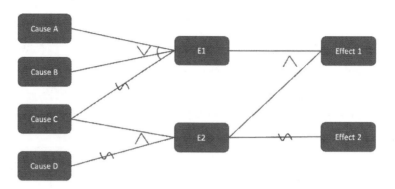

Figure 5.4 – A complete example cause-effect graph

Note the intermediate states **E1** and **E2** and the three-input OR gate leading into **E1**. This shows how causes **A** through **D** interact to produce effects **1** and **2**. Using this graph, you can determine the truth table linking these variables, as shown here:

A	B	C	D	E1	E2	Effect 1	Effect 2
0	0	0	0	1	0	0	1
0	0	0	1	1	0	0	1
0	0	1	0	0	1	0	0
0	0	1	1	0	0	0	1
0	1	0	0	1	0	0	1
0	1	0	1	1	0	0	1
0	1	1	0	1	1	1	0
0	1	1	1	1	0	0	1
1	0	0	0	1	0	0	1
1	0	0	1	1	0	0	1
1	0	1	0	1	1	1	0
1	0	1	1	1	0	0	1
1	1	0	0	1	0	0	1
1	1	0	1	1	0	0	1
1	1	1	0	1	1	1	0
1	1	1	1	1	0	0	1

Table 5.13 – The truth table for the cause-effect graph shown in Figure 5.4

I think you'll agree that the cause-effect diagram is easier to read, although the table explicitly lists all possibilities to save you from working them out. In practice, however, variables and their connections are rarely this complex. You could separate the causes leading to **Effect 1** from those leading to **Effect 2**, for instance, even if they share some common causes.

Frankly, if you're using this technique, I think you have too much time on your hands. The development team should be able to diagnose the causes of bugs with far less information than an exhaustive list of all the times it is seen. So long as you can provide at least one set of steps that reliably reproduce the issue, you shouldn't need to map out every single dependency.

> **Important note**
> I include cause-effect graphing here for completeness, but I don't recommend you use it in practice.

Having seen how we can map the effect of different variables, we now turn to the values those variables can take. There are common equivalence partitions that cause issues in many contexts that you should use in your testing, as described in the next section.

Testing variable types

In this section, we consider interesting values to use in common variable types, such as the contents of strings or numeric fields. These lists of different test cases are useful in many different scenarios. You should refer back to them throughout this book—they are used in user interface tests, in internal and external API fields, and as values in function calls. Your system should be resilient to exceptional values in these fields at all levels, starting with those entered by the user.

These lists use equivalence partitioning to divide up the space of possible inputs into different categories and pick one example from each category to check your system's response. Testing these invokes **Murphy's law**—if something can go wrong, it will. If your customers can enter these values, one day, somebody will do so. These aren't happy-path cases because many of these require deliberate malicious intent, such as SQL injection, and won't be entered accidentally. But so long as the input field could receive that value, your application needs to be able to handle it correctly.

Testing generic text input fields

The chances are that your application, whether desktop, mobile, or web page, has a text entry field or two, either for users to enter data or as part of an API. You can try a standard set of tests on every text field, then more specific ones depending on how a field is formatted. First, let's list the general cases:

1. A null value
2. A blank value

3. The maximum length value:

    A. If there isn't a limit, enter a ridiculously long value and see how the application responds

4. A value with a space or only comprised of spaces

5. A value with leading and trailing spaces

6. A value with uppercase and lowercase characters

7. A valid entry (for example, see the *Testing email text input fields* section)

8. An invalid entry

9. A value with Unicode characters (accented characters, Mandarin script, and so on)

10. A value with special characters (punctuation marks, such as `[{ ('!@£")}])`)

11. A value with **HTML** tags (`<b>bold</b>`)

12. A value with **JavaScript** (`<script>alert("Shouldn't show an alert box")</script>`)

13. A value with **SQL** injection (`Robert'); SELECT * FROM USERS;`):

    A. If you want to be evil, you can drop tables, but `SELECT` statements are less damaging

In addition to those tests, certain text fields have more specific formatting conditions, such as email addresses, passwords, or numeric values, as considered next.

Testing email text input fields

For fields containing an email address, you can check all the general cases listed previously and the following in addition:

1. The presence of a single @ symbol

2. The presence of a . symbol after @

3. Are email addresses with an extra . in the username treated as identical?

4. Are email addresses with a `+<anything>` suffix to the username treated as identical?

5. Does the username only contain Latin characters, numbers, and printable characters?

6. Does the username contain a dot as the first or last character or have two consecutively?

7. Is the username less than 64 characters?

8. Do quotation marks work around the username?

There are more complex rules governing the precise format of allowed email addresses. For more details, see `https://datatracker.ietf.org/doc/html/rfc5322`.

Real-world example – Signed in or not?

A new starter had trouble accessing an internal system in one place where I worked. He could sign in successfully but couldn't access any of the tools.

Different user groups had access to different tools on that system, so I checked his username, group memberships, and group permissions, and everything was set up correctly. Everything worked fine for everyone else.

The problem turned out to be that he logged in with a capital letter in his username. Login was not case sensitive, so he could log in successfully, but the check for group membership was case sensitive, so the system didn't think he belonged to any groups and gave him no access. Using capital letters was the key.

Testing numeric text input fields

For numeric fields, you can check the following variations in addition to the previous general cases for text input:

1. Non-numeric characters (letters, special characters, Unicode characters, and so on)

2. 0

3. Negative numbers

4. Decimals

5. Very large values

6. Very small values

7. Exponents:

    A. Does the textbox accept the letter e, for instance?

Separately, you need to test your application's handling of those values, as described in the *Testing numeric processing* section.

Testing password text input fields

Password fields may have a simple list of required conditions, or more complex heuristics, which gauge overall complexity. In those cases, complexity in one dimension offsets the lack of sophistication in another. For instance, if the password is long enough, it may not need to include capital (uppercase) letters, whereas shorter passwords need to contain capitals (uppercase) to achieve the same security.

Password complexity heuristics are challenging to test, and you need to know the algorithm to check that it is working successfully. For passwords that follow rules, you can step through each to check it is being applied, as follows:

1. Check the minimum length requirement

2. Check that passwords without capitals are rejected

3. Check that passwords without special characters are rejected:

    A. And which special characters are accepted

4. Check that passwords without numbers are rejected

5. Check that certain text strings are rejected (for example, `1234`, `aaaa`)

6. Check that dictionary words are rejected

Remember to test all the previous generic text input cases, such as whether the password fields are vulnerable to SQL injection attacks and whether they accept Unicode characters. All those cases apply here as well.

Testing time input fields

Date and time pickers may indicate your birth date, the pickup time for a parcel, when a booking is due, or a hundred other possibilities. If your application uses this input type, the following are the interesting values:

1. Times in the past and future

2. Times in the far future (for example, 10 years in the future)

3. Starting and ending at midnight

4. Going over midnight:

    A. Crossing the boundary into other weeks/months/years

5. Daylight savings changes

6. User time zones

7. Changing time zones:

    A. Time zone adjustments moving between days

8. Leap seconds

9. For appointments: all-day appointments, recurring appointments, recurring appointments with exceptions

As with the other fields, as well as checking that these values are accepted, you need to test how the system handles them in future processing.

Testing user-facing textboxes

As well as the values you enter into input fields, there are different methods of entering those values. For textboxes in your application, try using them in the following ways:

1. Copying from the textbox
2. Pasting into the textbox
3. Dragging and dropping to and from the textbox
4. Selecting everything within the textbox
5. Is the cursor displayed correctly?
6. Is the length correctly limited?
7. Is the character set correctly limited?
8. Does tab correctly move you between textboxes?
9. Does pressing *Enter* correctly submit the value?
10. Is the tooltip or alternative text correct for the textbox?

Testing file uploads

Along with text inputs, many applications need the user to upload files, such as video clips, documents, or other information. If your application includes that functionality, then these are different input types to check:

1. File types:

    A. Check the content type

    B. Check the file extension

2. Smallest/largest file size
3. Different filenames (see the list of preceding generic text inputs)

The preceding variables apply to any file type. For uploading images, consider these additional tests:

1. Smallest/largest resolutions
2. Unusual aspect ratios:

    A. Very tall and thin

    B. Very wide but short

3.   Advanced features:

   A. Interlaced

   B. Alpha channels

   C. Animated

With all these steps, there are both positive and negative versions—we can test that all supported file types work, for instance, and that other file types are rejected. Test that your application supports up to the maximum file size and rejects those above it. There are separate checks for how these files are processed and other security risks based on their contents. For more details on those, see *Chapter 9, Security Testing*.

Next, we consider processing these inputs, starting with tests to perform on numeric data.

Testing numeric processing

Once data has entered your system, consider how it will be processed. Are values simply entered, then displayed back to the user, or are they combined with other data for graphs and charts? Is any processing needed before data from different sources can be displayed together? This section considers the typical processing of numeric data types.

Wherever your system uses floating-point numbers, check on limitations from rounding. Where does the rounding occur in your design? Converting currencies is a common example of this, although many of those issues apply to any floating-point processing, not just that of currencies. The considerations when testing conversions such as between currencies are the following:

- How many decimal places does your system measure exchange rates to?

- Which exchange rates do you use?

- How often are exchange rates updated?

- When exactly during a transaction is the exchange rate applied?

  - If a transaction starts on day X with exchange rate one but finishes on day Y with exchange rate two, which exchange rate is applied?

- If transactions have multiple steps, which exchange rates are applied?

  - For instance, if a customer pays a deposit, then they pay the full amount, or if they buy a product, then they get a refund.

- Which currencies do you support?

  - What happens if there is a transaction in an unsupported currency?

- Are there any double conversions (from currency *A* to currency *B*, then back to currency *A*)?
- Is each value rounded in the same way before display?

  - Is a value sometimes displayed rounded and sometimes not?

It can be hard to trigger rounding issues deliberately, so plan it carefully, and it's helpful to have a large dataset of examples to double-check.

> **Real-world example – Inconsistent rounding**
>
> In one company I worked for, we displayed summary values to our customers in table cells shaded in different colors to provide a visual representation. The shading was based on the unrounded value, but numbers were rounded before they were displayed. That meant sometimes the same value was shaded differently – some instances of *47* were light green, and some were dark green.

Check that values are rounded consistently before they are used in any outputs, such as user interfaces.

Having stepped through the details of different test conditions, the next sections consider how to optimize your test plan and your testing, starting with hidden defects, which have the potential to introduce some of the longest project delays.

Uncovering hidden defects

Often, testing can be carried out in parallel, with many parts of the test plan conducted simultaneously. As long as they are independent, the only limit on the number of tests you can run at once is the availability of test systems or testers to carry out the tests. When two tests interact, for instance, by requiring mutually exclusive settings, they either need separate test systems, or you need to run them serially, one after another. Testing serially is much slower, and you should avoid it wherever possible.

Another case where testing has to be run serially is when a bug blocks further testing. That first bug must be fixed before you can run tests and find bugs in the remaining functionality. Any issues that couldn't be tested are *hidden* behind the first bug.

For example, if signing up new users doesn't work, then you won't be able to find bugs when multiple users sign up simultaneously. The bugs with multiple users are hidden behind the bug signing up new users.

Sometimes it's obvious that part of the test plan cannot be run until a bug is fixed, as in the preceding example. If a screen on your application doesn't load, for instance, then you can't find any other bugs on that screen. This is why exploratory testing is so valuable—it quickly identifies any issues that block large areas of testing and might hide other defects.

At other times, it's unclear that a particular code path isn't being run and could hide a bug. For instance, if an application crashes when it receives an invalid API command, that needs to be fixed before you can see whether it returns the correct error to the query.

Defect hiding is also an issue during load testing. A crash that occurs after one day of load testing will obscure crashes after three days of use. The lead-up to those issues might be visible – such as increasing memory usage or performance degradation – but the crash won't occur. Because the unit can't run longer than one day without restarting, any longer-term issues are hidden.

To find hidden bugs, you must run a complete cycle of testing: running a build, testing it, raising a bug, fixing it, deploying that fix, and testing again. Depending on your development processes, that may take some time, so these bugs risk delaying projects and releases. The only way to speed that up is to prioritize fixing bugs that might hide others. That's not always obvious, so keep your eyes open and use your experience.

Another area where your experience is vital is when error guessing. With limited time and resources, you must choose which areas to test most by making educated guesses about which functions are most likely to fail.

Optimizing error guessing

When designing your test plan, you need to identify the relevant inputs and variables, considering the partitions and combinations of partitions to test. You need to use your creativity to choose representative cases and examples to try. Be evil! Choose the worst possible examples, the tests that are most likely to cause breakages. What has the development team not thought of? What do they sometimes forget? What broke last time in a feature like this or in this area?

Error guessing is an official title for the ad hoc process of coming up with those test cases. It relies heavily on experience, so, like exploratory testing, it is best suited to experienced testers or those who can think up interesting new cases. Areas with previous errors are prime candidates to test with your new feature. As another of the ISTQB principles states, bugs cluster together and are not evenly spread throughout an application. By knowing about previous clusters, you can make your best guess about where to find others.

Note that the more unusual your test case, the less likely it is for a real user to encounter it, and the lower priority that bug will be. It is valuable to discover even obscure bugs in case they cause problems for users or indicate an issue that may have a more widespread effect. However, be aware that the most valuable bugs are those in the most common use cases, and bugs requiring artificially convoluted steps may not be prioritized. It is still worth trying these cases because obscure cases test both the rare and unusual examples. For instance, when you enter a non-ASCII string into a textbox, you are testing non-ASCII characters and whether that textbox works at all. That means you're gaining extra testing compared with entering an ASCII string, as described in the *Identifying worst-case scenarios* section.

Error guessing is not exhaustive, and you should only use it in addition to systematic testing. It provides an extra layer of checks, or it can help inform the generation of the test plan from the feature specification. However, always carry out a rigorous test plan too. Just because an area hasn't failed in the past and you think it's unlikely a defect will be found, carry out those tests for your new feature too. Then, also guess where you might encounter errors.

Error guessing is also a valuable part of white-box testing, which we examine in more detail in *Chapter 6*, *White-Box Functional Testing*. By understanding the architecture and implementation of the code, you can see where possible weaknesses might appear. If there's a calculation with a division, can you make that value zero? If two different modules have to work together, are they passing the necessary information correctly? Look for the weak spots in the implementation.

What are the known weaknesses in your system? Which functions are a perennial problem? And how do problematic features interact with the new feature you are testing now? Here are a few candidates:

- Web browser/operating system interoperability
- Upgrading/migrating database schema
- Restoring from backup
- Areas where information has to be sent from one part of the system to another
- Localization (translation and time zone differences)
- White-label branding
- Logging and events
- Errors and invalid inputs
- Behavior under load
- Behavior under poor network conditions

None of these will be a priority for the product management team since none are associated with delivering new user features. Still, they will affect many new features you develop, whether you want them to or not. Since these are important and regular sources of bugs, they are covered in more detail in other sections or chapters, so make sure they are part of your test plans.

Finally, on error guessing, look out for the edges of your feature. Some parts of the feature will be headline functionality, the areas that people are talking about and are of the highest value to the product management team. Those tend to be well-thought-through and have fewer issues. They require systematic testing, of course, but bugs are more likely to be in the other areas with a lower priority, which have had less thought devoted to them. These are the edges of the feature, away from its core functionality. These are areas such as the following:

- Functions that were dropped or added during the development
- Functions only used by a few users
- Functions that support the main feature
- Areas where the behavior changes between domains

Watch out for any functionality that is added or dropped (or both repeatedly!) during the development cycle. Changes like that require careful thinking through to catch all the knock-on effects. If a feature is added, you need to go back to the start of this book and work through exploratory testing, writing up the feature specification, and having it reviewed all over again. Likewise, if a feature is removed, even if the change appears obvious, you'll need to consider all the dependent and independent variables to see which need testing again.

Real-world example – What kind of calls?

I once worked on a video conferencing system that could perform many different types of calls—into conferences, directly from person to person, to groups of users, and so on. We were making an architectural change to improve the way calling worked, which required extensive testing, and we were introducing it gradually.

Initially, we would only use the new calling architecture for meetings, not for calling from person to person, so we concentrated our testing there. However, attendees could add other users to the meeting. That was a person-to-person call, so it opened up a whole new test plan. What if the people had called each other before, if they had never called each other, or if they were hosted on a different part of the system?

A seemingly small piece of functionality – the ability to add participants to conferences – greatly increased the necessary testing. We didn't spot that initially, which caused issues when we started testing it later.

Parts of the feature used by only a small percentage of users or that only exist to support the main feature (such as adding participants to conferences) are also areas that may have received less thought and may harbor issues. They can be difficult to spot since, by definition, they are considered less. It's your job to divide all functionality in a binary way—either it's fully implemented and tested or entirely excluded. Either way, you need to think through the consequences. Bugs hide in gray areas, so make everything black and white.

Look for edges in terms of functions, too—the oldest supported browser or the newest. What is the complete list of supported browsers and operating systems? Which is used least? This will be a lower priority for testing because you should clearly concentrate on the most popular cases, but there are more likely to be some issues in the rarer cases.

Experienced testers should perform error guessing because they are most likely to know the weak spots in a system. They gain that experience by paying careful attention to the areas where they've found bugs in the past, categorizing them, and recalling them for future use. That vital skill is using feedback in your testing, which is described next.

Using feedback

Test plans are not static documents carved in stone to stand for all time. They should be dynamic, living texts that evolve as you learn more about your features and products. Recall the testing spiral from *Chapter 1, Making the Most of Exploratory Testing*. Even after the detailed test plan is complete, you need further testing, specification, and discussion cycles to refine and improve your checks.

Those refinements can take several forms. Most benignly, you may need to add details you are happy with to the specification. Perhaps a particular input case or UI element had been missed from the document. If you find it during testing and it works as intended, all you need to do is write it up.

In my experience, such lucky coincidences are rare. If an element was missed from the specification, it's unlikely a developer will implement it exactly as the product owner intended. Most feedback is, unfortunately, negative—either bugs where the feature doesn't meet the specification or surprises in areas on which the requirements are silent.

Failure to meet the specification is simple enough. If the product doesn't match one of the requirement statements, you raise a bug. What you should look out for are themes within the bugs. Identify which features suffer from many bugs and delays and test them even more. As noted previously, bugs cluster together, so the presence of several in the same place suggests there may be more.

Look out for trends between features. The *Optimizing error guessing* section lists common areas of functionality, such as localization and restoring from a backup, that can be difficult to implement and may interact with many other features. You need to generate that list for your product. What areas consistently cause problems? Ideally, record the areas in which bugs are found in your bug tracking system so you can systematically log what causes issues. Otherwise, you'll have to rely on memory, which may make specific issues stand out while obscuring more significant trends.

If the feature specification fails to describe the behavior, then you will need a discussion with the product owner to determine what the behavior should be, then you'll need to update both the specification and the code. Does that omission suggest anything else that the requirements fail to describe? Maybe there is a class of inputs that hadn't been considered or a whole set of interactions. For each issue you find in the specification, see how it can be generalized.

Also, watch out for bugs that indicate whole classes of potential issues. For instance, if a web UI fails to display one error message, does it show any of them correctly? If an API mishandles one invalid input, does it break with other invalid inputs?

This is all vital information to feed into your test plan to generate other test cases. Follow your *nose*. If one area performs brilliantly and you can find no significant holes in its specification or functionality, then leave it alone. Concentrate on the parts that have shown problems and haven't been thought through. Those are the places to spend your time.

To spend more time on an area, you can choose other examples from within equivalence partitions, be strict about testing every supported platform rather than just picking the newest and oldest, and check that area's interactions with other apparently independent features. Usually, those additional steps wouldn't be necessary, but if a feature is struggling with bugs, it's worth spending the extra time to try to find more.

The other way to increase test coverage in a problematic area is to perform finer-grained checks on the product behavior as you use it. Logs, system interfaces, and monitoring systems provide vital feedback you should use throughout your testing, as described in the next section.

Determining what to check

So far in this chapter, we have considered many different tests to run, but we haven't covered the vital next step in the test process—what should you check to ensure the test passed? There are many levels to consider. Most superficially, you can tell whether the application continues to work as described. In our example of a signup web page, does the user receive an email after entering their address? For everything written and saved, you can check where it is subsequently displayed to the user. Is it correct in all those places?

For changes that transition your program into a new state, does it make that transition correctly in all cases? For inputs that trigger other changes in the application, do you have a complete list of those changes so you can check them all?

The feature specification should include the user experience for each output, so you'll need to refer back to that extensively for these checks. If anything is missing, for instance, the wording of error messages, you need to get them added and reviewed.

Another part of error guessing is knowing what to check. Perhaps there is a part of your product that has many dependencies and is liable to break due to changes elsewhere. Keep a note of those areas and routinely check them when there are changes, even apparently unrelated ones.

As well as customer-visible effects, you should also check other layers within the system; for example, were there any errors in the logs? For changes that result in stored data being changed, check that data – are the fields in the database being correctly populated? This requires white-box testing and is described in *Chapter 6, White-Box Functional Testing*. You'll need to work with the developers to find out exactly which database fields should change and which logs lines should be written to see any that are missing or incorrect.

So long as the logging reports issues, this can be the best way to catch unexpected behavior. Within automated tests, there should be a routine check of the relevant logs for any errors or warnings, and their presence means the test has failed, even if the behavior otherwise appears correct. Have a zero-tolerance approach to errors in the logs. As described in *Chapter 10, Maintainability*, all log errors need code change, even if only to downgrade the warning.

Real-world example – Correct rejections for the wrong reason

In one company, we implemented **Session Initiation Protocol** (**SIP**), a public protocol for making video calls. We went for a penetration test in which another company would send all manner of invalid messages to check that we correctly rejected them.

They ran the tests, and the results were great—we rejected all the messages. No matter what invalid input we received, none got through. However, looking at the logs, we saw that one of the early messages had sent our application into an error state. It would reject everything after that, even valid requests. We were rejecting invalid calls, but not for the right reason.

We had a bug, and the test was invalid. They needed to change their test procedure to include some valid messages amongst the failures to check that they hadn't completely broken the system under test, and we needed to fix our bug, which only the logs had indicated.

Remember to watch the logs as you test. However, you'll need to specify which logs those are. In a system of any size, there are likely to be many processes writing logs at different levels, and knowing which ones are relevant is often far from obvious. One of your first tasks is to identify important logs so that you can watch them all.

Load testing also presents a challenge for checking that your tests are working. Under load conditions, there will be a lot of activity and logging. It's best to track simple counts of actions successfully completed and overall system health to avoid being overloaded with data. For further details, see *Chapter 12, Load Testing*.

Finally, keep your eyes open for any other unexpected changes based on your input. This extends the preceding *Performing negative testing* section – everywhere you can check to ensure a transition is completed successfully, you can also check to ensure it correctly left other elements unchanged. If a code change has unintended consequences, it could result in failures in apparently unrelated parts of the product. That will depend on how well your product is architected to separate different parts of its functionality.

Real-world example – The identical speed tests

One application I tested involved software applications connecting to our cloud infrastructure. When endpoints connected, they measured the network and reported the bandwidth results so we could see the quality of service they could expect.

After one upgrade, the endpoints reconnected successfully, and the system appeared to recover perfectly. However, my colleague noticed that all the endpoints reported precisely the same network bandwidth. A bug in the reporting meant that the endpoint threw away the real result, and they all showed a default value instead.

Feature testing had missed that change, and we would have missed it in live usage too, except for the sharp eyes of my colleague. There was no written test for that, no procedure to say what to look for. You just have to keep your eyes open and follow up on anything where you think to yourself, "that's odd…".

> **Real-world example – The video glitch**
>
> My favorite example of an unrelated bug was in a video unit we sold. This was a hardware appliance for performing video conferencing, which customers would buy and own themselves. I sometimes noticed video glitches but couldn't reproduce the issue reliably.
>
> Eventually, after a lengthy investigation, I finally spotted the cause—when I made configuration changes on the unit, that caused the video to become corrupted briefly. The action of saving changes to the internal memory interrupted the processing of the media, and in a real-time system, even brief delays were immediately visible.

Such unrelated issues are tough to catch. An experienced tester performing manual testing is most likely to spot an unexpected interaction, but that is the most expensive form of testing. Inexperienced testers may not notice issues like that, and they are challenging to write automated tests for since they only perform the checks you have designed.

These examples demonstrate that checks in automated tests should be as broad as possible. In terms of architecture, checks for the system state should be in a separate module that can be improved independently of the tests. When you add a check for a new state, all tests should be able to take advantage of that, not just the one you wrote it for. Those additional checks will take time, so you may need to prioritize them if they slow down test runs. However, err on the side of including checks, even if they appear superfluous, as they are the only way to catch such unexpected interactions.

When designing checks for your test plan, curiosity is key, just as it was when creating the tests themselves. Some checks can be written into the test plan, and you can add as much detail as possible on the outcomes and user experience for a given change. Other bugs are due to unrelated changes in a part of the system that should be unchanged. You can't check the whole system after every test step, but automated tests should have extensive checking, even if it seems unnecessary. For manual testing, keeping your eyes open and noticing unusual events is essential.

While checking is vital to your testing, it can cause problems in automated tests. If tests check too closely, they can become brittle and prone to breaking after safe, correct changes. That results in false-positive failures and excessive maintenance, so it's essential to get it right, as explained in the next section.

Trading off precision versus brittleness in automated testing

In manual testing, the checks are as precise as the test plan specifies and the experience of the tester performing them. In automated testing, you have to decide the level of detail of the checks you perform, and there is a trade-off between the precision of your tests and how susceptible they are to break in the future, as shown here:

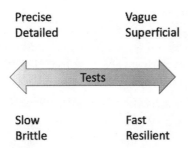

Figure 5.5 – Trading off precision versus resilience in tests

The more precise and detailed you make your tests, the slower and more brittle they will be, liable to break due to small or inconsequential changes. However, in making them faster and more resilient, they will generally become more vague or superficial. While there is no escaping that trade-off, some guidelines can help.

For system testing, you can apply the same rules as you did for the specification – test the behavior, not the implementation. It doesn't matter about the internal messages, the database values, or the application state, so long as the end result is correct. That lets the development team completely re-architect the code if they choose, and the automated tests should keep passing. That is a valuable use case for automated testing: to verify that a code refactor has left the behavior unchanged.

Automated testing requires a very controlled environment. Unexpected inputs result in tests sometimes failing, known as **flakes**, which obscure genuine problems with the code. It's vital to keep your tests as simple as possible, with as few dependencies as possible. Ensuring automated testing is independent of the implementation removes its main dependency, making for more resilient tests.

While some aspects of a program are clearly implementations – such as database tables – and others are clearly outputs – such as screens and web pages – others are intermediate. The HTML for a web page, for instance, is an output of the code but produces the final look of the screen. Should that be classed as implementation and ignored or as output and tested?

While individual cases may vary, a rule of thumb is only to test the final outputs. That is what your users will see, so that is where you should concentrate your testing. The development team is free to change any stages in generating that final output, which shouldn't affect the tests. For instance, very different HTML could produce the same screen, so the tests should focus on the result, not how it was achieved.

There may be exceptions to that rule if an interface is crucial to demonstrate that a system is working; integration tests, for instance, isolate the interfaces between different program modules to perform testing there. However, for system tests, the interfaces are the outputs of the application overall, so testing should focus on them.

The tests themselves can also have different levels of specificity. Should a test check for the presence of text on a screen or its location, for instance? How strict or lax should timeouts be? What tolerance should there be on bandwidth measurements? For each of these, the temptation when writing the test is to be very strict and then make them looser, as intermittent failures cause unnecessary work and investigation. This is a pragmatic approach since it leaves checks strict wherever possible and adds variation where needed. Ideally, these values are explicit in the specification, so you can set your tests to check them.

Another approach is to add more detail in problematic areas. The location of text can be checked by comparing screen grabs, for instance, and various services are available for that. For timeouts, you can break down the time taken at each step to see if any are longer than expected. You can add instrumentation to the generation and transmission of data when measuring bandwidth limits. All of that takes extra work, so at this point, you need to trade off the specificity of your tests with the resources you have available to build and maintain them. That detailed testing is possible at a price.

If the maintenance burden of your tests is too high, you will need to revisit your approach. Specific tests or certain checks within those tests may need to be disabled or quarantined to ensure tests pass reliably. Check your tests aren't dependent on the implementation or external factors, then examine which aspects of the tests are most important. Focus your checks there, and leave the others alone.

Brittleness shows the danger of having too many tests or them being too strict. That is an example of test prioritization, which is considered in more detail next.

Test prioritization

The ideas in this section, and all the following chapters of this book, describe a gold-plated, exhaustive test plan that will comprehensively test your product or new feature. You should definitely consider all the test cases described here, but that doesn't mean you should perform them all. You will be constrained by the available time and resources, which will vary depending on how critical the software is.

Test management is beyond the scope of this book, for instance, how to organize a test team, which roles should perform which tasks, how testing should fit into release cycles, and many other considerations. Here, I am solely concerned with designing test plans and the tests to run. That means I will list many tests you should consider, many more than you will be able to run in practice. You must choose which to carry out.

Even if you don't run tests, it's important to be aware of those you have left out and consciously decided not to run. That lets you gauge the risk of each release far more accurately than having patchy test coverage with no clear measure of which checks you are missing. Those tests should be documented so you can choose to run more if the risks increase, for instance, because you are making changes in that area of code.

Conversely, writing too many tests can result in an unmaintainable system where there are so many test failures that you can't see real bugs. As we saw in *Chapter 4, Test Types, Cases, and Environments,* there is a testing pyramid where you aim to have many unit tests, fewer integration tests, and the fewest system tests.

Which system tests you should run will depend on your system, but the following list presents guidelines that apply to many systems:

- Test all the core happy-path cases through your system

- Once a feature is working, test the worst-case scenarios to ensure tests are as efficient as possible

- Concentrate testing in areas where you've found bugs before; they are most likely to break again

- Have different levels of tests, some you can run on every change and a large set to be run nightly or on demand

- Perform extensive checks on logs, database state, user interface behavior, and so on for all the tests you run

I can provide no more than guidance, in this case; you will have to carefully decide exactly which tests to run on your system. Another gray area is where people's expectations about product behavior differ. That is the fine line between bugs and feature requests, which is examined next.

Comparing bugs and features

It can be difficult to distinguish between bugs and feature requests in software applications. Despite your best efforts to clarify the feature specification (see *Chapter 2, Writing Great Feature Specifications*), it is easy for ambiguity to creep in. Within those gray areas, your assumptions about what functionality should work may differ from the implementation.

For instance, sometimes new features aren't initially available in all situations. Maybe you can create users on your system, and you have recently added an API to your system, but for now, the API is read-only, and you haven't yet added an API command to add a user. APIs usually have a precise specification to say which calls have been implemented, but other interactions between features are less clear.

Other problematic areas are what should happen under degraded performance. On poor networks, what quality of service is acceptable? On low-resolution screens, how should the user interface adapt? Beware of your assumptions here; while you might expect worse performance under suboptimal conditions, the quality you expect might be different from what the product owner had in mind. You can end up raising invalid bugs about poor performance, which is expected, or, worse, accepting degraded performance, which should be better. This needs a detailed explanation in the feature specification. If you don't have those details, you need to discuss them with the developers and product owners to make it clear.

These gray areas are why you must keep asking questions and refining the specification as you test. If your checks are sufficiently detailed, you should find many questions to ask as you go along.

Summary

In this chapter, you have learned the key considerations when performing black-box functional system testing. This is the core of the testing since it ensures that all the main behavior of this new feature is correct, and further testing will build on these results. If the feature doesn't work correctly even once, then you can't check the complete user experience or its behavior under load.

Black-box testing needs to systematically cover the entire feature specification while also extending it by trying out ad hoc cases that weren't explicitly listed. You should also maintain a sense of curiosity to see what happens as you step through the feature's different states. You find all the best bugs when you go off the test plan, so always extend the cases as written to try new combinations and check other outputs.

This chapter reviewed the various ways to approach black-box testing, from API and CRUD testing, negative testing, and identifying worst-case scenarios to equivalence partitioning and boundary analysis, which apply over a wide range of settings. When dividing test cases into equivalent partitions, you must choose which particular case to trial. This can be informed by your previous experience, finding the known weak spots in your system since bugs tend to cluster together.

This chapter provided standard equivalence partitions for some common data types. It stressed the use of feedback and error guessing to let your application guide where you could concentrate your testing and finished by considering the precision of your checks, test prioritization, and what should count as a bug or a feature.

With the black-box testing complete, you can gain a lot of confidence that a feature is usable, and you can consider giving it to internal users or beta testers. The happy path and working cases have been verified, but the testing is far from over. Black-box testing will always be limited as it does not consider how the feature was implemented, which is described in the next chapter on white-box testing.

White-Box Functional Testing

"What is the heart but a spring, and the nerves but so many strings, and the joints but so many wheels, giving motion to the whole body?"

- Thomas Hobbes

The last chapter described the key approaches to black-box testing. By looking at the external behavior of a feature, thoroughly defined by the feature specification, you can test its primary functionality and ensure it meets all the requirements.

Unlike black-box testing, where the implementation of a feature is unknown, white-box testing lets a tester understand the workings of the code and design test cases to exercise it all. You'll now cast aside the naivety that was initially so useful to find surprises and unexpected behavior. Here, you need as much knowledge as possible to understand how and why the implementation works – the springs and joints of your particular application.

This will let you see dependencies that may not have been obvious: areas of code the developers had to rework, special cases they had to handle, or uncertainties and unknowns they had to deal with. Many important test cases won't be obvious simply by looking at the feature's behavior, and white-box testing is the best way to discover them.

White-box testing overlaps with unit testing, which tests functions in isolation rather than running as part of the whole system. This book concentrates on system tests since these offer the broadest test coverage, although this chapter also considers the implementation and measurement of unit tests. By focusing only on individual functions, unit tests are simpler and therefore easier to test, which is one of their main strengths.

In this chapter, you will learn about the following:

- The importance of code analysis to automatically find issues within a program

- Static testing to check and review code

- The different ways of measuring unit test coverage and their strengths and weaknesses

- How to test APIs, modules, and messages

- How to systematically test state machines

- How error guessing can be applied to white-box testing

- What to check during white-box testing

- Gray-box testing, which uses a combination of white- and black-box testing techniques

We begin by considering the advantages and disadvantages of white-box testing.

Advantages and disadvantages of white-box testing

White-box testing has its own set of advantages and disadvantages, as shown in the following table:

Advantages	Disadvantages
Can find issues without running the code	Requires testers with coding skills
Easy to automate	Hard to catch unimplemented requirements
Easy to measure coverage	Fragile to code refactoring
Can check all code paths	
Easy to investigate failures	

Table 6.1 – Advantages and disadvantages of white-box testing

White-box testing provides a new set of tools that complement and enhance the testing provided by black-box testing. White-box testing begins with you familiarizing yourself with the code partly by inspection but ideally with at least one session with the developers. When talking through their code, the developers may notice issues they hadn't thought of before or at least flag up limitations they were aware of and hadn't had the time or resources to improve. That walk-through is valuable, so make sure you schedule time for it.

However, that also highlights the first weakness: you need to understand the code you're being shown. If you are not a proficient coder in that language, your ability to perform code reviews will be limited. If no one on the test team has coding skills, then detailed white-box testing may not be possible, but even coding skills, you can still understand the modules and messages, internal states, and the transitions between them. That allows some white-box testing without the need to read individual lines of code.

Given that you have a handover and can understand the code, you can write unit- or higher-level tests to check the behavior of each function and their behavior together. You can measure your progress, and there is a clear place to stop when you have covered each new function. That's unlike black-box system testing, where there is always another combination of variables or another test environment you could try.

The test coverage can also be comprehensive, checking each line of code and each decision outcome. You can check each boundary condition, and if there are any failures, it's clear which line of code caused them. That differs from black-box testing, where it takes investigation to work out which line of code was running at the time.

On the downside, white-box testing may not find unimplemented requirements. If you only test the code that's there, you won't see code that is missing. Once unit tests are automated, they may fail if the code is refactored, even if the overall behavior is unchanged. Changing a function name might be enough to break white-box tests, whereas black-box tests only consider the overall behavior.

As with all types of testing, white-box testing is insufficient on its own but provides essential new ideas as part of a wider test plan.

Using code analysis

Most of this book is devoted to dynamic testing, in which you execute the code and check its functionality. However, testing can begin without running the application by looking at the code to see errors, inefficiencies, and unhandled cases.

The first stage of this testing is to scan the code automatically. Many applications are available to check for uninitialized or unused variables, possible divide-by-zero errors, and the like. These can be built into source code editors but you may need more advanced checks as code complexity increases. Ensure this analysis has run and passed before spending any time on manual testing.

This analysis can catch errors such as memory leaks and null pointers in lower-level languages without memory management. If your company uses languages like that, make sure those checks are part of your software development life cycle.

You can measure many metrics in the code, such as the number of comments, churn in each file, and the size of modules. While gathering the data is easy, that doesn't indicate what you should do with it. Code comments, for instance, used to be highly recommended, but in modern languages, it's possible to write far more readable statements. The best code doesn't need comments, so their presence is a mixed blessing as they take work to write and keep up to date. A discussion of coding best practices is beyond the scope of this book, but be aware of the possibilities of metrics you can measure and the pitfalls of aiming for the wrong targets.

Code analysis will produce an output of warnings and errors for you to triage and work through. It's important to introduce this early in product development because later on, the list of issues can become offputtingly long. If you are in that state, aim to work through a few each day to reduce the backlog. Once a build is clean, developers are far more motivated to keep it clean. Nobody will notice if a list of issues increases from 76 to 77, but no one wants to introduce the first error.

Other issues can only be found by running address-sanitized builds. These add tracking to each memory allocation and free commands to look for memory leaks or invalid access. These are massively useful for finding issues that are very difficult to find in any other way, although they come at a cost: the extra checks slow code execution, which makes it a less realistic test. Changing the code timing can also reveal other race conditions, which are valuable to find, even if they rarely occur under typical conditions.

Once your automatic checks have passed, then you can move on to manual checks and code reviews, as described in the next section.

Using static testing

Static testing involves carefully reviewing the code to think through its implications and possible issues. It lets you find bugs before the code is even run by highlighting edge cases that haven't been handled and good coding practice. If your company already runs code reviews, check that they always consider these cases and testing.

In terms of the review types listed in *Chapter 3, How to Run Successful Specification Reviews*, this is an inspection, stepping in detail through the code to identify and solve technical problems by domain experts.

Static testing should review the unit tests, which are written alongside the code. Apply the ideas in this book to ensure the unit tests comprehensively verify the individual functions within each feature. The tests can even be written before the code as part of **Test Driven Development** (**TDD**). In TDD, the developer writes unit tests based on their proposed implementation, which initially fails. As they write the code to fulfill those functions, the tests start to pass, and when all tests pass, the implementation is complete. Thinking through the planned implementation in that detail is a useful exercise, although it can feel slower to write the tests before the code.

The key areas to consider in static testing are as follows:

- Code format
- Code conciseness
- Defensive coding
- Removing extra debug logging
- Checking against the specification
- Design choices
- Unit testing

Each of these is considered in this section.

Code format

Static testing begins with style guides for your organization, such as the placement of brackets and tabs. If you've ever seen code such as the following, then you'll know the pain of varying function cases, bracket locations, and tab lengths:

```
function_a() {
        print("This is function A")
}


FunctionB()
{
   print("Function B behaves the same but looks different")
}
```

These have been the source of passionate debate in the past and were a fine example of bike-shedding, also known as the law of triviality, as proposed by C. Northcote Parkinson, where minor but visible changes receive far greater discussion than more important but harder-to-understand decisions.

These can also be checked by linting, which enforces a particular style to ensure that everyone in the development team works in the same way. Generally, the choice of style is less important than ensuring everyone is consistent.

Code conciseness

More interestingly, static testing examines the behavior of the code itself. Is the code **DRY** (short for, **Don't Repeat Yourself**) rather than **WET** (short for, **Write Everything Twice**) within reason? Writing code once makes it maintainable because if you need to change it, there is only one place to update it. Consider this example of a function to create a new user:

```
create_user(permission)
{
    if(permission == ADMIN)
    {
            user = create_user()
            make_admin(user)
    }
    else
    {
            user = create_user()
    }
```

```
        return user
}
```

Clearly, this can be simplified. Since both branches of the `if` statement create the user, that should be run once, beforehand:

```
create_user(permission)
{
    user = create_user()
    if(permission == ADMIN)
    {
            make_admin(user)
    }
    return user
}
```

This is logically identical but shorter, making it easier to read and maintain. Other examples are far more subtle or far-reaching. Writing neat, concise code sounds obvious but especially during updates, it can be tempting to make bare minimum changes, rather than refactoring large areas, which adds time and risk without altering the program's behavior. Also, sometimes it is best to explicitly write code out to make it easier to read, rather than rigorously adding indirection to always avoid repetition. The cost of other developers' time to read and understand the code can be greater than the benefits of conciseness. As ever, writing DRY code is a guideline rather than a rule.

Defensive coding

Do functions validate their inputs? Each function should make no assumptions about the data it receives and should discard and log any invalid inputs. Does the code raise understandable errors if it receives unexpected data? This is a vital part of code resilience, which is covered in greater detail in *Chapter 7, Testing of Error Cases*. You not only need those checks but also clear warnings to help you debug when that error occurs in practice. For example, the following checks should be present for a function accepting strings or integers:

```
create_user(str name, int age)
{
    if(name == "")
            throw(error, "Username is blank")
    if(age < 18)
            throw(error, "Users must be 18 or over")
    if(age > 130)
```

```
        throw(error, "Age value is too large")
    ...
}
```

This ensures the function will catch any errors and clearly state the problem it found.

Code functionality

Given that code is understandable, concise, and written defensively against invalid inputs, you can move on to its functionality. Remove any debug values or extra logging, of course, and check that all configured values are correctly set. Whether they're hardcoded or optional, the program default should match the specification.

Refer to the technical specification and check that each statement is correctly implemented. If you only check the code that is written, you won't spot absent functionality, so add an explicit step to check for anything the development team missed. Using the specification also provides an excellent way to run through the program flow from beginning to end.

Unit tests

At the lowest level, white-box testing involves writing unit tests to cover each line of code individually. You will need to identify the purpose and function of each line so you can write a test to check that the output is correct. That might be as simple as checking an assignment works or testing two branches of an `if` statement.

For most lines, the main challenge comes from deciding the variety of inputs they could receive. Datasets might be empty, variables could be null, or numbers may be out of range. There should be tests to cover those error conditions as well as the happy-path scenarios.

The principles for writing system tests listed in *Chapter 4, Test Types, Cases, and Environments*, apply just as well to unit tests: make each test independent of the others; each test should cover one piece of functionality, give tests clear names, and aim to have lots of tests that are clearly grouped and prioritized. With those goals in place, your tests can be thorough, easy to debug, and organized.

The tests you need will be as varied as the lines of code, but they are usually clear and have an obvious mapping to the code itself.

In terms of the project, reviewing the unit tests is an important handover between the development and test teams. Unit tests should be produced along with the feature, so your first task is to review what is already there to avoid duplication and identify gaps. This is where you start to apply the lessons from this book in terms of what should be tested.

Most of the tests in this book don't require programming knowledge, but when checking the code, you have to be proficient in whatever language is used. For this reason, these can be a more specialized form of testing. Identifying issues requires not only that you understand the code but understand it well enough to spot problems introduced by the developers. That isn't easy but is massively beneficial, and certain checks apply across a broad range of coding. Next, we consider the many different ways to measure the coverage you have achieved.

Measuring code coverage

At its lowest level, white-box testing involves stepping through lines of code to design test cases for them. The development team often writes the unit tests themselves. As such, I won't go into detail on their implementation, but as a tester, you can still check their design and coverage. There are nine major measures of code coverage:

	Coverage type	Detail
1	Function	Function coverage ensures that every function has been called at least once.
2	Statement	Statement coverage checks that each line of the program has been run at least once.
3	Decision	Decision (or branch) coverage ensures that each logical branch of a program has been run at least once.
4	Condition	Condition coverage ensures that each variable in conditional statements takes all possible values at least once.
5	Modified condition/decision	Modified condition/decision coverage ensures that each variable in a conditional statement has affected the statement outcome at least once.
6	Multiple condition	Multiple condition coverage ensures that every possible combination of variables is checked for each conditional statement.
7	Parameter value	Parameter value testing uses equivalence partitioning to ensure that all main types of parameter input have been tested at least once.
8	Loop	Loop coverage ensures that loops have been run multiple times.
9	State	State coverage ensures that each state in a finite state machine has been tested.

Table 6.2 – Types of code coverage

These different code coverage measures provide very different levels of testing, from patently incomplete to unreasonably exhaustive. To measure the coverage of your tests in each of these areas, you divide the coverage you have by the total possible coverage. That's laid out in the *Calculating code coverage* section.

As is often the case, the primary skill is deciding how much testing to perform by understanding the different approaches and choosing the one relevant to your project. The following sections show how to implement them so you can evaluate their strengths and weaknesses.

The types of coverage in *Table 6.2* are ordered roughly by the amount of testing they provide, starting from function coverage, which offers the bare minimum of testing.

Function coverage

The least-stringent measure of code coverage is **function coverage**. This ensures that all the functions within a module have been called at least once. That means that at least one set of function parameters has been tried, but this still leaves many possible statements and code paths untested. Just because you called a function doesn't mean you have run every line within it, let alone every code branch.

You can augment function coverage with other forms of testing, particularly parameter coverage, trying different function parameters, and decision coverage to test different code branches. However, on its own, it leaves significant gaps.

Like the other forms of code coverage, there is a simple formula to measure how much function testing you have achieved, described next.

Calculating code coverage

You can measure all these types of **code coverage** in an equivalent way. This is vital as it shows how much testing you've done and how much you still have to do. The calculation is straightforward: you need to know the total number of entities you are measuring, for instance, the number of functions for function coverage, and the number you have tested.

For example, if there are 20 functions in 1 module and you have tested 15 of them, then your test coverage is 75%:

Function test coverage = (Number of functions tested) / (Total number of functions) x 100%

Function test coverage = 15 / 20 x 100%

Function test coverage = 0.75 x 100% = 75%

That style of calculation applies to statements, decisions, and each of the other types of code coverage considered here. Various tools are available to automatically analyze your code and produce that measure to save you from doing it manually. Be sure to check which type of coverage your tool measures. The number is only meaningful if you understand what check it has performed.

The next most stringent form of code coverage, after checking functions, is to measure how many statements in the code have been tested, as described in the next section.

Statement coverage

The most basic form of code coverage is statement coverage, which simply checks that each line of code has been run at least once while checking for correctness.

> **Real-world example – 100% code coverage**
>
> On one product I tested, the development team proudly told me that they had 100% code coverage on a new module. Skeptical that anything could reach total coverage, I did some exploratory testing and rapidly found several issues.
>
> Going back to the development team, I asked what the 100% figure applied to. It turned out only the backend code had 100% coverage, not the frontend, where I had found issues. Also, it was only statement rather than decision coverage or other, more comprehensive measures. No code is ever fully tested, even if your code coverage calculation hits 100%.

Beware of statement coverage! While you may be able to report that 100% of your code has been tested, it is far from complete. Even data structures as simple as if statements and loops can pass statement coverage tests but still contain critical bugs, let alone more complex program flows such as object inheritance and decorators.

Consider the following simple example program with only four blocks of code to test:

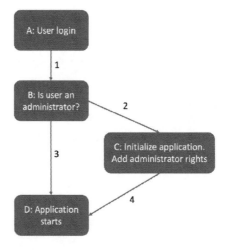

Figure 6.1 – Program initialization with a single if statement

Figure 6.1 is a *control flow graph*, which logically maps out different parts of a program's functionality. This allows it to be easily visualized and understood, which is particularly important when measuring the test coverage you have achieved and the gaps that might remain.

In the preceding example, by logging in as an administrator, you can test all code blocks with a single test. That moves through the statements in order – **A**, **B**, **C**, and **D** – and should pass correctly. However, running an `if` statement once is not enough – there are two different outcomes it can result in, and you need to check that both can run successfully. If the user is not an administrator, the program flow is **A**, **B**, and **D**. In that case, the application will start without passing through block **C**, which initializes the program, so it will fail.

Statement testing is also inadequate where compound or complex statements include multiple elements. If you simply count lines you have run, you may miss testing multiple statements on a single line. Even if you split out those statements, complex lines may require several tests. For instance, the ternary operator in **C** includes a conditional check and two output branches on a single line of code and would need more than one check.

It is good coding practice to keep statements simple and separate, as that not only improves readability but also means that measuring your statement coverage gives a more accurate view of the actual percentage you have tested.

Statement coverage has significant limitations as a measure of code coverage. The next level of testing provides far more comprehensive testing by testing each decision or branch within the code.

Decision coverage

In *Figure 6.1*, there are four code blocks: **A**, **B**, **C**, and **D**. While statement coverage tests each of those, it does not test the different paths between them. Those are labeled **1**, **2**, **3**, and **4** in the diagram. You can reach all four code blocks by only traversing paths **1**, **2**, and **4**. Considering decision coverage clearly shows you've missed out branch **3**.

In this case, branch **3** does generate an error – only block **C** initializes the application. If you are not an administrator, block **C** does not run, and the application starts before it is initialized. Even though you had 100% statement coverage testing, relying on statement coverage alone would miss a critical bug.

Decision coverage ensures you have taken all possible code paths through a given code block. This is also known as branch coverage since each decision generates another branch for you to test.

This provides far more complete testing than function or statement coverage and, while it still leaves gaps that we will consider later, can be a happy medium to ensure you have run all the critical paths.

The challenges of decision coverage are working out all possible decisions and branches. *Figure 6.1* has a clear `if` statement with two possible outcomes. More complex data structures, such as callbacks and object inheritance, will require careful analysis. In addition, it may not be clear what values you should try for different variables. Booleans can simply be set to true or false, but other fields have massive spaces of possibilities. As shown in *Chapter 5, Black-Box Functional Testing,* there are common categories you should try for common data types, but you will have to consider the specific values for your application. See the *Understanding parameter coverage* section for more details.

Decision coverage is also deficient when there are complex conditional checks. Consider an if statement with a three-way OR gate taking Boolean variables:

> If ((A || B || C) then …

You can reach 100% decision coverage with two tests:

- **Case 1**:

   A: true, B: false, C: false

- **Case 2**:

   A: false, B: false, C: false

That would result in the statement evaluating as both true and false, so the criteria for 100% decision coverage is satisfied. However, variables B and C were false throughout the test. If there is a problem when they are true, these tests will miss it. To catch those cases, you could use condition coverage.

Understanding condition coverage

Condition coverage is not practical to measure code coverage. It has neither the ease of measurement of decision coverage nor the thoroughness of modified condition/decision coverage described as follows. I include it here for completeness and to show how it differs from the other measures, but I don't recommend that you use it.

Consider an if statement of the following form:

> If ((A || B || C) then …

Condition coverage requires each variable to take all possible values at least once within the test plan. The preceding statement could be satisfied with two test cases:

- **Case 1**:

   A: true, B: false, C: true

- **Case 2**:

   A: false, B: true, C: false

Those two tests check that each variable can be set to true and false, and that the statement evaluates accurately in each case. However, condition coverage is sometimes a weaker criterion than decision coverage because condition coverage doesn't require you to test every outcome of conditional statements. The only requirement is that variables take all possible values.

In the preceding example, (A || B || C) evaluates to true in both case 1 and case 2. A separate condition of *condition/decision coverage* requires both that the variables take all values and conditional statements evaluate all outcomes at least once.

Understanding condition/decision coverage

Condition/decision coverage simply combines the requirements of condition coverage and decision coverage, requiring that each conditional statement evaluates both true and false and that each variable takes all possible values at least once within the test plan.

Consider the `if` statement again:

If ((A || B || C) then …

For the preceding statement, condition/decision coverage could be satisfied with two test cases:

- **Case 1**:

  A: true, B: true, C: true

- **Case 2**:

  A: false, B: false, C: false

In those cases, each of A, B, and C take both the values, and the statement overall evaluates to both true and false.

However, even with each of the variables taking each possible value, we still haven't thoroughly tested that `if` statement. Note that in the preceding two test cases, B and C being true never affects the outcome of the decision. Because A is true in case 1, the value of the OR statement overall will be true regardless of their values. To check if B and C are correctly evaluated, we need a stricter criterion known as modified condition/decision coverage.

Understanding modified condition/decision coverage

Modified condition/decision coverage builds on the other forms of conditional testing requirements and extends them. It requires the following coverage:

- **Decision coverage**: This means that each possible outcome from a decision is invoked at least once.

- **Condition coverage**: This means that each variable has taken all possible values at least once.

In addition, it requires that each variable has independently affected each decision's outcome at least once.

Modified condition/decision coverage requires not only that every variable in an expression should take all possible values but that each of them actively determines the outcome of the `if` statement. This checks for errors in the evaluation and checking of each part of a conditional statement individually. This level of coverage is vital to find bugs within complex expressions. Consider the `if` statement again:

If ((A || B || C) then …

With the following test cases:

- **Case 1**:

    A: true, B: true, C: true

- **Case 2**:

    A: false, B: false, C: false

While they meet the requirements for condition/decision coverage, the decision's outcome never relies on true B or C. If those conditions cannot be met, or if there is an error, in that case, these tests will not find it. To meet modified condition/decision coverage, we need a set of four tests:

- **Case 1**:

    A: true, B: false, C: false

- **Case 2**:

    A: false, B: true, C: false

- **Case 3**:

    A: false, B: false, C: true

- **Case 4**:

    A: false, B: false, C: false

In cases 1 to 3, each of the variables A, B, and C is true on its own. The expression will only evaluate to true if they correctly evaluate to true, so you have tested the expression's dependency on them. You then need a fourth test to check that the expression overall can correctly evaluate to false.

While this is useful when A, B, and C are simple variables, it becomes even more critical when they are complex expressions, possibly involving multiple function calls each.

Many compilers and interpreters will avoid evaluating code if they don't need to. In that case, if A is true, then (A || B) is true regardless of the value of B. There is no need to evaluate B, so the program may not do so. If B is a variable, that may not change the program's outcome, but B might be a series of function calls in its own right. While A is true, you are not running or testing that code. Only by requiring B to be true independently of A can you ensure that all the available code is run.

However, this has still not covered every possible condition. We have three Boolean values giving a total of eight potential cases. Testing all those cases requires a stricter criterion known as multiple-condition coverage and, while undoubtedly comprehensive, may require too many tests to justify.

Understanding multiple condition coverage

Multiple condition coverage is easier to understand and more comprehensive than modified condition/decision coverage: you must test all possible combinations for a given set of inputs into a decision. While good in theory, this rapidly becomes too time-consuming to achieve in practice and involves the repetition of very similar cases.

For our three-way OR conditional, multiple condition coverage requires eight tests in total:

If ((A || B || C) then …

The following test cases meet the criteria for multiple condition coverage:

- **Case 1**:

  A: true, B: true, C: true

- **Case 2**:

  A: true, B: true, C: false

- **Case 3**:

  A: true, B: false, C: true

- **Case 4**:

  A: false, B: true, C: true

- **Case 5**:

  A: true, B: false, C: false

- **Case 6**:

  A: false, B: true, C: false

- **Case 7**:

  A: false, B: false, C: true

- **Case 8**:

  A: false, B: false, C: false

It is simple to generate these cases, compared to working out which states are needed for modified condition/decision coverage, but they are very repetitive. It seems highly unlikely that it will work when A, B, and C are all true, for instance, but fail when A and B are true but C is false.

There is also a massive time cost associated with multiple condition coverage. If your conditional statement has *n* Boolean inputs, you will need 2^n tests to test it fully. That exponential increase based on the complexity of the checks makes it impractical to achieve compared to other measures of code coverage:

Code coverage type	Test steps required to test "If (A || B || C) then…"
Statement coverage	1
Decision coverage	2
Condition coverage	2
Condition/decision coverage	2
Modified condition/decision coverage	4
Multiple condition coverage	8

Table 6.3 – Number of tests required by different coverage types

This example starkly shows the measurable trade-off between the time you can devote to testing and the level of coverage you can achieve. See the *Choosing the appropriate test coverage* section for more on these comparisons.

While conditions will end up with binary choices within `if` statements, the variables feeding into them can be far more complex. They may be strings or function calls capable of taking many possible values. A further level of test coverage considers those inputs into conditional variables, as described next.

Understanding parameter value coverage

The inputs to the conditions we have considered so far were simple Boolean variables. In practice, conditional statements will operate on many variable comparison operators. Parameter value coverage works alongside the coverage types described previously by considering the different types of values variables can take within conditional statements.

Parameter value coverage applies equivalence partitioning to divide up the possibly infinite range of values into a finite subset suitable for testing. *Chapter 5, Black-Box Functional Testing*, describes common variable types and classes of values, such as negatives, decimals, and the value 0 for numeric fields or blank, capitalized, or special characters for string fields.

To satisfy parameter value coverage, each variable within a conditional statement has to include at least one value from each class of possible values. You will need to work out the classes of fields relevant to your variables and an example from each category to use in your tests, and you will need to repeat that for each conditional field. When you combine this with function coverage, you must pass each value into each function call to check for correctness.

Parameter value testing can rapidly expand into a vast test plan, so you will need to prioritize the tests you choose to include, both for the time they take to write and the time required to run them.

As well as `if` statements, loops have their own branching logic, which requires special consideration when evaluating code coverage. These are described next.

Understanding loop coverage

Along with `if` statements, loops are a fundamental aspect of code design. Due to their unique behavior, they also require dedicated test procedures. Statement coverage can be satisfied by only running the loop once, and decision coverage suggests you only need to check whether the loop is run or not. However, loop coverage is stricter and considers cases unique to running loops.

The main behaviors for loop coverage are as follows:

- Zero times around the loop
- One time around the loop
- Multiple times around the loop
- The maximum number of times around the loop

As with `if` statements, the first critical test is whether that branch is taken at all, so you need to check what happens if the loop is not executed. You then need two separate cases to cover if the loop is executed once or multiple times. Finally, you need to try the maximum number of cycles around the loop to check whether it can run successfully in the longest case.

For infinite loops, there is no maximum length to aim for, so you will have to set a pragmatic upper bound to reach instead. That should be longer than any customer can realistically trigger, or at least long enough to hit a steady state of repetition.

In his book *Software Testing Techniques*, Boris Beizer adds the following possible test cases for loops:

- One less than the minimum number of times around the loop
- A typical number of times around the loop
- One less than the maximum number of times around the loop
- One more than the maximum number of times around the loop

Not all of those may be possible for any given loop, and the bugs they find will be obscure. However, if you are after the maximum possible coverage, those are cases to consider.

Loops rarely exist in isolation. You will need to combine this loop testing with the coverage for branches described previously to check that `if` statements work correctly within loops at different stages. Between the many tests you can perform for both loops and `if` statements, you will hit a combinatorial explosion of possibilities to try, so you will need to prune those down. For more detail, see the *Mapping dependent and independent variables* section in *Chapter 5, Black-Box Functional Testing*. In general, you should aim to cover the most common, likely cases and identify unusual or obscure cases that have not been correctly thought through.

As well as `if` statements, loops are routinely nested within one another. Your most extensive possible test plan would be to test all the loop conditions listed previously against all the others for each loop. If the loops were nested four deep, that would give you $8^4 = 4,096$ different test cases, minus the cases where loops aren't run. To avoid that combinatorial explosion, you again need to identify which paths are either likely to see heavy use or are most likely to contain bugs. Using only the preceding four main tests reduces the number of tests to hundreds rather than the thousands in our example, so you will need to reduce that still further to produce a practical test plan. Again, this is where the skill of testing is required to identify the possible problems for your particular system.

These test cases have considered tests line by line, looking at individual `if` statements, function calls, and loops. You can also take a more abstract view of the program and measure coverage there, as shown in state coverage.

Understanding state and path coverage

Many applications include state machines for parts of their processing, which lets them transition from some starting state, through a series of temporary intermediate stages, to some outcome states, usually the success or failure of an operation.

The state machine should be included in the technical documentation for that code or may be recorded in the code itself, with a variable explicitly tracking the current state. If neither is the case, then getting that documented is your first task. Note that this is technical documentation beyond what is produced for the feature specification (see *Chapter 2, Writing Great Feature Specifications*). That specification only describes what the behavior should be; there are many ways it could be implemented, and you need those details here.

Once the states are clear, ensuring state coverage is as simple as checking your testing moves the application through all the available states. Consider this simplified example state machine, which sets up a new connection between two systems:

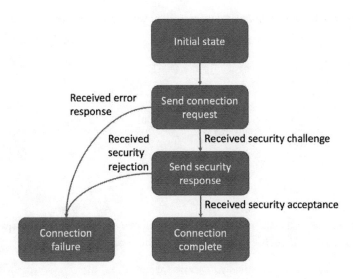

Figure 6.2 – A simple state machine

There is a single starting state and two possible outcomes, either success or failure. You can test this with two tests, one to reach each of those end states. However, state coverage is analogous to statement coverage and has the same weaknesses – at branches, it does not cover the different routes the application can take. We need a new measure of coverage, analogous to decision (branch) coverage, to count those other routes. That is known as **path coverage**.

Using path coverage, we need at least three tests to cover the preceding program, one for the success path and two for the failure cases. This simple example only serves to illustrate the different considerations. Any realistic program will be far more complex and will require additional analysis. This is an important topic, and there are more details in the *Considering states and transitions* section.

Choosing appropriate test coverage

Given the many different ways of measuring test coverage and the levels of testing they provide, you have to choose which is suitable for your application. That depends greatly on the risks associated with your program. If your software is for aviation or emergency services, lives may depend on finding bugs. If you work in automated trading or satellite services, tens of millions of pounds could be lost if there is a critical error. In those cases, modified condition/decision coverage could be a requirement.

If, on the other hand, you are working on a less critical area or with a smaller user base, a lower standard for testing might be suitable initially. You can always revisit the tests and require a higher standard later on, based on the bugs you find.

The lighter forms of unit testing, such as a statement or decision coverage, have notable advantages and disadvantages:

Advantages	Disadvantages
Quicker to write	Incomplete test coverage
Quicker to run	May give a false sense of security
Easier to measure	
Easier to understand	

Table 6.4 – Advantages and disadvantages of lighter forms of unit test coverage

Heavier forms of unit testing, such as modified condition/decision coverage, have the reverse advantages, being slower to write and run but, crucially, providing more complete test coverage.

Code coverage software can automatically measure the coverage you have achieved, although that is not without caveats. First, be sure what type of coverage it is measuring. If it is only statement coverage, be aware of the gaps that can leave in the program execution.

While it can be helpful to measure the coverage so precisely, beware of chasing numbers rather than thinking through the critical areas of testing. It might be better to leave some simple code areas with only statement coverage so you can run modified condition/decision coverage for particularly complex or sensitive areas. It is impossible to test code fully, so don't sit back and relax if your measure reports 100% coverage. What form of testing have you achieved 100% in? And what gaps remain? One crucial area is understanding the limitations of unit tests compared to system tests.

Systematically stepping through each line of code and trying each possible condition provides some confidence that there are no surprises at the lowest level. However, these are unit tests rather than system tests, leaving the possibility for unexpected behavior when two modules work together. In this section, we have strayed from the system tests that this book focuses on. As described in *Chapter 4, Test Types, Cases, and Environments*, unit tests can rigorously cover small sections of code but cannot find bugs that only appear when you run code together. Breaking down the code simplifies the tests that need to be written, which is why unit testing only gets this section rather than the rest of the book being devoted to the broader considerations of system testing.

Next, we turn to system-level considerations again, this time informed by knowledge of the application's inner workings, and look at how to test messages flowing between modules.

Testing modules and messages

When considering information flow within your application, you need to identify which information is local and remote for each module. How is the information passed around within the system?

This doesn't necessarily require reading the code but needs at least a block-diagram-level understanding of the data generation, storage, and movement.

The modules may be as obvious as different physical machines, or they could be separate virtual machines or containers, other services, or, at the lowest level, different blocks of code that can only be identified by code inspection. All of these require messages to be passed between them, which need to be specified and can host different classes of issues.

Watch out for third-party modules imported to perform specific tasks. The development team will be less familiar with their code, so they are more likely to be surprised, and any fixes may take longer since they will have to work around how the third-party module behaves.

Once you have identified the different modules, carefully list all the information passed between them. You need to test each field for the full range of values it can support in the same way you try the user inputs. Like black-box testing, look for equivalent partitions of data in the messages. For instance, you can apply the list of different types of text input to text fields passed between modules as well as when entered by users.

> **Real-world example – The secret new protocol**
>
> In one product I worked on, we displayed the details of our users' meetings that day, so they could dial in and connect to them. A new feature would give them their whole calendar on our app – not just today, but the ability to see future days' meetings as well.
>
> The feature was clear, and the user interface was well specified, so we prepared and ran a test plan thoroughly testing its functional aspects. When it went live, there were immediate problems. All the meetings disappeared – today's and those in the future, so they couldn't connect to any of them.
>
> Unknown to the test team, we had implemented a new protocol to pass information around our system to get the details of future meetings. While that had worked correctly in our small development and test environments, it couldn't handle the load of our live environment. We hadn't planned sufficient load testing and had a major test escape as a result. It showed that you can only fully test a feature by talking to the development team and understanding the implementation.

When considering messages between different modules within a system, there are three classes of errors to look out for:

- Errors within modules
- Mismatches of meaning between modules
- Limitations in the messages between modules

First are problems local to individual modules. You can find these with black-box testing, but by considering the code architecture, you can ensure you test every module, whereas you may miss some otherwise.

Secondly, when modules send information, two new classes of errors are possible: mismatches between the handling of some values and limitations of the transport. For simplicity, let's consider a client-server application with information being sent between them, potentially over the public internet. However, these considerations apply just as well to two code modules running within the same machine.

To find mismatches between different modules, you can again turn to the list of value types from *Chapter 5, Black-Box Functional Testing*, and make sure they mean the same to both the client and the server. For example, the client may accept negative numbers and happily send them off to the server, which then reports an error or treats them incorrectly. Part of the feature specification should state what happens in every case: if negative numbers are invalid, the client should reject them, so its behavior needs to change. If they are valid, then the server should be altered to accept them.

When raising bugs about mismatches between different systems, it can be difficult to tell which is in the wrong. The message may fail, but is that because the client has sent invalid information or because the server has rejected something valid? Only careful examination of the code, the message, and the specification can tell you for sure. Unusual but valid behavior from the client may trigger an error on the server. Then either side could be fixed, depending on how busy the development teams are and how extensive the changes would be to resolve it. Perhaps it is simpler to stop the client from sending the unusual message than to add support for it on the server.

> **Important note**
>
> The art of raising bugs is beyond the scope of this book, but beware when reporting bugs about messages between modules. It may be that quite different development teams are responsible for the client and the server, and each may blame the other for these borderline cases. Fixes can be delayed because both sides think it is the other's responsibility. Even if the behavior and the problem are perfectly clear, they may disagree about where to fix it. The different teams may need to meet and agree on the owner before it can be resolved.

The technique of error guessing from black-box testing is vital here too. Edge value and boundary conditions can also cause problems between modules. The client may accept values less than or equal to 100, whereas the server only accepts values less than 100. You may have covered these cases with black-box testing, but by examining the architecture, you can be sure that you have tested all the boundary conditions on all the module interfaces.

The third class of problem when testing messages between modules is limitations on the messages themselves. Possibly the client code happily handles negative numbers internally, and the server code handles negative numbers too. Still, the message implies that all numbers must be positive, and any negative numbers are to be converted to invalid values. The same tests that check mismatches between modules will also find issues of that type in the message specification, so these may not need more tests but may require a different solution to fix them.

Messages can also be limited due to their size. What combination of inputs will produce the largest possible message, for instance, the highest number of configured entities or the longest possible string values? You should try all of those on each message interface. Loading can also trigger bugs. This is considered in more detail in *Chapter 12, Load Testing*, so here I will just note that high loads may result in the application dropping messages or delays in processing. You can only ensure you have stress tested these interfaces by identifying all modules and their messages.

Real-world example – One too many edge servers

In one company where I worked, clients would connect to our infrastructure via several edge servers. As our client base grew, we did many new code releases and extended our infrastructure.

One day, we had reports of many clients failing to connect. We were baffled – there hadn't been a new code release, and the system had been fine the day before. The only change we had made was adding another edge server, providing extra capacity to connect to our system. We rapidly undid that change, and the clients recovered.

When they first connected, we sent the clients a list of possible edge servers. It turned out that that message was limited in length, and adding one extra edge server had made the message too long for the clients to read. We had to raise that limit before extending the system any further.

There may also be rate limits on the messages between different parts of the system, which can become overloaded, leading to dropped messages and errors. These are considered further in *Chapter 11, Destructive Testing*, and *Chapter 12, Load Testing*, but both these tests rely on you correctly identifying the modules and messages as part of white-box testing.

The testing of messages between modules also applies to messages on public APIs, considered next.

API testing

As described in *Chapter 5, Black-Box Functional Testing*, when APIs are released publicly, they can be tested using black-box techniques. There, you are checking publicly documented messages without knowing how the system implements message handling. APIs can also be semi-public, with some documented commands and others only available for internal use, or they can be purely internal.

The considerations that apply when testing those APIs also apply to messages between components within a system. The approach to testing them is simple enough: their documentation is their specification. There should be internal documents describing the implementation of internal protocols, just as there are for public interfaces, and you can design your tests against those. If that documentation doesn't exist, your first task is to ensure it's written.

Armed with that information, you need to systematically step through every field of every message to ensure it is correctly received. The skill is partitioning the inputs, as described in the previous chapter, to cover the important classes and identify dependent variables that need every combination checked.

Some fields will have a limited range of values they can take, so trying each one is a simple case. For freeform inputs such as text or numeric entries, see the list of different partitions in the previous chapter.

It is harder to identify which fields interact with each other and where you need to try every combination. For instance, you may need to check that every user type can exist in every state within a system. Most fields should be independent, and you do not need to check them against each other, which reduces the total number of test cases.

Testing external, third-party APIs is especially important because it can be hard to know in advance what data an external system might return to you. The API may be well documented, or you may be relying on previous messages to understand what it sends, in which case the data might change in the future. While systematic checks can ensure that your system rejects invalid data, you might have to accept it if a live system starts sending it to you. By testing, you can be sure of your system behavior, and by recording incoming messages, you can make sure your application correctly handles those cases in the future.

However, testing against third parties is both unreliable and antisocial. Other providers may not appreciate your auto tests constantly sending them repetitive requests. In addition, network issues or problems with the external system will result in test failures for you. Those need investigation but are not errors with your application and will waste valuable time you could spend elsewhere. It's far more reliable to test against applications and networks that you control. Then if there are errors, at least they are your errors to fix.

Real-world example – Beware stateful, dumb APIs

In one company, we used a third-party API for part of our functionality. We stored entities with the third party, so they had a list of everything that existed, and we kept our own list, which we used to access the entities as required.

Unfortunately, there was no correction mechanism on the interface, and no way to check our list against theirs and fix mismatches. Even more unfortunately, there were known ways we could get out of sync. If we deleted an entity and then restored it from backup, for instance, we would delete the entity on the third party but had no way to recover it. Then we believed that entity existed, but they thought it was deleted.

More unfortunately still, when we were out of sync, we got into a loop of infinitely retrying the doomed operation. We regularly had to manually fix issues because we were overloading the third-party service with the number of requests we made. The code was behaving as designed; the weakness was in the design itself.

As we saw in *Chapter 4, Test Types, Cases, and Environments*, you can test interfaces against stubs and mocks. Where resourcing permits, these are particularly useful for integration tests, so you can isolate different parts of the system and test only against them. On the plus side, this gives you complete control over the messages you send, so you can exercise every possibility. On the downside, they are expensive to write, especially if you already have an application that sits on that interface. A mock also risks finding low-priority bugs as it can send messages that the actual application never would. While they might provoke issues, that case would never arise in real life.

Where mock applications are vital is if you don't have a live application to drive the interface. For instance, you might provide an API from a server but let your users write client APIs against it. Then you may have to handle any input because external API users might send any inputs to you. In that case, prepare a client library so you have an application to test with. Scripts to use that library may be fully automated in test runs that perform actions, check outcomes, and report the results. Or scripts may be semi-automated, which need to be started manually and have a tester check them. Either way, you will need to write and maintain the code to send these messages.

The risk is that you end up testing the mock rather than the program itself. Ideally, scripts should be written by someone who didn't write the code implementation and share no common code. That way, they serve as a genuinely independent check on the live code. You should keep the mock as simple and reliable as possible, so you can spend your time finding bugs in the live code rather than the mock you are testing against. Despite their drawbacks, mocks are an important tool, especially for automated testing.

Testing against real third parties should be limited to a final manual check that the system works once all other tests have passed. The bulk of automated testing should use internal tools so you have reliability and control and can run at high rates to test for behavior under load. For more on those tests, see *Chapter 12, Load Testing*, and *Chapter 13, Stress Testing*.

Finally, check how much code the API shares with other interfaces. Ideally, an API is simply another route onto functions that run regardless of whether the API, user interface, or some other system calls them. Look out for functions where that isn't the case, and the API has its own implementation for some or all of its processing. Mismatches between its behavior and that of other interfaces can cause many bugs.

APIs can also cause the application to transition between different states, each of which you'll need to test separately. That requires extra consideration as part of white-box testing, which we consider next.

Considering states and transitions

Many applications will exist in different states during processing. Even *stateless* applications without persistent storage have transient state machines as connections are requested and confirmed, for instance, or they process incoming messages and send responses. An essential part of white-box testing is identifying and testing all those states, the transitions between them, and the errors that can occur.

Some states may be evident from the specification, such as users who have entered their email address but have not yet confirmed it or chosen a password and have not yet logged in. Those states and their transitions will already be covered as part of black-box testing.

However, many other states may not be obvious to users, which need to be discovered and understood as part of white-box testing. One piece of code might accept incoming web requests but then move them on to different threads or queues for processing. By working with the developers, you need to map out all those sequences to check the transitions between each state. This includes transitions leading to error states, which are often not apparent from usual user interactions. *Chapter 7, Testing of Error Cases*, describes that in more detail.

Having identified the states, you need to write tests to check each one. This will require you to visit all the states and traverse every transition. When you attempt to describe the code in a simple state machine, as described here, it may become apparent that no one diagram captures all the interactions, and the code can take different paths in different situations. This may happen if the developers hadn't thought of this code as a state machine and hadn't implemented it in a structured way. If that's the case, consider delaying the feature so that it can be done properly; otherwise, the complexity of a poorly implemented state machine might introduce many bugs.

For the different state machines, consider these questions:

- What is the starting state?
- Are there different configurations possible even from the start of the state machine?
- What are all the state entry points?
  - For instance, if you can create a new user from a web page, an API call, or an app, add a test for each
- Are there any states that loop back to earlier states?
- Are there any failure modes that move you between states?
- What are all the state exit points, including failure modes?
- Are any states really separate and behave differently based on a variable or environment?
  - You may need to split up a state if it has very different modes of working in different situations, especially if its inputs and outputs differ
- Have you identified all the transitions and added a test for each of them?
  - In all but the simplest cases, checking each transition requires at least as many tests as checking all the states
- What sequences of transitions might interact with each other?
- What are the end states?

You can generate many tests by applying those questions to the state machine for your application, as demonstrated in the following example.

State transition test example

Consider this example state machine:

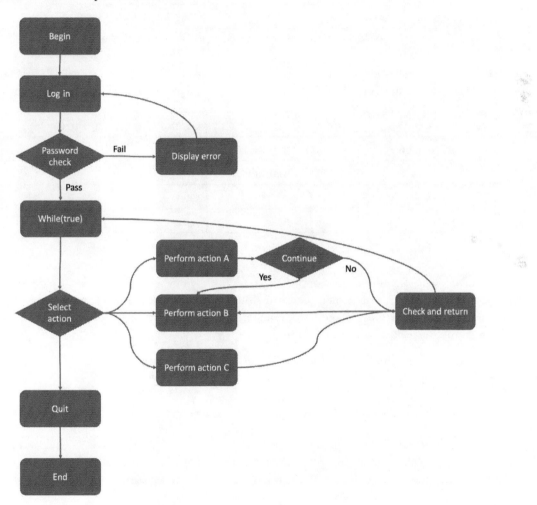

Figure 6.3 – An example state machine

In this simple application, users log in, then select from four options: action A, action B, action C, or to quit. Until they quit, the program loops so they can choose another action. Actions A and B are linked so that after performing action A, you can continue to action B.

You can test every state in this application with three tests:

Test	Login	First action	Second action
1	Fail, then Pass	Action A. Continue? No	Quit
2	Pass	Action B	Quit
3	Pass	Action C	Quit

Table 6.5 – Tests achieving state coverage for the example state machine

However, despite testing every state, you have not tested every transition. That doesn't check the option to continue from action A to action B. You need an additional test to check all possible transitions:

Test	Login	First action	Second action	Third action
1	Fail, then Pass	Action A. Continue? No	Quit	–
2	Pass	Action A. Continue? Yes	Action B	Quit
3	Pass	Action B	Quit	–
4	Pass	Action C	Quit	–

Table 6.6 – Tests achieving transition coverage for the example state machine

With those four tests, you can check all states and transitions. Look out for instances in your application when state coverage is not sufficient to provide transition coverage. Prioritize your tests so the important transitions do have tests, and if you choose not to test them all, make sure you have at least identified them so you can make an informed decision.

Even with all the transitions tested, there could still be issues depending on the combination of states the application passes through.

N-switch coverage

You have now tested all states and transitions. However, this program includes two loops. The result of one loop may affect subsequent runs. If a login failure simply adds an error message to the page, for instance, then two login failures in a row might show the error message twice. Or if action A is invalid after performing action B, these tests will not find that error.

Visiting each stage once is known as **0-switch coverage**, as named by Professor Tsun S. Chow in his 1978 paper, *Testing Software Design Modeled by Finite-State Machines*. He suggested measuring the sequences of states that you visit. If those sequences are one state long, you have 0-switch coverage. Considering a series of *n* states together, you have *n-1* switch coverage.

To achieve 1-switch coverage and find errors in sequences of two states in our example program, we need additional test cases:

Test	Login	First action	Second action	Third action
1	Fail, then Fail, then Pass	Action A. Continue? No	Quit	
2	Fail, then Pass	Action B	Quit	
3	Fail, then Pass	Action C	Quit	
4	Pass	Action A. Continue? No	Action A	Quit
5	Pass	Action A. Continue? Yes	Action B	Quit
6	Pass	Action A. Continue? No	Action C	Quit
7	Pass	Action B	Action A	Quit
8	Pass	Action B	Action B	Quit
9	Pass	Action B	Action C	Quit
10	Pass	Action C	Action A	Quit
11	Pass	Action C	Action B	Quit
12	Pass	Action C	Action C	Quit

Table 6.7 – Tests achieving 1-switch coverage for the example state machine

Test 1 covers the case of multiple login failures. Tests 1 to 3 cover the cases of login failure followed by each of the actions performed once. Tests 4 to 12 try the case of successful login followed by all permutations of pairs of actions A, B, and C in sequence. If there is a bug when you perform action B, then action A, this level of testing will find it.

Of course, with an infinite loop, you can extend this indefinitely through 2-switch, 3-switch coverage, and so on. These uncover bugs that are more obscure and less likely to be hit, so you can choose what level you want to achieve. A vital test principle is always to be aware of what you're not covering, even if you deliberately choose not to spend the time testing it.

Some combinations of transitions will be related, and others will be independent. We have considered multiple login failures and different combinations of actions, and both could hide bugs. But what if you have a login failure before performing actions A, B, and C? For 1-switch coverage, we should include those too. However, those two parts of the system are unrelated: once you have logged in, it shouldn't matter how many login failures you had previously. You can prune your list of possible test cases by identifying unrelated areas that aren't linked in practice.

In this case, there are so many combinations of actions, A, B, and C, that we will need to log in many times. In that case, you may as well add variety to the login since you will be running several other tests. Look out for other opportunities to add variation. If one area of the code is particularly complex and requires many tests to try all its paths, don't run all those paths with the same username, for instance. Since you are running those tests anyway, try them with many different usernames in case there is an interaction.

After each transition, you need to check the condition of the system. For state machines with an explicit variable tracking their state, you should start by checking that variable. Then consider the possible entrance and exit possibilities. This may mean that certain buttons or UI elements are visible to allow you to transition to the next step or that the application responds to specific API messages or inputs. Work out everything that distinguishes each state from the next so you can check them all.

Some programs are too complex to be described with a single-state machine. Those require a different approach to testing, considered next.

Checking asynchronous applications

The examples here have considered simple synchronous, single-threaded applications. In multi-threaded and asynchronous applications, different code sections can run out of sequence or in parallel depending on external events. While you can test that each function works correctly, it is much harder to test their interactions. You can't define a single-state machine, and it's best to find bugs with load testing. That is described in detail in *Chapter 12, Load Testing*.

Asynchronous applications involve sending messages from a subsystem of an application and pausing further processing or continuing with other tasks until it receives responses. That encompasses a vast range of possible uses, but there are a common set of checks to apply to them, as follows:

- Duplicate messages
- Out-of-order messages
- Missing update messages
- Missing response messages (timeouts)

This section considers each of these cases.

Duplicate messages

Using unreliable transport mechanisms, it can be hard to avoid sending duplicate messages without adding excessive latency. For each asynchronous message, how does the far end handle receiving duplicate messages? Is that subsystem guaranteed to be **idempotent**, such that receiving multiple messages won't change its state? Whatever the theory, check its behavior in practice.

Conversely, how does your application respond to receiving duplicate messages? If those are simple acknowledgments, they can be safely ignored. However, if you receive duplicate commands, it might not be clear whether both messages are genuine requests. Does your application disambiguate messages, for instance, with sequence numbers, in which case, does that mechanism work for all message types? If it doesn't, could duplicate requests trigger duplicate tasks, and what effects might that have? Duplicate data processing tasks might just result in pointless work, but user-facing requests such as sending emails might result in customers getting duplicate messages. Either case is a bug, of differing severities, and they may need significant work to avoid them.

Out-of-order messages

Asynchronous processes mean delays could cause messages to be delivered out of order. Consider the following sequence:

1. Master task spawns Child Task A.
2. Child A spawns Grandchild Task B.
3. Task B completes and signals its result to the Master, but the message is lost.
4. Child A completes and signals its results to the Master task.
5. Task B resends its result and succeeds.

From the Master task's point of view, this is invalid. Each task further down the chain should complete before its parent, but here Task B appears to have been completed after its parent, Task A.

Anywhere messages should appear in a given order, reverse them to check the warnings that are raised and what state it leaves your system in. It should be possible to check the state and automatically recover, despite the lost message.

Missing update messages

Often, two systems are designed to maintain the same state, with update messages indicating any changes. That might be a scheduling application reading your calendar, a statistics program reading sales figures, or one of many other similar situations. Update messages such as **webhooks** are an efficient way to stay up to date without the need for polling, but if a message is lost, the two systems will be out of sync.

What happens if your system receives an update for an entity it doesn't know about or discovers a gap in a time sequence? There should be dedicated logic to identify such situations and correct them, so you'll need to check if that works.

Missing response messages

The opposite case of receiving duplicate messages is if your application sends a command but fails to get a response within its timeout. Did the command not reach the destination, or did the acknowledgment fail to come back? In this case, your application needs a way to check on the status of the destination to see whether it has already acted on the command message. You could send another command, but that risks the destination carrying it out twice.

There are various techniques to avoid these problems, so if your application has this pattern, you'll need to discover which yours uses and ensure it works correctly.

All these asynchronous problems are likely sources of bugs. Your application will probably only encounter them rarely, so they may not be a priority, but they will happen eventually and could cause significant issues.

Error guessing and identifying problem areas like this are necessary for white-box testing as well as black-box testing. Armed with the knowledge of the code structure and implementation, you can choose where to test and how best to trigger issues, as described in the next section.

Error guessing

Just as you need to choose the values of the inputs you will use for black-box testing, you also need to select the values for white-box testing. These also require equivalence partitioning and the careful choice of examples to represent each partition. As ever, the requirement here is to challenge the code as much as possible and try to provoke errors.

The lists from *Chapter 5, Black-Box Functional Testing*, are helpful. Instead of integers being entered into a web page or sent as part of an API, in this case, they will be passed between functions, but the same range of interesting cases still applies. How does the function handle negative numbers, decimals, or large values? Likewise, strings and other data types.

Watch out for historical anomalies in the code. For instance, sometimes data or configuration is stored one way up to a certain release and then a different way after that. Sometimes it is worthwhile to go back and migrate the old data to the new system, but that can be uneconomical, leaving the old configuration in place for old entities. With white-box testing, you can see those hidden partitions that are not visible publicly. Most likely, both cases are supposed to function identically, but they require test cases for both the old and new versions.

Another great source of bugs is repeated areas of code. If the same or similar functionality is implemented in two different ways, the development team must remember to update both locations whenever there is a change. If they don't, users will see inconsistent behavior. White-box testing can reveal those poor coding practices and the bugs they cause, so watch out for them. The correct resolution is to refactor the code so it only exists in one place.

Functions have a range of valid inputs they can accept, so ensure that error checking is in place to handle any unexpected data. If a function assumes that a database query will return a single entry, what happens if there are multiple entries or none at all? *Chapter 7, Testing of Error Cases*, covers that error checking in more detail.

With the code available for inspection, you can see possible values that may cause issues in that function. You can find potential divide-by-zero problems or null pointers with code inspection. Finding these issues requires a different set of skills that were described briefly in the *Code analysis* section, and the variables types and the cases to consider (described previously) are a good start.

After each test, you then need to check the state of the system. White-box testing gives the ability to perform more thorough checks than other forms of testing, as the next section shows.

White-box checks

Just as in black-box testing, in white-box tests, you not only have to decide what test cases to run but also how to check that those tests have passed. When you have access to the code in white-box testing, you can do this at several levels.

At the level of individual lines of code under unit tests, you can specify the exact outputs of the different functions. Once again, this has all the strengths and weaknesses of unit testing – it is precise and comprehensive but cannot find errors when the functions are combined.

While running system tests, white-box knowledge lets testers see the code's behavior in more detail. This lets you find other classes of issues that might cause subtle or invisible problems for users, such as inefficiencies in the code or two wrongs making a right, as described next.

Checking code inefficiencies

Code inefficiencies can include code that initially tries to do the wrong thing but there are retries, which means the operation eventually works. This might not cause customers issues beyond an imperceptible delay, but it means the function wastes time on a pointless request every time it runs. You should raise these as bugs, as covered in more detail in *Chapter 10, Maintainability*. Have a zero-tolerance approach to errors, and understand every warning within the logs while testing.

Retries may not even raise warnings, in which case only code inspection or careful examination of the logs will show the problem. When message-sending fails, you have two chances to catch the issue – both the sender and the recipient should log the problem. If they don't, then logs also need improving.

You need white-box testing to determine whether the logs go to a sufficient level of detail. While there needs to be a summary log, suitable for someone not familiar with that area of code, the log also needs to have a level of detail so you can trace its main function calls to find unnecessary loops and repetitions, as well as the successful completion of functions.

Checking for two wrongs making a right

White-box testing also lets you find mistakes in the form of two wrongs making a right. In this case, a value may be written incorrectly into a database or populated in a message. Still, the consumer of that information expects the incorrect value, so the code works as expected in most situations. It may only break during different tests, which should use the wrong value, or when the code is next altered. This can be the case especially when a single developer owns code for both the reading and writing of a field. If they have understood the field value incorrectly, then the code for writing the value and reading it will be consistent but will not meet the specification. Only by examining the fields themselves can you spot that error.

Examining specific loglines is particularly important when testing for the absence of behavior, such as fixing an application crash. Sometimes it might be possible to run on the old version and reproduce the issue, but if that isn't realistic or possible, a log line can indicate that the crashing condition has been hit but is now handled correctly.

White-box testing lets testers check on the data structures written to longer-term storage, such as files and databases. These need to be specified by the developers since they are implementation details that neither the product managers nor testers will initially know. Once documented, testing can check these alongside the customer-visible effects of features.

In white-box checks, you are looking for invalid data within database fields. They should be made as strict as possible to prevent invalid data from being written in; if you find bad data later, it can be tough to tell when and why it was added, so it is far better to prevent it at the time. The requirements on database fields should have strict checking applied as early as possible because making classes of data invalid later also causes problems if some already exist. Then you need to migrate that data before upgrades are possible. Fixing databases later is an operational headache, so check that invalid data is correctly rejected as part of white-box testing.

Finally, in this chapter, we'll consider mixing black- and white-box testing techniques, known as gray-box testing.

Gray-box testing

In this chapter, I have drawn a hard distinction between black-box testing with no knowledge of the code and its architecture versus white-box testing with full access. In practice, that is neither realistic nor desirable. Some code architecture will be obvious even to casual users – an app is connecting to servers, for instance, or different development teams work on separate parts of the application, so the code is never truly black-box. Then you can proceed through levels of detail. Testers without coding experience can still understand the system's architecture, its modules, states, and transitions, which can be sketched as block diagrams. Beyond that, you can follow the flow of the functions, and finally, you can step through the code line by line.

Each level provides useful extra information; you can go as deep as time and your coding skills will allow.

In a complex, multi-layered system, for instance, it can be tempting to raise bugs against the visible interfaces to the system – against the customer app rather than the server backend, against the web interface rather than the database and processes that drive it. With good knowledge of the code architecture, white-box testing can guard against that. Even if it isn't clear where a problem lies, the user interface is often less complex than the systems it connects to, and those are more likely to be the source of problems. Knowledge of the different modules and their logs should let testers correctly isolate the problem before communicating it to the development team.

After initially performing exploratory testing from a naive point of view to mimic the customer experience (see *Chapter 1, Making the Most of Exploratory Testing*), part of the feature specification review should be to gather as much detail about the implementation as possible to inform the testing (see *Chapter 3, How to Run Successful Specification Reviews*). Some classes of bugs and conditions can only be identified by understanding how the code works, making white-box testing a crucial part of system test design.

Summary

In this chapter, you have learned about the importance of white-box testing and the strengths it brings to a test plan.

Code analysis and static testing let you find bugs before you run the application by analyzing the code itself. Unit tests can provide comprehensive testing of the lowest-level functionality, and its coverage can be measured in many different ways. These provide varying levels of coverage, so it's important to know how you measure your coverage.

By identifying the different modules and how information is passed around within the system, you can identify mismatches in module behavior or errors in system messages. The same considerations apply to API testing, where you can also step through the messages and fields using the guides to variable type testing described in *Chapter 5, Black-Box Functional Testing*.

Understanding the different states an application goes through means you can test them and their transitions thoroughly. At the lowest level, white-box testing involves checking each line of code, which is unit testing rather than system testing.

Throughout white-box testing, you need to use the techniques of equivalence partitioning and error guessing to decide on the best test inputs to cover the maximum number of cases. White-box testing also opens up much more detailed checking you can do, not just on the user-visible functionality but also checking on the contents of internal system messages and database entries.

Finally, we saw that the distinction between black- and white-box testing is artificial and does not occur in real life, where testers are always somewhat aware of the architecture of the code they are testing. And that is a good thing – the more details you know about the code's implementation, the better testing you can perform.

In the next chapter, we will leave the happy-path working case and consider what happens when the code goes wrong by examining invalid inputs and error cases.

7
Testing of Error Cases

"Experience is simply the name we give to our mistakes."

– Oscar Wilde

In the last chapter, you saw how white-box testing techniques improve test coverage by examining how the code works. Understanding your application's implementation lets you write more detailed tests covering more of the code behavior, in addition to the checks identified by black-box testing. This chapter examines how best to test the final aspect of core behavior: the code's response to error conditions. There are still many other aspects, such as how usable, maintainable, and secure the application is, but this is the last section of testing focusing on the code's active behavior, testing what it should do in different situations.

In this chapter, you will learn about the following topics:

- Expected versus unexpected failures
- Failing early
- Failing as little as possible, to avoid defect cascading
- Failing as specifically as possible to give user feedback
- Timeouts
- Network degradation
- Data failures
- Fuzzing
- User feedback

First, we will consider the advantages and disadvantages of error testing.

Advantages and disadvantages of error testing

Error case testing is unusual since it is separate from happy-path functionality, giving it a distinctive set of strengths and weaknesses:

Advantages	Disadvantages
May not have been considered by the product owners	These are rarer conditions, so these tests are a lower priority
May not have been considered by developers, so failures may be more serious	Can be difficult to generate specific error cases
Important to give user feedback if there is a problem	Difficult to tell the ideal behavior in a failure mode
Good error handling makes debugging easier	
Can help to find linked issues	

Table 7.1 – Advantages and disadvantages of testing error cases

Testing error cases is important because the product owners may not have considered them. They are usually more interested in the main functionality than what happens when things go wrong. The developers, too, are likely to devote more time to the working cases than the failure modes, so performing this testing is a necessary check.

When your program is working well, your users are likely to be happy with it; the test comes when there is a problem. Does it provide clear, actionable feedback about what the customer should do? Is it worth the user trying again? Might their internet connection be to blame? You must inform your users if the problem is in the program itself and can't be resolved by retrying.

Your program will inevitably hit errors during its usage; the challenge is how fast you can debug and resolve them. Good error handling allows you to rapidly see the cause of problems, rather than leaving you with a string of effects to pick through to find out what happened first.

By triggering one error, you can often uncover others. Does the application produce excessive logging when it fails? Does it have sensible retries and timeouts? You can only check these in practice by causing problems and observing the results.

On the downside, error testing is a lower priority. These cases are rarer than the happy-path tests in black- and white-box testing, and if they aren't, your program is in serious trouble. Because they occur less frequently, they will have a lower priority, so factor that in when prioritizing testing and bug fixes. However, their importance is also a function of the severity of the failure. While your test case might be rare, it is still a critical bug if it results in a crash or data loss. When people questioned how much time I devoted to testing error cases, this was often my answer: probably I will only find minor issues, but there may be a major problem waiting to be discovered.

Error testing can be challenging to carry out in practice, and it can be difficult to identify all possible errors and trigger them. They may rely on unusual timing or a rare response from a third party. You may need to produce new test tools or add debug functions to your application to reproduce these cases reliably.

Finally, error cases need special attention in the specification. It may not be clear what the ideal behavior is during a failure or what is possible for your application. As noted previously, the product owner is likely to spend less time on these cases than the main functionality, so the desired outcome might not be documented thoroughly. I've seen a class of bugs we shipped because testers assumed a particular behavior was acceptable and expected during error handling when the application could have behaved better.

Don't fall into that trap: spend time specifying the error conditions fully. With those strengths and weaknesses in mind, we will start by classifying errors your program might encounter as expected and unexpected.

Classifying expected versus unexpected problems

There are two classes of problems you might hit while testing. The first kind is an expected problem, for instance, an unusual or invalid condition coming in from an external system. Perhaps you send a message and never receive a reply, or the reply contains a blank required field. Maybe you only support 10 simultaneous sessions, but someone tries to connect an 11th. These cases will result in failures, but they are all expected. When your code is running in the real world, people may try to misuse it, and you have to be ready to handle that input. All the tests in this chapter are of this first kind – expected problems. Even if the *external* system you are talking to is another internal module, you have to be able to handle receiving any kind of rubbish back from it. Input validation is necessary on any interface.

The other class of problem is something invalid happening within code – attempting to use a null pointer, a calculation requires a division by zero, or a function should act on a list but the list is empty, for instance. Notice that the descriptions of these problems are different: they are all lower-level aspects of asking the code to do impossible things. With expected problems, I can list potential failure modes your code needs to handle, but I have no idea why a pointer ended up null or a list was empty – it should never happen. There's no telling what external conditions might cause such problems since they should be impossible.

Expected problems should generate warnings that the behavior isn't ideal, but your application should handle them gracefully with relevant feedback to the user. Unexpected problems should raise an error for the development team because they indicate that the code is at fault and needs to be fixed. We'll revisit this important point in *Chapter 10, Maintainability*. There is an open question of whether the code should continue when it encounters such an error or not. If it is safety-critical, it should stop and fail-safe; if you are providing a less vital service, continuing to run despite errors can offer extra resilience.

The point of testing for error conditions is to handle expected errors so they don't turn into unexpected ones. This chapter will consider many classes of possible failures that you can add to your test plans. They will *fail*, but that failure will be in a graceful, designed way, with no part of the application complaining that something impossible is happening. Your application should fail as early as possible when it detects an error to prevent failures from propagating through the system. That is one of the guiding philosophies for handling errors, as described next.

Error handling philosophies

In black- and white-box testing, the desired behavior is often obvious. The specification can help describe details, but you can often guess the intended behavior. That becomes much harder with error conditions. In these cases, your application will definitely fail; the only question is precisely how. The specification is now essential to describe the desired behavior as it will no longer be self-evident.

This chapter follows several principles for error handling that apply across a wide array of programming languages and environments. It will show you the importance of these principles and how to apply them to your testing:

- **Fail as early as possible**: Your application should raise an error as soon as it goes wrong to make debugging easier.

- **Fail as little as possible**: Failures should be graceful, with clear error messages to users indicating the problem. One failure shouldn't lead to a cascade of other issues.

- **Fail as specifically as possible**: As we'll see in the section on user feedback, the more precise you can be in your error handling, the better user experience you can provide.

We mentioned error conditions in *Chapters 4* and *5* on black- and white-box testing, and there is a lot of overlap. In practice, you shouldn't divide the test plan into success and error cases; instead, focus on one web page or API message and test all its scenarios together. However, the considerations for these tests are different, so I have devoted a specific chapter to them. I'll let you combine the ideas from black-box, white-box, and error testing together when you write the test plan.

Your application should detect problems as early as possible. That helps prevent their effects from spreading, gives more accurate feedback to the user, and makes their diagnosis easier. Your task as a tester is to generate those problems to check that the error handling code is behaving correctly. Trying error cases means that all the tests described in this chapter will *fail* somehow. However, they are intended to fail, and the pass mark is that they should fail gracefully, with good feedback to the user about what went wrong with no additional side effects. Your application should never crash, for instance.

Next, we will consider these principles in more detail, starting with failing as early as possible.

Fail as early as possible

Your application should identify failures as soon as they happen. That means problems should become expected failures close to where that input was received, which brings a host of benefits in terms of user experience, debugging, and resilience. You're aiming to avoid unexpected failures that propagate through the system.

Failing early in the release cycle

Failing early applies both to the project overall and within your application. In terms of the project, your goal is to catch bugs as soon after they are written as possible. In practice, that means writing unit tests alongside the code that constantly check the main functionality and error cases. Those will have limitations: being written by the developer, they don't have a second pair of eyes, so any misreading of the specification will be written into both the code and the tests. And since they are unit tests, there is a class of integration and system problems they won't be able to find. Still, contemporaneously written tests are an excellent way to start finding issues.

Failing early in the release cycle means that the test team has to be closely aligned with the developers to avoid delays between the code being available and being tested. Get a second opinion from the test team as soon as possible once the first version of the code is available. See *Chapter 1, Exploratory Testing*, for more on when exactly to initiate testing.

The focus of this chapter, however, is failing early within the application. By identifying errors and preventing further processing, you can accurately report the source of a problem in your program, rather than identifying its effects. That saves engineers time investigating how errors occurred. To demonstrate that, we will examine the case of a signup website and how well it handles errors in a user's email address. The following sections consider best-case through to worst-case examples, where the code at different levels fails to reject the input to see the relative effects of bugs at different levels.

Catching errors in the frontend

When your application encounters invalid information, the best possible response is to fix it automatically. If a field is left blank, it could be populated with a default value, for instance. In the case of our signup email address, if the user includes capital letters, they can be automatically converted to lowercase before the address is saved. Since email addresses are case-insensitive, uppercase letters mean the same as lowercase letters so no information is lost. However, automatic fixing can only be applied in specific instances where alternative inputs have an agreed meaning.

Inputs that can't be automatically corrected should be rejected as early as possible. There are strict rules governing the format of email addresses – they need to have precisely one @ symbol, for instance – and if a user doesn't meet them, you should provide instant feedback. In terms of program architecture, the frontend can do that:

Figure 7.1 – Invalid inputs blocked by the frontend

The frontend of your application may be a web page, a physical screen or buttons, an app, an API, or some other interface with external systems. The frontend systems can then provide immediate feedback to the user telling them what went wrong and why, so they can fix it.

Identifying invalid entries early requires you to be completely clear on what is and isn't valid. That should come from the specification, and those requirements need a test to check that your application rejects each illegal case.

Catching errors in the backend

If the unexpected input isn't caught immediately, it can cause issues elsewhere. If the web interface happily accepts invalid email addresses and sends them off to the server, for instance, it might return an error or fail to respond at all:

Figure 7.2 – Invalid inputs blocked by the backend

The backend of your application might be a web server, cloud infrastructure, or any code modules that don't deal with external interfaces. When receiving invalid information, it should raise a helpful error with details about what it received and why it is being rejected.

Remember, each part of your system should validate its inputs. Even if the frontend correctly rejects incorrect values, you can test that the remaining parts of the system also throw proper errors. These might only be theoretical, but deficiencies in the backend's response could be exposed later if the frontend is changed or another interface is added. To do that testing, you might have to send fake messages rather than using the actual frontend so that you can send values it would otherwise reject. That shows some of the tools you need to test error cases beyond what you need for black- and white-box testing.

> **Real-world example - The Danish bug**
>
> I once worked on a hardware platform that could be localized into many different languages. For one release, we prepared our updated text strings as usual but instantly hit a problem for our Danish beta users. Their equipment became unusable and wouldn't even boot. Unfortunately, there was a typo in the formatting of one of the Danish strings. A formatting check in the localization system had gone wrong, and the error propagated into our code.
>
> Our hardware also failed to check and it read the strings so early during startup that the error prevented the application from starting. A change as minor as updating text strings had crippled the units, and we could only recover them by booting into the emergency recovery image. Because we didn't catch the error early, it propagated through the system and caused a major problem.

If the backend doesn't handle invalid information cleanly, then there may be no useful information about why it failed. The user will see a general error or a timeout without indicating what they should change to fix the problem.

Debugging is also tricky. Your backend will throw errors that you have to monitor somehow. If the error message is buried in a log you never look at, you may not notice this is failing at all, and if the logs don't contain the values they received, you may not even see the invalid address that caused the problem. Fields that contain **Personally Identifiable Information** (**PII**), such as email addresses, have rules about how long that can be stored and who is allowed to access it, making debugging harder. See *Chapter 9, Security Testing*, for more details.

When you see the error, you need to analyze it to discover its source. You have to see the invalid value and understand its significance, and the further the error is from its cause, the more work you have to do as a tester or developer to understand it.

Catching errors written into the storage

Beyond the backend, your program storage can also reject invalid entries. That may be a database, a filesystem, or some other persistent store, and it can also validate its inputs:

Figure 7.3 – Invalid inputs blocked by the storage system

Checks by storage systems are generally less complex than is possible in the backend code but can still spot missing fields, excessive lengths, invalid data types, or other data format problems. Detailed checking for the syntax probably isn't possible, however. You should validate the values your storage accepts, such as the type of each database field, making them as strict as possible. Again, to test those types, you may need a dedicated tool to let you avoid checks in the rest of the system. Catching errors as they are written to storage is your last chance to find them when they are generated because once invalid data is written to storage, it becomes much harder to debug and fix.

Catching stored errors

Invalid data could stay for years in storage before being retrieved and used for the first time. Again, the code should check for any invalid data coming from storage, and you can add checks for that. To test, you may need to deliberately write invalid entries to storage if other parts of the system correctly block them.

When faced with invalid data, the behavior could be anything from full functionality, with your program happily sending rubbish data to your users, to complete failure where your application can't even start. As illustrated here, this is the case where the backend reads information out of storage:

Figure 7.4 – Invalid data detected when being read

Now you have three problems. In the short term, you have to find invalid data and fix or remove it to recover your app. Secondly, you also need to find out how the invalid data got into the database, which can be even more challenging. You have to check the history of the messages to see when this was written, and your logs may not go back far enough. Perhaps the user interface has since been fixed to block that error, so you cannot reproduce the problem. Maybe some interfaces, such as web and mobile apps, correctly reject the value, but the API lets them through. I've seen cases where we never worked out how bad data was written to storage.

Thirdly, depending on the failure mode, invalid data may have been building up for years, which means that as well as fixing the immediate issue and finding how the invalid data was written, you have to find and correct all the other invalid entries as well. The longer an error persists, the more work it creates for you.

The problems caused by invalid data grow over time. There is no hope of giving the user helpful feedback if the data sits in a database for a month before it triggers an error, so that is another benefit of testing error cases. If you discover your application accepts invalid data, you can improve performance to catch it earlier. That protects your application, makes debugging easier, and gives users an improved experience.

As well as catching errors quickly, your program needs to respond well, as described in the next section.

Fail as little as possible

What counts as a test passing when the functionality is failing? In the previous example, immediately identifying the problem and informing the customer exactly how to fix it is the best possible result. For external APIs, the criterion is similar – the best outcome is clearly stating in the logs or error messages which field caused the problem and why.

Sometimes, even the best failure mode is less than ideal. For instance, a failure to reach the infrastructure in a web application may result in a gateway timeout message. That is useless to end users – they are unlikely to understand it, and there is nothing they can do about it. The best thing you can do in that case is to show an unhappy robot or other symbol and let the user know they've done nothing wrong. They just need to wait, safe in the knowledge that somewhere on a distant console, a light has turned red, and an engineer is desperately trying to recover the service.

In each case, you will need to determine the best failure mode, by checking with the product owner. Often failure modes are not covered in feature specifications, but as they are user-facing, the product owner will want input on what to do. Ensure these are carefully documented during the feature specification review so you know what to expect during testing.

Even without a precise specification, some error responses are always wrong. Your application should never crash, for instance, or be left in a state that requires manual intervention to recover. The severity of a bug is roughly the chances of you hitting it multiplied by its effects when you do, minus any mitigations or workarounds you can put in place. While error conditions are unlikely to be encountered regularly, if they have severe outcomes then they are a top priority. That's why it's essential to test for them.

As described in the section *Classifying expected versus unexpected errors*, your application should be resilient to any possible inputs, checking and rejecting invalid ones as early as possible. Short of losing power, your program should keep running while ensuring errors don't propagate through the system. Users should receive understandable and usable feedback for each fault, as described in the section *Giving user feedback on errors*. If that's not the case, you can raise bugs for any examples of failures.

Aside from those extremes, there are many intermediate cases where you can choose whether to proceed with the processing or halt when encountering an error.

If your code controls a nuclear reactor or an airplane, then stopping completely at any unexpected conditions during startup is a safe way to operate. All inputs and data should be validated and understood before proceeding any further. For other applications, failing to provide service is the worst thing that can happen, for instance, on a website, a game, or a communications platform. In those cases, being resilient to errors, flagging them, but continuing to run may be the best outcome.

> **Real-world example – The fail-safe communication system**
>
> One communication system I worked on was designed to be fail-safe. While some minor errors didn't interrupt processing, others prevented the system from starting. A typical sequence for this was the following:
>
> 1. The system started correctly with valid data.
>
> 2. Invalid data was written to the database, but the system kept running as it hadn't detected it.
>
> 3. The system stopped, discovered the invalid data, and couldn't restart.
>
> The challenge was that this was a multi-homed system with many customers sharing one instance. A single error in a single part of a single customer configuration denied service for all the customers on that instance. Since this was a communication platform, there was little risk in starting up, even with errors. The worst that could happen was we would fail to provide service, and that was the result when the system failed to start. In that case, working around the error by disabling that configuration or that customer would lead to a more resilient system than preventing the instance from starting.

While continuing with processing may be a good outcome in lower-risk applications, an exception to that is when invalid data risks causing data loss through deletion or corruption. Failing to provide a service is not the worst thing that can happen if you risk losing customer data or configuration. You'll have to weigh the chances of encountering those problems for each input in your system to choose whether continuing despite errors is the best course.

If failures aren't caught early, you risk cascades of issues, as described next.

Understanding defect cascading

A single error can leave your system in an unknown state. Unless you have identified and replicated that problem as part of your testing, it also leaves your system in an untested state. Your application may work well, but there's a higher risk of issues than during regular operation. Triggering one error state is a great way to look for other problems.

Example problems that arise during error handling include the following:

- **Excessive logging** – It's vital to record information about errors, but if a failure is recurring many times a second, that adds load to the system, either in terms of disc usage or network bandwidth to report it. Using those resources can trigger further issues.

- **Lack of detail in logging** – A regular finding in post-mortem meetings after failures was that the logs were hard to use and didn't have helpful information. Use the logs while you're testing to discover weaknesses before the code goes live.

- **Lack of context in logs** – In a modern, distributed system, logs will be written by many different processes. You need an easy way to gather the relevant sections together to tell a coherent story about what happened.

- **Infinite retry loops** – Retries are useful when a module encounters an issue with an external system, but they need to be carefully handled. The application mustn't send the same message again forever – there has to be a timeout. Systems getting locked by constantly attempting an action that will never work is a critical issue.

- **Rapid retries with no backoff mechanism** – A special case of infinite retry loops is when a module attempts the action without pausing, sending messages as fast as it can. This obviously drains resources on both the source and destination systems, which can cause other problems.

- **Unnecessary dependencies between modules** – A major cause of defects propagating through an application is dependencies between subsystems. Some are necessary, but others can be mitigated or avoided altogether. Having redundant routes rather than single points of failure, queues in front of databases, and removing unnecessary lookups, for instance, let your application continue despite problems.

- **Modules failing due to the absence of others** – Each module should stand alone and be able to run independently. If part of your system has failed then some functions will be unavailable, but the other modules should identify and mitigate the failure as far as possible rather than failing themselves.

- **Modules failing to restart correctly** – A special case of modules relying on others is if one cannot start without the presence of another. Again, some of these dependencies are unavoidable, but check where they are necessary. By systematically disabling systems and restarting others, you can flush those out.

- **Lack of alarms indicating failures** – Another regular finding in post-incident meetings I've attended is the lack of monitoring indicating failures. When you add new features with new failure modes, you need to add a check for them. See *Chapter 10, Maintainability*, for more on monitoring.

Many other possible knock-on effects will be unique to your application, so once you are in an error state, carefully check the system. Subsequent issues may be subtle and apparently unrelated to the initial problem, so keep your eyes open. See *Chapter 11, Destructive Testing*, for more information on testing while in an error state.

> **Real-world example – Self-inflicted DDoS**
>
> In one company where I worked, we started to experience crashes and slowdowns in our cloud infrastructure. The effects were hard to pin down – the crashes seemed unrelated to each other and were mainly due to watchdog timeouts, although it wasn't clear what was triggering them. Eventually, we identified that disc usage was preventing the watchdog file from being written. Why was the disc so heavily loaded? Because large amounts of logs were being written, far more than in our previous release. Why was there so much logging? Because our clients were reconnecting at very high rates. Why were they reconnecting so often? Because there was no backoff mechanism to slow them down. Why were they reconnecting at all? Because a bug in our last release was causing regular disconnections.
>
> One bug on the client side had caused a massive cascade of issues throughout our system. With better discs, we should have been able to handle that rate of disc access. There should have been rate limits on our logging, and there should have been warnings about the rates we were seeing. There shouldn't have been so much written to the logs at all because the clients shouldn't have reconnected so quickly. We should have had warnings when they dropped at that rate, and they shouldn't have disconnected in the first place.

Putting strain on the system in one way can uncover a whole host of knock-on issues, so ensure testing these error cases is part of your test plans. Next, we consider the priority to place on error testing.

Prioritizing error case testing

For all the test cases described in this chapter, remember that the more obscure your failure mode, the lower priority the bug will be. Testing error cases is always less important than tests that cover the main functionality of a new feature since if they fail, that feature won't work at all. Error cases shouldn't usually happen, so their rarity lessens their impact. The more obscure the failure case, the rarer it is and is even less critical. Error case testing should be tempered with a knowledge of that priority. You can run this area of testing last, for instance, alongside the maintainability tests, which don't affect customers directly, and destructive tests, which are another failure mode.

On the other hand, it is difficult to know in advance how bad any failures will be. For instance, if there is a bug when adding too many users, you will probably receive an unhelpful error message. That is a bug, but not a high-priority one. However, that failure could be far worse, crashing the application or locking up a thread that, if repeated, would eventually stop your application from working at all. Until you've done the test, you don't know how bad the issue is, and the priority of the bug is a combination of how likely it is to happen and its severity when it does.

While there are only a few successful routes through code, there are many more possible failures, so it is possible to spend a very long time on these tests. Don't get bogged down. Ensure that more critical testing is covered first, and only return to examining error cases once you are confident in the other behaviors.

With that priority in mind, here are common failure modes you should check for in your code.

Testing beyond the limits

What are your system's limits, and what happens when you go beyond them? Part of the feature specification is to identify system limits and what values you are required to support. These can be difficult to judge, especially around loading. Having thousands of visitors a second to your website might be a problem you would love to have but, as a tester, it is your job to find out how well you can expect your site to perform.

System limits are of two types – policed and unpoliced. A policed limit is one in which the system actively blocks users from going beyond it. For instance, it might support 4 simultaneous players or a maximum group size of 20 users. You cannot configure the 5th player or the 21st user. That's as opposed to unpoliced limits. System rates are typically of this kind: how many connections per second can you handle? Some configuration limits may also be unpoliced, such as the total number of users on the system, since nothing in the code will prevent the database from growing. You should test these different types of limits quite differently.

Policed limits should have a user interface that lets people know they are at the limit and cannot do anymore. That limit should be apparent before users try to use it – the **Add user** button should be grayed out with a note saying why, for instance, instead of letting users click the button. *Chapter 8, User Experience Testing*, describes user experience issues like this in more detail.

However, even if there is a user-interface limit, you still have to test the system behavior when users try to go beyond it. Sometimes limiting the interface isn't possible, such as an API that could always accept more messages. On a web page, it's possible for one user to load a page to add an item, a second user to add the final item, then the first user to submit their request. Stale web pages could still make invalid requests, making this a more obscure case, but still worth trying.

As described previously, the pass mark for these blocking tests is that your application should return a helpful message to users. For example, a red bar stating **Error 652** is a failure; a pass is a message saying **Maximum number of users reached** or whatever text your user experience team has chosen.

As part of the feature specification, you need to carefully list all configurable entities to perform this testing on them. Where the limits are very large, you will need the scripts to drive the system to its maximum, as described further in *Chapter 12, Load Testing*.

For non-policed limits, the tests need to be different. There will be no user interface warning and nothing to prevent you from adding the 100,001st user; for instance, the system will just keep going. That means there is no user interface to test and no feedback to the user, so product managers and developers may argue that the limit can't be tested. However, it is still important to pick a number to test up to – see *Chapter 2, Writing Great Feature Specifications*. That lets you know when you are approaching the limit and heading into an untested configuration.

For non-policed limits, the failure modes are different. When you have a large number of configured entities, lists can become unmanageably long, or the system might slow down – web pages may take so long that browsers show warnings about the page being broken, for instance. In this case, you will need to decide the acceptable performance with the product management team. While pages technically still load, the user experience of using them and searching for information is terrible. The *fix* for these issues might include pagination for tables with a limited number of entries per page, navigation buttons, and search options.

It is worth loading the system up to these limits before performing other regression tests so that you can look for interactions. The effects of having a large system load may not be apparent and may cause issues or slowness in unexpected areas. Only by having that in place before running other tests can you find those cases.

Other non-policed limits involve the rates that the system can run at, for instance, the number of transactions per second, simultaneous users or the rate of updates, and so on. Again, you will need to pick the acceptable limit you want the system to support and have the tools to drive that load. And again, it is best to perform other testing when this load is present – while the system might be able to support a high transaction rate in itself, that may prevent other operations from completing successfully. You will need to work out the dependent and independent variables to decide which combination of load and functionality might interact and should be tested together. For further tests when running the system at its limits and beyond, see *Chapter 13, Stress Testing*.

Driving the system can result in it being so slow that certain operations time out while waiting for responses. This is such a common and important failure mode that it should have dedicated testing, as described next.

Testing timeouts

One crucial failure when communicating with any remote system, whether internal or external to your application, is not receiving any response. That lack of response could be due to network issues, a problem with the destination system, or the message being invalid. Whatever the reason, there is a new set of failure modes to look for in this case related to timeouts and retries:

- The presence of timeouts on all messages
- Appropriate timeout lengths
- The use of heartbeat messages
- Retries for failed messages

At the most basic level, you have to check that a reasonable timeout is in place. If we pick a simple example with a client sending a message to a server, we need to make sure that the client notices the lack of response and reacts to it. There are cases where clients will enter the state of waiting for an answer forever. That is the first class of bugs you can raise.

Next, is inappropriate timeouts. You may need to discuss these with product owners; again, this is an area they may not have considered but will have an opinion on since changing the timeout might have customer-visible effects. In APIs, the specification might state how long different states should persist, or applications should wait for different responses. If that is the case, then check against that specification.

Suitable timeout lengths vary depending on context. Timeouts being too short mean valid responses could be missed, and you generate unnecessary errors. You need to check those relative to the loading at the time; a timeout may be sufficient during light system load but too short when the system has a lot of activity and operations take longer. You should test timeouts against the worst case that the system can handle.

It's safer to allow timeouts to be too long, which is less likely to result in errors, although it may unnecessarily tie up system resources. An overly long timeout may look like an error to users, even if the system behaves as expected. Your users might give up rather than wait 10 seconds for a web page to load, for instance. That needs input from the user-experience team to determine the best reaction to a failed message.

Systems with continuous connections should send heartbeat messages to each other to check the other end is still running. You'll need to check the timeout on those messages and prevent responses so you can test whether the disconnection is correctly detected and acted upon.

A more subtle timeout issue can occur in complex systems with at least three machines communicating with each other. That is when the timeout for an initial message is shorter than subsequent ones.

Consider a system in which module **A** sends a message to module **B**, and module **B** then forwards that message to module **C**. The timeout on the message from **A** to **B** is 30 seconds, but the timeout on the message from **B** to **C** is 60 seconds. In that case, the failure mode is shown as follows:

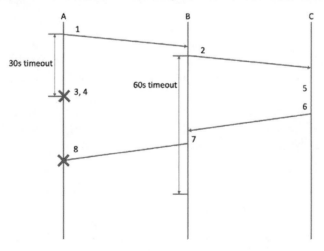

Figure 7.5 – Message failures with incorrectly figured timeouts

1. **A** sends a message to **B**.

2. **B** forwards it to **C**.

3. 30 seconds pass

4. **A** times out and fails after 30 seconds, returning an error.

5. Another 15 seconds pass.

6. **C** returns the answer to **B** within its 60-second timeout.

7. **B** sends the answer back to **A**.

8. **A** rejects the response because it has already timed out.

By the end of this sequence, **A** claims that **B** timed out, but **B** claims it responded successfully and has had its answer rejected. The logs can be challenging to read in this situation, but the underlying cause is simple enough – **A**'s timeout needs to be long enough to encompass all the subsequent timeouts downstream in the system. If those added together make for an unreasonable timeout at **A**, then the others need to be shortened. Alternatively, you need to give some feedback to the user that processing is continuing (see the *Giving users feedback on errors* section).

A final failure mode we will consider here is what the system should do after a timeout. Messages should generally be retried in case there was a transitory issue that was quickly resolved, but those retries need to be carefully implemented. Watch out for infinite retry loops. That critical bug will leave your system constantly sending out messages and spamming another system, waiting for a reply it will never receive. If the first 10,000 messages failed to generate a valid response, it's unlikely the 10,001st will.

A special case of the infinite retry loop is when the client retries at maximum speed, with no time delay. That will max out the CPU on the client while sending messages at the fastest possible rate to the server. Have a serious word with the developer in that case; their lack of care has produced a significant risk to system stability.

That leaves the client application in an invalid state, but can also be highly damaging for the server. If the server is unable to respond to some requests, then clients with this bug can result in a system effectively performing a **Distributed Denial of Service** (**DDoS**) attack on itself, as in the previous example. A large array of clients will constantly send messages to the server, which is unable to process them, causing a DDoS attack. Over time, any other clients attempting this transaction will end up in the same state and worsen the situation. A system that starts off running only a little behind can end up crippled by the cumulative load that this produces.

In that case, the safe method of failing is to implement exponential backoffs. The client should retry, but not constantly. Instead, it should retry with exponentially increasing delays between each message, for instance, trying at 1 second, 2, 4, 8, 16, 32 seconds, and so on. That will prevent a buildup of load on the server, while also letting the client detect any recovery. That exponential backoff should stop at some maximum value, for example, 5 minutes, so it does not grow to ridiculous lengths of time. All that needs to be captured in the specification.

These timeout issues can affect any of the states and messages in the system, so you need to test them all. Anywhere a module sends a message and expects a response can suffer from these issues, so the specification needs to identify them all as part of your white-box testing to let you check their timeout handling. Some system messages are evident from the customer-facing behavior, but others may be subtle implementation details. You need to identify and test them all.

As well as failing to receive any response, intermittent responses can also pose significant problems for an application, as described in the next section.

Understanding network degradation

Many applications rely on the internet to transport data, but some are more sensitive to poor network conditions than others. Programs that send video, for instance, or online, real-time gaming, rely on high-quality, low-latency networks. Their behavior under suboptimal conditions is vital to users' perception of their product since network problems occur with depressing frequency. Even for applications less sensitive to network performance, such as web pages, you can check how your application responds to problems.

Sources of network degradation

There are several types of network degradation for packet-switched networks such as the internet:

- **Packet loss**: The classic problem of networks, where sent packets aren't received
- **Latency**: The scourge of gamers is a delay between sending the packets and receiving them at the far end
- **Jitter**: The variation in the latency of journey times
- **Re-ordering**: Packets sent in one order are received in a different order
- **Duplication**: One packet is received twice at the destination

These problems arise because packets sent as part of the same communication may take very different routes to reach their destination and pass through many switches and routers. If one of those switches is overloaded, it may drop your packets or add delays. However, only some of your packets might take that route.

Note that there is an alternative to packet-switched networks. Circuit-switched networks, such as standard telephones, create a direct connection between two machines. They offer lower latency and suffer from none of the issues listed previously. On the downside, they need to be centrally controlled and configured – there's no option to simply share your Wi-Fi password and automatically let a new machine onto your network. Changing to a different Wi-Fi network takes a few seconds, but porting your mobile number to another provider requires a dedicated code and several days wait. In the end, the inflexibility of circuit-switched networks almost always makes them a second choice to packet-switched protocols such as TCP/IP, despite their potential problems.

Consider the following network, with a source sending packets to a destination. In TCP/IP, there will always also be a stream of acknowledgments flowing back from the destination to the source, but they can be ignored for this example, shown as follows:

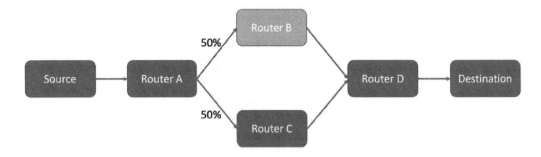

Figure 7.6 – An example network suffering degradation

Packets from **Router A** can take two routes to their destination. **50%** go through **Router B** and **50%** through **Router C**. Those routers are simultaneously taking lots of other traffic, and **Router B** is, unfortunately, failing to route packets.

If **Router B** drops all the packets sent to it, **50%** of packets will be dropped overall. Note that if there are acknowledgments and retries, these could be sent again and may succeed with a delay. For simplicity, consider this a UDP stream where packets are sent without retries. If **Router B** only drops half the packets sent to it, then the overall packet loss on this connection is 50% x 50% = 25%.

Instead of packet loss, **Router B** might be working slowly, adding delays on that route. Then, half the packets are delayed but the other half avoid the issue, so you will see high jitter – significant variations in the time it takes packets to arrive. Some might take 20 ms while others take 200 ms, and your application has to handle both cases.

Because of a variation in delays, packets might arrive out of sequence, as shown in the following example:

Packet	Time sent	Transit time	Time received
1	0ms	20ms	20ms
2	10ms	200ms	210ms
3	20ms	20ms	40ms

Table 7.2 – Varying transit times causing packet re-ordering

Packet 2 went through Router B and has a significant delay, so even though they are sent in the order 1, 2, and then 3, the destination receives them in the order 1, 3, and then 2.

Finally, many packet-switched protocols such as TCP/IP have retries built in. However, that can result in duplicate packets if timeouts are set incorrectly. See the example in the *Testing timeouts* section.

Let's repeat the previous example, but after 100 ms, Router A detects that packet 2 has not been acknowledged and sends it again:

Packet	Time sent	Transit time	Time received
1	0ms	20ms	20ms
2	10ms	200ms	210ms
3	20ms	20ms	40ms
2, retry	110ms	20ms	130ms

Table 7.3 – Varying transit times causing duplicate packets

The retried packet 2 goes via Router C and reaches its destination in 20 ms while Router B was still sending the initial attempt. This time, the destination receives the packets in the order 1, 3, 2, and 2. Your application needs to be able to detect and discard those duplicates.

Aside from degradations, there can also be problems if packets are larger than the maximum transmission unit for the network. That sets a limit, for instance, 1,400 bytes, on the maximum size of any one packet on the network. To send messages larger than that, you need to split the data across multiple packets, and the destination needs to reassemble them.

Real-world example – Too much debugging

In one place I worked, we used a third-party service for one of our features. Unfortunately, they were massively unreliable. We repeatedly pointed out issues and they finally devoted an engineer to investigate them. Immediately, there was a total outage. The system that seemed to have intermittent failures now didn't work at all. We cursed their incompetence and demanded to know what had happened.

To investigate the problem, it turned out they had added debug information to each message. That had taken it beyond the MTU of the network, without the ability to split the information across packets. Instead of some failures, now every message was invalid until they turned the debugging off.

If your application implements packet handling rather than using third-party solutions, you will need to test each of those cases.

Testing degraded networks

Often, network problems will be handled lower in the stack, with your TCP/IP or VPN provider responsible for the logic to handle cases of network degradation. However, if your application deals with network packets, for instance, using UDP streams with retries as part of your application logic, these tests need to be part of your test plan. Even if your application doesn't deal with packets directly, you can see how well it responds to poor network conditions.

The first point for network testing is that you need a solid network to test on. There's no point adding in network degradations if your network is already performing poorly in random and unknown ways. Make sure you can rely on your network before starting this testing.

Network emulators allow you to introduce the specific impairments listed in the *Sources of network degradation* section for your testing. Chrome has a few network throttling options in the **Network** section of its Developer Tools. On Linux, you can use **Netem**, Windows has **WinDriver** or **Traffic Shaper XP**, Mac has **Network Link Conditioner**, and there are many others available. Even more realistic is to use a separate box, such as **PacketStorm** or **Spirent**. Then, the source machine is unchanged and the network issues are purely external, as they would be in reality.

Be aware that unless you buy expensive hardware, these have relatively low throughputs – they can only handle a few simultaneous connections. If you put significant traffic through the emulator, it will drop packets because it can't handle the load. For those tests, use dedicated hardware solutions.

For testing, add specific impairments to check the response of your system. You can apply different levels of each type of impairment, testing the outcome at 1, 2, 5, or 10% packet loss, for instance, or different delays to introduce latency. In practice, however, impairments rarely happen independently; if some packets are dropped, others are likely to be delayed. Packet loss can also be random and evenly spread, or correlated and grouped in spikes of loss between periods of good connectivity.

The simplest setup is to physically place an emulator in line with the machine under test:

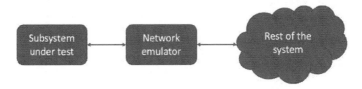

Figure 7.7 – A network emulator in line with a subsystem under test

That works for running tests locally, but a scalable solution requires you to be able to route packets to and from the network emulator to impair any connection. Be aware of the direction of the degradation – are you restricting packets to or from the system under test, or both?

With the impairments in place, measure the network conditions at both sides of the connection. This is vital to detect any unwanted impairments that may invalidate the testing and to check your desired impairments are applied correctly.

All those considerations lead to a massive space of possible combinations of network issues. You can choose those that are most relevant to your product and cause the most problems, and there are specifications and recommendations for patterns of impairments to consider.

During packet loss and high-jitter streams, the jitter buffer is a crucial part of the system test. The jitter buffer is a temporary store of packets as they arrive. During applications such as video streaming, packets are not played out immediately but stored for up to a few seconds. If the incoming stream is interrupted, the video can keep playing so long as the network recovers before the buffer is empty. A large buffer provides extra protection against network issues but delays the media stream. A short buffer plays media faster but offers little protection.

In practice, jitter buffer sizes will vary; during good network conditions, they will shrink since protection is not needed, reducing delays. On unreliable networks, the jitter buffer will increase, delaying the media but giving the best chance of continuous playback. If your application uses this technique, be sure to exercise both modes of working and the transition between them.

Even on a stable network, responses from remote systems may not contain the information you were expecting. That class of data failures is considered next.

Data failures

As well as failing to get any response, a much broader class of issues arises from receiving a message or input containing unexpected data. It may be surprising because your specification was wrong, or due to a gray area that was poorly specified. If the message's sender is another part of your system, you can choose where to fix it – should the sender change the message, or should the receiver accept it correctly? If the sender is a third party, your application must handle that input, regardless of the specification.

The most basic failure is receiving an error in reply. Each message you send out needs to be tested for a variety of possible error responses. The pass mark here, as elsewhere, is that these errors are expected so they can be handled gracefully and as early as possible. Both the message and the error should be comprehensively logged, so you can replay each situation and check new code against it. By catching errors early, you can return as much information as possible to users, particularly letting them know whether it's worth retrying that operation due to a temporary error or if the failures seem permanent.

Testing failures can be problematic with third-party systems because they may return an error once and then never again. To reproduce the issue, you may need a test harness that can mimic the external system but give you complete control over the responses it sends. There's work to prepare that mock system, so unless an interface is particularly problematic, it may not be worth the investment in time. Then code reviews may be the only preparation possible, checking that the application is ready, in theory, to handle different error replies without running it for real.

Once you are past timeouts and error responses, you are down to the level of unexpected data within the individual fields of a message. Here, the possibilities are endless and will depend on the system you are testing, but again there are many common themes you can add to your test plans.

A simple first case is checking what happens when different fields are missing. The external system might respond without specific data, and your program needs to be able to handle that. Missing data might be mandatory, and its absence might mean the transaction fails, or there may be optional data, and the message can still be processed without it. The specification needs to clarify the requirements so that you can test each field.

If the data is present, it might still be invalid. Here the list of possible inputs for the different field types listed in the chapter on black-box testing is helpful again. For strings, check long values, Unicode values, special characters, and so on; for numeric fields, check negatives, decimals, and numbers out of range. See *Chapter 5*, *Black-Box Functional Testing*, for the complete list.

At a lower level, database queries might unexpectedly return no results. There may be one result when the application is expecting several, several when the application only wants one, or the query may return a vast number of results. Check that your application can handle each of those scenarios.

Once you have tested each field, you need to check for any interactions or dependencies between them. Perhaps your application handles one field being missing but not two related ones. Again, there is no easy way to see those dependencies, so it relies on your skill as a tester. To catch combinations you haven't thought of, you can inject random data, in a testing technique known as fuzzing, described in the next section.

Fuzzing

Fuzzing involves generating randomized input to test the response of the system. You can use this technique to generate broken combinations and detect bugs when multiple seemingly independent fields are missing or corrupted in a message. Manually designing and implementing a search across all possible arrangements would be uneconomical, but an automated, randomized method can efficiently perform that testing.

To perform fuzz testing, pick an API interface in your system, one that is listening and accepting input. That might be a web server, a public API, or any other interface that could be inspected with a packet sniffer. That lets users see the format of the messages and shows where an attacker could to try to gain access.

Within that API, identify the individual messages to test, for example, `/user/create`. Then, list the variables within those messages, such as the name, email, and country location.

To be successful, fuzzed messages must be valid so they can be parsed and understood by the destination machine. Purely random messages will be rejected easily. Instead, the messages should be formatted correctly with valid field names, but invalid information should be placed in those fields. For an even wider test, you can also randomize the field names. The application under test will then attempt to parse the messages and have to handle the data it received.

It can be challenging to gauge the level of randomness required for fuzzing. A single invalid field may mean a message is rejected without checking the others, so limit the corruption of messages as far as possible. Instead of purely random inputs, you could randomly select from a prepared bank of invalid values. That increases the chance that the message will be processed properly, but limits the randomness of the list you prepared.

The OWASP Foundation has a great guide to fuzzing and available tools here: `https://owasp.org/www-community/Fuzzing`. Whichever tool you choose will require configuration to specify which aspects of a message should be fixed and which changed. Fuzzing is a significant investment of time and may only find obscure bugs unlikely to arise in practice, so it is only valuable on the most critical interfaces. It is also most useful on external interfaces, which may receive invalid data. Internal interfaces are even less likely to send each other the randomness described here, although it is still possible. Feedback from the system is valuable: if you have a protocol that hits errors that only fuzzing could realistically find, it is probably worthwhile for your system.

Finally in this section, we consider the feedback your application should provide to users during failures. These should be specified, and your testing should check them all.

Giving user feedback on errors

Every application will suffer failures at some point, either through internal faults or failures of third parties on which it relies. The measure of a great application is failing rarely, recovering quickly, and providing feedback while the problem persists. During error conditions, letting the users know what's going on is the difference between a good user experience and a support case.

> **Real-world example – Deliberately stopping the video**
>
> On one video application I worked on, we implemented protection against packet loss on video streams. One important tactic was to reduce the bit rate – if the available bandwidth had dropped, we needed to fit our video stream to the available speed. That meant reducing the quality of the video, and sometimes even stopping the video entirely so that the audio could get through and users could still talk to each other.
>
> Unfortunately, we didn't give the user any indication of what the system was doing or why. They just saw the video quality degrade, and their video stopped working. The feature only made it as far as internal testing before we had many complaints. We were taking reasonable steps to mitigate a real problem, but we couldn't ship the feature until we also gave the users feedback that their poor network connection was causing all the issues.

Alongside failing as early as possible, we can add the requirement to fail as precisely as possible. A poor application will just throw an error that a particular line of code encountered an issue. If you're lucky enough to have a stack trace, you need to examine the variables to find one that might be causing the problem. Good code will validate its inputs, raising an error if any are invalid, indicating which one and why. *Chapter 10, Maintainability*, has more information on the importance of that internal feedback. All the error types discussed in this chapter should raise internal events to let the development team see what happened and why. In addition, they should give user feedback.

When you know why a failure occurred, you can let the user know. Whether on a hardware screen, an app interface, an API response, a web page, or any other interface, the requirement is to be as specific as possible. If an external connection fails, the user's network may be down. That is a vital error to report since the user could fix it themselves.

Other errors are intermittent. If it is worth the user retrying the operation, let them know that. Again, give them as much information and power as possible. If they might be able to recover the system, tell them that. If performing the same operation is only likely to result in the same error, let the user know that. Don't leave them fruitlessly trying the same requests until they eventually give up, which is the worst possible outcome.

If a transaction could legitimately take a long time, then let the user know that. They should have immediate feedback that their request has been received successfully and that your application is working on it. That might be in the form of a spinner or an intermediate screen. Without that, you risk users retrying operations that were already in progress, creating additional system load, and possibly delaying their response even further. For more on user feedback, see *Chapter 8, User Experience Testing*.

Most errors are, almost by definition, unexpected. If you knew that your application could fail that way, you would have protected against it. In that case, be honest with your users, too – let them know that something unexpected has happened and the application needs to be fixed. That fix, at least, involves identifying this error specifically so you can provide a better error report and fail more gracefully.

Summary

In this chapter, you have learned about testing error conditions within an application. These tests are designed to cause failures, but they should be caught early and be as limited as possible by expecting the issues and handling them gracefully. Unexpected errors, especially ones that persist over time, cause a poor user experience, are difficult to debug, and may cause other, much worse problems.

To test error cases, you should push the system beyond its specified limits, try the timeouts on messages, trigger communication failures with network errors, inject invalid fields, and fuzz messages with random data.

Carefully consider the priority of the error case testing. It is a lower priority than the rest of functional testing, which guarantees a new feature or application is working in usual cases. Public interfaces or mission-critical applications must be resilient to errors and perform well during expected operations. Even for less critical applications, if you don't test for mistakes in advance, you will have to spend time debugging them when they appear in real-life situations. Whatever the error is, give the user as much information as possible to ensure the best experience.

In the next chapter, we will return to the customer-facing aspects of an application by considering testing for user interfaces.

8

User Experience Testing

"Less is more."

– Mies van der Rohe

In the previous chapter, you learned about common error types: how to provoke them and how they should be handled. While there were some gray areas on how best to deal with error cases, most were clear-cut – errors should be identified as early as possible to give the most helpful feedback to the user. In this chapter, we will examine an area of testing with even more gray areas – **user experience (UX) testing**.

Not every feature will involve UX changes. Entire teams are often devoted to internal processing or external APIs, which function without human interaction. If you only work within one of these areas, then you can skip this chapter for now.

However, your product does have to interact with humans, even if only during its installation and setup. UX has a disproportionate effect on how the quality of your product is perceived; so, while it might appear like window-dressing compared to the main functions of your system, you can significantly improve the perceived quality of your product by focusing on this testing.

In this chapter, you will learn about the following topics:

- How to approach UX testing
- Testing interoperability
- Testing displays
- Optimizing text on user interfaces
- Localization and time zones
- Menus and information display
- Loading and user interaction

- Testing documentation
- UX during error conditions
- UX feedback

UX design is a fascinating area with a large and growing literature. This chapter only provides an overview of the key techniques and considerations, so for more information, please research further. We will begin by defining exactly what we mean by UX testing.

Defining UX testing

You should question the requirements throughout your testing process, checking whether they still make sense or whether there are better ways the same goals could be achieved. This is particularly the case in UX testing when there are many ways to present the information and controls. Still, not everything is in scope for your testing.

The colors the designers have chosen, whether the interface is **skeuomorphic** or abstract, the font they've chosen – none of those are the test team's responsibility. There are two classes of such issues to check for. Firstly, you must check how easy it is to understand and interface. If fonts are hard to read or the colors make it hard to understand, those are problems that need to be fixed. Feel free to provide ideas and feedback on other aspects, but so long as your product reaches a minimum threshold of usability, trust your design team's decisions.

> **Important note**
>
> Skeuomorphic user interface design mimics real-life objects. Early versions of Apple's iPhone calendar app, for instance, had leather stitching around the edge and shaded buttons to make them look three-dimensional, as though you could press them. That's as opposed to buttons with a constant color or a flat design.

Secondly, watch for consistency within the user interface. While a green or blue icon is fine, your product shouldn't use green and blue icons randomly on different pages. This applies to products, too: if the fashion is for flat interfaces across your industry, you can question why your new interface is skeuomorphic.

Within those meta-requirements of being understandable and consistent, the design team has a broad scope to create interfaces. Your role as a tester is to point out anything that could be improved – anywhere you struggled to understand something or find what you were looking for, anywhere you could reach the same goal more quickly or easily. This chapter is filled with examples of common use cases to try on your product.

The subjectivity of UX testing means that raising UX bugs should be done politely and respectfully, even more than in other areas. Since there are often no clear answers, you will make suggestions rather than outright bug reports, and others may disagree. You should make your reports knowing that the developers and designers might have deliberately made the choices you are complaining about, and there may be different points of view. Unlike bug reports, where there is usually an obvious correct behavior, with UX, it's often much easier to find problems than to design great solutions. Tact, discussion, and cooperation are vital.

If your company has the resources, you should conduct UX testing with real users to gain their feedback with genuine first impressions of your new feature. However, before you reach that stage, the internal test team should check the functionality, find improvements, and offer ideas. With those ground rules in place, next, we will describe the advantages and disadvantages of UX testing.

Advantages and disadvantages of UX testing

Unlike functional testing, where there are several different approaches to testing similar functionality, the areas of testing we will consider in this chapter – usability, security, and maintainability – each require specific considerations and find issues outside the core functionality of the feature or application. So, that is its first strength – by considering usability at all, you can discover a new class of issues:

Strengths	Weaknesses
Best way to detect this class of issue	Mainly manual
Can find blocking issues	Subjective
Directly affects users	Difficult to predict what will cause problems for customers
	Costly to run usability studies

Table 8.1 – Strengths and weaknesses of UX testing

The major strength of UX testing is that it is the best way to find usability issues. The specification might state that a particular function should exist, and it does, but only if you successfully navigate four layers of menus and select three unrelated options. It's easy to hide features so that busy users never find them. After all the work has been done to implement a feature, UX considerations get it over the finish line so that users can use it in practice.

Far from being extra polish on a finished feature, UX concerns can require you to reconsider how entire features are implemented and presented. The sooner you find those issues, the sooner redesigning can begin.

> **Real-world example – Different kinds of muting**
>
> In the early days of video calling, we added a new feature to our product – the ability to mute other people during a conference. You could mute yourself on your video endpoint, or others in the conference could mute you. It was a significant feature to implement, but the idea sounded simple enough.
>
> However, if you mute yourself for privacy reasons, others shouldn't be able to undo that, so if you had locally muted yourself, only you should have the power to unmute. But if someone else had muted you, via a remote mute, they should be able to undo that. There were effectively two types of muting. How could we add that functionality without revealing that complexity?
>
> We couldn't, initially. After months of work setting up the protocol to communicate mute commands between different participants, we shelved the feature until we could work out how to present it to users.

UX testing can find blocking issues and should be prioritized accordingly, and it also directly affects your customer experience. Testing error cases, security, and maintainability are essential topics, but your customers won't immediately see their effects. A hacking attempt will fail, or you'll be able to find and fix a bug quickly, but from your users' point of view, nothing will have changed. UX testing, in contrast, alters how your customers see your product.

The first disadvantage of UX testing is that it is primarily manual. Some can be automated – such as checking links on a web page or the behavior in different languages and on different screen resolutions. However, the more challenging part of UX testing is judging how others will understand your product, which requires a tester.

UX testing is far more subjective than other tests, which clearly show errors or how a product diverges from the specification. Just because one tester finds something obvious doesn't mean your customers will, and vice versa. This can lead to debates about the correct implementation, which, while beneficial for examining the possible alternatives, also take time and resources. User interface reviews are vital for gathering opinions and ideas from the development team on the best way to present a feature. Even after those discussions, it is hard to pinpoint what customers will find surprising or confusing.

To find genuine customer reactions, you can conduct usability studies, although it requires significant effort to plan and run them and analyze their results. While they can provide valuable insights, you can only check a subset of your users, and their findings will never be complete.

Those are the weaknesses you need to be aware of and mitigate while you perform UX testing. First, we will consider the relationship between usability and the feature specification.

Understanding usability and the feature specification

You, and everyone on the development team, spend your working lives on this product and devote orders of magnitude more time thinking about it than your customers. They are teachers, entrepreneurs, or bankers who just happen to use your product, and if they can't work out how to use it in 2 minutes, they'll give up. They'll complain your product is a piece of rubbish and get on with their actual job.

UX testing can be broken down into two different sections. First, you need to ensure that the product conforms to the specification – are the user-facing elements present, do they look correct, and is the text as described? This is objective and automatable – does the implementation match the specification? If a button is missing or the color is incorrect, that can be found and fixed.

More often, problems are due to the specification, which is the second class of issues. Your feature might be implemented and working perfectly and match the specification, but users will still find it hard to navigate and use. After all the work of adding a new feature, usability problems can still render it useless, such as if it is hidden away in a menu or keyboard shortcut that users can't find. Usability is a vital part of customer-facing features.

You should review the specification as you do all forms of testing. Do these requirements make sense? Is there an easier way to achieve the same goal? Will this feature have undesirable flow-on effects? Ideally, you should have thought these through at the specification review, but it is never too late to raise them.

In UX testing, even more than in other areas, you should constantly review the specification. Is that the best place for a text box or a menu item? What did you find confusing? What is the best name for a new function? If you are in an organization large enough to have a dedicated UX team, they should have thought this through, but even then, there is always room for feedback and improvement. If developers or other non-specialists design the user interface, then your voice, as a tester, is just as valuable as theirs in determining the best outcome.

As a tester, you have the first view of a new feature as someone who is not closely involved in its design and implementation, so you have a unique perspective from which to comment. The naivety that helped you with exploratory testing is useful again here: how did you predict this feature will work, considering the product? If it behaves differently from your expectations, raise that as an issue. Of course, your naivety is far from perfect. As a member of the development team, you will have spent more time thinking about it than your customers ever will, increasing the importance of your findings. If you know the product well and still have trouble, your customers will likely fare even worse. Once you have acted as a newcomer, you can apply more knowledge using the techniques described here.

Feedback on the specification should be provided in a dedicated section of the feature specification review, as described in the next section.

Running UX reviews

The user interface presents so many possibilities, is so essential, and can generate so much discussion that it deserves its own review meeting. These follow the same guidelines as the main feature specification review, as specified in *Chapter 3, How to Run Successful Feature Specification Reviews*, although there are differences.

The guest list for the UX review should include the UX team, the developers, the project manager, and the testers working on the feature. The project manager and senior developers are still optional. This area benefits from multiple points of view, so make sure everyone can attend and is prepared to present their ideas. Having said that, from experience, it's good to keep the guest list as short as possible; otherwise, having too many opinions can make these meetings take too long.

The timing for the UX review is also tricky. The developers should expect this meeting, or they may consider the interface finished when, in fact, the review is just starting. Like the specification review, the UX review should come after exploratory testing when an initial feature implementation is available for everyone to use. Seeing how a feature works in practice is especially important for UX testing.

The UX review aims to gauge users' current expectations and how they will react to your changes. What do they already know? How far does this feature reuse existing designs and patterns, and how much is unique? How visible is the difference, and is that commensurate with this feature's importance? Placing a new option on your home screen makes it very easy to find, but if only 1% of your users need it, 99% of people will see a more complex screen for no reason.

Judging your customers' expectations is not an exact science, and debates in UX reviews can become heated. They are beneficial, however, so endeavor to keep them polite and respectful to gain the maximum benefits.

The best way to measure customer expectations is to perform usability studies so that you can watch a representative sample of users using your new interface. There are many options here, such as A/B testing, which involves offering two different views of a feature to see which has better usage, or recorded studies, where you video users trying to use a feature for the first time and check their response in detail. For more information, see the *Running usability studies* section. This research can provide fascinating feedback, but it is also slow and costly, only reaches a small subset of users, and explores only a few limited options out of all the possibilities. It may show where users have problems but not show how to solve them.

A theme we will return to throughout this chapter is that it's far easier to say something is difficult to use than to propose a solution. Keep this in mind when raising usability issues. You can help the designers by suggesting improvements, but don't be surprised if they aren't implemented as you proposed. Usability studies are just the start of another round of design, implementation, and review to improve the interface.

Next, we will consider the two main use cases for any application: setup and ongoing usage.

Setup versus ongoing usage

Your product is likely to have two very different classes of user stories: those associated with setting the product up and those with its ongoing usage. In terms of total use, the ongoing cases vastly outnumber the setup ones – that is, unless you're experiencing massive customer growth and turnover simultaneously.

Despite being the minority of interactions with your product, getting users onboarded takes a disproportionate amount of design time relative to other features. When first using your product, users will know the least but also have some of the most challenging tasks to perform around getting your product ready. Unless they can overcome that barrier, they'll never become regular users.

You should devote similar proportions of time to testing onboarding tasks as setup tasks. On the plus side, this form of testing needs very little test data or equipment. The whole point is that you are a new user with no prior history with the product. Your challenge will be faking a clean installation. You will likely have installed your product hundreds of times or run through those same setup steps. Are they only working this time because you have performed them before?

This means the first step to testing product setup is ensuring you can fully uninstall your product or create an entirely fresh account. To correctly test signup, you'll need to make sure your system is representative of a non-user. Does your uninstaller remove all the registry keys, all the directories, and all the configurations associated with your product? If not, you need to know the details of the installation so that you can perform the extra uninstall steps and check that they've been done.

> **Real-world example – A whole new node**
>
> At one place I worked, we ran a private cloud infrastructure that we maintained and expanded ourselves. Our latest release was running happily, and business was good, so we set up new locations to handle the future load.
>
> Unfortunately, the installation failed. The same hardware and software version we were using was taking live traffic across the rest of the cloud, but despite them being identical, in this new location, they failed.
>
> On investigation, a change we had made to one of the libraries had gone wrong, and a file was missing. So long as you upgraded from the previous version, you used the old file, and the system worked. However, new installations didn't have the file and could never start.

Whether the installations are internal or external, make sure they are part of your test plan for all your supported environments and configurations.

For UX, a driving principle is that, as Mies van der Rohe said, "*less is more.*" You're aiming to let users achieve their goals in as few steps and as few clicks as possible, and those should be clear. The difficulty is that making one task more obvious, by putting an option on your home screen, for instance, makes other tasks less prominent by making the home screen more complicated. Putting a thousand buttons on your home screen means that all those functions are just one click away, but it doesn't give the best UX.

Step through the onboarding journey while looking for any steps you can prune. Every piece of information a user needs to provide is a little barrier to them using your service. What can you put off and collect later when the system is running? Stick strictly to the shortest route to make your service usable.

How much knowledge do you need your users to have? Don't rely on anything. Even if they have personal information such as ID numbers or details, they may not have them to hand. Let users enter information in whatever order they want. This will create more work for the development and test teams – more options for the user means more internal states to handle and more code paths to test. However, this work is well worthwhile as it makes for a great UX.

For instance, you can still find examples of search boxes that require you to select which entity you are searching for: usernames, customer names, ID values, and so on. Compare Twilio's search box, where we are searching for a number, to Google's home page:

Buy a Number

Figure 8.1 – A Twilio search box

Here is the Google home page:

Figure 8.2 – Google's famously sparse home page

Every piece of information you require from a user is a chance for them to get it wrong. It's much better for the user if the application accepts all possibilities and works out what to search for, even though it will take more effort from the development team to code and for you to test. Balance those costs, but look out for similar opportunities in your application where you could ask less of the user and do more within the program.

Finally, during the onboarding journey, look for any knowledge you require from the user. Do they have to know a setting is under a particular menu, or what step they need to take next? Setup wizards and similar systems are designed to solve these problems by guiding users through the necessary steps. If your product doesn't have one, that is an important addition. Don't rely on documentation – build the signup sequence into your product.

Having logged in and got the product working, you can start looking for common issues with the user interface.

Testing the user interface's look and feel

The watchword for the look and feel of any interface is consistency – a small set of colors, fonts, and styles should be used throughout. Or, to return to the theme of this chapter: *less is more*. Fewer designs and colors provide a better experience for users.

As a tester, you can check that consistency. Do new pages use the correct company colors? Does the text use a consistent font that's a uniform size? Are the buttons and links the same size and design as others? If there is a genuinely new element, does it use the same style as others in a new way?

Typically, adding new features simply involves extending the styles already in use, but every so often, there is a project to rebrand a product. Due to the amount of work and the marginal gain this involves, I've only seen it done when absolutely necessary.

> **Real-world example – The corporate takeover**
>
> One successful company where I worked was bought out by a larger competitor. They were great, and the takeover was a success, but one of the main changes it involved was rebranding. All the logos, all the names in all the documentation, and all the web pages had to change. Copies of our logo had been everywhere, but we purged them all.
>
> The one place our name remained was in the messages we sent via our API. We supported standards-based messaging, and each product reported its version and manufacturer in its messages. We read that information and sometimes changed our behavior based on who they were. Since they might have done the same, we had to keep advertising our old name, just in case that broke anything. Changing everything else, however, was a considerable project.
>
> The punchline? Just as we finished and got everything updated, we were taken over by an even larger competitor and had to rebrand all over again.

If you're in a large company, there will be a design team responsible for keeping user interface elements consistent and designing new ones to go along with them. Then, you only need to check that the implementation matches their designs and that those designs make sense and are easy to use for you.

Check all the visible functionality. Standard tests should press every button and check every link. That is the simple, objective part of usability testing, and it's easy to calculate the percentage coverage and automate it. As well as the complex, subjective tests listed here, ensure those fundamentals are also complete.

So long as your user interface is clear and consistent and works on at least one device, you can expand your testing across the full range of platforms your product supports. This process, known as interoperability testing, will be described next.

Interoperability

Picture this scene: you've designed a beautiful website or app that is clean and straightforward to use with a clear flow between tasks and provides all the complex functionality of your application at your users' fingertips. This would be excellent, except it doesn't load on their device.

There will always be a wide variety of operating systems and web browsers being used and supported at any time, with a spread of percentages from new to old and between competitors. Which platforms and versions does your application support? That's the first interoperability question and will depend on the variety of versions your users are using. The product owner needs to trade off the technical effort of supporting those versions against the importance of those customers. You might include a version because many customers use it or because there's a smaller number of highly important clients. Whatever the reason for their inclusion, as a tester, you need that list of versions you support so that you can try them all.

If you are testing a hardware appliance, you are spared these considerations and have the luxury of using an environment you control. You'll just have to worry about different generations of your product and any component changes that might affect its behavior and performance.

There are far more software than hardware products, however, so if you are testing one of those, you'll need to prepare for interoperability testing. In a large company, it may be worth running a lab with different systems, and there are external companies able to test on different platforms. From experience, running a lab can be costly in terms of both time and money and it's a miserable task trying to keep old operating systems running correctly.

Real-world example – Juggling web browser compatibility

In one company where I worked, a customer reported being unable to add users. This came as a shock since no one else faced the same problem, and it turned out that they were using an outdated version of Firefox. It was so old that it was no longer officially supported, but it was the only version approved by the company's IT team. They were such an important client that we had to provide a fix.

We removed the offending function call, and they provided an installer for us to test since it was no longer available. Our application passed regression testing and rapidly went live.

Then, a different set of customers reported issues. In fixing the old version of Firefox, we had broken an old version of Internet Explorer. While we had run regression tests, we hadn't run the complete interoperability test plan. We made sure we included that for any future changes to our compatibility.

I recommend having two layers of interoperability testing: a sanity test that every build should pass and a more comprehensive set of tests to run when you have made changes that affect your interoperability. Within that extended test plan, look for any pages that are special or unusual within your websites such as WebRTC videos, embedded media, or any technologies not widely in use. Those are potential sources of bugs in general and interoperability bugs in particular.

As described in *Chapter 5*, *Black-Box Functional Testing*, you need to identify dependent and independent variables. Web browser and operating system interoperability are variables that interact with many others. If your test automation setup and time allows it, run those core tests on every version – for instance, creating, editing, and deleting a user.

With that test plan and the list of supported versions in place, you are ready to test and sign off the interoperability of your application. The last ongoing task is regularly reviewing the list of supported browsers and operating systems, removing old ones, and, more importantly, adding new ones. You should sign up for the beta programs of all operating systems and web browsers you work with to get an advanced warning of any compatibility problems. This will give you the chance to fix them before they are widely available.

Within each operating system, you need to consider the different displays it can work with since they will massively change the appearance of your product, as described in the next section.

Testing displays

A key variable in the user interface is the display showing your application. Whether high-resolution displays, mobile phones in different orientations, or web browsers that users can resize however they want, your application has to handle whatever it runs on. Again, if you're testing a hardware appliance with a built-in screen, you have it easy with only a single possibility to try. Otherwise, there are many options you have to cover:

- Screen/window resolution:

  - Maximum resolution

  - Minimum resolution

- Aspect ratio:

  - Landscape versus portrait

  - Extreme settings:

    - Tall and thin window sizes

    - Short and broad window sizes

- Changing resolutions dynamically:

  - Changing a phone screen from landscape to portrait and vice versa

  - Resizing a web browser

- Second monitors:

  - Using your application on a second screen

  - Dragging the window from one screen to a second screen

  - A second screen with a different resolution than the first

- Maximizing and minimizing the application:

  - On a second monitor

I have seen bugs in all those areas at different times over the years. Some are more common than others – low-resolution screens can cause UI issues, for instance, but users would have to deliberately reduce the resolution on a modern screen to ever see them. Problems changing from landscape to portrait were incredibly rare until smartphones became ubiquitous.

Web pages need to be designed to work on both mobile and desktop screens in both landscape and portrait orientations. This is a challenging job for the UX team, so check whether it works. Even if it works on wide and narrow screens, does it work for resolutions in between?

Ideally, this testing should also be automated. Tools such as **Chromatic** are available to take snapshots of user interfaces and warn you about any unexpected changes as code is developed. By altering the viewport size, you can take a snapshot of how the screen is supposed to look at a range of resolutions, then rapidly check new releases are unchanged. While these tools can perform simple tests well, for more complex scenarios such as second monitors and dynamically adjusting screen sizes, you may need manual testing. Saving the hardest cases for manual tests keeps them as short as possible.

Sometimes, there is no neat way to display information when the screen is small or has a low resolution. The user interface has to make tradeoffs and remove some information, and there is no way for it to display everything. This may not be a bug as such. See the *Comparing bugs to features* section for other examples. In that case, work with the UX team to find out the desired behavior and what they are happy with, even if there is no good solution.

Scroll bars

Aim to limit your application's use of scroll bars. Pages are much more usable if you can see all of them at once, although that requires careful design. Pages with lists can be paginated with search boxes, limited table widths, and text wrapping to ensure it fits into the available size. You'll need to pick a minimum resolution to work within; anything bigger than that will also fit. Double scroll bars anywhere in your application are a sign of lazy design, and you can raise that as a bug.

Using touch screens

How well does your user interface work on a touch screen? Buttons you can distinguish with a mouse might be too close on a small phone screen. Pages often need to be completely redesigned, making them much simpler for those devices. If your company hasn't got a dedicated UI for phones, you'll need to check how usable your current interface is. If your application does have a dedicated interface for phones, that requires a separate test plan.

Not all touch screens are small, so also consider tablet or laptop touch screens. Are the elements readable, and are all the buttons accessible? There are different keyboard options when entering text; are yours appropriate? Multitasking abilities are limited on some hardware; does your application handle losing focus and being reactivated? Do you have an app design dedicated to larger screens?

Once you have tested the look and feel of your app and the screen it appears on, you can move on to the content of your user interface.

Choosing clear words

Clearly labeling your application avoids a host of user-related problems. Giving understandable names to options and buttons is harder than it looks, however, and if those are confusing, users will resort to tooltips and help text that also has to be written. At a basic level, you need to check that all the text is legible and displayed correctly, but the greater part of testing the words is to ensure they are as comprehensible as possible.

While technical writing is a topic I love (can you tell?), I don't have space here to give an in-depth guide. As a tester, you won't need to know every nuance, but there are certain checks that you can perform across many functions.

The first is simply consistency. If a group video call is referred to as a *conference*, then it should be a conference everywhere and not referred to as a *meeting* half the time. They may be synonyms as far as you're concerned, but your application needs to pick one term and use it consistently. When an application reaches a certain size, and especially when two or more technical authors are working on the product, it's vital to have a style guide to ensure they use the same terms and phrases throughout the application.

Certain words are difficult to translate into other languages and might confuse readers who aren't native English speakers. I find this fascinating since wording that seems entirely equivalent to me appears very differently to novice speakers; for example, see the following:

- *Once* you have selected an option, then you can submit the change

- *When* you have selected an option, then you can submit the change

This is another example:

- The application *may* prompt you for your phone number

- The application *might* prompt you for your phone number

Once and *when* are used as synonyms, but *when* is more clearly about time and is easier to render in other languages. This is similar for *may* and *might*. While you can use either without changing the sentence's content, *might* indicates the conditional more clearly. *May* has several other meanings that make it harder to understand.

As a tester, it's not your role to design easy-to-understand language but look for any phrases you struggle with. Anything you need to read twice might cause far more problems for someone with less knowledge of English and your application. Again, use your naivety. Anything you have to try twice, anything you have to think about to understand – these aren't your fault. They show that your application is not straightforward and needs more work.

Features should be carefully named to make them as straightforward as possible.

Real-world example – Struggling to find a name

I once worked on an obscure piece of functionality that changed the participants you would see in a video conference in different situations. We struggled to find a snappy name for it on the settings page and ultimately gave up. We named the options *type 1* and *type 2*, and gave a longer explanation in the help.

Don't do that. Even if the name isn't perfect, always give your user some clue about what *type 1* refers to, and provide a detailed description elsewhere.

Once the text in your native language has been chosen, reviewed, and agreed upon, then you can start working on the translations. These come with their own set of testing considerations.

Testing localization

Getting a feature to work in a single language is usually a challenge, but usability must also consider working in different languages and geographies. Translation bugs can be critical blockers – recall the example from *Chapter 7, Testing of Error Cases*, of a hardware unit that couldn't boot when set to Danish. An error in rendering one of the variables in the string caused a critical issue, and we loaded the strings so early in the boot sequence that we couldn't even upgrade them. It needed emergency intervention to fix. So, don't underestimate the importance of translations and testing them well, even though they come with challenges. As with usability testing in general, there are both subjective and objective aspects to testing localization.

Objectively, all strings must have translations in place that render correctly. Remember to include both successful cases and error messages in your testing. When manually testing translations, it is a good idea to leave your product in the foreign language for an extended period when trying other features to see whether any issues appear in other situations. This provides much more comprehensive testing than only using translations when explicitly testing them.

Always check for the presence of translated strings, and test that they are displayed correctly. If your application is developed in English, then some languages, such as Mandarin, usually have fewer characters to represent the same string, which generally doesn't cause problems. However, other languages, such as German, have longer word lengths, on average, which means the translated strings need more space. This might mean they are truncated or wrapped around, depending on the size of the text box they are in. The second objective test for translation is to ensure the user interface still looks correct in the other language.

> **Real-world example – It's not what you say, it's the way that you say it**
>
> In a video conferencing system I worked on, we used an external company to connect callers who dialed in by telephone. They would be greeted with a prompt welcoming them and asking them to enter their conference number, provided by a text-to-speech system. We sent the text and an automated system to a third party to read it out. As well as English, we supported a range of other languages and would send a message indicating the text and the language to be used.
>
> Unfortunately, in one release, the French translation string was missing. We told the third party the text was French but sent English words. This resulted in us greeting our French customers in English, but with an insultingly thick French accent.

Presentation issues such as detecting text wrapping, pages looking incorrect in foreign languages, and problems in text-to-speech rendering are challenging to automate and may require a manual check.

Finally, on translations, you need to check the strings' content. Even if the translated strings are present and rendered neatly, they may still have typos or be mistranslated. It's best if you speak the language in question so that you can also comment on the quality of the translations and the presence of foreign text to avoid embarrassing omissions.

> **Real-world example – Half Mandarin**
>
> On one product I tested, we supported various languages and diligently tried them manually for each release. We verified that Mandarin characters were displayed for all our strings when set to the Chinese localization.
>
> Unfortunately, we had introduced a bug in our Unicode rendering and only displayed every other character. Alternate characters weren't shown at all, and the text was gibberish. Without someone who understood even basic Mandarin, we failed to spot that the strings were half the length they were supposed to be and had only checked for the presence of squiggly-looking letters.

String checking should be automated, although it may fail to detect strings that have not been translated. If only an English string is available, and the test system reads the strings from the same code, it may compare the English text to the English text and pass the test. To avoid that, you can keep a separate repository of strings in the test system, although that is a significant maintenance overhead.

A native speaker of that language should check the strings to verify the work of the original translator. Since you are unlikely to have a suitable range of polyglots in your team, you will need external help from other departments or a translation agency. Just as English needs a style guide, each language should ensure they are using the same terms and style consistently throughout.

You need to give translators the option not to update strings, even when the English changes. Previously, we saw an example of group video calls being called *conferences* or *meetings*. If we change the English from one to the other, foreign languages might be happy with the term they are already using and not want to change it. As well as tracking to ensure changes are picked up, you need the option to keep their existing strings.

Context can also be a challenge for translators. A string or a word in isolation could be translated in various ways, and they would need to see the application in use to know which is correct. If your translation system doesn't allow translators to see the strings in the context of the application, then they will need to propose a translation that can be added to a build they can use, then have the chance to give feedback and make changes before it goes live. This can be time-consuming, so it needs to be prioritized and started early in a release cycle.

With all that in place – strings translations that can be seen in context, reviewed by another native speaker, informed by their style guide, and with the chance for feedback – you will be set up to ensure consistently strong translations. It takes a lot of work with no easy shortcuts, however. Next, you must check that dates and times are handled correctly throughout your application.

Testing time zones

Since almost all applications report time in some way, nearly all applications will need to handle different time zones. Even if your customers are clustered in a long thin stripe along the Greenwich Meridian, daylight savings time and leap seconds can still cause issues. Here are the considerations when adding them to your test plan.

Let's examine the case of creating a conference since that demonstrates all the issues you are likely to come across. In that case, there are six time zones to consider:

- The initial time zone of the conference creator
- The initial time zone of the conference invitee
- The conference creator moving to a different time zone
- The conference invitee moving to a different time zone

- The initial time zone of the conference

- The updated time zone of the conference

In each case, you need to ensure that people seeing the conference both from within the time zone and outside it can see the conference reported correctly. Changing the time zone of the viewer should not alter when the conference occurs, although it should alter the time they see. To add extra complexity, use time zones that aren't on 1-hour boundaries, such as in India, to check that those offsets are applied correctly.

Times should always indicate which time zone they refer to, either explicitly or from context. It is no use showing the conference is at 2 P.M. if it doesn't say 2 P.M. in which time zone. You will also need to keep careful track of when these conferences are; this is an area where it's easy to make mistakes.

As well as time zones, daylight savings can cause problems if your application isn't suitably architected. Of course, the way to handle these changes is to use a single time zone, UTC, for all internal processing, only changing it to local time when it is presented. Due to this, there will be no problems with gaining or losing hours because the single time zone has not changed. Detecting problems with daylight savings time is difficult to uncover because it can be tricky to mimic a time change, but it's well worth persevering to make sure the times are presented correctly.

More obscure but possibly more damaging are leap seconds, which need to be inserted or removed to keep time as measured by atomic clocks synchronized with solar time. These cause problems because they alter the trusted time zone, UTC, from which you derive all others. Applications need to be able to handle even UTC not incrementing monotonically. Again, they are tricky to test in practice, but if one has been scheduled for the future, make sure you take the time to try it out. The problems they can cause go well beyond incorrect presentation: crashes and database corruption can result from code that assumes constantly increasing time values. They may not come from your code but from libraries that you use, so system testing is essential to work out the application's overall behavior.

Next, we will move on from the written word and look at what philosophies your app should take regarding the visual aspects of usability, starting with ensuring your application is accessible to all users.

Ensuring accessibility

How well can those with physical disabilities use your product? Most of the recommendations in this book are just that, recommendations, but accessibility requirements are enshrined in law in various jurisdictions. Failing to test this section of your product could result in lawsuits.

Luckily, the requirements for accessibility are generally good practice for all users. Here, we consider the example of testing web pages, although some of these considerations also apply to mobile and desktop applications too. For each web page, check the following:

- The title is present and clearly describes the contents of the page

- Each image has alternate text set so that screen readers can indicate its content

- Headings are present and are in a meaningful hierarchy
- The contrast ratio for your text is sufficiently high and configurable:

    - Avoid text of a similar shade or tone to the background; for example, gray text on a white background

- Check that the text is readable when enlarged
- Tab ordering:

    - Ensure that pressing the *Tab* key navigates through all the elements of your page
    - The ordering should be predictable and not have random jumps
    - Each element should be visibly selected when it's in focus

- Moving content should have the option to be stopped
- Flashing content should have the option to be stopped
- multimedia alternatives for videos and text
- Correct form formatting and error handling

Web page titles and alternate text for images should be present and accurately describe their contents. Headings should have a correct hierarchy, only stepping down one level at a time, and should match the content they present. Watch out for text color that is too similar to the background, making it illegible. However, the colors should also be configurable since some people with dyslexia need lower brightness (luminance) text to help them read.

Real-world example – People matching the background

Probably the craziest bug I ever encountered was due to luminance calculations – not of text, but within a video stream. The flagship product of one video conferencing company where I worked had an entire room dedicated to video calls. Everything was specified: three huge screens, the desk, chairs, and even a glowing blue wall behind the participants. When you ordered it, it arrived on a lorry.

However, sometimes, we saw video problems. If you waved your arm, copies of your hand were left behind as it moved, staying in the background. That didn't happen for our regular, cheaper video endpoints, so why did it happen here?

The problem was the blue wall. That shade of blue had the same luminance as some users' skin tones. If you converted the picture into black and white, they would be the same shade of gray. Our video processing only used luminance to detect motion, so it couldn't tell the difference between people's skin and the background and left patches of the wrong color as it moved.

Your website's text should be legible when it is enlarged because some users require that setting. It shouldn't overlap as it grows, and the text should wrap so that it can all be reached, rather than getting cut off or requiring people to use scroll bars.

Pages should have a reasonable tab ordering for users who cannot use a mouse. If you press the *Tab* key repeatedly, all the different elements of your pages should be highlighted in order. The selection shouldn't jump around randomly and each element should clearly show when it is selected so that users know where they are. Are all elements accessible by tabbing through them? And do all elements let you *Tab* away from them? For each element, you need to be able to select it and use it only when using the keyboard.

Moving and flashing content should be optional. This includes auto-playing videos and any scrolling text carousels. Users should be able to stop or hide that motion to avoid distraction. Media should offer alternatives – captions for those unable to hear the sound and audio descriptions for those with visual impairments.

Each element in a form should have a label associated with it, and those labels should be positioned consistently – to the left for text boxes and dropdown lists and to the right for radio buttons and checkboxes. Any required fields should be marked, and an error message should let the user know if a form is submitted without them. The other fields on the form should remain populated, even if there is an error, so that users don't need to fill out all the information again.

Many of these requirements are helpful for all users, not only those with accessibility requirements, so ensure you pay attention to these aspects of UX testing. Many tools are available to perform these checks across your site, making it easy to automate and check that changes are working well.

Once the structure of your pages and fields is correct, you can consider the information that is being displayed, as shown in the next section.

Testing information display

Keep the screens that display information as simple as possible. To return to the theme of this chapter, *less is more*. This is easy to say, and the more egregious violations of this principle are easy to spot. The trick is seeing them early enough and finding even the mildest of examples. This is a large subject and deserves a dedicated team to focus on it. Here, I will only cover some simple examples to look out for while testing, but I thoroughly recommend reading further on this fascinating subject. Within the Packt library there is *Practical UX Design* by Scott Farnanella or *Hands-On UX Design for Developers* by Elvis Canziba.

Real-world example – Too many axes

One company I worked for produced an internal tool in which graphs of network activity had eight different axes, all plotted on the same chart. Sending bandwidth, receiving bandwidth, packet loss, jitter, and latency all had lines that were superimposed over each other by default. If you ever see a graph like that, that's a bug to raise with the development team.

Here is an example of such a graph:

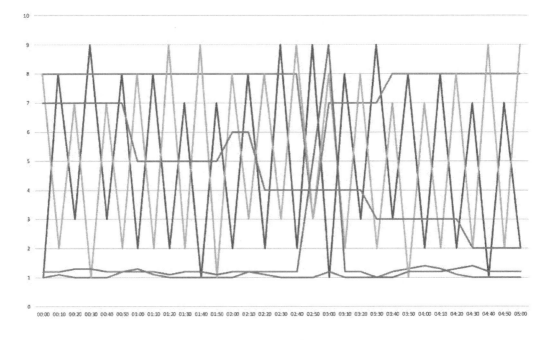

Figure 8.3 – An example of a graph containing too much information

Even if displays like this can be filtered and made simpler, they should not have to be. This applies to logs, tables, or anything else that can become too complicated. The default view should be readable and show you what you need without you doing anything. If not, raise that as a problem until it's fixed. Then, from this simple top-level view, give users the option to drill down into the details they need.

This section presents examples of poor UX practices to look out for when testing your product, as well as more successful alternatives.

Displaying information in tables

To keep tables simple, they should contain one piece of information per column. This may seem obvious, but it's very tempting to combine data, which makes searching, sorting, and filtering much harder. If the development team has implemented a table in that way, let them know they should make a change. For instance, consider the information grouping in this table:

User	Connection	Status
bob.bobson@example.com	UDP Rate up: 10 Mbps Rate down: 20 Mbps	Online 5 minutes
john.smith@example.com	TCP Rate up: 5 Mbps Rate down: 8 Mbps	Offline 5 days
jane.doe@example.com	UDP Rate up: 10 Mbps Rate down: 100 Mbps	On call 5 minutes

Table 8.2 – A table with too much information in each column

When arranged like that, the data is harder to see, and you can't sort the columns. Because there's no one data type that they contain, it's not clear what sorting would mean. Here's the same data, now with one kind of data in each column:

User	Connection Type	Rate up (Mbps)	Rate down (Mbps)	Status	Duration
bob.bobson@ example.com	UDP	10	20	Online	5 minutes
john.smith@ example.com	TCP	5	8	Offline	5 days
jane.doe@example. com	UDP	10	100	On call	10 minutes

Table 8.3 – A table with the same data spread across columns

Everything is presented more clearly in this version, and you can sort by each data type individually. It can be tempting to group information if you have so many different data points that there would be too many columns. It's best to break up the data if there is that much and make each table more specific or, if necessary, have a table you can scroll around rather than grouping entries together.

Also, avoid having two columns listing the same information at different levels – for instance, if there's a list of wholesalers and customers, but where customers might appear in both lists. Again, this makes searching and filtering harder:

Inviter	Invitee	Date
adam.blake@example.com	bob.bobson@example.com	2/1/22
bob.bobson@example.com	john.smith@example.com	4/3/22
bob.bobson@example.com	jane.doe@example.com	5/6/22

Table 8.4 – A table with the same data in two different columns

If Bob Bobson has invited 100 people, then finding the entry where he was invited isn't easy. If your users notice, they should sort by the date because Bob will have been invited to the service before he asked anyone else. However, such tricks shouldn't be necessary. This is an exception to the preceding rule that searching should be kept as simple as possible for the user by not giving them options. In this case, selecting which column to search for can usefully narrow down the result.

Visual elements

Colors can be a valuable tool for guiding users through complex workflows – for instance, always having one color indicates progressing to the next state or highlighting errors. They should be used sparingly, however. Only two or three meanings can be given to colors before pages become incomprehensible rainbows, so assign colors only to the most critical aspects of your page. The saturation of the colors is important too. Pastels and shades are less noticeable, so a page can tolerate more of them. If more than one color is fully saturated, the screen will be garish, especially if they cover a wide area rather than being limited to an isolated button or icon.

Colors should be consistent. Recall the bug from *Chapter 5, Black-Box Functional Testing*, where the same data points were displayed in different shades due to a bug in the rounding. If you are using color as an indicator, the same color should always mean the same thing.

Icons themselves need to be carefully chosen. Generally, they are small, so they can have a bold, saturated color. However, only use one unless you're deliberately aiming for a rainbow effect, such as in the Windows or Google logos. Otherwise, the main requirement is that the logo is distinctive and should be sufficiently different from any others that might be shown with it. Watch out for aspect ratio problems and incorrect resolutions in icon files to ensure they aren't stretched or degraded, even when displayed as thumbnails.

Testing notifications

Many applications make use of push notifications for users. These might be urgent and integral to a product, such as incoming call alerts on a communication platform or meeting reminders from a scheduler. Elsewhere, they can be reminders or prompts that don't require immediate action and are just designed to get users engaged with that application again.

With this form of testing, the first stage, as ever, is to identify the scope. What is the complete range of notification messages your application can send? Once you have that list, you can generate each, in turn, to ensure it appears correctly.

Common variables recur in this area: what happens if the user has blocked notifications? Does your application still work without them? Notification systems are implemented differently in different operating systems, so your test plan needs to try them all. Your application can receive messages both while running in the foreground or background. Does it display notifications properly in both cases? If it wasn't in the foreground when the message arrives, does it activate correctly and quickly enough for users to react, for instance, by answering the call?

Notifications can be of different types and priorities, so you must ensure you are sending the right kind. It's tempting to always send high-priority messages, although systems such as Apple's Push Notification system monitors and caps those. You might find all your messages are delayed if you attempt to abuse the system and claim that your daily prompt to use the app has the same importance as the next meeting starting. You may require specialist tools or code inspection to check which sort of message your application sends.

Information display overview

As mentioned previously, other than a few clear-cut cases, many user interface design decisions are subjective and don't have a clear answer. When raising this class of issue, remember to flag that it is a UX issue, which implies that others' opinions may differ. Spotting problems is vastly easier in usability testing than designing great solutions, and it may be that the design you think could be improved is, in fact, the least bad option, given the problems with other arrangements. Keep communication open. Discuss the issues and possible solutions, rather than assuming your proposal is the best or the correct behavior.

Many of the worst crimes against UX are perpetrated within internal tools as they are used far less and have a more forgiving audience than your customer-facing interfaces. Even then, developers should apply best practices in preparation for more important interfaces and help your internal processes.

These are just examples of problems I have encountered; exhaustive guidelines are beyond the scope of this book. Rely on your intuition. If you find something hard to use or difficult to understand, users who spend less time using your system will struggle even more.

Once a user can see this information, they'll want to interact with it, as described in the next section.

Testing user interaction

As with displaying information, there is vast and growing literature on user interactions; I will only list a few particular examples here. As ever, trust yourself – if something annoys you, if you make mistakes, or if you have to carefully think through steps when using your product, then others will struggle even more. The fault is not necessarily yours, so first, check whether your application could be easier for users to use.

A good interface will guide users from the general to the specific: I want to change how I'm viewing this page (so I select **View**), I want to zoom in (so I select **Zoom**), I want to zoom to 200% (so select **200%**). Are there clear routes through your application like that for all your user stories?

The other extreme is the **Linux** command prompt. While massively powerful and configurable, it provides almost no guidance. It's simply a prompt; all the knowledge about how to use it comes from the user. In a way, it's the worst possible user interface, one in which users are on their own. Consider your product – how much guidance does it give and how much, as with the Linux command prompt, has to come from users?

In this section, we'll cover some basics of user interaction that apply to many areas.

Counting user steps

Consider the number of steps a user needs to take to achieve a particular goal. Can any of them be removed? For many years, I worked on a product with a long list of customer names, with further details available via links. But the customer names weren't links. Every time I wanted to go to the customer page, I had to look up a customer's name, then go over to the other side of the screen to click the pencil icon to edit it, as shown in the following screenshot. The customer's name should have been the link to save that extra step:

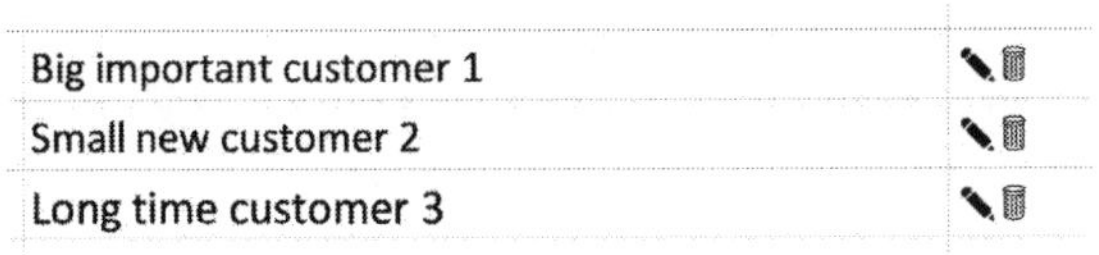

Big important customer 1	✎ 🗑
Small new customer 2	✎ 🗑
Long time customer 3	✎ 🗑

Figure 8.4 – Information displayed with the edit icon separate from the name

Even worse, the edit icon (the pencil), which we often clicked, was right next to the delete icon (the rubbish bin), which we rarely used and would cause serious problems if used at the wrong time. While not wrong, the interface invited mistakes. How easily can users make errors on your pages? Separate options as much as possible, especially dangerous steps you can't undo.

Each time a user has to click, each lookup and translation of information they have to do is another place where things might go wrong. This might mean looking up a user's email address, navigating from a menu to a submenu, or any of a thousand different interactions. If you see an opportunity to remove a stage, flag it up. Simpler workflows make life easier for you and your customers because you are a major product user, and it simplifies your test plan.

To tell which steps a user will need to take, you will need to consider the everyday tasks a user will perform. User stories often capture these, but they are beyond the scope of this book. Product owners and designers should use them as a significant input into the feature specification. While you can generally work just from that specification, when testing user interactions, it's helpful to go back to the user stories to see the overall flow of tasks on the product. Where do they start? What are they trying to achieve? What route do they take, and where do they end up? This will show you the different steps they must take and thus the ones you could avoid.

Required combinations of steps

Even worse than having steps you have to perform in order is having unrelated steps users have to do together – for instance, creating a user and adding them to security groups. Even worse are inconsistent requirements when the setup is sometimes automatic but sometimes requires manual steps.

This is a tripwire waiting to cause problems for unwary users, and again more often occurs in internal tools than in the interfaces you polish for your customers. Wherever inconsistency appears, it causes problems and supports cases when things go wrong.

> **Real-world example – Failing to enable the feature**
>
> In one company I worked at, we used flags to control the rollout of features to customers. First, they would be upgraded to the new version with the feature available, and then we would gradually activate them. The feature flag system had been implemented early in the company's history, but we had outgrown it. For instance, to enable a feature for 1,000 customers, you needed to send 1,000 separate messages, since the API was per-customer only.
>
> Even worse, for some (but not all features), you didn't just have to enable a flag; you also had to set the default to be enabled. Because it wasn't always required, this two-stage process repeatedly caught us out. It culminated in the rollout of a new feature being delayed for 2 months after we thought we had enabled it, but the default was still disabled. The feature was resilience to video errors, which we thought was happily working but was hard to see from normal usage.

Of course, the fix for requiring your users to perform unrelated steps is to combine them somehow. Sometimes, you can set a reasonable default – for our feature flags, assume that if the flag is enabled, the default should be too. If you add a user, maybe there are standard groups they should always be added to. When no single answer always applies, create a wizard or other interface to guide users through each necessary step so that they don't forget about them. Even within a wizard, give users the option to skip steps. Maybe you hadn't forgotten about adding the user to groups, but you don't know which ones they should be a member of yet. In that case, prompt the user to add the necessary information, but give them the option to skip steps if they want to.

Requiring restarts

A special case of requiring combinations of steps is when a restart is required for new settings to take effect. The rule here is that the user needs to be informed of what is happening and why to give them control over the process. I know I've experienced that sinking feeling minutes before an important meeting when a computer shows a glacial progress bar instead of starting back up. Help your customers avoid that fate.

When it comes to restarts, the settings have three possibilities:

- The settings take immediate effect and do not require a restart
- The settings don't take effect until the next restart
- Changing the settings causes a restart

Wherever possible, put in the effort to make settings take effect immediately, especially for anything customer-facing. That consistency is a massive help for usability. If you really can't spare the time for that, clearly label the user interface.

Even more importantly, highlight any settings that will trigger a restart. If you have a page full of settings and only a few cause a restart, you are highly likely to surprise and annoy your users. Let your users know what will happen, and give them the option to change their minds to double-check they are sure before initiating the restart.

Providing freedom and feedback

Routes through the system should offer the user as much freedom as possible. If a user loves keyboard shortcuts, make sure they're available for your new feature, along with menu items, or right-click options. Can the interface be used just with tabs and pressing *Enter*, as required for accessibility? These different possibilities add to the testing load but directly affect how your users experience your product.

A simple way to give users more freedom is to delay checking on fields until they submit a form. To change a date field from *1st September* to *31st January*, don't throw an error if they changed the day first and set it to `31st September` temporarily. Yes, it's invalid, but they might be halfway through a change and be about to change the month. That's a valid sequence, so there's no need to warn the user part way through. See the *Presenting errors* section for more details.

> **Real-world example – VMWare – Changing memory always gives an error**
>
> The **VMWare** interface for assigning memory to a virtual machine annoyed me as it always threw an error when changing measurement units. By default, the interface gave the memory size in MB, which was less than helpful for modern machines. Instead of saying a machine had 8 GB, for instance, VMWare would say it had 8,192 MB.
>
> To increase the memory from 8,192 MB to 10 GB, you needed to change both the value and the units. If you changed the units first, the interface would read 8,192 GB, and VMWare displayed an error that it was too high. Then, you would have to change the value to 10 GB to correct it. If you changed the value first, the interface read 10 MB, and VMWare displayed an error that that value was too low until you changed the units to GB. Whichever order you chose, VMWare always showed a warning.

While I can complain about unavoidable errors, this is a case where it may be the least bad option. VMWare wanted to let users know as early as possible that the values they had selected were invalid, and the cost of that was always displaying an error in some cases. The best fix would be to change the default measurement to GB, which is far more helpful for modern machines, and leave the checking for invalid values as is.

This demonstrates that checking for errors while a user is filling out a form can cause issues, but you should give users feedback as early as possible. If a system has reached its maximum number of users, for instance, then prevent users from even trying. They should not be able to reach the **Add User** page at all. That option should be grayed out with a message stating why. This avoids users from filling out lots of details before discovering that the operation will fail. See the *Testing error feedback* section for more information.

Recall *Chapter 5, Black-Box Functional Testing*, which lists string types to try in text boxes, modes of use such as copying and pasting, and responses to pressing *Tab* and *Enter*. You can combine those variables with the others in this chapter: does each text box still work well at low screen resolutions, with enlarged text, or using keyboard input only, for instance? Does each text box clearly state the inputs it accepts, and does it give a clear error when it doesn't get them?

Hidden tools

You must make user interfaces as obvious to use as possible and lay out clear paths for users to reach their goals. However, sometimes, you can offer shortcuts for those in the know. These extra features aren't necessary for users to use your product but make it quicker or better in some way. Generally, they use already visible buttons in a new way. There are many on the **iPhone**:

- Pressing the green call button in the phone app brings up the last number dialed
- Pressing and holding the spacebar lets you reposition the cursor

- Pressing and holding the **Send message** button lets you send the message with text effects
- The Apple symbol on the reverse of the phone is a configurable button

Among many others. These occasionally have clickbait articles written about them, publicizing their existence for anyone who hasn't found them yet. Like every feature, these need testing, but they occupy a unique position from a usability point of view. Hidden tools aren't a crucial part of any user journey but are a wonderful layer of polish. Usually, when you add a new option for a new feature, it comes at the cost of making a page more complicated, but by being hidden, these features avoid that.

Swiping on touch screens and touch pads can reveal hidden functions, such as bringing up options in messaging apps or moving between screens. With hidden options, make sure there are other ways to perform those actions and give hints about their existence where possible.

You should be wary of adding too many since users may accidentally trigger them and wonder what's happening. Another risk is that you don't optimize the more obvious ways of using your product because you know of the shortcut. Heavy users like you have a great experience, but most of your users may not. So, remember, these are shortcuts, not replacements for the main functions.

Otherwise, hidden features are a lovely addition so that power users can work more efficiently. The challenge is finding opportunities and ideas for them.

Irreversible operations

Irreversible operations need special consideration for usability. These include deleting information or removing configuration, which leaves the user with no way to recover the previous state. These should be protected with options to confirm the operation. However, they are imperfect, especially for heavy users who may get so used to agreeing that they also confirm accidental deletions.

It's more powerful to have a temporary, intermediate state that allows the user to recover information for some time. This might be a recycle bin, a *recently deleted* folder, the option to disable rather than delete users, or similar functions. On the downside, these create extra states you need to consider in all your testing.

Temporary states can have a multiplicative effect on your test plan – for every operation that you can perform on a user, for instance, what happens if you do that while the user is disabled? So, recovery features can come at a high cost in terms of the ongoing test burden but are a valuable addition to usability. If you don't have them, plan to add them in.

Another form of protection for unrecoverable operations is to require extra permissions to perform them. This restricts the number of users with access to those functions or can mean that users need to explicitly raise their access level to carry them out. Again, this helps prevent accidents, although it can be irritating to use regularly.

Menu systems

When my son was very small, he played games on an iPad. After a while, he learned how to use it himself. I still remember him, aged 1, selecting the app he wanted to use. This isn't a story about how amazing my children are (although they are, of course). It's about how fantastic the iPad user interface is: it is literally simple enough for a 1-year-old to use. It has no apps hiding in the **Start** menu, no icons that need double-clicking, no mouse to use, and not a single word to read. He could just see the picture he wanted and point at it.

While my son could navigate the iPad menu and play the simple games I'd downloaded, he still needed help every time he wanted to play because of the intermediate step – navigating the games' menus. They used lots of text rather than pictures and sometimes had the main menu and then a submenu to navigate, which was beyond my toddler.

This story has a few morals. The first is that a task is as hard as its hardest step. The iPad was simple and the games were simple, but the menus were not. The second is that there's no point in polishing the UX in one area if most customers fail to reach it due to a difficult or off-putting step earlier in the process. Finally, the most challenging step for users may not be initially apparent.

If you work on a small, new product, your company probably touts its simplicity as one of its selling points. Your product doesn't have many features yet because you haven't had time to develop them. If you are at that stage of development, these problems won't be acute yet, and the challenge will be arranging the interface so that it can grow successfully. This is difficult because it requires predicting which features might be required and where they could be put. With a strong enough idea of the architecture, this is possible, but it's harder because once you have a user interface in place, changes are likely to upset existing customers. They've learned to use your product in one way and won't want to change. Any user interface mistakes are compounded as your product grows, so spend the time getting each new addition right.

Still, those are problems for the future. If you're working on a mature product with many years of development, it will likely accrue menu items and options, like barnacles encrusting a boat. Anything customers wanted over the years is added on, and removing functionality is very difficult as, again, it may upset a customer relying on it.

Real-world example – The endpoint menu and the system menu

I once worked with a fantastic video endpoint. It was reliable, useable, and ahead of its time. However, its main menu always annoyed me. Half its main settings were under an option called *System Settings*, and the other half were under an option called *Endpoint Settings*.

But the system was an endpoint! I could never remember which settings were where, and half the time, I went looking in the wrong menu first. After years of development, there were dozens of settings under each heading, which only made the problem worse.

So, the first rule for your menu systems is to always find genuine distinctions between your headings to give your users the best chance to remember where items are. In the real world, there are gray areas and overlaps. A well-designed system enforces a structure that appears natural and obvious, but it took a lot of work to decide on that structure from all the possible options the designers had. Remember that users have a broader view than any single developer and will find inconsistencies or ambiguities between areas that are consistent within themselves.

Next, when designing menus, ensure the most used features are in the most accessible locations. Burying a commonly used tool three layers deep in a menu will annoy your users enormously, and the heavier the user, the more it will annoy them. Check out Ken Rockwell's diatribes on camera menu systems for great examples. For this, you'll need to know which options your customers use most – it may not be obvious how your customers like to use your product. If there are three ways to do the same thing, which do most people choose? Possibly different groups of users use your product very differently. See *Chapter 10, Maintainability*, for details on collecting that style of information.

Given that you have data or can at least make educated guesses, check that your menus are arranged suitably, and stay up to date as the product evolves. You will have to make tradeoffs and judgments about what percentage of users is worthwhile caring about. If 10% of people use a feature once a week, is that enough to have it on the main menu? Some customers will be more critical than others; perhaps you have a freemium model, and many of your users pay nothing at all. In such a case, how should their experience be weighed against paying customers' experience? As a tester, it's your job to ask such questions; answering them is beyond the scope of this book and belongs more in the domain of the product owner and UX designer.

Accessing features in multiple ways

Some features are so common that they are available via several different routes. In this case, as with so much UX, the key is consistency: however users choose to access that feature, they should get the same experience. The nightmare for users, and the bug for you to raise, is if different options provide similar but subtly different functionality.

Real-world example – The same page, only different

On one web interface I worked on, our customers had a settings page with two parts. The first was customer-facing, and another section was only visible to our internal staff.

We were users of our own equipment, so the *customer* I visited most often was our organization, to turn on new features or enable new configurations. For our organization, I could reach it in two ways – as an internal user or an admin. I repeatedly used the shortcut of being a real user, only to find half the settings page I needed was missing, forcing me to return to the same page from the admin route.

Test all the ways users can access each function on your product. The following are some examples:

- Main menu
- Right-click menu
- Keyboard shortcuts
- Commands revealed by swiping

Consider how functions are available – whether they're on an application, hardware, or web page. Are they on an admin interface or a customer interface? APIs or user commands? There may be many more for your application, and the goal for all those different methods is that they should behave in the same way.

Ideally, they share an implementation, and other than their external interfaces, the same code is run each time. This will guarantee identical behavior; otherwise, differences will creep in. Testing all the interfaces is the only way to reveal that.

Data structure design

Make your data structures and priorities match your user priorities. This can be particularly difficult to get right since it involves making your low-level data structures align with customer preferences and behavior. However, it's well worth getting right due to the ongoing pain it causes when it goes wrong.

Real-world example – I care about this, but you care about that

On one private cloud service I worked on, new users could be created on various physical servers based on variables such as the customer's location, the cloud server version, and the cloud server loading.

Unfortunately, the variables that our customers cared about didn't match up with the cloud decision. The cloud primarily used the server version to choose the location: it always used the lowest version for safety. Having identified the lowest version servers, it selected between their locations and which was most lightly loaded. However, our customers didn't care about the server version; they just wanted to be placed close to themselves geographically.

We discovered this after leaving a server running an old version in our Chinese data center. Being the safest option, the cloud placed all new customers from across Europe and the US there, despite us having much more geographically appropriate sites. This was a designed functionality rather than a bug, but we constantly had to manage upgrades and check user placement to work around that fundamental mismatch.

To identify this class of issue, you must notice anything mismatched between your product and your users. In the previous example, the cloud worked exactly as designed when it placed all new users in China. This wasn't a bug in the implementation but the specification.

Having altered the specification, fixes may require significant alterations being made to the product architecture. The mismatch exists for a reason, and the bug fix may not seem worth the effort of the necessary changes. Over time, however, these changes do pay back that investment. If you find areas where your product structure differs from your customer behavior and expectations, it's well worth fixing it up.

User interaction overview

For your product, look for different ways to achieve the same thing: the same option in two places, setup wizards, shortcuts, and so on. Consider different ways of navigating the page, such as the tab order on desktop applications and web pages. Which box is selected by default when you first load a page? Does pressing *Enter* correctly submit the information? These may seem like minor issues, but they can annoy regular users.

The field of user interactions is rich and varied, and I cannot do it justice here. These are examples for you to generalize from and apply to your application. Remember these guiding principles: identify and minimize the customer steps, give users a choice over their route, and don't throw errors during changes, but block invalid actions as soon as possible. How you apply them to your product is up to you.

The following section considers the product documentation and the tests it needs.

Testing the documentation

The best documentation is one you don't even need because your product is so simple and easy to use. However, to help any users having difficulty, there should always be a description of how to use it. Ideally, most users will never need to refer to it; if they can work out the product from its interface alone, they don't need documentation, and that's great. The docs are there for when things go wrong.

Testing the documentation first involves specifying what types should be present, and there is a wide variety to choose from:

- Static manuals
- Tooltips
- Help web pages
- Instructional videos

Traditionally, documentation would be a physical manual describing each aspect of the application's functionality piece by piece. Years ago, that would be printed on a dead tree; more recently, it would be a file you could download, but both options have been superseded. Manuals are slow to put together because you need everything ready before you publish the entire document, as opposed to publishing piecemeal as you can with the other types of help. Users have to navigate the document themselves to find the section they need, and it is limited to text and pictures.

Tooltips are a kind of context-sensitive help. Instead of downloading a document about the entire product and then finding the piece you need, a tooltip gives information about the user element they are currently looking at. On the plus side, these are simple and quick to read. However, they can't give examples, answer questions, or use different media types.

Help web pages combine the best aspects of tooltips and user manuals. Like tooltips, they are context-sensitive: a help button on each page can bring up documentation for that page. But unlike tooltips, they can go into greater depth with examples and step-by-step guides and can include pictures and other media. Because they are written per page, you don't have to prepare them all at once, but you can bundle help web pages into a document users can download if they desire.

Instructional videos show detailed guides about how to perform different tasks. They can be costly to set up and produce but provide an excellent description of the areas they cover.

If your application's user base is sufficiently large, you should aim to have tooltips, help pages, and instructional videos. As a tester, you must check that information is present and up to date, with no old screenshots or deprecated advice, and do that for each update.

Feature flags make rolling out new features much easier but can complicate the documentation. You need to ensure that all screenshots and videos show the application with the correct feature flags enabled. They should activate all the new features, but none of the in-development features that haven't been released yet.

Having checked its presence and correctness, the final check for documentation is its usability. Does it make sense? Can you follow it? And, most importantly, does it help you resolve your problems? I hate documentation so useless as to be tautological. The best help talks you through your problems. Compare these two tooltip texts:

- Username: The name of the user.

- Username: The name you will use to log in. It must be between 3 and 16 characters and include only letters and numbers. If your selected username is already in use, please choose another.

Only the second example helps you solve your problems and talks you through possible errors.

As well as documentation, error handling requires dedicated user interface considerations, as described next.

Testing error feedback

Testing the user interface for errors is simultaneously far less frequent and far more critical than that of your primary use cases. It is less important because, hopefully, users encounter error conditions far more rarely. However, once they've hit an error, they will rely on your interface to correct them and help them achieve whatever goal they were aiming for. While these might be rarer cases, handling them well is vital for users who need assistance. This section considers how to present errors and internal failures, how to find spurious errors, and how to avoid displaying errors in the first place.

Preventing errors

As described in *Chapter 7, Testing of Error Cases*, your application should catch problems as early and as specifically as possible. If there are problems in the user input, then let the customer know exactly what is wrong – is the entered text too long, or does it contain invalid characters? Is a number field too high or too low?

The best user interface prevents errors from even happening. If a field's maximum length is 20 characters, stop the user from entering the 21st. If only positive integers are valid, don't let users enter negative signs or decimal points. Protections like this stop errors before they begin. Ideally, your application should provide feedback if users hit these restrictions so that they know why their keystrokes aren't being accepted since it's immensely frustrating. Raise errors with the user as soon as possible, instead of letting them fill in an entire form and then letting them know they got half of it wrong, raise errors as they go.

Presenting errors

The best error messages let the users know what they should do next. There is a class of problems that users can solve for themselves, so you must empower them where possible, rather than them needing to call your support team, which will cost your company time and resources. Identify obvious, fixable problems and check that their error messages are clear. This includes cases such as the following:

- They've reached the maximum number of configured entities: The user needs to delete some entities or extend their allowance

- The feature is not available without a higher subscription: The user needs to purchase an upgrade

- The login session has timed out: The user needs to log in again

- The user's security credentials are incorrect: The user needs to enter the correct details

Following our general rule of making tasks as simple as possible, fixable errors should have links to take users directly to the page that lets them fix the problem so that they don't have to remember and navigate there themselves.

Errors should be as specific as possible. Consider the case of connecting two services. You run service A, in which users enter the address and access token for service B, run by a different company, *company B*. Unfortunately, the connection fails. You should let the user know the reason for that failure because the possible remedies are very different. Consider the different failure modes:

- The user might have entered invalid information: The user should correct their connection details.

- Service A might have had an internal failure and failed to send the request: The user should retry later or raise a support case with your company.

- Service A might have received no response from service B:

  - The destination address might be wrong: The user should correct the address

  - The network connection might have failed

  - Service B might be offline and not responding: The user should retry later or raise a support case with *company B*

- Service A might receive a `500 failure` message from service B indicating it failed: The user should retry later or raise a support case with *company B.*

- Service A might receive a `400 failure` message indicating an invalid token: The user should correct the token.

If your service simply says *Connection failed*, then the user won't know which of those situations has occurred. Should they double-check their access token or raise a support case? If service B has failed, you should let the user know that your service isn't at fault so that users don't mistakenly curse your unreliability. By being as specific as possible, you give the user the best chance to fix the issue.

Note that receiving no response has several possible causes. To help users diagnose that problem, you need to identify those causes and which of them is most likely. Then, you can present them in order for the user to work through them. In this case, they should check the destination address because they can fix that, but otherwise, they need to retry and raise a support case.

Just one action can have a host of failure modes. You will need to carefully survey them so that they can be tracked in requirements and included in your test plan. As you can see from the preceding cases, even simple functions can require many tests.

A final note on presenting errors: all these messages need to be correctly translated into every language you support. As described previously, this needs to be automated so that you can cycle through the possibilities for each failure mode you generate.

Avoiding spurious errors

Raising errors early can result in spurious warnings while you go through an intermediate step, as noted in the *Providing freedom and feedback* section:

- For instance, a date picker with dropdowns for the day and month is initially set to today's date: `5 - June`.

- You want to set it to the end of January, so you start to change it: `31 - June - error, invalid date`.

- The application has quickly and specifically identified that you've entered an invalid date, but only because you were partway through. Then, you make the final change: `31 - January`.

- We saw a similar example when selecting the disc size in VMWare. The error feedback was good; in both cases, the best solution was to be cleverer about the options you were presenting. In VMWare, they needed to choose a more up-to-date measurement of disc size by default. Here, you can swap the day and month fields: `June - 5`.

This little nudge should encourage users to select the month first so that the day can be validated correctly.

While preventing invalid inputs is usually good, it makes things worse in these situations. For instance, if the month is set to June, you can only give date options up to the 30th. Then, I can't select the 31st without choosing the right month first. As a user, that's likely to make my journey longer and more irritating as I discover I can't set the day, have to select the month, then return to set the day a second time. Enforcing such a flow limits user options and provides a worse experience.

> **Real-world example – Do not push this button**
>
> One cloud product I worked on had a dedicated admin interface showing its configuration and state. It also had a handy button to display the most recent error messages to diagnose issues quickly.
>
> Unfortunately, early versions of the product held those errors on the same disc as the running system. If the system's problem was being limited by disc I/O, the last thing it needed was a massive new database query to run, filtering all events for recent errors. During one outage where the system was providing a slow but usable service, I managed to crash it by pressing the button to debug. Make sure presenting errors to your users doesn't make the issue worse.

Why go into all this detail on error presentation in a book about testing? Especially around errors, there are many ways feature specifications could be implemented. The following is a perfectly reasonable requirement:

- Invalid dates are rejected with an error message

However, that still leaves the possibility of the poor user experience described previously. As a tester, you need to check not only that your product meets the requirement but meets it in a pleasing and understandable way. In the domain of UX, there are many options to consider and recommend, which is why I've described them in detail.

Policing errors

For policed limits, such as the configured number of users or connections, prevent users from going over the limit, but let them know why. Consider these:

- **1, Worst**: Let users try to add another user, then silently fail and discard their information
- **2**: Let users try to add another user, then silently fail but keep their information
- **3**: Let users try to add another user, then fail with an error message explaining why
- **4**: Prevent users from adding another user without explaining why
- **5, Best**: Prevent users from adding another user and explain why

Don't let your users waste their time filling in forms if you already know they will fail, especially if that failure is silent and throws away their work. If a form submission fails, keep it populated with their information so that they can try again, except for secure fields such as passwords and payment details that they shouldn't save.

Instead, gray out the **Add User** button with a note explaining that they've reached the limit. This prevents users from causing an error, helps us avoid wasting their time, and lets them know how to achieve their goals.

Spurious errors

When error messages are a part of your application, there are two ways they can go wrong: they might not be shown when they should or they might appear at the wrong time. As well as checking that invalid data displays the correct message, you need to check that error messages don't appear incorrectly. I've seen errors pop up when you type the first character into a text box but disappear when you enter the second, or appear if you click on a text box and then click away again.

Unfortunately, these tests are tricky to automate. You'll need to know the error messages for each element on your pages and add checks to ensure they don't appear. In practice, these can be simpler to run manually since you can easily spot if anything untoward is present.

Internal failures

Finally, consider the feedback you give users if your system cannot process their responses. Perhaps a third party you rely on is unavailable, or an internal part of your system has failed. Returning error messages or displaying obscure failure screens is unhelpful. The error you show to users should be general; they don't know the system's architecture, so all you can do is advise them to try again or, more likely, return later when you've had a chance to resolve the problem. For more details on triggering internal error states, see *Chapter 11, Destructive Testing*.

Even if your system isn't experiencing a failure, its behavior under load can be quite different from running under ideal conditions, as considered next.

UX and loading

You should combine UX testing with load testing to check the behavior in the worst cases. While response times and pages may be acceptable under light load, this could be very different when the system is busier. See *Chapter 12, Load Testing*, for more details. Loading issues can manifest in several ways.

The most obvious is lists that grow in size. If there's a page or a menu with a list of items that can increase over time, such as users or customers, ensure you have proper pagination and searching in place. When the lists are short, you can get away with loading and displaying the whole thing at once, but that rapidly becomes unmanageable if your system experiences any kind of popularity and growth.

Pagination involves loading a certain number of entries, with the remainder split over other pages. The number of entries per page should be configurable, and there should be options to jump to the next and previous pages and the first and last pages. A search feature should be available to search the entire list for anyone who had been relying on their web browser's search feature previously. If those features are missing, raise the task to add them.

As well as static loading of entities, usage also counts as load. Check that response times remain reasonable. It does not matter if your app loads all the correct information if it takes 5 minutes to be ready; no user will wait that long. Response times should form a part of all UX testing, and those should have been explicitly stated in the feature specification. Keep checking those times as you add more system activity and scale.

Next, we will consider gathering more feedback on the user interface by running usability studies.

Running usability studies

A theme throughout this chapter has been the limitation of your point of view and the importance of gaining feedback from real users to find the areas that confuse them. At different times, you can use your naivety about a new feature, for instance, to play the role of a customer, but there is no escaping your experience since you work with your product so much. For that reason, getting feedback from real users is a vital part of UX testing, even more than beta testing or other types of testing the product with users.

There are many different ways to gather feedback from users, of which we will consider four key ones here: recorded sessions, questionnaires, A/B testing, and instrumentation.

Recorded sessions

Recorded sessions involve gathering volunteers and presenting them with the new feature and a task to complete. They get no other instructions but are advised to *think out loud* to explain what they are doing and why during the recorded session.

On the downside, this is an artificial setup. The user might be performing a task very differently from their everyday workflow, and they are aware of being filmed, which will change how they behave. Still, seeing their thought practices, wrong turns, and assumptions can be fascinating. Another disadvantage of this approach is that the result is an unstructured video recording that needs to be analyzed and broken down into usable findings. To work out that, for example, 70% of users couldn't immediately find your new option, you will need to carefully watch all the videos to see how quickly users found it. It's a time-consuming process, but one full of information if you can take the time to extract it.

Questionnaires

A more structured approach that takes less effort to implement is to send out questionnaires. This won't uncover all the subtleties and assumptions of a recorded session but will let you know what issues your customers are aware of and what they like and dislike about using your product. Be aware that not everyone has time to fill out a questionnaire and your responses will more likely be from unhappy users. There may be many more happy users who don't have the time to fill out a form simply to tell you that everything is fine.

Questionnaires can ask closed questions such as which options users prefer, but even more interesting can be the open questions. How do you perform that task? How do you use this product?

In the early days of the development of **Microsoft Excel**, the engineers were proud of its mathematical functionality. You could program complex, interactive equations to present detailed financial and other numerical data. Then, they asked their customers what they used Excel for. They discovered that a major use case was simply storing lists with it. I know I do. The designers had never considered that important, but based on that feedback, they added features to make managing lists easier, such as the ability to define a table with filtering and sorting on different columns.

Who knows what surprises are waiting for you to discover about your product?

A/B testing

A/B testing provides even more structured feedback by offering two or more different versions of a user interface to different groups of users. This is backed up with instrumentation to detect different usage: which buttons and options did they use? A/B testing is used extensively in sales and marketing to determine which adverts customers engage with most, but it is also helpful in purely technical contexts. For instance, does the option for your new feature fit better in one menu or another? Should the button be placed in different locations on a page? While you should still discuss this internally to decide on the best options, you can then present a selection to users to see which is used most.

The disadvantages of A/B testing are that it requires more development time. Unlike questionnaires or recorded sessions, A/B testing needs software changes to prepare the different options. It also needs a system to collect and present usage information. If you do this repeatedly, this becomes easier, but there is a cost to set it up and use it for each new feature. The options are also limited to those you place in front of customers. Maybe all the alternatives you present annoy users, but this method will only let you compare pre-selected choices.

On the plus side, you get very realistic feedback. These are normal users acting in their usual way, not while being recorded or answering questions about their behavior. You can also gather detailed information – for instance, how many milliseconds it takes a user to go through different steps in a process. This data is structured so that you can automatically generate graphs and charts of the results without reading freeform questionnaire replies or watching and categorizing video responses.

Instrumentation

The final method of user feedback considered here is similar to A/B testing but without providing alternatives – tracking user behavior through instrumentation. When you release a new feature, you can gather feedback on how many people used it and how they did so – for instance, by using menus or keyboard shortcuts.

This form of tracking is vital for monitoring sensitive steps such as user signup. Getting new users is essential for any application, especially those aimed at the consumer market and without a hardware component. Signing up always requires a few steps of setup and gathering information, even after these have been simplified as far as possible, so it's important to track how far users get. If 90% of users open the application and enter their name successfully, but only 50% go to use the application, you need to find out why there is such a high failure rate and make that step easier.

Tracking interactions within your application provides the least UX feedback but is also the cheapest to perform. Once a method for gathering and presenting this information is running, adding a new feature has little extra cost. Events tracking different user actions should be added routinely to aid testing and bug diagnosis (see *Chapter 10, Maintainability*, for more details about that). On the downside, it will only show how your existing application performs. You need to use one of the other user feedback methods for other perspectives and ideas.

While you can raise possible issues as part of your testing, they will often need to be investigated with usability studies to confirm whether they are a problem. What might be obvious to some people will be obscure to others, and vice versa. This is especially the case when working out user expectations and determining which issues are features and which are bugs, as discussed next.

Comparing bugs and feature requests

Often, there is a gray area between a bug and a feature request, especially in user interface design. For example, old feature A works, and new feature B works, but you can't use features A and B together. Whether that is a bug or a feature depends on your users' expectations – would they think those features should work together? This is context-dependent and may require usability studies to figure out.

As a tester, you can discover and highlight these limitations. In a mature product, interactions between features may not be apparent and might have been missing from the specification. They will require knowledge and imagination to find whether you are using automated or manual testing.

In terms of wording, spelling and grammar mistakes are bugs; improving the phrasing is a feature request. Text wrapping awkwardly is a feature request, but having it overlap and become unreadable is a bug. Improving hard-to-find elements is likely to be a feature request, but if an option is unavailable, that's a bug. I've seen web pages where the scroll bars were missing and the **Apply** button wasn't accessible at the bottom of the screen. You could only use the page by tabbing to it or changing your screen resolution. Not all issues are so clear-cut. Discuss this with your product manager and make your case for improvements.

Summary

UX testing is a complex but vital part of feature testing. It is far more subjective than other areas, and clear-cut bugs are interspersed with choices that are tradeoffs or matters of opinion. Respectful discussions, which are important throughout testing, are especially needed here.

Some of those gray areas depend on user expectations. What might a user reasonably expect from your new feature? If that functionality is missing, is that a bug or a feature request? This needs consideration from the product owner, UX designer, and yourself.

In general, when performing UX testing, always look out for anything confusing that you struggle to remember or have to attempt twice. If a function is challenging for you, who uses this product full time, it will be even harder for your customers who only have a few minutes to devote to mastering it.

When you've found a problem, remember that identifying an area for improvement is vastly easier than finding good solutions to improve it. Make suggestions and offer ideas, but also defer to the design experience within the team.

In the next chapter, we will move on from aspects of features that directly affect your users to protections we hope they will not even notice: security testing.

9

Security Testing

"Si vis pacem, para bellum," adapted from Publius Flavius Vegetius Renatus

("If you want peace, prepare for war")

In the previous chapter, you learned about techniques you can use when performing user experience testing. Although it may not appear as important as the actual functionality of your application, this is a prominent area that has a massive impact on your customers' experience of your product. Next, we come to another place of testing where the importance may not be immediately obvious but can harbor some of the most severe bugs your application can suffer from – **security testing**.

Security testing is an extension of functional testing with a specific focus on security issues. There is an overlap with the tests described in previous chapters, such as text field inputs, but here, we will consider specific examples and tests for security-related topics. Security testing aims to ensure the **CIA** triad of the **confidentiality**, **integrity**, and **availability** of information. Data should be confidential, only available to the correct owners, and always accurate and available.

In a way, security testing is the opposite of user experience testing. UX testing is unique to your application and subjective. Security testing, in contrast, involves so many shared technologies and techniques that many bugs are well known. The main advice here is to not perform security testing on your own. Use some of the widely available tools that search for known issues for you. Your role is to guide and augment that testing with considerations specific to your application. As with other areas, this is a vast and growing area of software testing, of which this chapter only provides an overview.

In this chapter, you will learn about the following topics:

- Defining your attack area
- Security scans and code analysis
- Tests for logging in
- Tests for string and file inputs
- Common web attacks

- Handling personally identifiable information
- Bug bounty programs
- Security beyond the application

Security testing is fun because you get to be an attacker, attempting all manner of invalid access and incorrect behavior to gain more permissions and control than you are allowed to ensure your application blocks them all. As the Latin adage at the beginning of this chapter states, only by preparing for attacks can you ensure your application will survive peacefully and securely.

Advantages and disadvantages of security testing

Like user experience and maintainability testing, the key advantage of dedicated security testing is that it is the best way to discover this critical class of issue for your business. Its main advantages and disadvantages are summarized in this table:

Advantages	Disadvantages
The best way to discover security vulnerabilities	Requires a wide breadth of testing
Many tools available	Requires dedicated knowledge and skills
Easy to automate	Constantly evolving security vulnerabilities and threats
	Only part of a broader security story

Table 9.1 – Advantages and disadvantages of security testing

Unlike exploratory testing or user experience testing, where a lack of familiarity can initially be an advantage, security testing requires domain knowledge from the start. This chapter will provide an introduction to that, and there are many other books and tools to automate and make this task easier. Security testing also requires a breadth of knowledge from testing user interfaces and APIs, web technologies, through databases, and down to networking and even hardware issues. This chapter will give you an overview of all those areas and their initial approaches.

On the plus side, focusing on this area is the best way to find security-related issues as they require dedicated tests and tools. There are some overlaps with other areas – such as the inputs used when testing error cases in black-box testing – but generally, these are tests you would not otherwise run. Since security is a shared issue for so many companies, many tools are available to help you with this form of testing, and it's easy to automate. In this chapter, I will describe some of the techniques they use so that you understand what kinds of testing they are doing and why.

Security threats are constantly evolving as new systems introduce new weaknesses and new vulnerabilities are discovered. In this area, more than any other aspect of testing, it's vital to stay up to date since you can't rely on past test results to indicate that you're currently secure.

The security of your product is a much broader problem than the tests you run. It starts with the design, includes the coding, and reviews, and extends into your organization's policies on everything from network design to door access controls, from email policies to password requirements. The **ISO27001** specification provides a comprehensive list of security considerations, most of which are beyond this book's scope. Here, we will only cover part of the story – the technical security of the product you ship. We will start by listing the different types of attacks.

Attack types

The security threats to your application fall into two classes – acquiring access to restricted information and gaining control of private systems. The first class is easier and more common. Data leaks involve anything from accidentally allowing public access to data stores to using outdated cryptographic hashes, giving sufficiently resourced attackers the chance to break their encoding. It's harder to control remote systems, but anywhere there is an input there is a chance to enter invalid data that will trick your application into obeying an attacker.

As a simple example, a 404 content injection attack involves creating a link that makes a trusted third party display a message of your choice. For example, you can enter `www.example.com/visit_my_company` in your browser. If `example.com` is vulnerable to this attack (which it isn't, in reality), it would display an error such as **The URL /visit_my_company was not found on this server.**

You have now made `example.com` display text, which you chose. While it is in an error message, you can craft the text to make it appear realistic, and guide users from that trusted site to a malicious one you have prepared.

This chapter describes how to test for common attacks that seek to reveal your information or control your system. This can be a thankless area of testing; if you do your job well, no customer will ever notice. A failure, however, could leave your company at risk of paying millions of dollars to ransomware attackers or in regulatory fines, not to mention the reputational damage, so pay close attention.

Next, we will consider the first stage of securing your system: discovering its attack area.

Discovering the attack area

What is an outsider's view of your company from a technical viewpoint? The first stage in security testing is working out your public presence, which is your attack area. You most likely run many public machines both for your company and the product you provide. Even if you only have a website, that is your attack area.

Are you sure about which machines are public? Search for all the records under your primary domain. DNS records are easy to add but difficult to remove – it is hard to be sure they're not used by some rare but essential service. They tend to accrue over time, so if you are in a mature company, there may be many. Scan them all to see whether a machine is running on that address. Anything you find in your scan is part of your attack area.

Similar logic applies to any public IP ranges your company owns and runs. Some of these may be directly related to running your product, while others may host internal machines for your company's use. Again, there will be machines you know about, but you need to scan the whole range for any others you weren't aware of.

And finally, check for all machines hosted out of cloud providers. These should have DNS records and be found by the first scan, but they may not. You need to include all the machines on all the cloud providers your company uses for the scan to be complete.

This book is about testing new features of products, so many of these services are beyond the scope of what you strictly need to test. If your VPN server is insecure, that is not a job for a software tester unless you are in a tiny company where everyone chips in with everything. However, products often have a presence on the web, and the only way to discover any old testing servers that everyone had forgotten about is to do a complete scan. Once you have the full list, you can divide it into those owned by the IT or operations teams, as opposed to the ones you are testing as part of product development. Shut down any servers you no longer need to reduce your attack area.

With that list of machines, you only need to identify different server types. If you have 10 edge servers with shared configuration, then you only need to test one of them. To be sure, you need a configuration management system that enforces the same settings everywhere. If you are manually configuring them in any way, you will need to run a scan against all of them to check that there are no mistakes. Repeat that categorization for all your other servers. How many different types do you have?

As well as public machines, compile a list of internal servers and server types. If a device inside your network has been compromised, what connections could it make, and what other access could it gain? You will need an inventory tracking system to log the machines on your network, as well as their types and owners. You can also run network scans internally to identify any addresses in use that aren't in your inventory.

Armed with the lists of addresses for internal and external machines, you can move on to running security scans.

Running security scans

While this chapter describes some core security testing requirements, it is unusual because this area has so much shared code and common vulnerabilities that third-party companies have extensively automated it. Don't start security testing from scratch; you will never achieve the depth and breadth of knowledge compiled by third-party tools.

Security scanners can quickly find common security issues such as these:

- **Unnecessarily open ports**: Accepting inputs to services you don't need unnecessarily increases your attack area

- **Out-of-date software and libraries**: Libraries are kept up to date with the latest security fixes, so running old software leaves you vulnerable

- **Out-of-date security hash functions**: Older, less secure hash functions can be compromised. meaning attackers could break encrypted communications

- **Connections that don't require encryption**: Accidentally sending messages in clear text allows eavesdropping

- **Common web security vulnerabilities** (such as CSRF, CORS, or content injection): See the *Testing web application security* section for more details

These are just examples among many possible findings, and each will be prioritized by the security scan. These can be broken down into a grid of how easy they are to exploit and the impact they would have if they were:

Impact Likelihood	Negligible	Minor	Moderate	Major	Severe
Highly likely	Low	Medium	High	High	High
Likely	Low	Medium	Medium	High	High
Possible	Low	Low	Medium	Medium	High
Unlikely	Low	Low	Medium	Medium	Medium
Highly unlikely	Low	Low	Low	Medium	Medium

Table 9.2 – Determining the risk of a vulnerability given its impact and likelihood

So, if the likelihood of a vulnerability being exploited was **Unlikely**, but its impact was **Major**, the overall risk would be **Medium**. To help you choose a security scanner to use for your testing, OWASP maintains an extensive list of different security scanners here: `https://owasp.org/ www-community/Vulnerability_Scanning_Tools`.

Security scan results

Your aim with this testing should be to use the available tools against your attack area, then augment that testing with checks customized to your application. Security scanners can check for all the issues and vulnerabilities in old versions of operating systems and web servers and any problems with their configuration. Your task is to understand what these tools are doing and to extend them.

First, security scans run **Nmap** or equivalent port scanning software to discover all the open ports. Some ports are used to provide your product's service, but are there any surprises? Are any ports open but don't need to be? The next simple step for security is to disable all the unnecessary ports on your machines, which quickly and simply blocks access to potentially vulnerable services. For services you require, ensure they are set to secure versions. Port 80 HTTP interfaces should redirect to 443 HTTPS, and similarly for FTP and others.

Real-world example – The over-enthusiastic security scan

In one company where I worked, we ran regular scans of our external addresses, then set up the same company to run a scan from inside our network.

The scan began, and machines immediately started to lose connection with one another. It was run out of hours, so it took a few minutes to spot the issue and identify the cause, but we rapidly shut the scan down, and our systems recovered.

The security scan had found open ports and had tried to connect. The connections had failed, but even the attempt was enough to knock out the live connections between machines and cause the communications failures we'd seen. We updated our systems before attempting that scan again.

For each open port, you need to list all the supported protocols. Most of the time, there will be a one-to-one mapping, such as one port for SNMP or telnet. But one port could support multiple protocols – for instance, both an API and a web interface could be available on a web port. You must list all the available protocols, not just the open ports.

Scanners are limited in how much they will use your application. Some only scan addresses and ports, while others load web pages and check for common vulnerabilities. However, to completely test your particular application or web page, you will need to design a custom set of tests to exercise your specific features.

Security scan reports can propose many low-risk recommendations, such as disabling ping responses. Even the critical errors need careful triage; you might be running an application with a known vulnerability but never exposing it due to how you use it. Security scans can't tell that. They simply look at the version number, so you need to consider each report individually for what it means for your application.

It's best to use scanning tools in conjunction with code analysis to detect issues, as described next.

Running code analysis

Part of your security approach should be source code analysis, which can identify security issues before the application is even run. This is a form of **static testing**, as described in *Chapter 6, White-Box Functional Testing*. Like linting, this automatic check can detect potential security issues such as being vulnerable to SQL injection attacks or buffer overflows.

Many tools are available for such analysis, and the development team should ensure they run one before the code reaches the test team.

Such tools are easy to run and can be built into deployment pipelines to check each code change. However, they can flag false positive results, and it can be challenging to uncover some classes of vulnerability, such as authentication or access control. They also can't find configuration issues, as they only examine the code rather than how it is deployed.

Despite its weaknesses, code analysis can quickly find important classes of bugs and is a necessary step before proceeding with security testing. Before running the code and starting dynamic tests, there is one other static check to perform.

Upgrading everything

Upgrade everything now. The first finding from any code analysis or external security scans is reporting any versions that are out of date. Hosted services might take care of some of this for you, but you must regularly update any versions you control. Operating systems, web servers, programming languages, and all their related packages and extensions must be periodically upgraded. Schedule a repeating task to stay up to date with the latest patches and releases. Dependency management systems such as **Poetry** can ensure packages stay up to date during development.

While it is easy to say you should keep everything up to date, performing those upgrades and resolving any dependencies can be very difficult. Compared to adding new features, performing an upgrade that gives no tangible benefit can be a lower priority since, in the best case, your application works exactly as it did before.

In addition, making low-level changes like these risks introducing serious errors that are hard to predict, so you will need to run an in-depth set of regression tests to verify there are no breakages. The longer you have left it and the more out of date you are, the more painful it will be. However, upgrades are necessary, and all your other security measures rely on applying the latest updates and patches. So, bite the bullet, get it done, and stay up to date in the future to make it an easier task.

Given that code analysis and the security scan have passed, and you are running the latest versions, you can begin security testing in earnest, starting with the most basic security function: logging in.

Logging in

Logging in is vital to many applications, so much so that many standard frameworks provide this functionality. Here, you should use white-box knowledge: how much does your application use a standard framework, and how much have you implemented for yourselves? If you rely entirely on a third-party framework, you can keep your testing brief and focus elsewhere because others have tested and used that code. Even then, you need to check that it has been used correctly, such as requiring a login for all restricted screens. If your application implements most or all logging-in functionality itself, you need a far more comprehensive test plan, as described here.

Logging in comprises two functions: authentication and authorization. Authenticating involves verifying the identity of a user and proving they are who they say they are. Authorization grants access to some parts of your application based on that identity. At a basic level, there may be administrator and user privileges, where some pages are only accessible to administrators. The following sections consider testing those two functions.

Authentication

Your application can authenticate users in many ways, from traditional usernames and passwords to sending verification codes, time-based one-time passwords, biometrics, and **multi-factor authentication** (**MFA**). Since passwords are still ubiquitous, we will begin by discussing them, then move on to general issues. When using usernames and passwords, consider these requirements as standard:

- The application should not indicate whether a username has already been signed up
- Input fields should be resilient to injection attacks (see the *Testing injection attacks* section)
- All passwords should be suitably complex
- The application should handle multiple logins by the same user
- Users should be logged out after some time
- There should be a mechanism to reset a user's password, which requires the user's current password
- If the user has forgotten their password, they should be able to reset it using a pre-verified mechanism, such as an email
- When resetting a user's password, all current sessions should be logged out
- There should be rate limits on login attempts
- There should be a logout button that prevents any future requests from succeeding until the user logs in again

Each of these deserves tests in your test plan. The following sections describe these in more detail while considering tests for usernames, passwords, and the login session overall.

Tests for usernames

The first operation users perform in many systems is picking a username, so make that process as painless as possible.

From a security point of view, it's best not to indicate that an email address or username is already in use. That data leakage may be innocuous for most services, but if, for instance, you are providing a web page to help people cheat on their spouses, any information leakage is a critical bug.

When attempting to reset your password, you can give a conditional message: *If an account exists for that address, we have emailed instructions on how to reset your password.* That explains what is happening without admitting whether the email address is in use.

Login attempts also shouldn't indicate whether a username is already using your application. Don't have two different error messages, one for an incorrect username and another for an incorrect password; just say that the combination doesn't work. Look out for more subtle indications too, such as the speed of the response. If the username is incorrect, your app could respond quickly that the login will fail, whereas performing the necessary hashes to check the password might take longer. The same processing should occur for both failures – check the password hashes even if the username is incorrect so that processing time doesn't indicate whether the email address is in use.

However, it's harder to avoid leaking information when initially signing up for a service. Silently failing because a username is in use is unhelpful to a user, compared to telling them they should try an alternative. You'll have to weigh the security benefits versus the user experience costs for your service to decide what error to display.

For hardware servers, the login screen should give as little information as possible about the system to avoid helping attackers. This may be a page available on the public internet, so displaying the manufacturer and version of a server allows attackers to look up potential exploits. If only authorized users should be accessing that server, keep the login page as simple as possible. On web services where you hope the world will connect, you can make your login page more inviting.

Consider different email addresses that route to the same account. The email specification states that `joe.bloggs@example.com` and `joe.bloggs+anything@example.com` are equivalent, known as **sub-addressing**. Anything between a + and @ symbols in the username is ignored for the process of routing the email. Addresses with dots added to the username are also equivalent. Not all email providers support those functions, but Gmail supports both. Since the strings are different, most applications treat them as entirely different users, even though they are routed to the same person. How does your application handle that case? So long as it works, it's an invaluable tool for generating many test accounts.

Tests for passwords

Passwords should enforce complexity requirements to prevent users from entering overly simple passwords. When lists of stolen passwords are published, the most common choices are depressingly obvious, showing how tempting it is for users to pick easily-guessable options. However, the fault also lies with the services that allow those passwords. Make sure your application requires better security from your users.

Stricter password rules can be as simple as requiring different classes of symbols, such as numbers and special characters. It can be more effective to use an algorithm to detect the overall complexity of a password by taking many factors into account, including length and common character combinations. However, those requirements can be harder to describe to users.

There should be a limit to how many guesses a user is allowed within a given period. This blocks attempts to guess users' passwords by firing many automated login attempts. If anyone exceeds the limit, they need to wait a configured period to try again. You'll need to determine how many guesses should be allowed and how long the backoff period is, and all those values should be recorded in the feature specification.

There needs to be a mechanism to reset the password, requiring the user to reenter their current one as a precaution. Once they've reset their password, that should invalidate all older sessions.

> **Real-world example – How not to reset a password**
>
> On one service I used a few years ago, I forgot my password. They didn't have an automatic reset mechanism (the first red flag), so I had to email their customer support to regain access. They helpfully emailed my password to me so I could log in again, in plain text, in the email body. Needless to say, I canceled that service as soon as possible and warned them about their security policy.

All user passwords should be hashed rather than stored in plain text; it should not be possible for you to email a user's password back to them or read it at all. That is the absolute basic requirement for password security, but it has to be stated once. If the user forgets their password, it is gone forever.

However, it should always be possible for users to reset their passwords, usually by emailing a reset link to create a new one. For automated tests, you'll need a system that can receive and parse emails to check that, and many services offer that functionality. Your email needs to be worded carefully to avoid being blocked by spam filters; emails encouraging users to click on links can rightly be treated with suspicion. You'll need to regularly check that a defined list of common email providers has accepted them.

As well as the user's primary password, remember to also hash any other passwords or PINs they have to enter as part of your service. If they can password-protect documents or recordings, for instance, that field needs to have hashing, just like their login. If any of those sensitive fields are visible in the configuration or the logs, raise that as a bug.

> **Real-world example – Too much marketing spam**
>
> In one company where I worked, we started to get complaints that our emails were blocked as spam. This was disastrous – our service used emails to invite users, tell them about meetings, reset their passwords, and other critical features. They had worked before and hadn't changed but were now being rejected.
>
> It turned out an enthusiastic marketing team member had run an email campaign that had generated so many complaints that some mail providers had blocked our domain. That prevented other marketing emails but also emails crucial to using our service. We rapidly got in contact to get our domain off those lists and gave the marketing team a dedicated domain for future communications.

Does your application work with password managers? Many users don't remember all their passwords but instead use one master login to a password manager, which can then store very secure, random strings to log in to different sites. Those managers work hard to be compatible with websites, but there can be issues, especially around the interface. For a complete check, you'll need to try the popular password manager services against common web browsers.

API authentication

As well as users, consider all programmatic access to your application. APIs typically use either challenge-response authentication or authentication keys to grant access. Both types require a standard set of tests:

- Valid authentication details should be accepted

- Invalid authentication details should be rejected

- Authentication details can be updated, after which the new details are accepted and the old details are rejected

- Authentication details can be revoked, after which they are rejected

These can be used at each layer of your system, from external APIs, between internal modules, down to databases and data stores, so check the behavior at each level.

Tests for login sessions

Test that all pages/screens requiring a login can only be accessed by authenticated users.

Your application should handle multiple logins. The simplest is to only allow one session at a time, logging out any older sessions when a new session starts, although that limits the user experience. If you allow numerous live sessions, then you have to handle users submitting out-of-date information. Let's look at the following case:

- A user loads page A in browser tab 1

- The user loads page A in browser tab 2 and makes a change

- The user submits page A in browser tab 1 with out-of-date data

The application should store user state per session rather than per user so that multiple logins on the same account can use the application simultaneously. For sites with simple, atomic actions such as creating users, that is less of a problem. However, in applications that include short-term states, such as being halfway through a learning exercise or test, things could go wrong if the same user is using them twice.

Users should be logged out after a certain period, which is a simple, albeit time-consuming, test. If that value is configurable, you can reduce it to shorten your wait.

Finally, the **Logout** button should instantly ensure that no further requests are accepted for that session. In a simple application, that is easy to implement and test. However, as applications grow, if a single token is used for logging in to different parts of the application, you need to check that it is invalidated everywhere without waiting for the timeout.

Other login methods

Ideally, there should also be MFA using a separate secure mechanism such as a text message or email. The importance of that will depend on the sensitivity of your product; it would be a higher priority for banking or medical applications, for instance. You can also use SSO from various providers to avoid many of those issues and leave these security considerations to them. Whichever additional methods your application supports also need a section in the test plan.

Another way to avoid these issues is to require time-limited sign-in codes. This means your application doesn't need passwords and leaves security issues with the email provider. On the downside, temporary codes make signing in longer since you must request a code, check your email, and then enter it instead of entering your usernames and passwords. Still, they can be helpful in applications where you sign in for a long time, such as chat apps.

One issue with such codes is when cloning a PC. Here, two applications can end up with the same unique token, which causes bugs. That's difficult to avoid in practice, other than advising users to log out before cloning.

Logging in is crucial to so many applications that it needs significant testing in even the most commonly run test plans. Remember to test the negative cases – verify users who should have access and check that unauthorized access is rejected. Every method you support and every screen involved (such as signing up, logging in, password reset, and logging out) all need to be thoroughly covered.

Once logged in, the next question is how much access you should have. That is determined by authorization, which is considered next.

Authorization

Once a user has logged in, you must check that they have the proper privileges. Authorization schemes can vary from a distinction between admins and users to an entire system of group memberships and multiple permission levels. The critical point here is the negative testing – attempting invalid access. With a lower-level login, can that user reach unauthorized pages? The links might be hidden, but can you access the pages by entering the URL? In addition to higher privileged pages, can users see information from other users? Those are standard checks to run every release.

> **Real-world example – Signed in or not?**
>
> A new starter had trouble accessing an internal system in one place where I worked. He could sign in successfully but couldn't access any of the tools.
>
> Different user groups had access to different tools on that system, so I checked his username, group memberships, and group permissions, and everything was set up correctly. Everything worked fine for everyone else.
>
> The problem turned out to be that he logged in with a capital letter in his username. The login process was not case sensitive, so he could log in successfully, but the check for group membership was case sensitive, so the system didn't think he belonged to any groups and gave him no access. Using capital letters was the key.

Privilege changes are also important. If a user has had access revoked, does that take immediate effect? Does it apply across the system? If the user is logged in at the time, do the changes affect their current session, or are they logged out? They shouldn't be able to continue with their old permissions just because they were logged in at the time.

Privilege escalation attacks aren't easy, and some simple steps limit the possibility of falling victim to one. As mentioned previously, keep up to date with your system's latest patches and releases to avoid falling prey to any known bugs. Limit the number of accounts with admin, root, and high privilege levels. Regularly review which logins need increased permissions. The fewer accounts, the less chance one will be compromised. Within those accounts, check for default or weak passwords, and set up MFA where possible.

Once a user has logged out, you need more negative tests to ensure they no longer have access to any pages, and that you can then log in as a new user. Can you only see the new users' pages and none of the previous users'? Are notifications sent for the old user even though you're logged into a new account?

How quickly can you log a user out? In the event of discovering a compromised account and a rogue employee, you need to be able to rapidly revoke their access to all your systems. If you have to wait until user lists are synched overnight, they could do significant damage in the meantime. Check how fast users lose their permissions, and check every system that login applies to, not just your core applications. Are they deleted from your test accounts? Check anywhere that maintains user lists and doesn't synchronize them with the main one.

When you have logged in with the correct credentials, you can begin testing in earnest.

Testing injection attacks

Any inputs into your system are a possible way for a hacker to gain access or inject malicious data. Everything entered into your system should be checked, and as a tester, you get to play the role of the hacker, probing your application's defenses. We met some of these attacks in *Chapter 5, Black-Box Functional Testing*, and the different input types users can enter. In text fields, the primary attacks are **SQL injection**, **HTML injection**, **code injection**, and **Cross-Site Scripting** (**XSS**) attacks.

SQL injection

SQL injection involves entering a string that, if naively copied into a line of code, will perform unauthorized database changes instigated by an attacker. Consider this snippet of Python that uses a string without validating it first:

```
SQLCommand = 'INSERT INTO users VALUES (username);'
```

This works fine if `username` is `"Simon Amey"`:

```
SQLCommand = 'INSERT INTO users VALUES ("Simon Amey");'
```

However, it leaves it open to attack if the `username` string contains control characters:

```
username = 'Simon Amey"); DROP TABLE users;':
```

This now makes the string look like this:

```
SQLCommand = 'INSERT INTO users VALUES ("Simon Amey"); DROP
TABLE users;");'
```

Adding semicolons to the string has split the command into three. The first command inserts the new name into the users as expected, but that doesn't matter because the second command drops the whole table. The third command, with the closed bracket, is the remains of the initial string and is invalid.

To prevent this, all control characters should be escaped so that they are read as characters rather than acted on. There are simple functions in the different programming languages to achieve that. However, developers must remember to run that function on every text input field, so it's your job to see whether they've missed one.

HTML injection

A similar vulnerability leads to HTML injection. Strings entered by the user are often presented back to them within the user interface and in emails. If text inputs aren't validated when entered, they may be written into HTML and change the page's look. At a simple level, you can test for this by adding HTML tags to your inputs:

```
username = "<b>Simon Amey</b>"
```

If your username appears in bold, then the inputs aren't being validated, and malicious users could disrupt your pages far more than just changing how their name is displayed. Remember to check all inputs displayed to the user anywhere in your application. In one system I worked on, our web pages were protected against this attack, but the HTML characters took effect in emails sent out to users.

> **Real-world example – Testing the test tracking system**
>
> We recorded security tests in a test tracking system at one company where I worked. We entered the different cases, such as the input being too long and containing HTML or JavaScript tags.
>
> When we read that test later, the page failed to display correctly – the test tracking system suffered from the bugs we were looking for in our product. It rendered HTML tags and executed JavaScript, showing popup boxes whenever we returned to that test case. It made the system unusable. Although it only affected test cases we wrote and viewed ourselves, it didn't look like we could affect anyone else. We reported the bug to their support team, but it still hadn't been fixed months later. Our product didn't suffer from any of those issues.

Code injection

Code injection attacks attempt to exploit weaknesses in coding implementation to execute arbitrary, malicious code on the server. Much like SQL and HTML injection attacks, these rely on unsanitized strings from the user being trusted and used in internal functions.

One type of code injection attack relies on functions such as `eval()` that exist in PHP and Python. It takes a string as an argument but then executes it as code. This is a powerful way to solve some difficult programming challenges, but its use is heavily discouraged because of the associated security risks. While exceedingly difficult to exploit (the likelihood is highly unlikely; see *Table 9.2*), its impact is severe because it can let an attacker run code and potentially remotely control your server, giving it a high severity and a medium risk overall.

To exploit this issue, an attacker would need to find a point in the code that used an `eval()` function on a string that could be altered by user input. That is a thankfully rare occurrence but watch out for any possibility of it in your application's code.

Another method of code injection is the famous **buffer overflow attack**, in which an attacker writes too much into a fixed-length buffer. This fills the buffer with data, then writes over other sections of memory. That other memory can include the return pointer for the function, potentially letting the attack redirect program execution to their own, malicious code. This class of vulnerability is again difficult to exploit in practice but has severe consequences.

Higher-level languages with error checking such as Java and Python are immune to this type of attack, but if your application uses lower-level languages such as C or C++, you will need to check for it.

Cross-site scripting attacks

The final example we'll consider here is in the same family, where unvalidated inputs allow malicious users to alter a website's behavior. This time, rather than HTML or SQL being added, scripts are run on whoever reads that page. This is an XSS attack. This time, the malicious input includes HTML tags to add in commands from a scripting language, typically JavaScript:

```
Username = "Simon Amey<script>alert('Test')</script>"
```

If this is naively stored and presented on a web page, an alert box will pop up, providing an obvious and safe way to check that this vulnerability is present. If it is, malicious users could add far more damaging code. Again, this needs to be checked for all inputs.

The following section considers vulnerabilities associated with uploading files to you application.

Validating file inputs

Any files that users can upload to your system also need to be scanned for malicious content. For the filename, check all the variables listed in *Chapter 5*, *Black-Box Functional Testing*. These tests are standard across many applications, and this section draws heavily from the **OWASP** website, which I highly recommend you visit for further reading and details.

Testing file uploads

For the file uploads, consider testing the following requirements:

- Only authorized users should be allowed to upload files
- Only accept specific file extensions
- Check the file type rather than relying on the Content-Type header
- Check the minimum and maximum file sizes
- Virus-check all files
- Protect the file against **Cross-Site Request Forgery** (**CSRF**) attacks (see the *CSRF attacks* section for more details)

Acting as an attacker, you should attempt all those attacks to see whether your system is vulnerable.

Within the file, does your application scan and protect itself against common attacks? There are several common enough to deserve dedicated tests:

- Billion laughs (`.zip` or `.xml` bombs)
- Exploiting vulnerabilities in file processing
- Overwriting system files
- XSS or CSRF

The **billion laughs** attack includes a `.xml` file with 1 entity with 10 sub-entities, each of which has 10 sub-entities, and so on until the whole expands to a billion different entities. In a famous example, those were simply strings saying *lol*, hence a *billion laughs*. If an application naively attempts to parse the file, that can drain resources to the point of causing processes to be killed for requiring too much memory. Other attacks of that form are also possible with nested `.zip` files, which expand to enormous sizes.

Vulnerabilities in file processing can be exploited when commonly used tools suffer from security issues. Then, carefully crafted files can give unwarranted access, up to remote code execution in some cases. You can avoid these by always staying up to date and checking for the tell-tale signs of files attempting to use those exploits, such as your monitoring flagging up multiple upload attempts and scanning for known vulnerabilities. Look for whichever exploits are doing the rounds as you read this.

Testing file storage

Once your files have been uploaded, you need to test their storage. Consider the following tests:

- Are uploaded files encrypted at rest in your chosen storage location?
- What processes can access the files?
  - Check that both the necessary access is available and that other processes can't access them
- If the files contain **personally identifiable information** (**PII**), are they stored in the correct geographical location?
  - See the *Handling personally identifiable information* section for more details
- What are your storage limits, and when will you hit them at your current rate of usage?
- What are your storage costs?
- What are the maximum upload and download rates your application can support?

Any of those questions can uncover a critical issue with your storage model.

File uploads can also attempt to overwrite system files by including the same name. Again, check your system and add blocks against them. XSS and CSRF attacks will be considered in more detail later.

File uploads are common to both applications and websites, but there are classes of security concerns that only apply to web applications. These will be described in the next section.

Testing web application security

There are many common web security issues that you should protect yourself against, of varying degrees of severity. If you run a bug bounty program with these present, these are likely to be the first reports that you get. You will receive many duplicates of the same basic issues, so these are the faults to fix first to encourage researchers to explore more deeply.

Some tools step through these kinds of attacks, but here, we will describe how these attacks work and why.

Information leakage

An attacker looking for vulnerabilities to exploit needs to know what system they are attacking: what kind of web server is this, and what version is running? Web servers generally present this information in headers because it may help client web browsers with compatibility, but that information is not usually needed. Instead, it lets attackers know what exploits are likely to work, so it's best to disable it. There are settings to implement that, which vary between different servers; whichever you use, make sure that's in place.

Avoiding information leakage can go as far as security scans, which recommend disabling ping responses to obscure even the presence of servers. However, these are usually discoverable using **Nmap** – if they are on the network, they should respond to some requests at least – so unless you only allow specific IP connections, you may as well leave pings active for use by the operations team.

Balanced with common sense, give away as little information about your system as possible.

404 content injection

As we saw previously, if a user types an invalid URL, you shouldn't echo their text back to them, or if you do, it should be checked to ensure it isn't vulnerable to HTML content injection, as described previously.

While it doesn't give access to any data, the problem with this attack is that an attacker can put their words on a site you own.

For instance, going to the site www.example.com/wrong might display an error message on the form:

```
The URL /wrong was not found on this server.
```

This is a genuine page served by www.example.com, but now, it has the text you entered in the URL as part of the page. Despite the words surrounding that, it might trick a user into reading your message. Here, we have simply used the word wrong, but an attacker could direct users to an alternative, malicious website:

```
%2f%20This%20site%20is%20on%20maintenance%20Please%20
visit%20www.devil.com
```

If the web browser is also vulnerable to HTML content injection, you might be able to make the malicious URL a link to encourage victims to click on it. It is simple enough to alter the configuration to set up a customized 404 page that is displayed to all invalid URLs and doesn't echo back the user input. This makes your brand look more professional by letting you choose how that page looks, and where to redirect people.

Even when browsers are protected against simple content injection attacks, as described previously, encoding control characters in the URL can trigger other issues. The `..%2f` sequence translates into `../` when encoded in hexadecimal format. It causes different errors compared to simply adding an invalid URL, so also check those patterns.

Clickjacking

You should make sure your application's web pages have their **Content Security Policy** correctly set or the older **X-Frame-Options HTTP header** to prevent your site from being loaded as a frame on another, possibly malicious location.

Clickjacking works by overlaying an invisible frame over a valid frame that the user wants to use. The user attempts to click on a button on the visible frame but actually clicks a hidden button that grants the attacker extra privileges or access.

To prevent that, you can specify that your page cannot be loaded as an iframe within a page on another domain. These are options you can enable for your site and then leave in place; if you don't, then bug bounty researchers will remind you about them.

Long password attack

When logging into a website, the username is simply compared against the list of users configured on a system. The password, however, isn't stored in plain text but is hashed, so any password a user enters has to go through a computationally intensive transformation before it can be checked.

Usually, people log in rarely enough, and with passwords short enough, that even though password hashing takes some CPU time, it is well within a server's capabilities. However, if the password field isn't limited, an attacker could enter a colossal password, say a million characters long. Running the hashing algorithm on that can require so much CPU time that other login attempts fail, causing a **Denial-of-Service (DoS)** attack on the server.

All text fields should have length limits applied to them, especially the **Password** field, because of that vulnerability.

Host header attacks

Every web request contains a host header indicating the website they are trying to reach so that a server hosted on a single IP address can host several different sites. DNS resolution on the domain will direct requests to that server; then, the host header tells the server which site the request is for.

A **host header attack** involves sending an invalid domain, one not hosted on that server. Your application should reject that, but a poorly configured server might redirect the request to the specified domain. This implies the server trusts the host header field, even though it can be set by clients, possibly maliciously.

This doesn't cause a problem on its own, but it can be used in conjunction with other attacks to reroute requests from a trusted domain to malicious ones. The configuration is simple enough: web servers should only accept requests for domains they host and reject anything else.

CSRF attacks

CSRF attacks can occur when a user is logged into vulnerable site A but then visits malicious site B. Without protection in place, site B can include a link to site A to perform some action, and because the user is logged in, the browser will automatically have the session cookie, which gives access. That malicious request could retrieve information or make changes, such as altering the email address for the account to provide the attacker with more privileges.

You can check this on your system by seeing whether the credentials are stored in cookies on the user side. If those are all you need for access, then the site is vulnerable. The protection here is to add a CSRF token included in each request. Every form on your website needs to add that, so check whether any were missed.

CORS attacks

Cross-Origin Resource Sharing (CORS) allows websites to load adverts or other information from other sites rather than hosting everything locally. A strict policy should ensure resources are only loaded from necessary sites; however, policies require manual updates, so there is a temptation to make them too lax and accept requests from too many places.

As with CSRF attacks, CORS attacks can occur when a user is logged into **Vulnerable site A** but then visits **Malicious site B**. The victim executes a malicious script on site B, which issues a request to site A:

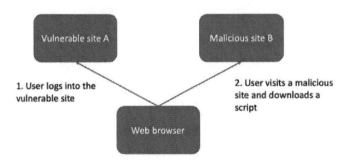

Figure 9.1 – CORS attack stage 1

For the attack to work, site A must have an open **Access Control Allow Origin (ACAO)** policy and an open **Access Control Allow Credentials (ACAC)** policy. If that is the case, the request is validated, and credential information is sent from the browser to **Malicious site B**:

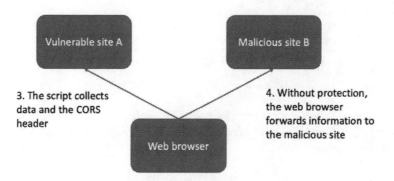

Figure 9.2 – CORS attack stage 2

Look out for wildcard checks – if your site accepts data from example.com, does it accept requests from malicious-example.com or example.com.malicious.com? The pattern matching should be exact and exclude prefixes and suffixes.

All these exploits are well known and have mitigations available. Test them all, and keep up to date as new ones arise. The following section deals with a security concern that is always present: managing sensitive personal information.

Handling personally identifiable information

You will almost certainly need to store PII somewhere in your application, so you need to be sure it is saved securely. PII includes the following:

- Names
- Dates of birth
- Birthplaces
- Names of family members
- Access keys
- Usernames or aliases
- Credit card numbers
- Email addresses
- Telephone numbers
- Physical addresses
- Social security or national insurance numbers
- IP addresses

- Passwords
- Personal photographs
- Passport information
- User gender

Some jurisdictions, such as **General Data Protection Regulation (GDPR)** regulations in the EU, include a further category of sensitive personal information that requires separate handling. This includes the following:

- Medical information
- Financial information
- Biometric information
- Education information
- Employment information
- Sexual orientation
- Political opinions
- Trade union membership
- Genetic data
- User race or ethnic origin
- User religion

Sensitive PII could put users at risk if it was disclosed and warrants further security concerns such as requirements to be encrypted at rest and in transit. You'll need to check whether your application deals with that data and the requirements for it.

The first step to securing PII is not to collect it if you don't need it. Unless you have a good reason, don't ask users for their data, which avoids all subsequent headaches about securing and managing it. Watch out for inadvertently gathering data. It's unlikely you'll accidentally ask users for their religion, but do your logs record your visitors' IP addresses or the URLs they visit?

What information do your logs record? This can be vital for debugging but should be as limited as possible. Check where the logs are stored and who has access to them; again, limit that. There will be logs throughout the system, from the communication layer down to the database, so check them all.

> **Real-world example – Touch tones in logs**
>
> One product I worked on used **Dual-Tone Multi-Frequency (DTMF)** digits – touch tones – where telephones sent numbers to our service. These performed various actions, and we recorded them in our logs for debugging purposes. Sometimes, these were used to choose from a menu, but our system could call other companies such as banks, and people could use DTMF to enter their credit card numbers, which also ended up in our logs. A security review discovered that issue, and we removed that logging.

Having reduced the amount of PII you collect, record exactly where it is copied and saved. Some jurisdictions require data to be stored within its geographic region, so ensure you have a list of those requirements and understand where you hold information. What copies do you make of the data, and are they stored in the correct region? If you have separate systems for statistics, logging, backup, or testing, check that they also conform to any geographic restrictions on storage.

The next step is to use PII as little as possible. User identities should be converted into **universally unique identifiers (UUIDs)**, and those should be used in any messages or URLs that need to be unique to a user. PII should be stored in a single, secure location and copied as little as possible. Again, look out for any values recorded in the logs where data is entered or used.

An important test is to look for PII copied to other locations. Items to check include the following:

- Source code
- Cookies
- Databases
- Files
- Configuration

You can use regular expressions to search for common patterns such as credit card numbers and email addresses in those locations.

The next part of protecting PII is to delete it when it is no longer needed. There should be a policy to say how long you will keep personal information and systems in place to delete it when it is no longer needed. Some data is naturally time-limited, such as browsing history or call records, and that should be aged out after some period. Any information still being used, such as usernames, can be kept as long as needed, but you should also have a policy to identify and remove stale accounts.

Despite that, you might want your application to maintain statistics for far longer than your other data, at which point it needs to be anonymized. For instance, you can keep the number of unique users per day without storing exactly which users they were. That can let you graph usage over time without the need for PII. That anonymization also needs to be tested – is it running correctly and removing all the necessary information? Again, you can search the anonymized data for any of the data types listed previously. This time, the search results are simpler to filter because there should be no PII of any kind.

PII is massively helpful to companies but requires strict requirements for handling it. Track its complete life cycle: where is it gathered, stored, used, anonymized, and deleted? You need to check each step.

In the next section, we will look at a simple way of outsourcing some of your security testing by running a bug bounty program.

Running a bug bounty program

Security testing is one area that is particularly easy to outsource. You should keep up to date with the latest security warnings that affect your application, but you can also apply for ethical hackers to try to find weaknesses in your application. Running a bug bounty program requires an investment of your time to answer the reports and a budget to make payments for valid discoveries. However, it is a quick way to get feedback and alternative points of view on your application's security. You can advertise your program on common forums and your site, and part of being a researcher is finding those adverts.

Security researchers should be familiar with the latest tools and know how to check for the latest vulnerabilities. This can save you time to concentrate on other aspects of product testing without having to recruit someone and make the long-term commitment of paying their salary. Researchers are particularly good at finding common problems on standard interfaces, such as missing security configuration on **Apache** or **Nginx** web servers. They can quickly make sure you don't have any glaring errors.

More in-depth researchers may request a test login, which can give greater access to the system if there isn't a free signup option. In this case, you can provide them access, ideally, to a test system that is separate from your live installation. They can then perform potentially destructive tests and attempt to extract data from the database without gaining access to genuine customer data. Requesting a login is a good sign that a researcher wants to spend more time investigating your application, so do encourage that and help if you can.

There is a law of diminishing returns to a bug bounty program. Researchers will probably find some simple, common problems, and you will receive duplicate reports of the same vulnerabilities until you resolve them. Often, these are minor issues, so they aren't a high priority to fix compared to other changes you want to make in your application. However, you need to fix or otherwise remove interfaces to encourage researchers to look for more exciting problems.

The downside of a bug bounty program, besides the resources required to run it, is that most researchers will use the same simple tools to attack the same interfaces, particularly web interfaces. If your application uses other protocols, researchers may not attack those interfaces at all. When I worked for a video conferencing company, almost all the reports were issues with our web portal and the machines we hosted. None found weaknesses in the protocols we used for video calls – **H.323** and **SIP**. That probably matches the skills of malicious hackers – they are also more likely to attack standard interfaces. However, to ensure that those other protocols are secure, you will probably have to test them yourself. Don't assume that because you have no bug bounty reports about an interface it is secure; more likely, it means it is not being tested.

To get ahead of any bug bounty researchers, look for any old machines and interfaces away from your main application that also need to be secured.

Avoiding security through obscurity

Does your application have any backdoors? For debugging or administrative purposes, does it listen on any ports? Have any superuser accounts been added for emergency access? In larger companies, this is the responsibility of the operations team, but if you can, also check them from a test perspective.

When you discovered your attack area, were any admin interfaces left open, such as **telnet** or **SNMP**, that needed to be secured? If possible, close these down; otherwise, you must ensure they are secured through the necessary passwords, access restrictions, and keys. Security requirements can often be combined to greater effect, so apply as many restrictions as possible.

Never rely on security through obscurity. If an interface is publicly accessible – whether it's an open port or a particular URL – assume it will be found. The question is, what could an attacker learn from that interface, or what access do they gain? Restrict logins and apply all these security recommendations to those pages too.

There can be a great temptation in security testing to concentrate on the main interfaces. They are big, public, and obvious. So, consider the non-obvious cases – what about the disaster recovery access? What old systems are still running, and what deprecated interfaces are still available? What DNS records are still active, pointing to old servers? Those obscure, low-priority, little-used interfaces are where your real security risk lies, so this is the time to concentrate on them.

Considering security beyond the application

This chapter has focused on testing your product and the technical weaknesses it may have. This is only one aspect of system security and not the most important one. If you want administrator access to a rival's system, the easiest way isn't to discover a privilege escalation bug – it's to trick an administrator into telling you their password. Social engineering with phishing emails is a huge problem that requires training, policies, and technical solutions such as email filters.

Internal policies are vital to security, such as requiring laptop hard drives to be encrypted and using a password manager to secure logins, along with 2FA. Wherever possible, these shouldn't be company policies advising users what to do but should be enforced on all users' devices.

Security is an area where the smallest gap can undo vast amounts of hard work, and it's easy to be lulled into a false sense of confidence. Just because you have excellent security in one area doesn't mean your security is excellent overall. Strong protection against social engineering means nothing if your database is left exposed on a public site; great security testing of your product is pointless if your colleagues might leave an unlocked, unencrypted laptop on a train. Security requires a holistic approach, of which this chapter only considers one part. This part is your responsibility as a tester, but it is not the whole story.

Summary

In this chapter, you have seen many examples of security processes and tests you should run on your application. The first step in security testing is identifying the attack area – what different kinds of servers do you have, which are public and private, what ports do they have open, and what protocols do they support? Armed with that information, you can perform security scans and design test plans on the relevant machines.

We described running security scans and code analyses as the first steps for testing security, and considered the main areas of security vulnerability, including logging in, privilege levels, and user and file inputs. We looked at web server misconfigurations that can lead to security problems and considered PII, which is particularly sensitive and needs to be identified throughout your system, along with a process to ensure its deletion.

Finally, we looked at systems around security testing of the application, including running a bug bounty program and security systems for your company as a whole. These are significant topics, and this chapter was designed to suggest further research rather than being a complete guide. Still, a security discussion does not end with just the security of your application.

In the next chapter, we will consider an area of functionality just for internal users – maintainability. While it doesn't affect the customer experience of your product, checking that it is easy to maintain will make life easier for everyone in development so that you can make all the other improvements faster.

10
Maintainability

"Temet nosce" (Know thyself)

- Ancient Greek aphorism, here given in Latin.

In the last chapter, we examined security testing and the unique checks related to securing your application. These are vital tests that need special consideration because they do not form part of the core functionality of your product or feature. This chapter considers another area that can be overlooked: **maintainability**. Unlike the other methods of functional testing, maintainability is not customer-facing, so it is a lower priority when time is short. However, getting this area right makes working with this application easier for everyone involved – testers, the support team, and the developers assigned to fix and improve the code.

You need to consider your code's instrumentation carefully – what events should it report on its behavior? Only by gathering this information can the product managers know which features are important and which are rarely used in practice. It can be tough to set the level of logging and events so that you can easily filter the important messages. This needs to be tested too.

In this chapter, you will learn about the following:

- The requirements for monitoring new features
- How to use monitoring to enhance your testing
- The testing of maintenance operations
- The requirements for logging
- Ideal logging usage

Out of all the areas of testing described in this book, this one is closest to my heart. If you get this right, debugging all other testing areas becomes simpler and, more importantly, quicker. Good logging means that testers and junior developers can resolve issues without needing help from senior team members, making the entire development process faster.

Know thyself and know thy app! Great maintainability lets you understand your application, so spend the time learning how to get this foundation in place. However, it requires special consideration, so this chapter explores its possibilities and pitfalls. First, we consider the maintainability use cases for the internal teams using your product.

Understanding maintainability use cases

Testing maintainability features is a form of black-box testing that checks functions that a specific group of users needs, so it is quite separate from code maintainability.

Code maintenance requires that your code is well architected, with minimal dependencies and clearly defined interfaces between modules. It needs a clear directory structure and comments to allow developers to easily find code and understand it, among many other considerations. However, these are outside the scope of this book and aren't the focus of this chapter.

Maintainability, here, refers to product features for users inside your company. That includes groups such as the following:

- The operations team ensuring a hosted application runs reliably
- The support team triaging customer issues
- The product owner checking feature usage
- The test and development teams debugging errors

You might release a brilliant new feature that your customers love, but it writes no logs and is completely opaque. When it fails, you have no way to see why. In that case, first, you must update the code to add log lines. This lack of logging is a bug you should identify during your testing. Other examples might be

- Your next release might pass all its tests with flying colors, but the upgrade is missing a database migration so the operations team can't roll it out live.
- You release a feature and your product owner thinks it is a big success, but it has no metrics to see if customers have actually used it.
- You release a feature and it seems to be running well, but later you realize it has been broken for a week and you had no monitoring alarms to warn you.

These classes of problems are unique to internal users and can often be neglected or misunderstood. However, out of everyone, internal users will spend the most time interacting with your product, and the problems they encounter cost your company time and money.

This is a distinct set of requirements that need dedicated tests. Each of the previous problems is a bug, either in the specification or implementation, and it's your job as a tester to find them. With that in mind, next, we consider the advantages and disadvantages of maintainability testing.

Advantages and disadvantages of maintainability testing

An alternative to explicitly performing maintainability testing is to try to maintain your code and see what happens. You'll soon discover which logs are unclear and which problems are impossible to debug due to missing information. Your task is to speed that process up by predicting what you need. The advantages and disadvantages of maintainability testing are as follows:

Advantages	Disadvantages
The best way to discover maintainability issues	Not a priority for product development
It makes your life easier	Requires knowledge of user experience design
Speeds up the development process	Hard to predict what information you will need
	Benefits from feedback late in the development cycle

Table 10.1 – Advantages and disadvantages of maintainability testing

The biggest issue for maintainability is its low priority. It doesn't directly help customers, so there is always a challenge to give it sufficient consideration. Testers can be less willing to raise maintainability issues, developers are less inclined to work on them, and product managers are unwilling to spend time on them. Maintainability improvements often need to come *for free* – by being included as part of other work that is considered a high priority. As with so many aspects of development, excellent maintainability can be achieved very quickly if you know what is required and don't have to think it through from first principles or learn as you go along. In the long run, great maintainability testing is a huge benefit for your product, but it takes time in the short term. This chapter aims to make great maintainability as easy to achieve as possible.

However, designing good maintainability requires a good knowledge of user experience design. You need to consider different use cases, as testers' tools and approaches might differ from developers'. As a tester, you will need to let the engineering team know what you need and argue for it.

This is especially hard because it can take time to determine the most important information. It's far easier to see what you need when using the product, but by then, the development team may have moved on to other work. Often, requests for improvements to maintainability will come sometime after that code is live and the team is working on other features. The product manager may be reluctant to devote time to an area that should already be finished. There's no easy way around this other than planning or arguing your case that the feature is not yet complete. Ideally, you should add time to revisit functions after they have shipped to make changes based on live feedback. If nothing needs changing, that is a bonus, and you can use that time elsewhere.

Planning maintainability work is challenging because every issue you debug is unique. You are not polishing a single happy-path scenario for users – every problem is different, probably because it wasn't considered fully during the development process. Maintainability is one unhappy-path scenario after another, so predicting what you need is always tricky. However, some guiding principles apply to many situations, and we'll consider those here.

Good maintainability helps everyone on the team. You can debug issues faster, understand the code better, and get greater visibility of what the code is doing and why. It's well worth putting the time in to ensure your product is easy to maintain. Next, we will consider the three main goals of maintainability.

Goals of maintainability

The maintainability of your product includes three main use cases, which we will discuss in this chapter:

- To quickly know if your system is suffering from degraded performance, for example:

  - Checking on hardware health

  - Checking on system resources

  - Identifying patterns in software issues

- To easily maintain and improve your system, for example:

  - Seeing the current running state

  - Performing upgrades and improvements

  - Enabling new features and capabilities

- To debug specific failures, for example:

  - Why didn't a user receive their password reset email?

  - Why did a web page fail to load?

  - Why did the application fail to update to the latest version?

Maintainability is closely tied to observability because you can only make improvements if you thoroughly understand your product's current running state. This section considers these three use cases in more detail.

Tools for observability

Complex products with multiple interacting systems will generate extensive data indicating their performance. Rapidly diagnosing issues depends on using various data types to gain an overall view of your system. The four main data types for observability are as follows:

- **Logs**: Logs are the most traditional method of observability, being statements your application outputs as part of its operation. There is a spectrum of formats, from plain text logs stored locally in simple files to the structured output you can search and filter on dedicated web interfaces. As well as a particular message, logs will almost always include the following:

  - Timestamps

  - Severity

  - Which part of the system they were written by

  The challenge with logs is managing the huge volume that can be generated and sifting them to find the key lines. Logs will be a major part of your life as a tester, so it's in your best interest to ensure they are written well. Like no other part of the system, when it comes to testing logs, it's personal.

- **Traces**: Traces let you track a single request through your system to see the services it interacted with, for instance, from an **Edge server** through a **Gateway**, to a core machine and then the **Database**:

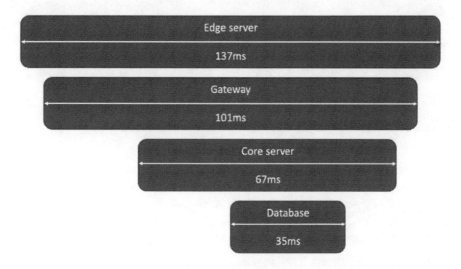

Figure 10.1 – Tracing a command through layers of a system

You can see the relevant loglines and timings and quickly zoom in on the source of a problem if one of the steps fails. On the downside, you'll need to set up tracing across your system to avoid having gaps in the analysis. This might be an enormous task in a mature, distributed system, but is hugely valuable.

- **Metrics**: Metrics are measurements of your system's performance that are sampled regularly, then gathered and presented in a central location. This can be everything from disk, memory, and CPU utilization to database latency and response times up to configured numbers for entities and rates of application operations. These measures and their graphs provide an invaluable view of the workings of your system. You'll need to check that these produce correct output, so you can use it to identify issues while you test. If these measures cross the configured threshold or have anomalies detected, then they can raise error events to indicate the issue.

- **Events**: The final type of observability data is events. These are more abstract than logs. Whereas logs might record output from each function involved in creating a user, an event will simply record that user X has been created. This lets you plot data points easily to measure trends over time and correlate additional data. If your user creation event includes information about which country they are in or what method they used to sign up, you can monitor that information and how it varies too.

  Generating events from loglines is a shortcut, but it isn't ideal. Events should be generated deliberately so they are independent of refactoring the code and can include all the information you need. Using a logline may break if the log wording is changed and might not record the right details, although it is quicker if you can configure event generation but not make code changes as easily.

  An important subclass of events is **alarms** that indicate issues with your system. These alerts get the operations team out of bed at three in the morning, or if they are less severe warnings, give developers a to-do list of problems to investigate. Sometimes events and alarms are generated from other data types, such as error log lines or metrics showing issues, for instance. In that sense, they are outputs from other forms of observability. At other times there is logic in their generation – if so many log lines are seen within a specific period, for example – so they can be separate, or written entirely independently of any other logs.

Each form of observability works with the others, solving a different problem and providing another part of the picture. Metrics will tell you about the health of your hardware and the load on your application, whereas events will give the headlines of operations that have occurred. Traces will tie related functions together across disparate machines, and logs will detail exactly what happened. You will need each to debug issues you find in your system.

As a tester faced with a new feature, the questions are: Are the right tools in place to ensure this feature can be maintained and upgraded? When there is a problem, will we be alerted quickly? Based on that alert, can we quickly diagnose the issue? Failures in any of those areas are bugs you need to raise. We will consider each of those three key use cases next.

Identifying system degradation

Consider this scenario: to improve system performance, your product has added a queue in front of its core servers. You've tested its functionality and security, applied stress and load testing, and everything looks good. But your queuing feature isn't ready to go live until you can measure its performance and detect when it has failed.

Of the four types of observability data listed previously, metrics and events are the most important for identifying system degradation. Standard metrics should be measured for every standalone machine, including the following:

- CPU
- Memory
- Disk usage
- The number of threads or processes running

These should be monitored automatically for any new machine you start to run. Then, add load metrics specific to this application based on the events it generates. For our queue, for example, measure the following:

- The rate of requests arriving
- The rate of requests being serviced
- The response time
- The current queue length
- *Dead letters* (requests that can't be processed)

You will need to design the metrics for the applications in your system and the events to track its primary functions. Based on those, you can choose what alarms you want to raise. For the queuing system, this will be issues such as high rates of requests arriving, slow servicing of the queue, increasing queue length, and lots of dead letters.

When you have identified the relevant metrics and placed alarms on them, you are ready to enable that part of your system. For more on detecting degradation, see the *Designing monitoring* section.

Improving your system

As we saw in *Chapter 8, User Experience Testing*, you aim to let users complete their tasks in just a few obvious steps. The same applies to monitoring and maintaining your system. You need to make it as simple as possible to roll out changes and upgrades, ideally automating the entire process from a change being approved. Other core maintenance operations include the following:

- Testing the upgrade process
- Configuration transitions
- Security updates

- Database migrations
- Capacity expansion

Those topics are considered in more detail in the *Testing maintenance operations* section.

Debugging issues

If your system is running the correct version with the proper configuration and you still hit a problem, then you need to go down to the next level and look through the logs. Work through common failure modes for your product and explicitly plan out how you would diagnose them. What information do you start with? How do you know where to look? How many steps does it take to get there? Traces can be an invaluable way to link processes in disparate parts of a system and identify the sources of issues.

At some point in this process, you cannot specify debugging steps any further. You have no idea what kind of issues might be reported next or what failures you might find in your testing today, but you know the sort of issues you've hit in the past and the errors you've had to investigate. By extrapolating from them, you can see the kinds of problems you might face in the future and take as many steps as possible toward a solution. See the *Using logging* section for more detail on what you should require from logging on your system.

In the following sections, we'll walk through the primary solutions to those three main use cases: what logging you need to debug issues, how to test the maintenance operations that improve your system, and the monitoring systems you need to identify system degradation.

Designing monitoring

Monitoring involves checking system performance metrics and regularly running simple automated checks. These overlap with tests you should have run before release, but they fulfill a different function since they find test escapes and operational issues affecting your live environment. Since monitoring checks are run after a system's release, they are not tests as such but have so much overlap with your test plan that they're worth considering here.

Being a tester, you'll interact with the monitoring in two ways:

- Firstly, you're a user, using monitoring to check for errors on your test system. New code must complete its test run without causing errors in the monitoring system.
- Secondly, you need to ensure that every new feature has relevant monitoring. If your system can now fail in a new way that you're blind to, that's a bug that needs fixing.

Monitoring requires a dedicated system that gathers all monitoring data so it can be aggregated, processed, and presented to users. Programs such as Nagios, Datadog, and Amazon CloudWatch perform this function, and a prerequisite for monitoring is that you have set up your chosen system ready to receive this information.

Instrumentation

The requirements for each new feature should specify what measurements you need to take from it. How often is that function invoked? From which interface? What was the outcome of the request, and what did the user do next? The product owner should routinely ask for this information, so if they don't, double-check with them. This information can be provided with events, and checking they are correctly generated should be part of your testing.

Careful instrumentation and analysis can provide fascinating insights into your product's usage without having to ask your customer for feedback. See *Chapter 8, User Experience Testing*, for more details.

Filtering alerts

Aim to have three levels of alerts in your system: **critical**, **error**, and **warning**. Instead of basing these on the state of your system, it's more pragmatic and useful to define these based on the action you should take:

Alert level	Action	Examples
Critical	Requires immediate attention	System unavailable
		Users unable to sign up
		Data loss in progress
		A minor function is unavailable
		An error preventing internal users from doing their jobs
		Consistent rejections from third-party systems
		Security issues
Error	Requires attention	High disk usage
		A transient error not currently occurring
		Intermittent rejections from third-party systems
		An internal problem with a workaround
		Unhandled exceptions
Warning	Does not require engineering attention An expected failure	An outgoing API request fails
		Customer mistakes (incorrect passwords, misconfiguration, invalid API queries, and so on)
		Temporary loss of connection
		Attempting to access an invalid address on your server

Table 10.2 – Alert levels and their definitions

The most important part of monitoring is critical errors that indicate an ongoing outage. These require constant, careful tuning to ensure that you check every relevant metric, but you have to ruthlessly remove spurious errors so that alerts correlate to genuine issues. In monitoring, adding checks is relatively easy; avoiding false alarms is a much tougher job.

Every critical and error-level alert must require manual intervention to either fix or downgrade it. You can't leave any of them alone. If it doesn't need someone's attention, it should be downgraded so you can see other errors more clearly. See *Chapter 7, Testing of Error Cases*, for more on the distinction between expected and unexpected errors.

Possibly the easiest *fix* for an alert is simply to downgrade it. Suboptimal but possible scenarios should be logged as warnings, for instance, occasional rejections on a third-party API. You can't stop them from happening and want to record that there was a problem, but they'll be retried so no action is needed from the development team. That's a warning.

There is a gray area between warnings and errors. A one-off rejection by a third-party API is only a warning, but 100 in 5 minutes is an error, or possibly a critical ongoing outage. Some warnings need to be promoted to errors based on their frequency.

When a developer writes the code for one part of the system and it fails, they may be tempted to raise it as an error since their function was unsuccessful. However, that may be a minor part of the system, or there may be retries or fallbacks designed to correct that state without intervention. They mustn't fill the logs with error messages, which may obscure far more important problems. Errors should only be for impossible states of the system. Anything bad but possible is just a warning.

More problematic are the cases where a single error has two causes; a common, boring one and an important, rare one.

> **Real-world example – It's always packet loss**
>
> In my video conferencing days, we regularly received reports of poor video quality. However, they were almost always due to packet loss on poor networks. The support team patiently guided our customers through troubleshooting, generally finding a different network that performed better, to show that our equipment wasn't at fault, which was almost always the case.
>
> Because there were so many reports and there was a well-known cause, when we did have a bug in our decoder, it took us a long time to isolate and fix it. We needed more than a report of an issue – we needed a consistent pattern of problems, even on reliable networks, before it was escalated to the development team to investigate.

The solution for serious issues hiding behind a common one is to monitor them separately, to find a difference in the conditions, which lets you raise two different alarms. Then, one can be downgraded to a warning, and the other left as a critical alert.

When filtering errors, expect to be under constant attack. On a public web server, amateur hackers will regularly try to reach configuration files for common servers in an attempt to access your system.

So long as your security configuration is correct, these will be rejected with a 400 error. Since this is a predictable problem, you can't add an alarm for it. If you want to raise alarms about incorrect access, you need to find a different way.

> **Real-world example – Raising client-side errors**
>
> One company I worked for wanted warnings if any of our systems received 400 errors when communicating internally with other parts of our system. Unfortunately, the servers they contacted were public and constantly returned 400 errors to attackers trying to access invalid addresses.
>
> We couldn't add an alarm on the server because of all the attacks, but we could raise a critical alarm if one of our clients received a 400 error while querying an internal system. Since we controlled both the client and server sides of those requests, an error response showed a misconfiguration in our system that we needed to fix urgently.

Performing active checks

In addition to passively checking for errors in your system, your monitoring should actively perform actions to ensure that key functions are working. Typical monitoring checks include the following:

- API queries to ensure the API is running and returning responses correctly
- Loading landing pages
- Connecting clients
- Signing in
- Signing up
- Performing a simple standard operation, such as creating a new entity

You should run these checks on both user-facing and administrator interfaces, raising different alerts for each.

Monitoring checks will typically run every few minutes, with frequencies varying from every 30 seconds for brief, lightweight checks, to once an hour for non-critical systems or checks that involve significant complexity or cost. You should run checks as often as possible to detect outages quickly. The goal is to identify problems before your users. The worse the outage is, the easier it is to find with monitoring, but the less time you have before your customers hit it too.

Monitoring creates a dull background noise you must filter out of the logs. You'll need to remove any users and other entities your monitoring makes, and this deletion is a useful check that removing configuration is successful. Ideally, mark all entities created by monitoring as test entries that can be deleted. Filtering monitoring usage out of logs can be harder but is worthwhile to make the actual activity easier to see.

System resources versus customer outcomes

The most vital checks are of customer-facing outcomes: can users actually log in? These checks are far more useful than checks on the internal system state. Outages fail to correlate with resource monitoring in both directions: a machine may have an unacceptably high CPU load, but the service is still available and working. Conversely, your application may be down even though resource loads are fine.

Consider customer-facing metrics, such as the following:

- Screen loading success rates and times

- User action success rates and times

- Connection success rates and times

- Download success rates and times

- Upload success rates and times

If your application lets users upload data, for instance, then there should be metrics tracking every upload attempt, whether it worked, and how long it took. You should be able to produce graphs to easily see anomalies, and to run anomaly detection software to produce automatic alarms if there are problems. All of this relies on having metrics in the first place, so it is important to test that they are present and working.

As defined previously, approaching system resource limits is an error-level event: it requires intervention but is not a current outage. This event should warn you in time to mitigate it. In practice, if your system is awash with error-level events that you don't triage regularly, you will need to escalate approaching resource limits into critical alarms so you can act on them, but this sort of inflation in error classification isn't sustainable. You need to downgrade your current, spurious errors to let you see the real ones clearly.

Hierarchies of system failures

One failure can have many expected effects. For instance, if a hardware server fails, it's not a surprise that none of the machines it hosts are running. In that case, you'll be flooded with errors, listing all the different machines that are unavailable, and the knock-on effects throughout your system. To quickly identify the hardware failure's root cause, you'll need to set up hierarchies of dependencies within your monitoring.

By letting your system know that specific machines rely on that hardware, if it fails, your monitoring can ignore those alarms and only report the root cause, speeding up your diagnostics.

Automatic problem reporting

As well as errors from your servers, you should ensure that your clients or any other remote programs report issues to you. Clients connected to cloud infrastructure should regularly upload their logs and inject events into your event management system, whatever that may be, including errors that require attention, such as crashes.

Even software following the traditional model of an application installed on-site or on users' computers should also report crashes back to a central server. These reports should include a complete dump of their logs and state to allow for thorough debugging without needing any extra information from the customer.

Monitoring overview

Monitoring is not a replacement for testing; it's a tool you can use to detect issues while testing and it's a functional area new features must consider. If a new function introduces a failure mode – a new subsystem that can crash, for instance – you need to ensure those issues are reported back into your main monitoring system. A new function that can't be monitored, or requires its own unique process, can't be easily maintained and needs to be changed.

In the next section, we will move on from monitoring your system overall to internal operations, which are another crucial part of ensuring your system is maintainable.

Testing maintenance operations

While only internal staff perform maintenance operations, they are often among the riskiest on your system. Upgrades and configuration changes are the sources of most outages, in my experience. You'll need to test the content of each modification, but this section considers changes in the abstract – what should you try for every upgrade?

> **Real-world example – Which version is that?**
>
> I once tested a minor plugin that supported our main product, which was installed locally on a desktop. We shipped the first version, then a couple of maintenance releases. Only after a couple of versions did we realize there was a piece of functionality that we'd missed. Users kept reporting issues that we thought we'd already fixed. Were our fixes failing, or had the user not upgraded? The first question that the support team asked was what version they were running.
>
> Unfortunately, the plugin didn't report its version number anywhere, not on the user interface and not in the logs. Instead of being able to tell what was happening, we had to advise users to upgrade just in case they weren't up to date. Not reporting the version was a slight oversight, but made the support team's job much harder.

Firstly, all parts of your system need to report their current version and running configuration. That's not the version that's supposed to be running and the configuration it's supposed to have – your system needs to report what is actually in use. Sometimes showing the configuration is more straightforward because you just read the contents of the configuration files. It takes more effort to check the machines and see what was actually applied. However, pushing configuration can fail, leaving it out of sync with reality. If you don't have a quick way to check your system's state, that's an important feature request.

Worst-case maintenance operations

Carefully consider maintenance operations, as they can have a multiplicative effect on your test plan. Backup and restore is one such process, covered in *Chapter 11, Destructive Testing*; other examples are upgrades or migrations between servers. For every new feature that you add, you'll need to check it works correctly for those operations.

To test these, it's helpful to prepare the most convoluted, complex configuration possible for a customer, a user, or whatever entities your application deals with. Ours were known as *evil organizations*. Add all possible types of extra details, with multiple instances if possible. Then, perform upgrades, migrations, and restores to see if all the configuration survives. Where settings are mutually exclusive, you will need a set of evil organizations to cover them all and have at least one massive evil organization. This tests loading on the system, even though it may be too slow for regular use. If those evil organizations work, then simpler entities should be fine.

Real-world example – Losing our largest customer

Often your most important customers are also the largest ones, who push your system to its limits. At one place I worked, we needed to move our largest customer to a new geographic node. This meant a migration, copying all its data from a source node database to the destination. That would involve downtime, so we scheduled the maintenance for overnight. I started the command and waited. These operations were slow and would take minutes at the best of times, so with that many users, it wasn't a surprise when this took over an hour.

Then it hit an error. After all that waiting, the operation had timed out. I was frustrated but not worried yet; our system was designed to only delete information from the source once the destination copy was complete. A rollback should have left us back where we started, but unfortunately, it didn't. The failure meant the configuration never arrived at the destination, but the source thought the operation was a success and deleted it. I frantically triple-checked both locations, but the customer had vanished.

We'd tested failures where the destination rejected the transfer but not where the destination accepted it but took too long. I scrambled to restore the configuration from the backup and got them back online in their original location before they came online for the morning.

Centralized commands

Rollouts should be centrally controlled with commands to completely upgrade the independent parts of your product. This can be difficult in a varied environment with legacy systems, but you will be upgrading it a lot, so it's well worth the effort to improve the process. Likewise, the configuration should be centrally managed to provide easy visibility and control.

In *Chapter 8, User Experience Testing*, I discussed the problems I'd encountered with locally configured feature flags. When you have a local configuration, there is no easy way to set it and check it across your entire infrastructure. The wrong way to solve this is to add a checking mechanism – you'll still have thousands of individually configured settings, but you can search for discrepancies. This is a waste of your time, as it needs constant checking and fixing. To solve the problem for good, a better fix is to make the configuration centrally controlled. Best yet – use an external service that your application queries and gives you visibility and control.

Watch out for backsliding in the development team. Possibly your system already has excellent centralized management, so your job as a tester is to ensure that you maintain those high standards. On a rushed project I once worked on, a new feature was enabled with a database field. We had a perfectly good system for allowing new features, but the developer hadn't used it. That's a maintainability issue for you to catch.

Testing upgrade types

Upgrades are some of the riskiest operations on a live system, both at the point when you ship bugs live and due to the risk of the upgrade process going wrong. You need to test this process, checking for failures for each upgrade type in your product. In a heterogeneous system, there will be a different process for each kind of server, and various upgrades even within the same server. Consider cases such as the following:

- Edge servers/load balancers
- Gateways
- Core servers
- Databases
- Web server versions
- Serverless cloud infrastructure
- OS upgrades of all the systems listed previously

Upgrades are generally the first operation you test. They get on the new code running, ready to perform all the other tests, but ensure you perform upgrades realistically. You may have development shortcuts to get you running faster, and those are fine for everyday use, but make sure you have at least one test to go through the customer steps.

Testing upgrade control

Upgrades should be tracked, with a complete history available for running versions and configuration. This control also lets you roll out versions easily and see the requested settings. Remember that the running version may differ, so don't simply trust that your configuration has been applied.

Real-world example – What was running on the 16th?

In one company, we carefully tracked the version history of our servers, but our client's software version was just controlled with a configuration setting.

After one release, a new error appeared. Looking back through the logs, we had first hit it several days before, around the time of the upgrade. Had this new release introduced an issue? If we rolled back to the previous version, would that fix it? That depended on when exactly we had performed the upgrade. Without a version history, we had to trawl through the logs to piece together what had happened.

While core servers and configuration may be tracked, are all your settings controlled that way? New settings or features, such as DNS, may simply be set rather than version controlled. Is the configuration described all the way to the server level, or does it assume a set of servers are in place and you must keep them synchronized? For maintainability, get as much configuration as possible into your settings files.

Once configuration files are ready, you can run extensive checks on them before they go live. Does it correctly reject invalid inputs such as the following ones?

- Invalid syntax
- Code versions being unavailable
- Duplicate addresses and IDs
- References to other machines and configurations being unavailable

It's vital to get this feedback as early as possible instead of having to loop through the entire cycle of upgrading in practice, which can take minutes or hours.

Testing upgrade processes

Certain upgrade types can avoid downtime by running the old and new versions simultaneously and directing traffic to the new instance. If that's the case, you'll need to verify that system is in place and working. See the *Testing transitions* section for more details.

If there's downtime, you'll need to check its duration for any errors. Upgrades should be as automated as possible, with checking, scheduling, uploading code, restarts, and further checking performed without manual intervention. This automation is a massive benefit, but you need to check its functionality, including the following:

- Upgrade scheduling:

  - Refer to the time tests in *Chapter 5, Black-Box Functional Testing*

- Downtime during upgrades:

  - Duration

  - Errors while coming back online

- Dependencies are upgraded in the correct order

- Upgrades are as conservative as possible

- Upgrades under heavy load

- Upgrade failure cases such as the following:

  - An invalid upgrade image due to the following:

    - Incorrect sizes

    - Corrupt contents

    - Hash validation failing

  - A failure mid-upgrade due to the following:

    - Lack of system resources

    - Communication failure

  - Failure to start the new image

- Recovery checks such as the following:

  - Machines are running

  - All processes have restarted

  - Network access is available

  - The application is responding

Ensure upgrades are run in the proper order. If an image needs to be uploaded to intermediate servers, check that it's there before it's required, for instance. Upgrades should be as conservative as possible. It's tempting to add an upgrade or restart for a service just in case, which adds unnecessary load on the system. If one service isn't being developed but is upgraded at the same time as a rapidly developing service, it can have orders of magnitude more restarts than necessary. This slows down the upgrade process for no reason.

Client upgrades

So far, we've considered server-side upgrades, but some products also have to control client rollouts. If you have a web application, your clients are browsers, and you don't need to worry about their upgrades. Similarly, if you're testing an app, then the App Store or Play Store will perform upgrades, and be grateful they handle that complexity. If you have dedicated clients connecting to your infrastructure, however, you will need to manage those upgrades, which can be a challenging task.

> **Real-world example – Breaking down upgrades**
>
> At one place I worked, we specified a single version of client software that could connect to our cloud. When we pushed upgrades, clients went offline until they had downloaded the new code and could run it. We performed upgrades at night, so if users left their clients online, they wouldn't even notice, but if they connected in the morning, then they'd have to wait for the upgrade. That was fine until we gained large numbers of users.
>
> We only supported a few simultaneous downloads, so clients had to wait until their turn, all while being offline. It caused many support cases, so we fixed it by letting clients connect to older versions of the software and download the new code in the background while running. Until then, the poor operations team had to stagger upgrades, only doing a small fraction at a time so we could complete them quickly.

When testing client upgrades, consider the following:

- Slow internet connections, causing long downloads:

  - What is the timeout?

- Connections with significant packet loss

- Interrupted connections

- Mass simultaneous requests for upgrades

- Server restarts during downloads

- Limited client resources preventing the upgrade:

  - Insufficient disk or memory

Both client and server upgrades should be backward compatible whenever possible, but if there's a breaking change, you'll need to test the process that forces clients to upgrade. Where you support previous versions, you'll need to check that the oldest supported clients still work with the latest infrastructure to ensure that backward compatibility works in practice.

Recovery and rollback

Testing rollback mechanisms is usually low down the priority list since it's an operation you never plan to use. However, on the day you need it, rolling back becomes the most critical task in the world, so make sure you try it in advance.

There are several ways of performing a rollback; you'll only need to test the one you plan to use in practice:

- Roll back to a fixed state
- Revert a change
- Manually undo a change
- Make further changes to affect a fix

If you can take a snapshot of your system code, you can roll back by reverting to that snapshot. You'll need to separately fix your code to make sure the bug isn't deployed again. That automates returning to a known-good state and is the best recovery method if it's available. Reverting the change is also a controlled way to return to the previous state, although the code needs to be rebuilt and redeployed, so this can take longer.

Unfortunately, simply reverting the code to a previous state isn't possible if there are stateful changes such as database migrations or cache updates. Then, you'll need manual steps to roll back those data stores, as well as move to older code.

Finally, instead of reverting the change that caused a breakage, you can update the rest of the system to support the altered behavior. This may be tempting if you want the breaking change but had released it too early when its dependencies weren't in place. Instead of moving backward, you could update those dependencies and ship the change correctly.

This is the riskiest form of fix because you start running the new code in an untested configuration. Having shown that your testing did not catch the initial problem, shipping untried code even faster to fix it is dangerous. If the change is simple enough, and you can perform sanity testing in advance, this route might be best.

These tasks are headaches for the operations team. As a tester, needing a rollback probably shows that your testing was inadequate and needs to be improved. Your job is to learn from any test escapes and test that steps such as reverting to snapshots and reversing database migrations will work correctly if needed.

Testing transitions

Suppose that your current live version is working well, and the next version with a new feature fully implemented and rolled out has passed testing. But how do you get from here to there? While some features are simple and only require a single upgrade or feature flag, others require several steps in their rollout.

The classic example is removing a database column, which must be deprecated first. Simply removing a database field in a single step risks system failures until you upgrade the database and all processes that access it. Depending on how long your rollouts take, this could take a significant amount of time.

To catch these transient issues, you'll need to monitor your system during the upgrade and follow up on any problems, even if they appear to resolve themselves. Rollouts can be far quicker on test systems with the same logical setup as the live system but at a smaller scale. A brief problem on the test system might translate to a far longer one in production, so monitor your upgrades for any errors and then follow them up.

Where an upgrade has several distinct steps, you will need to check the functionality of each one. When handing over between *blue/green systems*, this has three phases:

1. Run the upgraded system alongside the live system:

   A. Check that both work as expected

2. Direct traffic to the upgraded system:

   A. Check that the new system is processing requests correctly

   B. Check that the old system is unused

3. Decommission the old system:

   A. Check that its removal hasn't affected live traffic on the new system

You will need to break down each step for more complex transitions and design test plans for each phase.

Testing maintenance operations overview

Maintenance operations are some of the riskiest changes performed on an application. They can involve fundamental changes to how a system works, and they are generally rarer than customer operations. Configuration management, upgrades, and system transitions all need to be carefully tested for each release to check that they work correctly for new functions.

When there are failures and you need more information to diagnose the issues, you will need to turn to the logs. As your primary debugging tool, you need to ensure that each new feature is writing logs well, as described in the next section.

Using logging

Logging is the most useful form of output from your system for diagnosing issues and understanding the details of its behavior. This section considers how logs should be written so that you can use them to the best effect.

Finding "the" log

It's vital that you get the correct information to the developer to help diagnose an issue in their code. While I always try to include the relevant information, I've lost count of the number of times a developer has asked me for *the* log. It's a simple enough request; the only problem is the word *the*. Which log do they need for any given issue? Within that log, which line is the clue? Other sections of this chapter will recommend approaches to finding problems within logs; here, we consider finding the correct log in the first place.

> **Real-world example – Logging on dual redundant hardware**
>
> In two of my jobs, I've improved the presentation of logs, and in both cases, I've been incredibly glad that I did. At one company, we made redundant hardware systems for processing SMS text messages. Two blades ran live simultaneously, both handling the system load, each writing logs of the messages they sent and received.
>
> This made debugging a nightmare because the messages were interleaved between the two logs. I wrote a program that downloaded the logs from both blades and arranged them in time order so that you could see the overall flow of messages through the system. This wasn't the most complicated program ever written, but it made our lives much easier.

Users of the system must have a minimum level of knowledge, such as where the logs are and how the different parts of the code interact. Where necessary, you can document the steps users should take, for instance, by writing a troubleshooting guide that considers the most likely failures and the areas to check in each case.

For instance, if a user didn't receive their password reset email, you would first check the system that sends out the emails, which is likely to be a third party. Was the email sent at all? Did the destination acknowledge receipt? Or did the request not make it that far? If not, you need to check the part of your system that sends those requests. If that is also missing this request, then look at the web page itself – did the page send the information correctly?

Even better than documenting the systems involved in different processes is automatically gathering the logs you need. Adding traces to your system lets you link together transactions from different parts of your system. A little work in this area can have a transformative effect, as described in the next section.

Understanding the debugging steps

Debugging can have the kind of user experience that would make a professional UX designer break down in tears. While the user experience may be atrocious, that's okay because very few people carry debugging out, and all of them are paid by your company. The difficulty of debugging – both the complexity of the tasks it requires and the problems you are trying to solve – highlights some of the fundamental ideas behind user experience design, for instance, the number of actions a user has to perform to reach their goal.

Once you know which logs contain the information you need, you can work out how many steps it takes to retrieve it. What information do you start with – for instance, the email address of the user who experienced the issue? Does the log you need contain that email address so you can search for it? Or does the log contain a unique identifier that you'll need to look up?

Break down each step to see what a tester or support engineer would do in practice, and look for areas that can be improved. Do you need to add identifiers into a log to make it easier to search? Is there anywhere you need to do a database lookup to convert between different identifiers? Can you write a tool to make that step easier, or use the same identifier everywhere, so you don't have to convert it?

When it comes to identifiers, make sure you have as few as possible. For example, for a customer name, you might have one user-facing, editable identifier and a second unique identifier used throughout the system. It is surprisingly easy for identifiers to proliferate, especially in a complex product. Part of maintainability is making sure that doesn't happen.

One product I worked on had six different identifiers for our customers: the frontend had a database ID and a different ID when loading web pages, as well as the primary identifier, which was shared with the backend. The backend had another database with a different ID, as well as a final ID (I was never sure of its purpose), not counting the actual customer name. Wherever related logs use different IDs, you need to translate between them to track a command through the system. Every translation is more work for you and another place to make mistakes, so if you see a new identifier creeping into usage, raise that as a maintainability problem.

In a distributed system with multiple servers handling each request, check how easy it is to track messages through the system. If you have 10 different edge servers, do your core servers record which server they received messages from so you can check back through the system? How obvious is that step? Do you have to look up IP addresses, or is it named? Is it written in the logline with the user identifier, or do you have to search back in the log for the transaction? Each requires a different step, and each step takes time to perform and is a chance to make a mistake.

For example, if a user complains that a particular web page is failing to load, but it works fine for you, you'll need to check the logs to investigate their failure. A typical process might be as follows:

1. Using the user's email address, look up their ID in the database.

2. Use that ID to find which server answered that request.

3. On that server, find the correct log.

4. Search in the log for the ID, and find the lines processing that request.

5. The request was handled successfully and sent on to a subsystem for processing; look up which subsystem took the request.

6. In that subsystem, find the correct log.

7. The subsystem log only includes a different ID, so convert the main ID to the subsystem ID.

8. Search the subsystem log for the subsystem ID and find the lines processing that request.

9. Find the error and start to investigate why it happened.

Sound familiar? This is the problem that traces are designed to solve. The first block of processing, or *span*, generates the identifier and then includes it in its message to subsequent services. You'll need to translate from the user or customer you're interested in and obtain that transaction ID, but with it, you can instantly retrieve the relevant logs from across your system. If you are suffering from these issues, this is the best solution.

If you can't implement complete tracing, *steps 1* to *5* could be handled by a single tool. Enter the user's email address, and it will convert it to the ID and find all server logs for that user, including the subsystems that handled each request. Similarly, for *steps 6* to *9* – you could specify a transaction, and a tool could look up the relevant lines for you. So you need at least two steps – to look up the user in the main system and then look up lines on the subsystem involved. Even without that automation, you can avoid *step 7* by using the same ID everywhere. You could avoid *step 6* by having one log link to the other.

How many steps does that kind of debugging take on your system, and how could you improve it?

The importance of messages

Different logs are written for different types of users. In particular, the developers will need records that detail the exact working of the code, so they can trace where problems came from. On the other hand, testers and support engineers only need to identify where a problem occurred, and within which system. A simple rule of thumb is that non-developers only need to worry about the messages sent within the system. Give them a log where they can see the messages, and that should be enough to isolate issues.

Logging the messages first lets you see all the inputs and outputs to your system. Whether API commands, web requests, or information from client applications, one of the most important interfaces is where your system interacts with the outside world. A whole host of problems start there, so make sure your logging records exactly what you sent and received.

Split the logging into different levels for the developers and testers. The testers only need to worry about the messages at first, and that will let them track down the source of issues. Did we receive an invalid request? Or was the request valid, but one subsystem failed to handle it? The message between the systems will indicate this.

> **Real-world example – Displaying messages**
>
> The second tool I wrote to help debug messages was for a hardware system for video conferencing. Each call required dozens of messages to be set up. There was a great interface that recorded every message, its title, where it was sent from and to, and when. But even that interface struggled when you had many people simultaneously dialing into a call.
>
> You could download an `.xml` file with the messages, so I wrote a web page that loaded those files and split up the messages into a table, where each conference participant had their own column. You could see at a glance which message came from each caller, including us, so you could focus on the ones with a problem. Again, it was a straightforward program but it really clarified what was happening.

On the other hand, the developers need to know how a message is handled. What is the state machine for the subsystem, and how far through did the message get? This level of detail is vital but should be hidden away from the testers. As a tester, you only need to trace the problem based on the messages sent. The best testers will get to know some systems they have worked on and may use the developer logs too, but it shouldn't usually be necessary for a tester to trawl through the developer logs.

It should be possible to refactor an area of code and not change the messages it sends. The message logs should be completely unchanged, even if the developer logs are different. Only the developers need to know about the implementation, so long as the behavior is correct when testers use it. This distinction in responsibilities should also be present in the logs that the different groups need to work with.

Note that for this purpose, timeouts also count as messages. Failing to receive a response causes the next stage of processing to start as if a message had arrived, so timeouts should also be logged at this level.

By only recording the messages and not every function and state transition, it should be possible for testers to learn what a healthy message sequence looks like and to rapidly see any problems or divergence from it. If a log has 50 messages, for instance, then a tester has the hope of remembering that. If a log has 3,000 messages, then that won't be possible. Focusing only on messages lets testers learn the system successfully.

Simple logs also help newcomers to learn faster. This might be a new member of the test or development team or someone from another team whose investigations have led them in this direction. How quickly can they understand what this code is doing? Again, having a simple, short log recording the messages in and out is an excellent first step; then, they can check the full logs when they know the location of the problem.

Having a message log brings many benefits, but only if done well. The following section considers exactly how messages should be logged.

How to log messages

It's not enough just to log the messages in your system; you have to log them well. Here is a short checklist to make sure they include the key information:

- Are all the messages in and out of the system recorded?

- Messages between subsystems should be recorded; messages within subsystems should not.

- Does each message include its name, a timestamp, and a clear description?

- Is the content of each message available?

- Does each message clearly state where it is sent from and to?

These may seem obvious, but it's easy to leave gaps. Standard components, such as web servers, should log the messages they receive but you need to ensure that any custom protocols are also logged. They are also more likely to have issues and need logging since they've had less testing and usage overall.

It's easy to miss messages such as DNS lookups, which are vital to send a message but aren't part of the main flow. Many protocols are text-based, making them easy to record in logs, but binary protocols also need to be registered. They need to be translated. This will be more work, but it's vital to also be able to read them.

While external messages and messages between your subsystems should be recorded, internal messages within those subsystems shouldn't be added to the log. They would add too much information and aren't necessary at this level. The message log is there to identify which subsystem has a problem. When you have determined that, you can go down to the next level and see its internal messages. They shouldn't be included in the message log, however.

Each message should have a title so that you can see the entire sequence of requests, just by seeing their names. You should be able to see that at a glance, so if message 37 was an error, you don't have to walk through 36 successful steps. Features such as these transform the workflow of everyone using the logs.

While it should be possible to see the names of the messages, once you have identified which one is the problem, you need to see its entire contents and those of the messages before it, which may have triggered the error. Summaries or headers are no good; at this point, you need to see the value of every field. Each message should also have a timestamp synchronized across the system. With the **Network Time Protocol** (**NTP**) everywhere, the days of mismatched clocks are thankfully long behind us.

The wording for each message should be clear. Ideally, an engineer who has never read this log line before should be able to tell what is happening. That may sound like a low threshold, but logs are sometimes more like notes that are highly dependent on context.

For instance, in one system I used, when a server received a request, it produced a log line saying, *"Dispatched message ABC…"*. A message arriving caused a log line saying it had been sent! It wasn't completely wrong – the request arrived from a third-party system and was sent on to an internal system for processing. However, I was much more interested in the external message flow than the internal one. You must raise these issues with the development team or train testers to fix them.

It may seem like a small change, but making your log lines understandable will help all your future debugging.

Finally, each message should record where it came from and where it was sent. This sounds like a simple requirement for a message but isn't always the case. Being able to deduce it from context isn't enough. Maybe some message types are always sent in a particular direction, but others might not be, and adding this information helps people to learn and remember what is going on. For external messages, you might log IP addresses named with a reverse DNS lookup, if possible. Messages between different internal subsystems should always have names.

Real-world example – Subsystem in the middle

The architecture of one system I tested involved a core controller, a subsystem for sending and receiving messages, and then interactions with third parties. Unfortunately, its logging was hard to use, and it didn't clearly record the sources and destinations of messages.

When debugging one issue, we could see that the messaging subsystem had received a command to cancel a transaction. But had it arrived from outside, or had it come from our controller? Missing such a basic piece of information meant we couldn't tell whether the problem was ours or the third party's, and we couldn't debug further without additional information.

The Goldilocks zone of logging

You will need to tune the level of logging from your system to get it exactly right since it can be tough to predict in advance. Some logs are too noisy, producing millions of useless lines; others omit vital information, which you only notice when you can't debug a critical issue. That delays fixes until you can release extra logging and wait for the problem to happen again. Both too much and too little logging are problems you need to fix, and the **Goldilocks** zone of sufficient logging lies somewhere in the middle.

The massive benefit of tuning the level of logging from your system is that users of that system can learn precisely what a successful sequence should look like. If there are tens of lines, you have a hope of remembering them all so that you can spot absences or anomalies. If there are hundreds of lines written for a single action, that becomes impossible.

Logging is such an essential part of your job as a tester that it must be written well. If you can't change the logs, go on whatever courses you need and set up mentorships so you can in the future. Changing log lines is simple and safe in the code but can transform the experience of debugging an issue. Combine the motivation with the ability to empower those who care. Testers are the biggest users of the logs, so you should be able to change them as needed.

Loglines should each be a readable account of a single action. I've seen loglines that simply stated *OK!* or *User added*. But what was okay? Which user was added? In structured logging, metadata sometimes provides more context, but the text itself should be comprehensible. The goal is for someone new to that area of code to be able to read the log and understand what has happened without extra details.

Any numeric fields should be labeled in the logs. While the developer might know what they all mean, newcomers won't. I've seen log lines with the following form:

```
Message received. 4: 243, 7: 32, 14: 23833
```

The ENUM field values are only useful for developers who have worked on the code for so long that they've memorized them. Naming fields is another small change that can transform the experience of using the logs, as you no longer have to look up what each field means.

Examine the logging for each new feature, checking for spam or gaps in the amount it provides, and that each line is an understandable sentence. If possible, fix these issues yourself.

Logging usability

The interface to read logs is also important to get right. The ideal is an interface that is aware these are messages and displays only their names, expanding them where necessary. This lets you quickly see an overview of what happened and examine the critical sections in more detail.

Visibility is vital. Seeing an overview of messages at a glance lets you instantly spot oddities. Maybe you were investigating a problem with a particular hypothesis in mind. If it takes effort to look through logs, then you will only realize you are wrong after you've taken the time to check that idea. Easily seeing summaries of events, especially the messages in and out, gives the chance to spot oddities and find other leads. If accessing the logs requires work, you are less likely to see problems.

Logs can be displayed in various ways:

- Network traces with no formatting
- Network traces formatted by a plugin
- Text logs
- Formatted logs
- Dedicated tools

While network traces will show you the messages being sent, a raw log requires significant effort to use. As well as setting it up on the correct interface, it needs to filter key messages from all the other traffic. Each message then needs to be decoded to understand its content. If these are text fields, some may be readable but you'll still need to know the meaning of each field. Crucially, it won't show you the names of each message so that you can narrow down the failure points.

One way to improve that is to write a plugin. If network captures are your best tool, make sure that you at least have a plugin to make them readable. When properly filtered and decoded, network traces can help to track messages in and out of your system. However, they still need to be captured at the right place and may not track messages between internal systems. It's much better if logging is higher in the application, only using network captures as a last resort.

Most simply, applications will write out text logs of their actions. This is better than nothing, but logs are most valuable when they can be filtered and searched. For standard log formats such as web server logs, there are numerous solutions to read these text logs and process them. For more custom logs, you need to do more work to make them easily searchable, and text logs can't provide a summary of just the message names, leaving you having to scan through all their contents. Structured logging fixes both those problems, so if you are using simple text logs, that is an important feature request.

When logs are structured, for instance, as JSON or XML, tools can filter on key fields such as time and severity. For more customized handling, for example, identifying log lines with message names versus those describing internal processing, you need tools to read out the logs in customized ways. Using dedicated tools to view structured logs is the best choice. These might be custom-made within your company, or numerous commercial options can be configured to view your logs. With this in place, you can easily see messages.

This is all very well, I hear you say. It would be lovely to have logs that clearly presented all and only the messages between the different systems in our product, but we don't have them. Our logs are a mixture of messages and implementation, scattered across various servers and accessed by hand.

This section showed what you should aim for. If your logging isn't like this today, plan to improve it by doing a little work alongside each release. Start with the most pressing issues – maybe your log lines are incomprehensible and need to be rewritten, or perhaps you need a new tool to view the logs. If you are adding a new feature, make sure its log lines are clear and understandable. All these investments pay back when investigating future issues.

Logging overview

Logs are a major part of your role as a tester, so pay close attention to getting them right. Check them as you use a new feature, even if everything is working and you don't need their output, to see how the code reports its activity. You need to check that the logs are written with the right details, are easy to find, and contain sufficient information to debug issues. There should be black-box level logging that records the messages sent between systems for testers to use, and white-box level testing detailing the code behavior for developers. This will need constant tuning as you see how it behaves in practice. With high-quality information displayed in easy-to-use tools, you have the best view of your application's behavior, ready to understand any surprises and fix issues.

Summary

In this chapter, we've seen the importance of testing the maintainability of maintenance operations, system monitoring, and logging. None of these functions are customer-facing, but each has a massive impact on the engineering team working on the product and, through them, the improvements they can deliver to customers. How fast can your company fix bugs, recover from outages, and roll out changes?

Those things affect customers, and they need maintainable code. That doesn't happen on its own; if you don't check that the requirements for maintainability are written and implemented, it's possible no one else will. This piece of testing is in your own best interest.

In the next chapter, we'll consider destructive testing in which you deliberately degrade your system to see how it copes with internal issues. These are vital to recovering from errors but can be hard to plan for, making it a critical area to test.

What we learned from Part 2, Functional Testing

Part 2, Functional Testing, has considered the behavior of your application in a wide range of situations, from security to usability to core application functions. These are all functional tests: when you do X, your application does Y. In that simple view, you check if your program's output is correct for all the relevant inputs.

That may sound exhaustive, but there are still types of testing we have not covered yet. In *Part 3, Non-Functional Testing*, we will consider destructive testing, in which you deliberately disable part of the working system to check its resilience and ability to recover. Load testing ensures that your application performs consistently within its specified limits, with no unexpected latency or intermittent errors.

Finally, stress testing checks what happens when your system is pushed beyond its limits and its ability to protect its core functions even when asked to do unreasonable workloads. Some of the most serious bugs can only be found with these stringent tests, so they are also vitally important.

Part 3 – Non-Functional Testing

Once the functional testing is complete, you can be confident that the feature under test will work as designed. But there is still more to check – what is the maximum load this feature can sustain? If there is an outage, how does the system behave, and how does it recover? Under load, are all features still available? This section considers the usage of the feature under extreme conditions, how to generate that load and the tests that should be run.

This section comprises the following chapters:

- *Chapter 11, Destructive Testing*
- *Chapter 12, Load Testing*
- *Chapter 13, Stress Testing*

11
Destructive Testing

"Is this a dagger which I see before me,

The handle toward my hand?"

- William Shakespeare, The Tragedy of Macbeth, Act 2, Scene 1

Destructive testing is a great way to find defects. By deliberately triggering specific errors, subsequent problems often occur. Even more so than error testing, as covered in *Chapter 7, Testing of Error Cases*, destructive testing gives you the chance to take the system out of its usual modes of operation to check its subsequent behavior.

These tests cover disabling communication with remote systems to check on retries and recovery. Your system cannot guarantee it will ever receive a reply to a message, so these scenarios need to be checked. Some subsystems are designed to be redundant, so we also consider testing that resilience. Disabling other subsystems will cause functional failures, so this measures their extent and recovery. Unfortunately, failures in remote systems will happen one day, so checking their behavior is a vital source of real-world bugs.

This chapter also covers backing up and restoring. Until you have practiced restoring from your backups, they may be useless, so to have any faith, you need this form of testing. Your backups may rarely be used, but on the day that they are required, you'll be glad you flushed the bugs from the system.

We'll cover the following topics in this chapter:

- Advantages and disadvantages of destructive testing
- Failover testing
- System shutdowns
- Communication failure
- Chaos engineering
- Backup and restore testing

If you enjoy kicking sandcastles over at the beach just to watch how they crumble, these are the tests for you. After all the hard work of carefully building your system and getting it running perfectly, you can deliberately destroy it just to see what happens. The question for this chapter is, can your system run even in a degraded state? This is the time to take up your metaphorical *dagger*, and any other tools at your disposal, to break your system.

Advantages and disadvantages of destructive testing

Destructive tests cover a range of conditions that other areas of testing don't touch. There is a class of bugs that you can only find with these tests, so make sure you include them in your test plan. The following table describes the advantages and disadvantages of destructive testing:

Advantages	Disadvantages
The only way to detect this class of issue	Tests rare cases
Verifies your resilience and recovery plans	Requires specialist environments, tools, and tests
	Need to filter valid failures from invalid ones

Table 11.1 – Advantages and disadvantages of destructive testing

After completing destructive testing, you will have much greater confidence in the resilience of your system to handle a wide range of adverse conditions.

On the downside, these tests can be de-prioritized compared to the core black- and white-box functional tests. This is particularly dangerous because system failures happen regularly and trigger issues. These cases may appear rare, but you will come across them before long.

These tests can be slower to run due to you needing to wait for timeouts or system recovery and require dedicated environments, tools, and configuration. Because they disrupt the system's performance, they will delay other users if they are run on shared systems. Ideally, all these tests should be run on a separate installation if you have the resources and the time to set that up.

These tests also need dedicated tools to trigger specific failure modes and specialist configurations. This higher barrier of entry can cause delays, and, like all non-functional tests, they should be run after the functional tests. You can only test system recovery if it was running correctly in the first place.

The final challenge for destructive tests is identifying valid and invalid failures. When part of the system is down, some functions will be unavailable, so you need to be clear on exactly what the behavior should be in those circumstances. This detail might not be in the specification, so it will need to be added. Finding errors and diagnosing issues is also harder because the system will have many alarms due to the planned outage. Nevertheless, finding unnecessary dependencies and parts of your application that could keep working, despite a partial outage, is important information for your company.

Destructive testing is an extension of testing for error cases, as described in *Chapter 7, Testing of Error Cases,* but those tests involve sending invalid data to a working system. The difference here is that you deliberately disable your system in some way. This is also known as **failover** or **disaster recovery testing**, which tests a unique set of circumstances. First, we will look at disrupting parts of your system that shouldn't cause outages, also known as failover testing.

Failover testing

Some parts of your system may be resilient to specific points of failure, so a great place to start destructive testing is to ensure those failovers happen successfully.

Designing destructive testing requires detailed knowledge of your system's architecture. Which elements interact with each other, and what is the failure mode for each of them? What classes of redundancy are used by the various parts of your system? Ensure you understand these workings and how your system should behave in failure cases.

Classes of redundancy

Redundant systems could include a pair of switches both capable of routing all the traffic, multiple web servers to which traffic can be sent, and database systems such as **Cassandra** that are capable of continuing when one node is down, among many others. Redundancy may be at the hardware or software level, although the approach and items to check are equivalent in both cases.

The important distinction for your testing is the failover strategy used by your subsystems, as illustrated here:

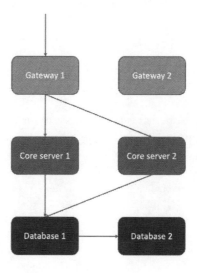

Figure 11.1 – Different failover strategies at different application layers

In this example, the pair of gateways work in a live-standby configuration. Only one accepts traffic at any time, but the system is capable of automatically detecting a problem with the live unit and using the backup instead. To test this, disable the live gateway and check that the automatic detection and rerouting properties send traffic to the second unit within the required timeout.

At the next stage, the core servers are configured in a live-live configuration, with both accepting live traffic simultaneously. Failover for this arrangement is faster since one server remains online and accepts traffic, so only transactions in flight during the failure should be affected. Once the gateways recognize the outage, they should reroute all traffic to the remaining server. Again, your task is to check that the outage is detected and that the system responds quickly and correctly.

At the lowest level, the databases work in a live-standby configuration, but unlike the other servers, they are stateful, with the master live-streaming its state to the backup. If you lose the master, you will lose any transactions it hadn't had time to synchronize. Again, your system must detect the failure, reroute the traffic, and mark the backup database as the master. On recovery, the previous master database needs to resynchronize and become the backup, as described in the *Failover recovery* section.

> **Real-world example – Failing the failover server**
>
> I once worked for a company that hosted a private cloud running in a cold standby arrangement. Our core database ran in location A, with a backup ready to be brought live in location B. The control system to perform the failover was also hosted in location A.
>
> This was a bad arrangement. Location A had an unreliable network and one day, we lost contact for several hours. Our main database went offline and, of course, we also lost the control system. Our backup database was reachable in location B, but we couldn't tell the rest of the system to use it. Make sure you separate your core servers from the ones controlling any failovers.

If your system doesn't have these automatic failover mechanisms in place, then implementing them is a priority. Testing non-redundant systems will be described in the *System shutdowns* section.

Performing failovers

Before performing a failover, ensure that your system is running correctly. You must start from a known good state before disrupting it. First, start a task to check a particular function – for instance, regular requests of a web page, running a ping command, or an ongoing action such as a video call. Then, shut down the subsystem under test. You need to check the behavior over two different periods – during the transition and after the failover when the system has recovered.

Throughout destructive testing, there are two failure modes to consider: **graceful shutdown** and **hard shutdown**. A graceful shutdown means invoking the software to stop itself, giving it time to finish any operations it was performing – for instance, closing external connections and completing I/O tasks – before stopping the software. The alternative is a hard shutdown, where you kill the process or otherwise completely stop the service without warning.

It can be helpful to ensure that graceful shutdowns are indeed graceful and cleanly finish their operations, but for destructive testing, hard shutdowns are the more interesting case. They test all the conditions graceful shutdowns do and more because they check that systems can recover from interruptions. Hard shutdowns also mimic crashes or hardware failures more realistically. In this case, systems will be interrupted rather than having time to finish their operations. While it can be useful to test both, hard shutdowns are the priority. If you only have time to try one type, use that one.

During the failover measure, ask yourself the following questions:

- What is the user experience?

- What monitoring alarms are raised?

- What errors are shown in the logging?

- Are there any unexpected side effects?

- What is the load performance?

To measure the user experience, you can set up a repeating check that runs throughout the failover event. You should see a pattern of successes, then failures, and then successes, with the failures lasting no longer than it takes for the system to recover. Those repeating checks can test multiple levels, such as client connections, web page loading, and system actions such as creating new entities. Likewise, your monitoring should report how long the system was unavailable, if it can detect issues as short as a failover. Error logs should definitely report the problem.

To measure load performance, run a load test while performing the failover. Instead of creating entities one at a time to measure the functionality, create them at the highest rate the system can sustain. This is likely to trigger failures, so you will need to decide what success rate is required. For a longer discussion on that class of tests, see *Chapter 13, Stress Testing*.

You can also add impairments to mimic real issues. There is the risk that your test environment is too perfect and controlled, which doesn't represent the live system well. You can add all network impairments described in *Chapter 7, Testing of Error Cases*, such as latency and packet loss, to see how that affects the failover times, alarms, and user experience.

Remember to leave the failover in place. Problems may only become apparent after minutes or hours in the new state, such as memory leaks or performance degradation, so don't be in a hurry to recover the service. Leave it disabled while performing another test to check that the system can function well while failing over.

Failover error reporting

Check that your application raises alarms while a subsystem is down. Generating a warning for a machine being offline is simple enough; hopefully, that is already in place. It's harder to filter out alarms that are just effects of the main issue. If a web server is down, you shouldn't have 10 errors from the edge servers telling you the same thing. As we saw in *Chapter 10, Maintainability*, alerts can be made dependent on each other so that it's easier to find the source of the problem.

More importantly, are there any errors that shouldn't be present? Are there any unexpected failures that could be avoided? Check your monitoring carefully to ensure the failure is as limited as possible.

In the logs, checks the errors that are raised in the same way. Many alerts will be related to your deliberate outage and, unlike monitoring, the knock-on effects cannot be filtered out. Again, you are looking for any extra errors beyond what you expect in that state.

Failover recovery

The main pass mark for failover testing is that the system should recover within the specified timeout. If it doesn't, that's a major bug to raise.

Given that the system does recover, carefully check that all key aspects are working now that you're on the backup system. This will vary, depending on the part of the system you are testing. The primary functions, such as loading pages with one web server/database node offline, are easy to check. But can you add new users? This operation requires pages to load, and the database's writes and reads, for instance. The details will depend on your system, but if possible, perform an entire regression test run while one part of the system has failed.

After the failover, you should measure the following aspects:

- How long does the system take to fully recover?
- Is all functionality restored?
- What monitoring alarms are still being raised?
- What errors are shown in the logging?
- Are transactions dropped, or does the system recover within its timeout?
- Measure server metrics for the remaining machines, such as the following:
  - CPU usage
  - Memory
  - Disk usage
  - Thread/process counts

The time taken for a failover to occur is one of the main differences between a graceful and hard shutdown. During a graceful shutdown of a redundant aspect of the system, the downtime should be minimal as it closes its current transactions and lets the other parts of the system know that it is going offline. In contrast, during a hard shutdown, there will be a delay waiting for a timeout while other parts of the system realize that the service is offline and initiate failovers. Measure the time carefully, from shutdown to full recovery. You'll need to work with the development team to specify the expected time and how long would be too long to wait.

Compare the failover time to the transaction time for your system. If your web requests time out after 10 seconds, but failovers take 12, you will drop requests that began at the start of the failover. Those that started partway through the outage will succeed when the server recovers. Check your retry times and timeouts compared to your failover times; waiting a little longer for retries could make many more transactions succeed.

Measuring the system's throughput once it has failed over should be part of that regression test plan, as described in *Chapter 13, Stress Testing*. The product specification should state the capacity when in failure mode. Should the system be capable of the same loading even when failed over? Or should the system be capable of more than twice the load you usually receive, so running at half capacity is still sufficient for your service? This is your chance to measure that degraded performance in practice.

System recovery

Finally, recover the disabled subsystem and ensure your application returns to its initial state. No monitoring alerts should persist, and all transactions should continue as normal as the system comes back online. Recovery is the most important step and shouldn't require manual intervention. Any additional actions you have to take can be raised as bugs or feature requests for future improvement.

For stateless systems, coming back online is simple – they just need to be running. It's more complex for stateful machines, which will need to resynchronize. For databases, this means copying the transactions they missed while offline. For processes that periodically read data, they must go back and catch up for the period they missed. In my experience, this area has rich pickings of bugs. Refer to the list of variables you can test for time fields from *Chapter 5, Black-Box Functional Testing*; you can reuse them here. What happens if the outage runs past midnight? Or the synchronization has to copy from another time zone or across a daylight savings change? This involves complex logic that you need to test.

After failover testing, you must move on to any parts of your system that aren't covered by redundant systems and will affect the live service.

System shutdowns

Which parts of your system are single points of failure, and whose removal will disrupt the service? Like failover testing, for these services, you can mimic crashes, hardware failure, loss of power, or cloud computing services being down – anything that makes a subsystem unavailable for a prolonged period. Examine your system architecture again to identify all the possibilities so that you can work through them systematically.

Testing during a shutdown is often complicated due to the exact behavior not being specified. In some organizations, it is difficult to carefully define the behavior of a fully working system, let alone cover the different failure modes. Work with the developers and product owners to determine the performance in these situations.

In addition to single points of failure, you can trigger multiple outages or major outages – rather than simulating losing one switch, for instance, what happens if the entire site or cloud service has an outage? You may have no failure plan in place; if your cloud provider goes down, you might expect your service to be down until they recover. If so, make a note to plan for that contingency, at least in terms of communication. In operations, my motto was that everyone has a bad day. To control your service's uptime, you must test backups for all your subsystems.

Shutdown test plan

Having identified the systems to disable and the behavior you should observe in that situation, you can now run through a test plan for shutdowns:

- Check the degraded functionality of the overall system

- Check the behavior of other services

- Check the loading of the degraded system

- Check the monitoring during the outage

- Check if the recovery is successful

- Check the behavior after recovery

First, test the system's functionality to ensure the outage is limited to the subsystems you have shut down. Are there any further issues? If possible, run adapted regression testing, identifying which tests should still work. Are there any functions that should work but have been disabled by the outage?

> **Real-world example – Non-redundant VPNs**
>
> At one company I worked in, we had two offices and could connect to the VPN of either. If one site lost its connection, we could connect to the other. However, when one office went down for real, we lost access to its LDAP server. Users connecting to the other site couldn't authenticate, so we couldn't connect to either location.

Look out for any surprising losses in functionality when half of a redundant system is down, especially any that defeat the whole point of having redundancy. These may be hard to work out, so a practical test is the best way to be sure. Usually, these inefficiencies cause no problems other than imperceptible delays and loading, but during an outage, they can significantly degrade behavior. Removing unnecessary dependencies is vital for the day when you face such an outage for real.

Next, test for incorrect behavior in the remaining system. For example, check for repeated retries sending constant messages. These might be from applications back to the server or between servers within the system. There should be exponential backoffs to limit messaging, which rapidly increases the time between messages to reduce the load both on the sender and the receiver. Without those backoffs, it's easy for you to DDoS yourself as your applications all spam your servers with messages when they fail to receive replies. It might look funny when a single application gets itself in a loop, but when a hundred thousand users can't reach your service when it's recovering from an outage, the humor wears off.

Shutdown error reporting

System errors should be reported back to the user. There will be expected errors, but they should be controlled and informative, saying that the system cannot complete their request temporarily. They shouldn't give incorrect information, such as suggesting the user immediately retry, and they should be explicitly designed rather than silently timing out or presenting web server errors or backtraces. Those are bugs that need to be fixed.

Check the monitoring during the outage. Make sure there are accurate error reports that track exactly what has failed. Even better, add dependencies to your monitoring so that the system expects specific problems to follow from one core issue. For instance, if one server goes down, you don't need 20 messages from your other servers telling you they can't reach it. It's much better to have a single, clear error rather than sifting through many consequences. For more on that, see *Chapter 10, Maintainability*.

Next, when you restart the server, does the system fully recover? Are there any manual steps you need to take before the service is restored? Those are improvements to make for the future. This may include VMs that have not been set to start on boot, services starting in the wrong order, or other common issues on a restart, but the system should be able to recover automatically. Anything else adds delays and risk to recovery from an actual outage.

Killing processes

As well as long-term outages simulated by failing over and shutting down the system, you can also mimic crashes by killing services. As mentioned previously, the critical test here is to ensure they recover without manual intervention. There should be errors and failures while the service restarts, but it should come back cleanly.

First, make a list of processes you can test. If you have an application communicating with central servers, this will start with the applications themselves, edge servers, core servers, and the database. Within each server, consider any web servers or other communications, then all processes and regularly scheduled jobs that run there.

As this is a quicker test, you can try this at many points within the state machine for your product. You can try this at several points in the signup cycle for a new user, for instance, or when receiving different API commands. Check what happens if a crash occurs during an upgrade, startup, or shutdown. The system should be left in a consistent state when it recovers – if a user needed to confirm their email address, for instance, is that still the case when the system comes back? As we saw in *Chapter 6, White-Box Functional Testing*, you need to identify all the different states and verify each.

While restarting services, look out for errors related to database entries. Database changes that should be performed as a group need to be committed in a single transaction, and this form of testing is one way to find those that aren't. A crash interrupting an unprotected transaction can leave the database in an inconsistent state. Consider a Users table, where each user has related statistics in another table:

Users		
ID	First name	Second name
123	Alice	Smith
124	Bob	Jones
125	Charles	Brown

Statistics		
ID	User ID	Stat 1
32	123	4
32	124	7
34	125	2

Figure 11.2 – Database tables before adding entries

The user ID in the Statistics table is a foreign key in the Users table. Whenever a new user is added, you need new entries in both places:

Users		
ID	First name	Second name
123	Alice	Smith
124	Bob	Jones
125	Charles	Brown
126	Daniela	Wilson

Statistics		
ID	User ID	Stat 1
32	123	4
32	124	7
34	125	2
35	126	0

Figure 11.3 – Database tables after successfully adding an entry

One table has to be written first, however. If the Users table is updated, then the application suffers a crash, and it could be left in an inconsistent state:

Users		
ID	First name	Second name
123	Alice	Smith
124	Bob	Jones
125	Charles	Brown
126	Daniela	Wilson
127	Eliza	Taylor

Statistics		
ID	User ID	Stat 1
32	123	4
32	124	7
34	125	2
35	126	0

Figure 11.4 – Database tables interrupted during writing

The transaction should be protected so that if you can't write to both tables, the operation completely fails and writes to neither of them. However, if that's not the case, then you may be left with a user partially created. They will appear in the application but fail as soon as they use their statistics and need to be manually fixed.

It is not easy to trigger a crash at precisely the right time, so killing processes isn't a great way to find this class of errors, but it is most likely to encounter issues hit by real crashes. For example, the longer a database transaction takes, the more likely it is to be hit by both your testing and a real-life crash.

Code inspection is a better way to find these errors, which involves identifying the database operations that have to succeed or fail together. They are hard to find in testing, but deliberately slowing down database operations with debug commands or other I/O loads increases the chance of hitting errors.

Starting back up

Shutting down is easy; the trick is starting back up again. This also needs a careful test plan:

- Do all the machines automatically restart?
- Do all the necessary processes start?
- Are there any dependencies on startup?
- Do processes start in the correct order?

If you are adding a new machine or process to your system, check that it has been set to restart and in the correct order relative to its dependencies. Starting too early or late might cause delays or, in some cases, prevent it from booting at all.

If a startup is successful on its own, try shutting down combinations of services simultaneously to see if they can recover together. There can be many combinations, so prioritize those that rely on each other and interact in some way. For example, if both services require the other to be running, both being down would prevent either from starting.

> **Real-world example – After you. No, after you**
>
> In one company I worked at, we introduced a new protocol between our core servers. They had been mainly independent before, primarily communicating via a shared central database, but now, they could talk to each other directly.
>
> This change introduced a host of problems, not least when we did the first upgrade after running the new system. The new protocol failed to start on our servers and the reason, it turned out, was that we'd upgraded them at the same time. So long as one side of the protocol lost connection, it would retry and eventually connect. However, if both sides went down simultaneously – for instance, due to an upgrade – it went into an error state, and neither side could recover. Restarts worked, but not simultaneously.

While restarting may generally work well, does it still succeed when your system is under a realistic load? Here, you will need load-testing tools to mimic your users: client connections, online players, data processing, or whatever service you provide. How well does your system cope while starting up while being hammered with connection requests or with a long processing queue waiting? That's the situation you'll face if there's a crash during live operations, so that's the one to test.

Next, we will consider a more subtle form of destructive test, where your system continues to run but different subsystems can't communicate.

Communication failure

As well as shutting a service down, tests should introduce another common, realistic problem – **communication failure**. Like system outages, these are real scenarios: blocking communication simulates a network outage while all the services are still running.

Blocking communication allows for a more specific test – you can let most of the system continue as normal and just restrict access between two particular processes. This can test specific failure scenarios, although they may be less realistic. You should work through different options, varying between large realistic outages and small specific failures that are less realistic but test distinct failure modes within the system.

You can also alter when communication failures occur. During a message sequence, test what happens if you fail to receive a reply to each message. Like white-box testing state machines, this ensures there is correct error handling at every stage. This will need careful scripting so that you can coordinate sending messages with the network degradation on the destination machine.

When blocking traffic, always block the receiver rather than the sender of the message. While testing a service, it can be tempting to block its messages, as shown here:

Figure 11.5 – Blocking the service under test from sending messages

Since you are working with it already, this is often easy to do. However, blocking the sender lets the server know that the message failed, which will trigger a different error case compared to not receiving a reply. For a realistic outage, you need the receiver to fail to respond:

Figure 11.6 – Blocking the remote service from receiving messages

This might be harder to configure, as it needs to accept all other traffic, but setting up such filtering is necessary for a realistic test.

Communication failures are harder to emulate than shutdowns. It's simple enough to turn off parts of your system! Communication failures, in contrast, will need dedicated tools to simulate a network failure in a controlled way, such as **iptables** and **netem**.

Whichever method you use, it's helpful to run the same tests as for system shutdowns: check the system's overall functionality for issues in other services, as well as loading, monitoring, and recovery.

Next, we will look at how to automatically perform destructive testing to look for possible issues using Chaos Monkey.

Chaos engineering

While it's good to think through which combinations of systems and services you can disable and restart, there is always the possibility that you have missed something. For confidence in your application's resilience, you can implement Chaos Monkey to automatically cause failures throughout your system.

This idea was made famous by Netflix, which introduced a program called **Chaos Monkey** to deliberately disable parts of their system. The best way to ensure you are resilient to any outage and can recover from it is by routinely doing it for real. Recall the options listed in the *Classes of redundancy* section:

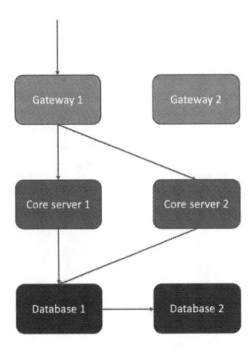

Figure 11.7 – Different failover strategies at different application layers

The gateways represent systems that run in live-standby mode, with only a single server taking traffic, but a backup ready to come online. The core servers run live-live, with both taking traffic, and the database is also live-standby, but with replication to keep their state synchronized. Chaos Monkey will periodically disable different servers, testing each kind of resilience and recovery for your particular subsystems.

Its actions are limited, for instance, to disabling only a single subsystem at a time. To apply this to your architecture, you will need to list the relevant machines and identify which are supposed to have redundant systems in place. Then, Chaos Monkey will periodically select an item from that list at random and disable it, measure the key performance metrics (see the *Failover testing* section), and then re-enable the system and measure again.

An even better test of your resilience is to leave system-level regression testing running in parallel with Chaos Monkey to ensure that all functions are available while different subsystems are disabled. Where systems are independent, it should be possible to disable them simultaneously and see no effect – for instance, turning off one switch, one edge server, and one database to let the system run on the other half of those pairs.

Chaos Monkey provides resiliency load testing. While performing a single test might show that the system can recover successfully, can it recover every time? Are there timings or external scenarios that might cause it to fail? You can build confidence that the system can recover across various situations by repeatedly triggering different failures in the same area. We'll see more benefits of load testing across multiple domains in *Chapter 12, Load Testing*.

Using Chaos Monkey is analogous to fuzz testing on interfaces (see *Chapter 7, Testing of Error Cases*). Rather than thinking through different problematic situations and combinations, you can add the possibilities and let the program work through them randomly, eventually covering all options. If you are truly confident, you can run this on your live instance, although I would recommend a dedicated test system first. When running successfully, you have far more confidence in your system, its performance when degraded, and its recovery.

Next, we will consider testing your backup and restore process.

Backup and restore testing

A crucial part of destructive testing is ensuring your backups can restore your system correctly. Your backups are worthless until they've been tried in practice. This is a significant operation and highly disruptive, so as with all destructive testing, you'll need a dedicated test environment for it. The following is a checklist of tests to run around backup and restore:

- Is the system fully functional during backups?

- Are there different types of backups you can restore from?

    - Partial or full backups

    - Different database systems

    - Streaming replication versus from one point in time

- How long do backup and restore operations take?

- Is there a warning if taking a backup is disrupted?

- Ensure you can restore from all backup types

- When restoring from a backup, is everything replaced?

- Are any manual steps required when restoring from a backup?

Taking a backup can be a disruptive operation in itself since it involves database tables being locked and operations being paused while copying. There are ways around these issues, but if related data is stored in separate locations, it may be necessary to lock different parts of the system while copies are taken to ensure consistency. Improving those issues can mean a major system re-architecture, so they are tough to fix. You can provide measurements on which functions are disrupted and for how long. Moving backups to the quietest periods of the week can mitigate their disruption, but data storage must be carefully designed to avoid issues.

Do you take different types of backups? If so, you will need to practice restoring each of them. For instance, if you have a streaming-replicated database, can you failover to the other unit? They contain up-to-date information, so if data is deleted, that deletion will be rapidly copied to the backup too. To recover lost data, you also need regular static backups. They will be outdated and won't contain the latest changes, but they will let you go back to an earlier version if recent changes have been problematic. You need one test for each kind of backup you keep.

How long is it acceptable for backup and restore operations to take? Daily backups ideally take less than 24 hours, but you will have to judge how long is too long for your system. Since that depends on the quantity of data, you will need a large test installation to check it. Otherwise, you can measure the backup time from the live instance. More important, though, is the restoration time. In an emergency, how long would it take you to recover? You will need a large amount of test data to replicate this, but it is essential to know because it can be a long time for a large system, depending on your tools and architecture.

Your backup process should be resilient to failures. If you have a distributed system with data stored in different locations, a failure in one place needn't mean the backup fails overall. If you have 10 data stores and one is unavailable, you can back up the other nine and raise a warning that the backup only partially succeeded. Even within one database, you can perform a partial backup to save only some of its data. If you have that in place, then you need to test that you can restore both full and partial backups and that those partial backups leave the system in a consistent state afterward.

Check that your monitoring system covers the status of your backups. If you deliberately disrupt it by stopping it completely or partially, do you get a warning to let you know? This should be as specific as possible; if the backup partially succeeded, does the monitoring process show you which part failed and why? The alarm should be clear about how out of date your backup is now and when the last backup succeeded.

Whether streaming from replicated or static files, partial backups or full, testing the restore process is the most crucial part of the process. You need to try all backup types, clearly recording the system's state beforehand to ensure the changes are rolled back. Does the backup include all the configuration for the system, or is any missing? Look out for any recently added features, especially for supplementary data stores. Is anything stored outside your primary database, such as data files or logs? Check their state – how do the logs appear after they've been restored? Are there different steps to follow to restore other parts of the system?

Is your system left in a good state after performing a restore? If there are multiple data stores, do you have to restore all of them simultaneously? What happens if you don't? Do your backups contain enough information to perform all those restorations and are they automatic run from a single command? Or are there multiple steps?

Keep careful track of all the manual steps required when restoring from a backup. If you have different data stores, do they each need separate steps and is the ordering important? Wherever possible, write a script to ensure that all the steps are taken in the correct order. In a distributed system, you may need to have access to many different subsystems, with enough permissions to read and write all the data there. Do specific steps have to be performed in a given order? Again, a script will guarantee that happens.

What checks can you add during this process to ensure that each step has succeeded before proceeding to the next? If there are several manual steps, then these checks need to be documented, but you should also raise an improvement to make them part of your script. If the script discovers any failures or surprises, it should stop in case continuing the restoration would leave the system in a bad state, but it should always be possible to override those checks. It might be less work to let the restoration continue and then fix the issues than it is to fix the problems and then restore. There are likely to be manual decisions during an operation as serious as restoring from a backup, so make sure any script gives you the option for that to happen.

Once you have restored your system as completely as possible, look out for subsequent bugs. For instance, are any sequence numbers repeated when you take the system back to an earlier state? Does that work successfully for both full and partial backups? Do connections still work to external systems, especially those that contain stored data? You can test this in both directions – if you delete data, is it restored correctly, and if you add data, is it removed correctly by the restore process? Is the state completely synchronized with those external systems, or is there a mechanism to detect inconsistencies and report them?

Real-world example – Only restoring half the configuration

In one company I worked at, our service stored some files in an external service. We maintained references and retrieved them from the service when our customers requested them. When we deleted a customer, we deleted their files on the service and our reference to them.

Problems arose when restoring from backup. The sequence was as follows:

1. Take a backup.

2. Delete a customer.

3. Restore from backup.

In that case, we deleted both the file and our reference to it in stage 2. In stage 3, we restored our reference, but we couldn't recover the deleted file. We were left with a broken reference, and our system had no way to reconcile and fix the difference.

Restoring from backups rarely happens, but on that day, you need confidence that it will work. I've never personally been bitten by a restore operation failing. Still, there are tales in the industry of nightmare scenarios, lost weekends, and missing data as engineers struggle to recover systems affected by failures or attacks. It's a vital part of testing, so check it regularly.

Summary

In this chapter, you learned about the importance of destructive testing and the main areas it covers. Deliberately degrading your system by stopping services or servers, blocking communications, triggering failovers, and restoring from backups are all vital areas to cover to ensure your system will perform well in live environments. None of these areas test features that customers use. They generally have far less development time devoted to them than features that provide users with more functionality or improve customer experience. However, without checking this behavior, how the entire system runs is at risk.

With areas of the system designed to be redundant, you need to ensure those failovers occur correctly. The monitoring process should report the error, but the overall functionality should not be changed. There may be a period of transition while the system detects the issue and reroutes traffic or processing, so you need to measure that time and ensure that full functionality is restored once it is complete.

For areas that are single points of failure, check the behavior when that service is down. There will be some service degradation, but it should be limited to the function provided by that service. Again, does the monitoring rapidly and correctly report the outage? Does the rest of the system keep functioning correctly? Are there any invalid behaviors in the rest of the system, such as constant retries? Does the service recover successfully once the service has been restored, without further manual steps? If the answer is no to any of those questions, then there is a defect in the system.

Communication failures are effectively similar to parts of the system being offline since they prevent particular messages from being sent. This is the realistic case of a temporary network outage, so you must ensure your service can survive. Are retries sent correctly, and does the system report the errors back to the user in a controlled and helpful way? Killing processes to simulate crashes requires similar considerations.

Once you have verified your system's resilience, you can implement Chaos Monkey to constantly cause system issues. This provides much greater confidence that your system can fail over and recover from errors across many scenarios rather than just a single test.

We also considered backing up and restoring your system. This is a major operation that is rarely used, but you need to ensure it will work correctly. As a tester, it's your job to provide that confidence. All backup types need to work, and you need to check the recovery of all the elements in your system.

In the next chapter, we'll leave the system running happily but test your system's maximum performance. Load testing checks that your application can handle peak activity and lets you plan for the future while proving test passes weren't happy accidents and can be repeated many times across many different situations.

12
Load Testing

"If you can fill the unforgiving minute,

With sixty seconds' worth of distance run,

Yours is the Earth and everything that's in it,

And – which is more – you'll be a Man, my son!"

– If by Rudyard Kipling, from the book Rewards and Fairies

In the previous chapter, we saw the importance of destructive testing and trying the failure modes of your system when different services are restarted or offline. In this chapter, we will turn to another vital aspect of non-functional testing – **load testing**.

Load testing is non-functional because it provides no new checks of the functions of your system. All the tests you run here should have been covered before in black- and white-box testing to ensure they work in at least one scenario. Load testing extends that testing to determine the limits of your system – how does it perform during periods of peak activity? Are operations resilient and reliable even when running many millions of times? How fast does your system run during high loading? What CPU, disk, and memory resources does your system need, and are they reasonable?

A separate question involves what happens when you go beyond these limits to deliberately restrict system resources, run for excessive periods, or apply too great a load. This will be considered in the next chapter, *Chapter 13, Stress Testing*. In this chapter, you will learn about the following topics:

- How to identify load testing operations
- Understanding load testing variables

  - Static versus dynamic
  - Soak testing versus spikes in load

- Designing load-testing applications
- What to check while load testing
- How to find race conditions in asynchronous systems

- Identifying coding inefficiencies

- Checking the performance of your system

- Filtering loading errors

- Debugging loading issues

The question for this chapter is, can your system fill each unforgiving minute with 60 seconds' worth of program run?

Advantages and disadvantages of load testing

As with many of these sections, the advantage of load testing is that it is the only way to find this class of bugs, and there are no alternatives. Only by deliberately loading the system can you discover interactions and limitations when your application performs many actions quickly. These are very difficult to predict and plan for, which is why this testing is so essential. Other advantages and disadvantages of load testing are as follows:

Advantages	Disadvantages
The only way to find this class of issue	Requires dedicated tools
The only way to measure system performance	Requires high-quality tools
Uncovers hard-to-find issues	Harder to debug
Finds software inefficiencies	Less realistic scenarios
	Expensive

Table 12.1 – Advantages and disadvantages of load testing

The other major advantage of load testing is that it is the only way to measure system performance. While the specification might state that the system is capable of handling some amount of load, that is not a value the development team can simply type in. It results from the interactions and performance of various factors interacting with each other. It is challenging to predict; the only way to be sure is to test it in practice.

To find errors that only occur once in a thousand times, you'll need to perform that function a thousand times, on average. They may be rare but depending on how often your customers use that function, this may happen daily. These are crucial issues that the product owner and development team won't find by giving the code a quick try, but they will affect your users. They are difficult to reproduce and isolate, so they need a dedicated test plan.

Load testing also finds inefficiencies in your application. For example, if a core function takes 10 times as long to run in your latest release, this is where you should see that. The function might work and pass all other forms of testing, but when you perform thousands of them each day, your system won't handle the load and will start to fail.

Real-world example – Reading events since the beginning of time

One of the worst bugs I ever shipped could only have been found with load testing. At one cloud provider where I worked, we started to see slow responses and crashes from our units. They appeared seemingly at random, although they mainly affected our busiest sites hosting some of our biggest customers.

These issues were a nightmare to debug since our logs at the time were held locally on units, which were slow and unresponsive. Because our system still provided some service, we couldn't take units out of commission once they were in this state. Sometimes, the problems would be bad enough to cause crashes, but they returned in the same condition even after a restart.

Eventually, we tracked the issue to disk usage, then to the database, and then to one particular command. Our previous release added an inefficiency that searched through every event stored on a unit. The more time that passed, the worse the problem became until the units slowed down and crashed. It had survived all our testing but failed under load.

Load testing is one of the hardest areas to perform and debug. It requires dedicated tools to generate traffic, a realistic system to run against, and sufficient resources to load it heavily. Load testing tools have to be of high quality, too. If you are looking for a failure that only happens one time in a thousand, then you need your tools to be at least that reliable; otherwise, they will fail before your system. If they fail earlier, you will end up searching through many spurious errors or, some classes of issues may not appear at all. For instance, if your test system leaks memory faster than the system under test, you may never uncover the real issue.

Load testing generates many ancillary problems, from disks filling with logs to email spam and database tables bloated with test data. Along with performing the loading, you will need scripts to clean up after yourself. This may mean rotating logs, clearing database entries, or putting restrictions on what actions the tests perform, for instance, preventing them from sending emails. All that is extra work but it's necessary to have these tests run smoothly.

Debugging load tests is especially hard given the number of operations going on simultaneously. During load testing, the logs will be full of traffic, and multiple services will be in use simultaneously. Picking apart the causes of problems is difficult, especially as you search for issues that do not appear during lighter loading.

There is a major class of issues that you only hit when performing load testing. For instance, deleting a user before it has been fully created may leave the database in an invalid state. While a genuine issue, it will never be encountered by a real user unless they are making and deleting users within milliseconds of each other. That's something load testing does, but no real user ever would.

You need to filter out that class of error. To do that, you can alter the load tests to work around system limitations, especially by slowing them down to more realistic speeds. Alternatively, you can trigger the issue but filter it out and ignore it or, if the development team has time, actually fix the problem on the system. While that might sound like an obvious choice, fixing an issue that only testers will ever see is not a high priority. They could work on other bugs and features that will have a more direct customer impact instead.

Load testing is often expensive, either in terms of the dedicated hardware it requires or the compute time on cloud services you have to pay for. That's in addition to the time it takes to set up a run. You will need a dedicated environment to run load tests since they are antisocial and may impact other operations. You can't rely on valid test results if load testing occurs simultaneously. That alternate system takes resources and time to set up.

Despite these weaknesses, load testing uncovers such critical bugs that it should be a crucial part of your test program. First, we will consider the technical requirements to carry out any load testing.

Prerequisites

Successfully performing load testing has several prerequisites beyond that of other forms of testing:

- **A dedicated test environment**: Taking the system to its limits may cause other tests to fail, so they should be run elsewhere.

- **A complete test environment**: To see realistic loading issues, you will need a complete, realistic system with the correct subsystems and resources in place.

- **A reliable test environment**: You need networks without packet loss and systems without other recurring issues before you can reliably find loading issues.

- **A loaded test environment**: Add at least as many entities as are present on your live system.

- **Load generation tools**: To rapidly create entities and perform actions on your system:

  - This includes generating web requests or a database load, simulating client connections, or data processing tasks. For more details, see the *Load test design* section.

All these need to be in place to carry out the tests in this section.

> **Real-world example – The dummy hardware**
>
> In one video conferencing company I worked for, we had a dedicated test environment. However, the hardware for video processing was expensive and unnecessary for many of the tests. While we had some real hardware, others were just virtualized, providing the same functionality but capable of much lower performance.
>
> That arrangement caused regular headaches and every few months, a tester would complain about tests failing when they were running them on the wrong hardware. Finally, we bit the bullet and purchased enough hardware so that the entire system could run realistic tests.

While load tests have more prerequisites than functional tests, you can still perform them early in the release cycle if you have sufficient warning and planning. Since load testing can take significant time and is a great way to flush out issues, it's well worthwhile getting organized to run it as early as you can.

With a realistic, reliable system in place, you can start to plan your load testing, starting by identifying which operations produce load on your system.

Identifying load operations

A massive surge in traffic might be a good problem, but when someone famous retweets your brand or your latest advert goes viral, that may be what you face. How will your system perform? That could be your one chance to make a first impression on thousands of potential customers, so you want it to be a good one.

What are the key operations of your system? These are functions your application runs repeatedly and that might cause a burst of load. Users signing up, logging in, and logging out are three common examples. If administrators can manage other users, then the creation and deletion of accounts are two others. Otherwise, your load testing will depend on your business: the number of simultaneous games you can run on your servers or video calls, the data you can gather, the processing you can perform, the downloads you can sustain, and the page impressions you can render. The possibilities are many and varied.

Go back to your core use cases and break them down into stages. What if a thousand users performed them simultaneously? There will be a whole series of operations a user will go through, so pick out each step as a requirement for your load testing.

> **Real-world example – The halftime break**
>
> I worked for a company that manufactured hardware to deliver SMS messages, back before smartphones when texting was the main way people messaged each other. I was onsite in Athens to commission equipment as it went live when Greece reached the European Championship semi-finals. Our kit would instantly face a massive test.
>
> I could see the SMS traffic across the country, in real time, for the network we were supplying. It built up to a peak before kickoff before thankfully dying down during the first half. Traffic plateaued again during halftime, and I braced myself for the final peak as the game ended. We had performed well, and I didn't want to push our luck.
>
> But the game went to extra time, prolonging my nervous wait even longer. After another dip, there was one last surge at the final whistle, which gradually died off into the evening as the Greeks celebrated their win. My hosts were doubly happy about the performance of their network and their team.

You must have tools that can stress each function of your application individually so that you can choose exactly how to combine them. You can plot curves of variables against each other. For example, your system may support 100 simultaneous downloads and 300 logged-in users, but can it do both simultaneously? Perhaps it can only manage 50 downloads and 100 live users. You don't need to plot a detailed graph, but you'll need to pick representative points to see how the variables affect each other.

It's no use being able to support 100 downloads only if no users are on the system because, in practice, there will always be users. You may need to pick ratios for your loading variables – two logged-in users per download, for instance – so you can specify your system's capability under realistic usage.

System performance is often under-specified, as described in *Chapter 2, Writing Great Feature Specifications*. Perhaps no one has ever considered the maximum rate of sign-ups your application should be capable of. The product owner may not have a strong opinion, and the developers might not know what rate the system can support. In these cases, pick an agreed rate and test up to it. You're aiming for a value far beyond practical usage and within current capabilities to keep the product owner and development team happy. Once you've picked that number and tested it, set your monitoring to warn you if you ever approach it in live use. You may be able to go beyond it, but that needs another, harsher test.

Dynamic versus static load

You can put two different forms of load on your system: large numbers of entities or significant rates of change. For instance, having a million users configured on your system applies one form of loading; creating one user per second involves the second form. For each of the core operations you have identified, test both a large static configuration and a rapid rate of usage.

You will need to look out for different styles of issues in various cases. With a sizeable static configuration, consider low-level processing such as the following:

- Database query times

- Data processing times

- System resource use:

  - CPU

  - Memory

  - Disk

  - Internal resources such as file handles, database connections, addresses, and so on

Also, consider the effects on the application overall and frontend behavior:

- Loading times of interfaces, especially those that rely on filtering entities from long lists of entities:

  - APIs

  - Web pages

  - App screens

  - Downloads

- User experience problems:

  - Drop-down lists that are unworkably long

  - Lists that make pages screens slow to load

  - Lists that require searching or filtering

Problems with static load will be considered further in the *Raising system limits* section. However, usually, when I refer to **load testing** in this chapter, I am not referring to a large steady-state load but instead dynamic, rapidly repeating operations. The many possible checks for those tests will be described in the *What to check during load testing* section.

Soak testing versus spikes of load

For each loading operation, whatever that function is, you can load it with a spike of the activity or apply sustained usage. The pass mark for a spike of activity within the system's capabilities is that the system should be able to batch, record, and smooth the work so that it all gets done and returns to its previous state. For testing beyond those limits, see *Chapter 13, Stress Testing*.

Your application should specify what load it can sustain in terms of constant use and peak activity. For instance, your application might handle 5 sign-ups per second on average over a minute, with peaks of 10 sign-ups per second. If you had 10 sign-ups in one second and 0 the next, that averages to 5, and your system should successfully process them all.

You need two tests, both of the peaks your application can manage and the sustained rate it should maintain over the long term. Those ongoing tests are known as **soak testing**. They ensure the application doesn't have any memory, CPU, or disk usage bottlenecks where the application can't keep up and will eventually fail over time.

That's a very different test from ensuring sufficient buffers and queues are in place to store and process spikes in load, and you need to try both.

Loading combinations

You can perform load testing on many possible operations, but there are even more combinations. Can you sign up new users while many people log in and out? Can customers place new orders if there are lots of downloads in progress? The possibilities are endless, so you will have to select key functions that interact, such as those requiring database updates to check for contention or excessive disk access.

To find unexpected combinations, set up a randomized load test that runs different loading scripts in parallel with each other and checks system performance. I'm a great believer in searching for the unknown unknowns – the interactions that no one has thought of, not even you. Try things for the sake of trying them, even if there is no reason to suspect a bug. Of course, prioritize the higher-risk areas, but test it all. Just because the development team can't imagine a bug doesn't mean there isn't one.

Your system can exhibit emergent behaviors: complex patterns arising from simple entities interacting. In nature, these produce beautiful effects such as the symmetry of snowflakes or murmurations of starlings. In your application, their results are likely to be more pernicious, with operations that work individually interacting and blocking each other when combined under load. These can be very hard to predict, which is why this testing is so important.

Randomized load testing is an excellent example of checking for unexpected interactions. As noted in *Chapter 6, White-Box Functional Testing*, high transaction rates for one operation might prevent others from completing it. So, mix and match loading combinations to see which affect each other, measuring the success and response times of all the operations as you perform them.

For all these cases, you will also have to decide what it means to pass a load test; see the *What to check during load testing* section for more details. To continue that example, the system may perform hundreds of downloads while users are logged in, but the downloads and signing in take 10 times as long as usual. Slowness is often a symptom of overload, and you will have to choose how slow is too slow along with the product owner.

Next, we will consider how to run load tests and the programs to generate this load.

Load test design

While some aspects of testing, such as exploratory and user experience testing, require manual steps, most testing should be automated, and some, such as load testing, absolutely require it. There are many tools available to produce these kinds of requests, such as **LoadNinja** or **WebLOAD**, so if they are suitable for your application, I recommend using one of those to get started quickly and see what is possible.

If your application requires other protocols or you want more control over the load test behavior, you can prepare your own scripts. While they may appear as simple as looping through some fixed behaviors, writing a good load script is deceptively complex, so check on the plugins and extensions available in other tools. Many are also open source, so you can take a branch to customize them.

First, we will consider the case of a client-server architecture in which you are load testing the server, such as a web application or mobile application connecting to core infrastructure. If you want to write your own load runner, consider the following factors.

Load runner architecture for client-server applications

To test application servers, you need to mimic many clients performing realistic connections to them. These should be simplified versions of real clients capable of running multiple instances on a single machine, receiving commands to initiate different tests, and passing their results back to a central location.

To prepare your load test implementation, you'll need to architect your code so that tests can run in parallel. In general, you want three layers in your architecture: performing individual actions, combining sequences of actions, and overall control over starting and stopping different arrangements, as shown here:

Layer	Purpose
Test control	The logic and intelligence for choosing which test sequences to run
Test sequences	Sequences of actions, such as create-check-delete-check loops
Individual commands	Individual actions such as creating, checking, and deleting entities

Table 12.2 – Layers of load testing logic

For instance, one script might have actions such as creating and deleting users, which is the lowest level. The mid-level script constantly loops, creating users, checking for their existence, deleting them, and then checking their removal. That script takes variables such as usernames and delays between cycles. These lower two levels can be distributed across many remote machines to increase the load you can produce.

A top-level script sits above, running user creation for 5 minutes, for instance, then loading up to the maximum number of configured users and rerunning it.

By clearly separating the layers, you can easily swap out the method of user creation – for instance, using an API instead of a web page – while leaving all the other logic of your load test intact. You can alter the rate of the stress test and, most importantly, you can choose how to combine them without affecting how they are run.

Other load runner architectures

There are many other architectures and interfaces on which you can run load testing and also use those same three layers of test control, sequences, and individual commands:

- Database read operations, performing queries on tables
- Database write operations, adding and changing data
- Mixed database operations
- Batches of data processing such as generating statistics and machine learning

For each layer of your system, consider its inputs and how to take them to their limits, both in terms of the number of messages they receive and the volume of incoming data.

Load runner interfaces

Then, you need to choose what interfaces to use when loading your system. These fall into three classes:

- Realistic clients such as web pages or applications
- APIs or public, programmatic interfaces
- Dedicated interfaces for debugging

Each option has strengths and weaknesses. Using genuine clients means your testing is as realistic as possible, and you are mimicking the behavior of large numbers of users. On the downside, you face all the complexities and limitations of the client code. Any bugs or instabilities it suffers from will limit your testing. You are also testing against an interface that isn't designed to be used by a program. Web pages may change without warning, leaving you having to refactor your tests to keep them working, and you're likely to suffer from inconsistent results.

APIs don't suffer from that problem. They are published and are guaranteed to be backward-compatible between releases unless you are given a fair warning about deprecated functions. This makes them far more reliable, although they are less realistic. You are also constrained by the commands and information available from the API. You have a unique use case because you are trying to load the application, so there may be significant omissions that limit your testing.

To get precisely what you need, you must design it yourself, with a dedicated interface for testing. That gives you control over what commands and information are available if you have the time to add them to your program. You can also fix any bugs and extend them to meet your needs while guaranteeing backward-compatibility.

On the downside, a dedicated interface is the least realistic. You may hit issues that only affect that route and which no customer would see, and you may miss the bugs customers encounter when using real clients and interfaces.

None of those options is perfect, so it can be best to use a combination to ensure you have some realistic testing and the control you need.

Load runner functions

Scripts to simply apply load to your application are not enough; you also need scale, visibility, and control.

For small applications, you may be able to generate the scale of load you need on a single machine, firing off requests at rates far higher than any practical usage by a single user or web browser. For larger applications, however, you will need a set of worker machines, guided by a controller, working together to load a given target. You will need different worker and controller scripts and a protocol to control their actions and get feedback on their results.

Load test results are complex due to the volume of information they produce: timings and many possible outcomes from many actions simultaneously. For further details, see the *What to check during load testing* section. At this level, be aware that you'll need to pass results up through your architecture, from the individual calls to the controller's user interface. You'll also need aggregation to summarize the outcome and easily flag anomalies. With that data, you can generate all sorts of graphs and charts to visualize your results.

Once you have that visibility, you need to act on it, not least by stopping your load tests when they hit a problem. That can be as simple as halting a script, but in a distributed system, you'll need to pass that command down to other processes or machines and ideally have them clean up their current actions before exiting cleanly. In more complex implementations, you'll want the ability to start, stop, and alter different types of load testing in real time, and produce new combinations. Again, that requires messages and functions in the scripts running the load.

Next, we will consider a specific type of load testing: raising system limits.

Raising system limits

Load testing is required for one specific form of feature enhancement: raising application limits. Your product currently supports 50 simultaneous users; if that increased to 100, would it still work? The first test you need to do is load the system up to that level to check for internal limits.

The complexity of these changes is often underestimated because testers perform most of the work rather than developers. Usually, features require more time from developers than testers because designing and implementing a feature takes longer than testing it. That means companies typically have more developers than testers to reflect that difference. However, when raising an internal system limit, the development work may be as easy as changing a single number, from 50 to 100, for instance. On the other hand, the test work may involve developing new tools to reach that higher limit and, once reached, running an extensive test plan.

In a complex system, there can easily be resource limitations that make seemingly simple changes harder to implement.

Real-world example – Out of addresses

In one company where I worked, our clients constantly communicated with our cloud. We could only support so many connections, but we needed to raise that value as we grew. The change was as simple as increasing a static limit, but each connection also required an internal address. We increased the configured limit but couldn't reach it in practice because we ran out of addresses.

The first test when raising system limits is to ensure that the whole system can support increasing that number with no hidden restrictions. Are new entities created successfully up to the new limit, and are they fully functional? Maybe you can create that many new users, but you have run out of file handles, so they can't upload profile pictures. Whatever entity you support more of, thoroughly test it when fully loaded.

Then, design a test plan to check the system behavior at the new limit. For a central function, that may need to be an extensive test – for instance, increasing the number of users can have ramifications across the product: on any page that displays users, any database searches based on the users table, and anywhere user lists are searched or filtered. Those may not be obvious, so you'll need to run a detailed regression test plan.

Look out for user interface effects. As described in the *Dynamic versus static load* section, high levels of static load can mean lists become so long they are slow to display, hard to filter, and challenging to search. You'll need pagination and searching to deal with that and indexing on database tables to ensure timely retrieval.

A special case of increasing system limits is raising internal limits, such as the number of threads performing some processing or the number of database connections. While these don't have effects directly visible to customers, they can have consequences across your system, so the key is always to hit the new limits at the same as realistic levels of other types of load to look for issues.

The checks you run when performing load testing are complex enough to deserve special attention, as described in the next section.

What to check during load testing

You should watch for monitoring alarms during all your tests, but especially with load testing, which is designed to exercise uncovering system issues. If there are memory leaks or leaks of other resources, this is the test to find them. Load testing has to be performed by automated scripts, but writing the checks is at least as much work as generating the load. A single command to change the system's state may need many tests to verify it. Write a generic check function that you can expand for whatever tests you are performing, and use your system monitoring; see *Chapter 10, Maintainability*.

At the most basic level, you can run load testing and check for any catastrophic events – the application crashing or unhandled exceptions. The next level of checking is verifying that each operation is successful. For every user creation command, for instance, check that a user exists. You should also routinely check the logs for error messages. For that to be effective, you'll need to purge the logs of spurious errors to let you see the real ones, again, as discussed in *Chapter 10, Maintainability*.

This makes load testing sound perfect and pristine – that the system behaves impeccably until a fault causes an operation to fail and an error to appear. In practice, unfortunately, load testing is far messier, with a far lower signal-to-noise ratio. You'll see many temporary errors that work when retried or slow operations that are borderline unacceptable. Sifting through them is so complex that it deserves its own discussion, as presented in the *Filtering load test errors* section.

With those basic checks in place, and given that you can distinguish real issues, you can plan sweeping tests of system metrics. You'll need to adapt these to your product, but check this list for each machine and subsystem in your service:

- CPU:

    - High sustained levels

    - Spikes of usage

- Disk:

    - High usage

    - High rates of increase

- Memory:

    - High usage

    - High rates of increase

- System resources:

  - Handles

  - Addresses

  - Database connections

- Rate of errors

- Packet loss

- Latency on operations

Each of these has a distinctive pattern that indicates issues. For CPU usage, you are looking for plateaus during which the CPU load is maxed out, showing that other processing may be delayed. Spikes in CPU load also indicate temporary issues. Measuring CPU usage is complex and dependent on memory latency, so in practice, it can be more helpful to measure how much CPU time is free. Dips where this approaches zero indicate overloading.

For disk usage, you are looking for unexpectedly high use, sudden jumps in usage, or continuously increasing usage. If logs and records aren't regularly cleaned up or moved off critical servers, this is the test that will highlight it.

Memory leaks

Look for similar patterns in memory usage: regular increases or the tell-tale sawtooth wave, which indicates crashes due to memory being exhausted:

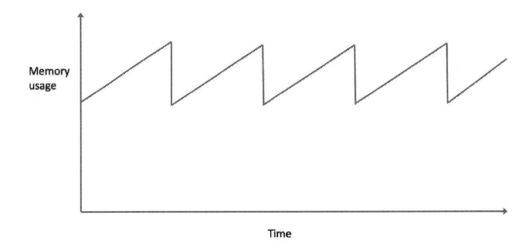

Figure 12.1 – A sawtooth pattern of memory usage indicating a memory leak

In this case, the memory usage increases linearly over time, and each drop in the sawtooth wave represents a crash, which recovers application memory. Those crashes are likely to be catastrophic and noticeable for stateful machines, but for stateless machines processing temporary transactions, you may need dedicated monitoring to detect them.

Real-world example – The countdown to Christmas lunch

It was a week before Christmas, and the office was relaxing. We had shipped our last major release of the year, and for lunch we had booked a swanky local restaurant for our Christmas lunch. Then, a warning light appeared on our monitoring system.

It was nothing urgent, just a high-memory warning from one of the busiest nodes in our cloud. We ran a private cloud with servers we maintained, so this was our responsibility. Was the new release using more memory? Looking at the graph, we saw the inexorable upward trend of leaking memory. The warning had appeared because it had crossed the 80% usage threshold and would only keep rising. Checking the gradient, we even knew when it would crash: in a couple of hours, right in the middle of Christmas lunch.

We could restart it before it crashed, but that outage would be the same length, and if you were going to suffer downtime, lunch was the best time since it was quietest. We had load-tested some operations before release but missed the one with this error. The development team set about investigating while we prepared to check its recovery and answer the inevitable support queries. Christmas was canceled.

Some memory leaks are in background tasks that run regularly and produce an obvious pattern; others only happen under specific circumstances. It can be difficult to separate legitimate increases in memory use due to storing more information from bugs that use memory but never free it. Load testing helps uncover those issues by performing so many operations that any problems become apparent. However, you have to cover a live system's full range of functions, or you risk missing the trigger of a memory leak. If you only perform an operation once as part of functional testing, the change in memory usage will be imperceptible. This class of issue requires load testing.

System resource leaks

A similar pattern to a memory leak can also affect internal system resources. If there is a finite pool of addresses, handles, connections, or IDs designed to be reused, then neglecting to recover them will result in a leak, eventually leading to your system running out and failing in some way.

> **Real-world example – The last database connection**
>
> In one company I worked at, we hit an outage due to running out of database connections. The only symptom was sporadic failures because we had no monitoring in place, so as well as increasing the connection limit, we also began to record the number of connections.
>
> Months later, we hit the limit again, and again the monitoring failed. Why hadn't it reported being out of connections?
>
> The reason was our check to read the number of database connections also needed to connect to the database. When the system had run out of connections, our monitoring could no longer reach the database to tell us.

If system resources aren't correctly reused, then one day, you will run out. That might be longer than the age of the universe, depending on the number and your rate of usage, or it may surprise you much sooner than that. Try to identify all those resources and IDs, since adding checks and warnings for them is trivial. As a fallback, extensive load testing should burn through resources far faster than live usage, so that will flush out any issues.

Reporting results

The trick to reporting load testing results is aggregation. When performing so many operations across many parts of the system simultaneously, you are generating a tremendous amount of information. Unlike functional tests, where you can examine each feature and its behavior individually, during load testing, you need to summarize the overall results. You will need to measure all the system metrics, as described in the *What to check during load testing* section; then, in addition, the results of the load operations themselves. The key measures are as follows:

- How many operations were performed
- Inbound and outbound data rates
- How many successes and failures there were
- Minimum, maximum, average, and standard deviation of operation times
- Summaries of failures and excessive latency
- Any errors and warnings that were generated

These measures can be taken at each layer of your system, such as from load balancers, core servers, and databases.

First, you need to record how many load operations you performed and their success rate. Recall *Chapter 5, Black-Box Functional Testing*, and the different methods of checking API call results. Ideally, you need a separate check on a different interface to verify that an operation was successful. In addition to measuring the success, record the time that takes to look for delays. All these should be fed back to the load runner interface so that they can be summarized, and graphed with unexpected results highlighted. For example, a summary might contain the following data:

Test ID	1
Time	20.43 minutes
Requests	103,472
Successes	103,244
Failures	228
Success rate	99.78%
Minimum latency	10.3 ms
Average latency	15.98 ms
Maximum latency	302.44 ms
Inbound data total	10.3 GB
Outbound data total	30.4 GB

Table 12.3 – Example load test result output

Visualizing load test results is vital to identifying trends and highlighting issues. In this example, the maximum latency (302.44 ms) is significantly larger than the average (15.98 ms). There were over 200 failures, but you don't know when they occurred. Were they grouped together or evenly spread? By plotting the results over time, you can investigate further. Perhaps there was one period of high latency that then recovered, in which case you need to check the logs at that time:

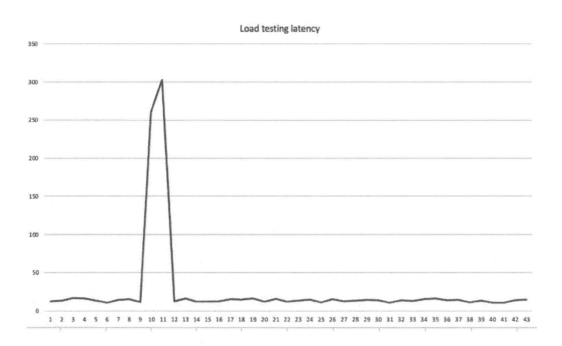

Figure 12.2 – Example load testing output with a period of high latency

Or perhaps the results were getting steadily worse over time, indicating you should run your test for longer and examine the system resources being used:

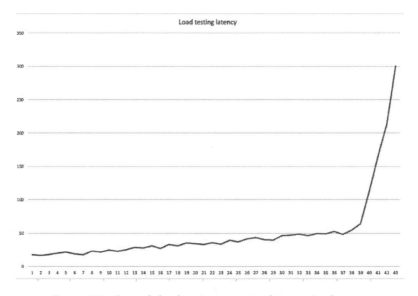

Figure 12.3 – Example load testing output with increasing latency

Only by visualizing your results can you see the pattern of failures, and so infer their underlying causes. If all you have are summaries or, worse yet, reams of unaggregated logs, you won't be able to debug effectively.

Finally, you need an easy way to check for any errors or warnings. Running a system under load is likely to generate many of these, so you need to filter out the expected problems, leaving only the new and interesting ones to be investigated. Do the failures correlate with the period of high latency, or are they separate, indicating that they're due to different causes?

Examining load testing results can be the most time-consuming part of the whole process, so it's well worthwhile polishing these interfaces and making them as painless as possible. It takes care and attention, because problems in load testing are often far from obvious, as described next.

Defect hiding

Load testing uncovers some of the toughest bugs to find and fix, especially because one issue can obscure others. On the user interface, in contrast, you can see multiple problems simultaneously, but that's not always the case with loading. If your application crashes after 3 days of loading due to a memory leak, that will hide the fact that it also crashes after 4 days due to an ID rolling over. You will need to test, investigate, fix, and release a new build for the first issue before you can start to look for subsequent problems.

Because of this, loading results are often on a measured scale rather than passing or failing. You can measure your **Mean Time Between Failures** (MTBF) while running under load, which averages the time before a malfunction for any reason. You can then convert the MTBF into a pass or fail result – to pass, load testing must run successfully for more than a week, for instance.

> **Real-world example – Checking the crash frequency**
>
> One of the most challenging bugs I ever encountered stemmed from a known issue. On a hardware platform for video conferencing, we suffered from a known but infrequent crash. Even under loading conditions, taking millions of calls, it took a month or more to hit. No customer was likely to see it, and almost certainly not twice. It was a known issue, very difficult to diagnose, and we lived with it.
>
> Coming up to the end of a long waterfall development cycle, we noticed that this crash wasn't happening every month anymore; now, it was happening every few days. It still required loading conditions, but it was much more frequent. It had gone unnoticed for months because it was a known issue that we routinely ignored.
>
> Suddenly, we needed a fix for a very difficult issue, which added a long delay to the end of an already long project because we hadn't spotted it earlier.

Another measure is the rate of failures you see. In a simple, synchronous program that executes from beginning to end, you can expect the same result every time you run it with the same parameters. However, very few systems are so simple. There will typically be multiple different systems interacting, often sending messages to one another and performing other processing while awaiting the result. These asynchronous systems are far more efficient and scalable but introduce new classes of issues such as race conditions.

Again, rather than a simple pass or fail result, you may end up with a failure rate: say, one in a million transactions fails. Along with the product manager, you'll have to decide what result is acceptable and counts as a pass. Load-testing bugs can be challenging to find and fix, so the effort to resolve those issues must be weighed against other tasks the development team could be doing. No application is perfect; if you think yours is, that probably shows you haven't tested it enough. If you test thoroughly enough, you'll always find a bug, and if you haven't found a bug, then you haven't tested well enough yet. The sign of a great product isn't having any bugs; it's having small bugs you understand.

Asynchronous processing and race conditions require special consideration and are described in the next section.

Race conditions and asynchronous systems

Unlike synchronous applications, which will execute from beginning to end deterministically every time based on their inputs, asynchronous applications depend on external independent systems. Those systems may be external, third parties with which you share information, send commands, or separate parts of your internal implementation.

Testing these interactions requires different approaches to find another class of bug. Consider an asynchronous application that sends requests to two different external systems and then waits for their responses:

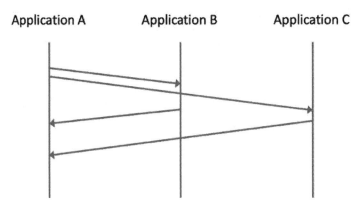

Figure 12.4 – Sending messages to external systems and receiving replies in order B then C

Application A has a bug and relies on responses coming from **Application B** before **Application C**. Generally, that is the case, and **Application B** processes the queries faster and returns its responses first. However, if **Application B** is ever delayed, **Application C** will return first and trigger the bug:

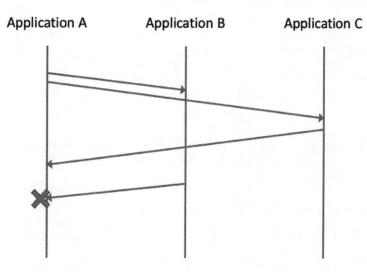

Figure 12.5 – Sending messages to external systems and receiving replies in order C then B

This is a **race condition**, a particularly nasty class of bugs to reproduce and isolate. After all, **Application A** does the same thing in both cases, but the outcome is very different.

Load testing is one way to trigger these issues. If **Application B** is delayed one time in a million, then running tests a million times would eventually hit the bug. That is not a very elegant solution. The other way to trigger these cases is to identify the commands and external calls and deliberately add delays to alter the order of responses. That is helpful testing, although it requires debugging functions in the external applications to introduce latency, as described in *Chapter 11, Destructive Testing*.

However, that testing requires a complete list of external messages, knowing which messages might interact, and the ability to trigger delays. Load testing will find which interactions matter in practice and flush out unknown unknowns that no one had thought of.

In the next section, we will consider a particular source of loading on the system – when starting up and shutting down.

Startup and shutdown

One vital test for your application is how well it starts up and shuts down. While your system might work well running in a steady state, how long does it take to get there, and can it start quickly when under load? For an operations team, the ability to restart a system is an emergency fallback to recover from unknown states, so it has to work. Worse, applications might crash at any time, and you need to know they can recover without manual intervention, which would make outages stretch into minutes or hours instead of seconds.

For each release, check how long your system takes to start up. Have any inefficiencies or extra processes been introduced? As with many gray areas, you'll have to work with the product owner to decide the time limit. There are two cases to consider – one where your whole application or one subsystem is restarting without any load. The other is to restart one part of your system while it is loaded. Measure the performance in both cases. Recovering from outages is described further in *Chapter 11, Destructive Testing*, but it is also part of load testing to restart your system with ongoing operations.

Another type of *startup* is when enabling a new feature. The whole system might run happily in a steady state, but starting a function with wide-ranging effects can require significant resources. This can be harder to identify – most features won't cause problems, so you'll need to watch for ones that will.

Real-world example – Turning on reading conferences from Outlook

In one company I worked at, we had a scheduler that let people create meetings in Outlook. As a new feature, we would also read their Outlook calendars and display those meetings in our application. It was a complex feature, requiring us to reconcile meetings created in Outlook with those we'd made, but it finally passed the testing and we turned it on for live users.

Immediately, there were issues as the system tried to load meetings from users across our system. That load resulted in us writing massive logs, which slowed the application so much that requests started to fail. Those requests immediately retried with no delay, causing even more load, logging, and failures.

A feature that had worked perfectly well in our small test environment was not ready for the numbers present on our live cloud.

For features that add significant load to the system, ensure you test them with high operations rates and large static configurations such as large numbers of users. What happens if many of its transactions fail? Also, check the retry behavior to ensure retries are properly implemented and to look for excessive messaging or logging, which could result in cascades of defects. See *Chapter 7, Testing of Error Cases*, for more on that.

Next, we will look at coding inefficiencies that load testing can flush out.

Loading inefficiencies

It's very easy to write code that works well but scales badly. Load testing is your chance to expose those issues by running new features with the heaviest loads your system is designed to sustain. Recall the example of the database query, which read all events since the beginning of time, gradually slowing the system down as time went on. There are many other examples.

> **Real-world example – 80 participants hang up**
>
> In one video company I worked at, we increased the maximum size of our meeting from 40 to 80 users. It was a massive project requiring changes throughout the system, but we finally got it running and were delighted to see so many participants connect successfully. There were huge congratulations all around; then, we finished the meeting, and all started to hang up.
>
> However, that hanging up took a strangely long time. Panes flickered back and forth, and commands became unresponsive, but finally, after several confusing seconds, everyone disconnected.
>
> Our algorithm for working out who should be shown in a conference didn't scale well, it turned out. When participant number 80 hung up, the system recalculated where the other 79 panes should appear for the remaining 79 participants. Then, it calculated 78 panes for 78 participants, then 77, and so on. It only processed further commands after it worked out what it should display. Since people generally hang up very quickly at the end of a meeting, calculations that had been fine with 40 participants became noticeably slow with 80.

Look out for n-squared relationships between the number of entities and the processing required, as when calculating conference panes in the preceding example. A good code review can find these coding inefficiencies, but they aren't easy to spot, and testing is the surest way to catch them. The steps you need were listed previously – identifying the entities in your system, taking them to their maximum values, and then performing a range of normal operations to ensure you still get good response times.

In the next section, we will look at messages between modules and the limitations they face under loading conditions.

Loading messages between modules

Load testing involves firing many messages at an application's external interfaces, but internal messaging will also have high usage when the system is busy. Another class of issues arises from overloading those communication flows.

Do your internal messages have suitable queues, retries, back-offs, and failure modes? This is another class of issue best probed with load testing to ensure there are no hidden bottlenecks within your system.

This section is hard to describe because both the causes and effects are indirect and can be difficult to trigger with system testing. You will have to check with the development team which operations will cause the highest rate of internal messaging within your system; this is an area where you need white-box insights. It won't be clear what symptoms internal message failures might produce. Operations could time out or fail; the system might be left in an inconsistent state, with some processes believing a task was complete and others believing it had failed. Fixes for these failures include adding queues or batching messages together to avoid high message rates arriving at the destination.

This is one area where the tests and their effects depend very much on your particular application. There are essential bugs to find, but you will have to work with your developers on how to exercise them and check the results.

Next, we will consider the performance of our system, measuring its current baseline so that it's ready to be compared to future releases.

Performance testing

Is your application slower than the last release? Some services, such as web servers, have relatively low resource requirements and are unlikely to be constrained under normal circumstances. Other applications will hit the limits of the available network, disk access, memory, or processing. You will see symptoms such as increased latency on operations or rising failure rates, which indicate that your system cannot maintain this level of activity.

Programs tend to become larger and more complex over time, which always carries the risk of slowing them down. Whatever limits your system is hitting, part of testing is to ensure that this release doesn't accidentally have lower performance than the last.

> **Real-world example – The accidental load test**
>
> In a company that provided SMS text message infrastructure, I was onsite to perform user acceptance testing with a large customer. We worked through the test plan, successfully demonstrating all the functionality such as read receipts, redirects, and statistics monitoring.
>
> After finishing one test, I noticed an anomaly: the system reported it was processing 50 messages per second when it was supposed to be idle. I double-checked our loading program but nothing was running. Where was the load coming from?
>
> We investigated but couldn't see the source of so many messages, so we decided to repeat the previous tests. Sure enough, partway through, the load on the system jumped to almost 100 messages per second. It turned out we had configured a loop in our redirects. Two systems diverted the same message back and forth as fast as they could, with no protection to stop it. Sending a second message into the loop had doubled the problem. We quickly removed the redirect and added a feature request to prevent it in the future.

Identifying bottlenecks

When you encounter stress or load test failures, it is likely to be because a single subsystem is overloaded. *A chain is only as strong as its weakest link*, as the saying goes, and your application is only as fast as its slowest component. When you start to hit performance limits such as high latency or failed operations, you need to track down the source of the issue.

This is a great test for your monitoring and logging, as described in *Chapter 10, Maintainability*. How easy is it to isolate an error and identify the source of the problem, among thousands of operations? That should indicate the subsystem that triggered the problem.

To diagnose the issue, examine those logs and the metrics you measure for that subsystem. It is running out of CPU or memory resources, or program resources such as processes or threads? Are queues becoming full or are operations timing out?

When it is unclear where a problem originates, you can experiment by increasing system resources and rerunning your test. That is especially the case when using cloud computing services where it is easier to assign more resources.

To resolve bottlenecks, you can either expand vertically, by giving more resources to the same applications, or horizontally, by deploying more subsystems that can be used in parallel. Scaling vertically is usually easier to start with as it changes only one aspect of the system, but there is a limit to how fast one subsystem will be able to run. For a longer-term solution, you may need to re-architect your system to be able to use multiple subsystems simultaneously.

Load tests in the release cycle

The critical tests here are a set of standard operations you can run on each release – possibly you process the same file or perform the same task – and record the system resources and time it takes. That sets a baseline to compare against future releases. Your testing is a comparison: if this release requires more resources or time than your baseline, that is a failure until the product owner and development team agree to the new behavior.

A short, sharp load test can be added as part of your CI tests to check the performance after every change. It is very easy to add a database query or function call that is a huge drain on system resources but works fine in limited test environments and only shows issues on realistic data rates or database sizes. Once you have these tests set up, make sure they are run regularly.

For real-time systems, even a tiny delay can be a critical bug. If you take 1.1 seconds to process 1 second's worth of video, for instance, your video calls won't go well. For systems with less time pressure, you can decide what performance you are happy with and set that as your new baseline.

So far, we have described load testing as simple and obvious, with clear passes, failures, and questions that need to be decided. However, actual results from load testing can be far more complex and require skill and experience to read.

Filtering load test errors

Load testing is messy. This is the most challenging form of testing, requiring all functions and logging to work reliably and a stable, robust system from which to run tests. If functional testing is a scalpel carefully probing your application, load testing is a rugby tackle, using brute force to take it down. When you run load testing, many operations coincide, and the system runs in ways it never usually does. While this may trigger genuine issues, you'll also hit a large class of problems that are only ever seen under loading conditions. These aren't useful to find or fix; so, the best option is often to work around them.

> **Real-world example – Users left behind after load testing**
>
> When we started load testing in one company I worked at, one of our first tests was to load user creation. We ran a simple loop that created and deleted thousands of users and instantly hit a problem: a small percentage of delete operations failed, leaving users that had been created but not removed. We happily reported the issue we'd found.
>
> There was a race condition, not in our product but in our loading script. In our distributed system, it took some time to make the user, so occasionally, we deleted the user before it was fully created. The delete operation failed, then the creation operation finished, leaving the user in place. You would only hit that bug if you deleted users milliseconds after creating them, so while you might hit that problem in load testing, no user would ever see it.

There are several classes of spurious errors you are likely to hit when driving your system so hard. You need to be aware of each of these so that you can work around them and find real issues instead:

- Problems driving the interface
- Problems with reporting and logging
- Problems with your load application
- Unrealistic operations

As described in the *Load runner interfaces* section, there are several ways to create load on your system, from user-facing screens and pages to dedicated debugging interfaces. Any problems with the debug interface are not interesting to customers and only affect your tests. While they might be a problem for load testing, they are a low priority compared to issues that impact your users. Load testing actual pages can also uncover spurious problems, which only occur if you use them programmatically instead of as a real user.

For these issues, and many in this section, the best short-term solution is to work around them. It might not be worth the development team's time to fix them compared to other work, as no user will see these problems. Change your load tests to avoid failure and keep going until there is a lull in development, and these can be improved. Often, the solution is adding a delay to make the load scenario more like actual usage.

Next, you may hit problems with reporting or logging. Log files may be too large or not rotated correctly, APIs may not be able to handle the volume of requests, disk contention might cause failures, or there may be other similar problems. Again, these issues are aspects of the load test rather than anything a customer is likely to see. APIs should meet their specified performance goals, but those may be significantly lower than the rates you want to run loading at. To work around this, you can change the method of obtaining load results, such as by writing a dedicated results file and turning down the logging sensitivity so that less is written.

Result sensitivity

There can be bugs in your test code, in the script that applies the load. Does it have sensible timeouts set on messages? Do you want retries or to report every failure? Does it handle errors from the application correctly?

There is a trade-off between the resilience of your tests and their sensitivity. If an operation fails but works when retried, do you count that as a success or a failure? You will need to get to know your system and how reliable it is. If there is a known issue either in your code or the system as a whole, be ready to filter out those issues. The risk is that a new, important issue manifests in the same way, and you fail to find it.

Unfortunately, there are no easy answers here, so you need to pay close attention and regularly tune your filters. Accepting retries for operations will make your error reporting quieter and let you see new issues clearly, at the cost of possibly missing some errors. Following up on every failure lets you see everything, but can be a huge task.

Loading reliability

Your loading tools have to be highly reliable. If your scripts fail every hundredth transaction, that will drown out any real failures that happen every thousandth transaction. In general, load scripts are much simpler than the main application, but if you use tools, such as clients to connect to your servers, then you rely on the stability of those clients. You have to fix issues there before you can load your infrastructure properly.

It's very easy to set a load test running for the weekend, only for it to fail 20 minutes after you leave. These scripts are highly likely to see timeouts and errors, so you need to build resilience, ideally with a system that will restart the main process if it stops. You will also need persistent memory so that a load test can pick up where it left off rather than relying on the state stored in memory.

Load testing, by definition, is unrealistic. No one would be able to perform the rate of transactions you are proposing. The aim is to condense many days or weeks of real usage into just a few hours. If that condensation process produces issues, such as trying to delete users before they were fully created, those aren't interesting problems, and you need to work around them.

As you can see, a host of problems can arise from loading your system. You will have to get to know your application's behavior to filter out the uninteresting errors associated with your testing from the real issues your users could hit. Distinguishing those is one of the hardest jobs in testing, so be ready to practice and learn a lot. Even once you have isolated a genuine issue on your system, debugging issues found in load testing presents unique challenges, as considered next.

Debugging load test issues

Functional testing, as described previously, is like taking a scalpel to your application and carefully probing individual functions. Ideally, each tester has a dedicated system, or at least of the core elements, so that you can completely control what happens there. When there is an issue, the logs are silent except for the single operation you performed, aside from any regular background processing. It's easy to isolate useful information.

When load testing, that's not the case. Having created a million users, finding the one that failed can be challenging. Performing even a single operation can have a cascade of effects across your system. Creating a single user might involve loading an interface, accepting input, sending that to the backend, and writing it to storage. There may be many other impacts, depending on your system's architecture.

To debug issues successfully during load testing, you must be thoroughly proficient at debugging functional issues. You need to know the logs, where they are, and what they should look like. You need to be able to search and filter them to know which fields are available at each level of the system. And you need to be able to step between different subsystems to trace an operation through various stages to find where the problem arose.

As with the rest of load testing, this is where your skills are put to the test. Testing has a lovely learning curve – you can start acting as a regular user, exploring standard functions, then gradually dive deeper into your system, automating routine tasks and refining your checks to detect subtle issues. Load testing is a complex challenge as in addition to all the expected operations, new, emergent behavior appears. This is your challenge.

Summary

Load testing uncovers some of the hardest-to-find and most important bugs in your system. These are issues that you'll never hit by just running some exploratory testing. They require dedicated tools and skills to discover and even more to isolate and debug.

In this chapter, we described identifying load operations, the differences between static and dynamic load, and soak testing versus spikes of operations. You need to consider the design of your application for load testing, the interfaces it should use, and the functions it requires. There are different bugs when raising system limits, looking for race conditions, inefficient programming, or testing the messages between modules. You need to create a performance baseline to check for higher resource usage and look for defects that obscure other problems.

Finally, we considered the challenges of filtering and debugging load-testing issues. In the next chapter, we will go one step further and apply load to push your system beyond its limits to test how it copes with usage over and above its design parameters.

13
Stress Testing

"OVERWORK, n. A dangerous disorder affecting high public functionaries who want to go fishing."

– Ambrose Pierce, The Devil's Dictionary

We now come to the final form of testing considered in this book: **stress testing**. These are some of the hardest tests to run and the most stringent checks on your application. Stress testing is a combination of testing load and error cases, as you push your system beyond its limits.

In the last chapter, we considered load testing, which ensured an application could perform up to its required performance. If a website can handle 10,000 simultaneous users, testing must reach that number without seeing a degraded performance. The pass mark for these tests isn't just completion, but also the time taken for each action. Stress testing comes next, going beyond system limits.

How does your application cope when the 10,001st user attempts to join, a user tries to extend their connection beyond the maximum time limit, or the system runs short of memory? As with both load testing and error testing, these are rare events but are also those most likely to cause invalid behavior and encounter critical issues.

Like error case testing, these are tests that are designed to fail. The pass mark is that the user experience should be understandable and that the system recovers correctly afterward. This is another area that is often underspecified, so if you didn't cover it in your specification review, your first task is to determine precisely what should happen in these cases.

It's time to be really cruel to your system, to twist the screws and turn it up to eleven. Spare no mercy! It's time to be as evil as possible with no holds barred. Your system will fail; the question is, can it pick itself back up again?

In this chapter, you will learn about the following:

- How to test excessive transaction rates
- Checking policed and unpoliced limits

- Identifying positive feedback loops

- Testing graceful degradation

- How limiting resources affect your system

- Soak testing and spikes of load

- Checking for successes and errors

As ever, first, we will consider the advantages and disadvantages of stress testing.

The advantages and disadvantages of stress testing

As one of the most extreme forms of verification, stress testing has a unique set of strengths and weaknesses:

Advantages	Disadvantages
The only way to find this class of issue	Requires dedicated tools
Discovers the limits of your system	Requires high-quality tools
Uncovers hard-to-find issues	Harder to debug
Finds software inefficiencies	Less realistic scenarios
Prepares you for overload scenarios	Expensive
	Difficult to tell the ideal behavior in a failure mode

Table 13.1 – The advantages and disadvantages of stress testing

Stress testing is the only class of tests where you push your system beyond its limits and check the application's behavior when dealing with excess failures. It's the only way to find the errors under load and uncover the real limits of its capacity. Your requirements might state a number you should reach, and your design might have a theoretical limit, but the only way to tell for sure is to push your system until it breaks. Now's the time to run those tests.

Like load testing, stress testing finds issues that will not appear in any other tests and requires dedicated tools and time to run. It uncovers coding inefficiencies that might not arise in any other condition. Most of all, stress testing gives you peace of mind. Once complete, you definitely know what your application can handle, and you're ready for the day the load becomes too much.

On the downside, stress testing suffers from all the disadvantages of both load testing and error case testing. It requires dedicated tools of high-enough quality that the system under load will fail before they do. Failures are difficult to debug because so much happens simultaneously, and like testing error cases, it's hard to tell what the correct behavior is when failing. It's also expensive to run and tries rare cases of loading that would only occur in your marketing team's wildest dreams. Just in case your company's next tweet goes viral or a celebrity mentions they're addicted to your product, you'd better make sure you know what to expect if half the internet suddenly decides to use your application. We start by considering that case: breaching your specified transaction rates.

Stress test architecture

As with load testing, the architecture of a stress test involves identifying the inputs to the various interfaces of your system and sending high data rates in terms of the number of messages and message sizes. For client-server applications, that means having many mock client interfaces.

Many third-party applications can provide this functionality, such as LoadNinja and WebLOAD, or the basic commands can be written in simple scripts. However, full functionality, including control and reporting results, is a significant task, which is why third-party tools are so useful. See *Chapter 12, Load Testing*, for more details.

Breaching transaction rates

What if your application grew to 10 times the size? 100? 1,000? This might be a problem your company would love to have, but on that day, a vast numbers of users will get a first impression of your product. You only get one chance to give them a good experience, and stress testing is your chance to ensure that you achieve this.

For all the transaction rates that you can load test, you should also stress test beyond those limits to see your system's performance. In practice, you should run these tests together: load your system within its specification to check for successful behavior, then keep turning up the rate to check what happens when it's overloaded. In the same way that testing error cases is an extension of functional testing, stress testing is an extension of load testing.

You will need to produce a list of transactions relevant to your application, but consider the following examples:

- The rate of web page requests
- The rate of client connections
- The rate of client requests
- The rate of user signup
- The rate of user sign in

For stress tests, you must decide what acceptable behavior is. The following graphs show the number of transactions requested versus the number your application can process. A steady gradient indicates success – you receive 5,000 requests and send 5,000 successful responses.

Let's say that your application is required to handle 10,000 **requests per second** (**rps**), and you test up to 20,000 rps. Eventually, all applications will fail under **Denial-of-Service** (**DoS**)-style attacks, where they are so busy handling incoming requests that they cannot process them correctly. The question is, what are your system's limits, and how well does it behave beyond them?

In this first possible result, the application handles the load with ease:

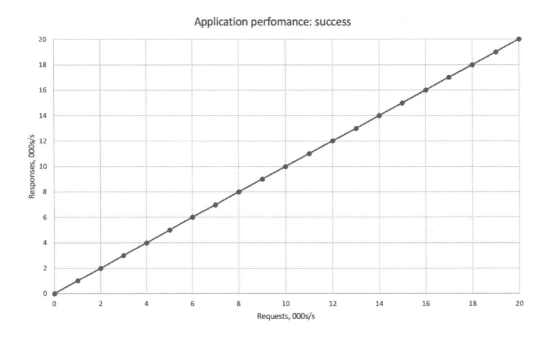

Figure 13.1 – Handling additional load successfully

The gradient is steady past 10,000 rps all the way to 20,000 rps. In this test, your application can successfully process twice the specified load. Ideally, you need to keep testing to see where it fails, and you can let the product owner know they can specify a higher transaction rate, if they'd like.

The following case is more realistic, where the application fails to process additional transactions beyond its specified limit of 10,000 rps:

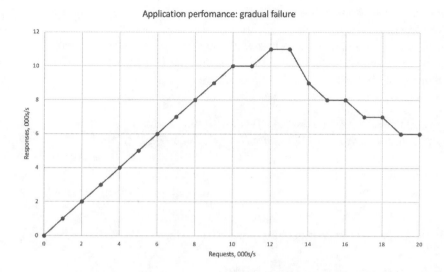

Figure 13.2 – Handling additional load with gradual degradation

The gradient is steady past 10,000 rps indicating the product can successfully meet its required performance, but beyond that, it spends so much time rejecting excess requests that it's unable to handle the new load. Queries start failing between 10,000 and 11,000 rps, so you have no headroom. Your application can only just handle its specified load, so if live usage reaches that limit, then you imminently need to find ways to improve its performance. However, that is not the worst possible outcome, as shown in the following graph:

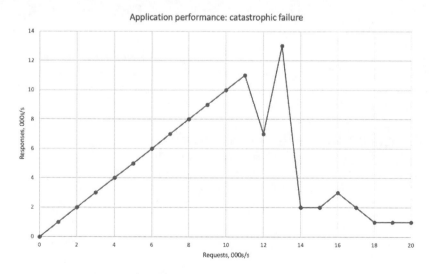

Figure 13.3 – Handling additional load with catastrophic failure

In this final example of output from a stress testing graph, the gradient is again steady past 10,000 rps but then enters a chaotic phase where the success rate varies wildly before settling at a permanently low rate. If you see this pattern, don't trust the chaotic section of this graph, as it is likely to change every time you run the test. It indicates that the application cannot maintain that workload and is hitting internal limitations. Beyond a certain point, in this case, around 13,000 rps, the performance crashes, and only a tiny proportion of requests complete successfully.

Stress testing is designed to find these kinds of drop-offs in performance because they can be a source of major outages if they happen in live use. The product owner then needs to judge how likely that rate of transactions is in practice. Possibly the limit of 10,000 rps is way above your usual load, and you'd be delighted to have that much traffic. Or maybe you're already approaching that limit, and the next successful promotion or viral advert could push you over. By being aware of these problems, you can prioritize their fixes.

In the next section, we will consider limits that are policed and which should reject excessive usage.

Policed and unpoliced limits

Rate limits are usually unpoliced – if you go over the specified rate, the application will do its best to service requests or perform the requested action. As we saw in *Chapter 7, Testing of Error Cases*, there are also policed limits, such as the number of configured users, which are designed to reject requests after a specified limit.

That might be a configured number of some entity, the maximum simultaneous connections, or the maximum number of operations your system can perform in parallel. Whatever the limits are in your system, identify them all and test what happens when you go beyond them. These tests are designed to fail, so the only question is, does the application fail gracefully, letting users know why their request can't succeed?

You can also stress test these limits, repeatedly attempting to add more entities or connections beyond the maximum to ensure that an attack of that kind can't degrade your system. This checks to ensure there isn't excessive logging, memory leaks, or any other problems that only occur when you try an invalid operation at scale.

Identifying positive feedback loops

Positive feedback loops can cause chaotic behavior and catastrophic reductions in performance, where adding load increases failures, which adds even more load:

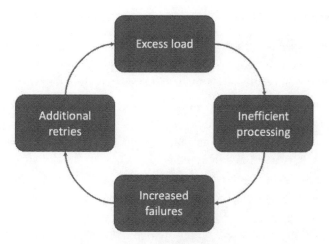

Figure 13.4 – A positive feedback loop of loading failures producing even more load

Inefficient processing can be due to failures requiring more system resources, for instance, due to writing large error logs or remote calls to indicate a problem. Additional retries can be caused by faults in the client logic, such that some failures lead to even more requests and even more failures.

Recall the example of self-inflicted DDoS from *Chapter 7, Testing of Error Cases*. There, positive feedback resulted in more load and even more failures. We saw an example when we read conference details from Outlook for all our users: the system was overwhelmed, and writing the logs for all the failures only slowed it down further.

Often these failures are emergent behavior, complex interactions that aren't predictable from any single part of the system in isolation. This is the strength of system testing – it's the only way to identify these interactions.

The solution for this class of issues is back-offs and prioritization to ensure critical work is done to resolve the situation. Logs don't matter if your service is down; if you have to choose between logging or a live service, keep your application serving your users until the situation improves. As we saw in *Chapter 10, Maintainability*, maintaining service in overloaded conditions requires concise logs, even during error handling, and carefully set priorities so other processes have access to resources.

When systems are down, retries should gradually take longer. Exponential back-offs work well, sending messages at 1, 2, 4, 8 seconds, and so on, as the chance of a rapid recovery dwindles the longer the problem lasts. This prevents your clients from causing your servers issues, especially if they are shut down while heavily loaded, and many clients try to connect simultaneously on their return.

Whenever you find a case like that, it's a bug that urgently needs fixing as it is likely to cause outages. In that case, the developer hasn't considered what will happen when there's a failure. At the other end of the spectrum are problems you deliberately plan for: handling the overload with graceful degradation, as described next.

Graceful degradation

Mainly, stress testing involves taking already present functions and using them excessively, but there is one aspect with dedicated code: graceful degradation. For functions that you expect to be overloaded but you still want to provide some service, your system can detect that state and adjust.

Possibly that doesn't apply to your system, in which case you can skip this section. However, keep it in mind for specification reviews: if you don't deliberately handle the case of overload, what do you want to do? Sometimes you can police a limit and prevent additional load by rejecting excess requests. In other situations, you have more subtle options.

> **Real-world example – Counting the frames**
>
> In a video conferencing company I worked for, we implemented graceful degradation in case the load on our system got too high. Our first line of defense was the best: if we couldn't handle the video processing load, we would leave everyone connected at the same video resolution but reduce the frame rate.
>
> It's very hard to see the difference between 30 frames per second, which we usually sent, and 20 frames per second, but making that reduction reduced our video encoding load by a third. It was a neat way to protect our system with minimal user impact. The challenge was testing it: we had to rely on the statistics for the video stream because the difference was imperceptible.

The primary method of graceful degradation is to slow requests down. Whether internal processing or responding to external queries, taking more time allows your system to handle a spike in load. Where you have queues or buffers in place, you'll need to check that they work up to their configured limits without losing messages. When you go beyond their configured limits, are rejections sent correctly?

Behavior under load can be tough to test, so you will need excellent instrumentation to log the rate of messages arriving, being rejected, queued, and processed. It should be possible to tally totals and plot graphs so you can see what is happening because if there is an issue, it can be challenging to spot and debug issues when the system is so busy. You'll need to both generate the load and closely measure system behavior before you can successfully run these tests.

An alternative form of stress testing is to use the same load but reduce your system's capabilities. How well does your system cope with constrained resources?

Limited resources

As we saw in the *Identifying positive feedback loops* section, resource constraints often form an essential step in exacerbating overload conditions. Some coding inefficiencies can be flushed out by realistically loading common operations, such as memory leaks or excessive disk usage. Others are more subtle and are best revealed by restricting resources.

Real-world example – 32 times 2 or 8 times 8?

One video conferencing company I worked for used standard servers that they owned and ran. I looked after procuring new blades, each of which ran with 64 GB of memory. We usually installed 8 lots of 8 GB memory sticks, but for one order, I bought two lots of 32 GB instead. That meant there were fewer components to go wrong, gave us more room for expansion in the future, and saved us some money.

The new blades came online and ran for several weeks before we got reports of higher packet loss rates. These were initially dismissed as poor networks (recall the challenges of filtering alerts from *Chapter 10, Maintainability*); however, it soon became apparent that we were the source of the loss. Buying a quarter of the number of memory sticks had advantages, but it also meant we had a quarter of the memory bandwidth, which relied on communication with eight different slots. The effects were subtle but, under load, our processing couldn't handle the restriction and dropped video packets.

To perform this form of testing, you need to limit one of the core processing limits in your system, such as one of the following:

- CPU
- Memory
- Memory I/O rate
- Disk space
- Disk I/O rate

The aim is to find how close to these limits your system currently runs. If you only have to reduce these metrics by a few percent before you start seeing failures, you are running dangerously close to your threshold. Conversely, this test might indicate that you are paying for more resources than your application needs to meet its performance requirements. It's important to run comprehensive checks while in this state. For more information, see the *What to check when stress testing* section.

Real-world example – Sharing with the monitoring system

On the same system that ran standard servers, we used virtual machines to run various applications on the same hardware. One day we saw slowdowns and crashes on two of our core servers. There was nothing special about them until we realized they ran on the same physical blade; servers on other blades weren't affected.

Those servers also shared a physical blade with our monitoring system. It turned out that the disk I/O for monitoring had reached sufficient rates and there was not enough left to run our core servers. We needed to separate that machine and buy more performant disks to ensure our core servers could maintain their function.

Another way to limit resources is by restricting the machines used within the system. If you usually work with four edge servers, can you handle the required capacity with only two? Again, this will only be needed rarely but can happen in the event of an outage. As mentioned in *Chapter 11, Destructive Testing*, you need to check that your system can successfully failover onto backups and still process the required load. Wherever you have redundant machines within your system, stress test the failover scenario.

Restricted system resources might seem like a problem low on the priority list, but the condition can arise from surprising causes. We've seen examples of incorrect hardware, positive feedback loops in the software, failovers, or sharing resources with problematic applications. It's essential to know how close you are to those limits and what problems you might suffer when you breach them.

In the next section, we turn to stress testing over long periods, known as **soak testing**.

Soak testing

What if someone decides to play your game for 24 hours straight, host a meeting that long, or leave an operation running for weeks at a time? The next type of stress you can apply to your system is to perform valid and invalid actions over extended periods beyond their design limitations. Some of these limits will be policed with checks to ensure nothing takes longer than a specified time, while others will be open-ended. Some actions will change your system's state, and others are individual operations you can apply repeatedly. That gives a matrix of possible cases, with examples here:

		Policed operation	**Unpoliced operation**
Valid operations	Ongoing state	Game length Call length Processing time	Web session length
	Separate operations	Transactions per day Operations available on a free plan	Signing up Logging in

		Detecting heartbeat timeouts Killing long-running transactions/processes	System degradation
Invalid operations	Ongoing state		
	Separate operations	Incorrect password attempts	Signing up too many users Creating too many entities Accessing invalid URLs

Table 13.2 – Different classes of soak testing tests

Some valid, ongoing states have time limits applied to them. You should have checked these as part of functional testing to ensure that users are kicked out of calls or games when they reach the maximum time. At a lower level, tasks and processes should have a time-to-live value to shut down infinite loops or stuck operations. Do these protections work correctly?

Some valid states don't have time limits, for instance, a web session with constant activity. If that's the case, you'll need to pick a value to test up to, so you can sign off on its performance. That can be a large value, say a week, so any session shorter than that should also work.

When stress testing individual and repeating operations, you should check for policed limits. Maybe only so many transactions are allowed per day, or users on a free plan might be limited in how many entities they can create. Stress test these rejections – do large numbers of them cause any issues? Extend the stress testing we've already described, for instance, logging in or signing up over hours or days, to ensure your system doesn't have any subtle problems such as memory leaks when processing them.

Examples of invalid ongoing states are those we considered in *Chapter 11, Destructive Testing*. You can test your system's response by disabling or degrading part of it. Some of these connections will have heartbeats, so check that their absence is detected and acted on correctly. Killing long-running or struck transactions is another example. Other degraded states won't, and can't, be policed. In terms of soak testing, how does your system respond to subsystems being offline for an extended period? A dual redundant system might failover and work correctly, but does it still work an hour or a week later?

Invalid individual operations can be policed, such as logging in with incorrect passwords. After too many failures, this should be locked and fail even if the user does attempt the right combination.

> **Real-world example – Invalid password attempts**
>
> In one company, we assigned the task of updating our root server passwords to a junior member of the team. A little while later, he returned, distressed that he was now locked out. Privately cursing his incompetence, I smiled and went to help. Sure enough, neither the old nor the new password worked. He must have changed it to something else, and we were now locked out. Then we tried one more time, and it worked – the new password was correct. We logged out and tried to log back in, and it failed again. How could a password work intermittently?
>
> We had forgotten about a monitoring system that ran in the background, checking login. It attempted regular logins with the old password and repeatedly locked us out. After the timeout, we had a brief window where the server accepted our password before the incorrect logins blocked us again.

Finally, many invalid, separate operations aren't policed, such as signing in too many users, creating too many entities, or attempting to access invalid URLs. You can check that these are rejected, then stress that operation over long periods to check for excessive logging, resource leakages, or other subtle problems.

Next, we consider the opposite case – brief spikes of high load.

Spikes in load

A more typical case than constant load is a short peak of high load. That might be due to people simultaneously dialing into their 9 o'clock meetings, a new update that users are eager to see, or a promotion starting. Your marketing team's job is to generate this traffic, and it's often very bursty. Can your system cope?

Testing queues

As mentioned in the *Graceful degradation* section, this is a test of your system's buffers and queues. Are they the right size, and do they fill up and empty correctly? You'll need to identify all the queues designed to spread the load in your system to check their behavior and the locations which should have a queue but don't.

Queues are particularly important for varied workloads where long, resource-intensive jobs compete with fast, little tasks. You have to ensure small tasks can still be processed quickly, even if large jobs are taking up resources. For instance, if you have multiple clients making requests to a central server, it may be able to handle light loads, as shown on the left in *Figure 13.5*, but not keep up if all clients want to use your service simultaneously. That's illustrated on the right, where the server drops some requests:

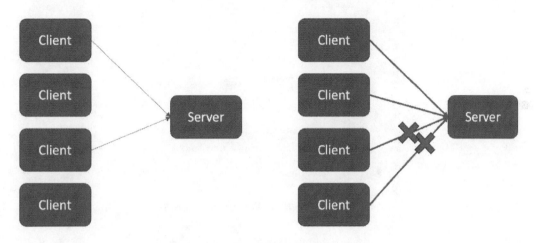

Figure 13.5 – A server fails under a heavy load

Implementing a queue provides protection against this issue:

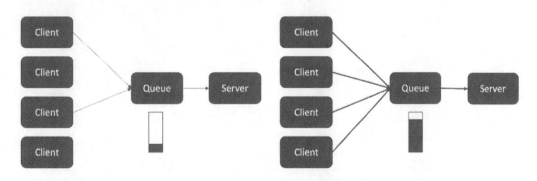

Figure 13.6 – A queue handles a spike in load

During periods of light loading, the queue is empty and just forwards requests, as shown on the left of *Figure 13.6*. During high loading, on the right, the queue successfully accepts all the **Client** traffic but limits the tasks sent to the server. It stores the excess, and the **Queue** function fills up. When the traffic becomes lighter, the queue sends stored requests to the server, keeping it busy even though the clients are now quiet:

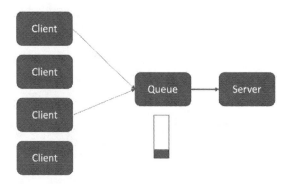

Figure 13.7 – A queue empties after a spike in load

With little traffic arriving, the queue empties its contents, sending them on to the server at a steady low rate, ready for the next burst. For example, if a server has a limit of 2,000 rps, without a queue, a 2-second peak of 5,000 rps will result in failures:

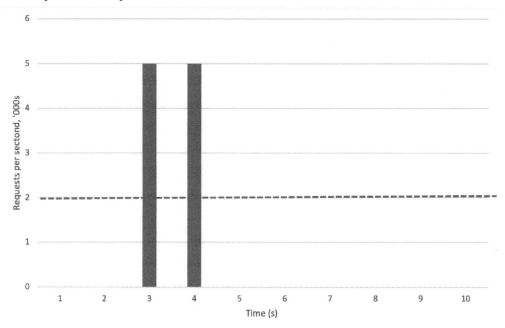

Figure 13.8 – Peaks of traffic overwhelm the server

A queue would smooth that traffic. It would still send a total of 10,000 requests to the server, but instead of 2 seconds of 5,000 rps, it would send 5 seconds of 2,000 rps, staying within the server's capabilities:

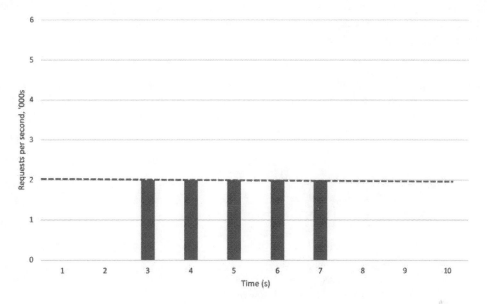

Figure 13.9 – A queue spreads out the load

The queue would smooth this traffic to keep it under 2,000 rps for an extended period.

Queues are a vital part of large systems, but they have limits and add complexity that (you guessed it!) needs testing. What is the maximum rate the queue can accept? What is the maximum backlog it can store? Your specification should state the number of transactions per second that the system should support, how that is averaged over time, and what peaks should be possible. If you have a peak of five times your average in 1 second, then no traffic for 4 seconds, on average, your system should handle that if it can buffer the peak and process it gradually. Check precisely what your system can support, or let the team know the reality if no one is sure.

When one queue is insufficient, several may be necessary to handle the spikes in load. Again, that is possible at the cost of increasing the complexity further. Queues also add a delay to the processing of tasks. Usually, this is brief, but that can't be guaranteed. You'll need to test that any requests traversing the queue are resilient to those delays. If the queue doesn't guarantee requests are delivered in order, **First-In-First-Out** (**FIFO**), then you will need to consider out-of-order execution. If requests interact and depend on one another, that may cause major problems.

What is the client's behavior when the queue's limits are breached? What visibility do you have of the queue's performance? Does the queue forward requests at the right level to the server? If the queue sends too many tasks, the server will still be overloaded; if it sends too few, it reduces the system's capacity. If your system includes queues, all those questions should be steps in your test plan. If the queue receives invalid requests, it must report those back to the client and flag an error instead of the main server doing it.

Where you have a distributed system with multiple servers ready to handle traffic, you'll need a system to direct the traffic to those locations. Load balancers also need to be tested – they'll have an algorithm to select destinations, from something as simple as a **round-robin** to complex load-based choices. Stress testing is your chance to check its routing during regular operation and when the system is overloaded.

The final test we consider in this chapter is also the toughest: stress testing the system while deliberately adding errors.

Stress testing with errors

Despite the harshness of tests that push your system beyond its limits, lab testing still misses conditions that will be present in real-life usage. The day your advert goes viral and loading jumps, you will still have all the packet loss, latency, and even the chance of internal failures of a typical day. For a complete test, remember to include these low-level issues in your testing.

As with load testing, to apply controlled errors, you must start with an error-free system (see the *Technical requirements* section in *Chapter 12, Load Testing*). To perform any of the tests in this chapter, you need a reliable setup with all the resources and equipment of the live system on controlled networks without packet loss or other issues. From that start point, you can apply loading and degradation combinations. Recall the sources of network degradation from *Chapter 7, Testing of Error Cases*:

- Packet loss
- Latency
- Jitter
- Re-ordering
- Duplication

Then add a realistic background level of everyday tasks:

- Sign up
- Sign in
- Data access
- Configuration changes

- Application updates
- Requests for invalid URLs

Include anything else that happens on a typical day. On top of that, apply your stress scripts to probe the behavior you want to test.

> **Real-world example – Too hot to handle**
>
> In one company, we supplied a custom-designed hardware appliance and started experiencing rare crashes on some customer sites. We'd never hit this problem internally, and on an investigation, the crashes were impossible – the code couldn't fail in the way the logs showed.
>
> It's always tempting to blame a crash on cosmic rays flipping a bit, but in this case, that really looked like a possibility until we noticed the environments that these units ran in. They were all in hot countries, with crashes during the summer months. They were running inside the temperature range we stated, but after retesting our chips at high temperatures over an extended period, we hit the same issue. For once, it wasn't a software issue at all.

Once all that testing is running, monitor its output, as described next.

What to check when stress testing

As with load testing, you need to constantly check your system during stress tests. First, carefully review your monitoring as described in *Chapter 10, Maintainability*. Track any errors or alarms generated during your tests and errors in the logs. That should be a given during any testing but is especially true here.

Stress testing is an external pressure you put on your service – an expected problem. As such, even stress testing shouldn't show any errors. In my experience, that won't be the case, so one of your first tasks will be to raise those alerts with the development team to either fix or downgrade to a warning.

Recall the list of system metrics from *Chapter 12, Load Testing*. All those measures are also important when running stress tests:

- CPU:

  - High sustained levels
  - Spikes of usage

- Disk:

  - High usage
  - High rates of increase

- Memory:

  - High usage

  - High rates of increase

- System resources:

  - Handles

  - Addresses

  - Database connections

- Rate of errors

- Packet loss

- Latency on operations

The same metrics of load performance also apply:

- How many operations were performed

- Inbound and outbound data rates

- How many successes and failures there were

- The minimum, maximum, average, and standard deviation of operation times

- Summaries of failures and excessive latency

- Any errors and warnings that were generated

What you should see during stress tests are many warnings about failed operations. Count those as carefully as possible – do they match the number of failed operations in your stress tests? Does the number of successful operations, plus the number of failure warnings, equal the total number of actions you attempted? Check for any discrepancies.

A particularly pernicious bug is dropped log messages. This can easily happen in a distributed system when one source of logs produces them faster than their destination can process. It's so damaging because the failure is often silent. By definition, it's the logs and alarms that warn you about problems, and those are missing, so you have no warning. Missing logs can delay and disrupt the diagnosis of many other issues, leaving you with unsolvable puzzles and impossible events. If one log line should always follow another but in this case it's absent, you can waste time investigating why that code didn't run correctly before realizing the code was fine, and the log line was missing.

Stress testing is an excellent way to verify your logging system under the highest load it needs to sustain and to check that you see the correct logs, warnings, and errors.

Then you need to check the results of each load operation. As described in *Chapter 5, Black-Box Functional Testing* – don't just read API return codes, but perform a second check, ideally from another interface, to ensure each operation has its intended effect.

As with load testing, the trick is to aggregate the results and see your percentage of failures. That's the measure to test against the requirements. Stress testing is more complex than load testing because you will expect some rate of errors, so you will need to add both and compare the totals.

To diagnose errors, you'll also need to use the same techniques as when load testing, as described in the *Identifying bottlenecks* section. This time you'll have to filter out the expected errors to isolate the genuine problems, but you should use the approach of starting with the logs and examining the system resources for machines under load.

There will likely be many transient issues, and you must prioritize which you investigate. Problems in stress testing often aren't clear-cut, so you'll have to choose where to spend your time. Be disciplined and try not to get side-tracked by checking unimportant problems. Only check those that happen most often, or have the worst effects. The others can wait until they become a bigger issue.

Summary

Stress testing puts all your skills as a tester to use: you need to identify all your system's functions: black-box and white-box testing and all the error cases that can occur, as well as using all the visibility you put in place from monitoring and logging, the degradations from destructive testing, and all the tools from load testing.

With all those tools in place, you can perform tests specific to stress testing. We saw how tests could breach transaction rates with policed and unpoliced limits. We considered the performance of the code, either deliberately handling excessive operations with graceful degradation or suffering from stress-related failures, such as positive feedback loops.

Loading on your system can take different forms – with soak testing over long periods or spikes of load, which can be mitigated with queues. Excess loading can also be caused by limiting system resources, which introduces its own class of issues, as does introducing realistic errors, such as network delays, into your testing.

Finally, we looked at what to check during load testing, ensuring you saw warnings for failures but no errors, and that the logging worked correctly.

If you can marshal all of your skills, stress testing probes your system to its limits, letting you thoroughly understand its behavior during any realistic scenarios it will face while running live. If it passes these tests, you have genuinely put your system through its paces and gained the highest confidence in its performance. Congratulations!

Conclusion

Congratulations on reaching the end of the book! You have just learned a vast amount about software testing, which I painstakingly pieced together after decades of research, training, and trial and error. I've worked on a wide variety of products in many different roles and with many amazing engineers. If you can apply these lessons to test your product, you will uncover a host of issues and be able to release code with far more confidence.

This book describes just one step in the software development process: what tests you should run against your code. With an application sitting in front of you, what should you do to uncover its defects and gain confidence that it is of high quality? Testing is a vital step to ensure software quality, but it is far from the only one.

This book hasn't covered important topics such as designing quality in code and code testability, test team organization and approaches, investigating and raising bugs, or managing risk and release sign-off. For those, you will need other books. Here, we have solely focused on designing detailed, comprehensive test plans.

If you test carefully enough, you will always find a bug; if you haven't found any bugs, then you haven't tested carefully enough yet. Great products aren't those without bugs; they're the ones in which the bugs are small and understood. Not every issue is worth fixing, and when you test, you'll find all kinds.

Testing is like fishing. You can't guarantee you'll catch a whopper, but by using the best techniques and looking in the most fruitful areas, you give yourself the best chance. Sometimes, you'll catch minnows, and that is part of the process, because only by testing in detail will you land the huge targets that you're after. This book is your guide to successfully fishing for bugs.

There is a lot that can go wrong with a software application. Computers are some of the most complex machines ever built, from semiconductor doping to making sub-microscopic transistors for the CPUs as part of integrated circuits running operating systems, including vast bundles of libraries and languages that make programming possible. Even relying on all those layers to perform perfectly, the workings of any modern, commercial program routinely elude even the brightest minds to fully reason about. That's where testing comes in.

Anyone using your application is implicitly testing it, so the test effort can be spread among many people, from developers and product owners to support engineers and your end users. However, that usage will generally test a few core functions and user-facing cases. Dedicated testing uniquely steps systematically through an application's functionality.

In *Chapter 1, Making the Most of Exploratory Testing*, we saw the testing spiral, starting from the initial feature specification and implementation, cycling inward through loops of testing, results, improved specifications, and further discussions. This is an iterative process as the team together discovers the limitations and possibilities of their design. As a tester, you need to be part of those early discussions, to learn about the feature and to request any changes, such as debug interfaces or the logging you will need to use. The tester's task starts in earnest once the first implementation is complete, with exploratory testing to fully understand the changes.

Testing requires a detailed feature specification to work from, laying out in detail how a feature is supposed to work. Relying on intuition and assumption isn't enough. In *Chapter 2, Writing Great Feature Specifications*, we saw how to write great feature specifications that capture those details without describing the implementation, and *Chapter 3, How to Run Successful Specification Reviews*, showed how to get that reviewed and agreed upon by all the relevant stakeholders. Armed with a comprehensive description, informed by the product owner's requests, the developer's knowledge, and your exploratory testing and questions, testing can begin.

In *Chapter 4, Test Types, Cases, and Environments*, we saw the testing pyramid and the importance of using a variety of unit tests, integration tests, and system tests. Of those, unit tests should be the simplest and most numerous, as they are the quickest to run. Since they have the fewest dependencies, they are the most reliable, but by definition, they only test small parts of the behavior. System tests are more complex and harder to run but can uniquely discover bugs that only appear when the whole system is run together. Because of that, system tests are the focus of this book.

Chapter 4, Test Types, Cases, and Environments, also described how to write tests, ensuring they each test one thing but are independent, clearly named, grouped, and prioritized. We saw that tests need to be designed to fit into the release cycle – a few key tests that can be run against every build chosen from a much larger bank of exhaustive tests that are run more rarely.

Chapter 5, Black-Box Functional Testing, began to describe the tests themselves, starting with black-box testing techniques such as equivalence partitioning and boundary analysis. During black-box testing, you can use your naivety to take on the role of a customer and see what they might assume and what might surprise them. That's a useful new perspective to bring to the team before you learn more about the inner workings of a feature that is necessary for white-box testing, as shown in *Chapter 6, White-Box Functional Testing*.

All these test techniques have strengths and weaknesses, and only by combining them can you achieve great test coverage. While technically part of black-box testing, it is useful to consider error cases separately as they have a unique set of user interactions, which was described in *Chapter 7, Testing of Error Cases*. *Chapter 8, User Experience Testing*, discussed what to look for when testing user interfaces in general. Being visible, these are some of the simplest tests to run, although, with no obvious right answers, they can also lead to the most contentious discussions.

Security testing has much stricter rules, and *Chapter 9, Security Testing*, showed how to secure your application. Security issues are numerous and are common to many applications, so security testing is best performed with an external tool, although it is important to understand its tests and findings.

Maintainability is an oddity as it does not affect your user's experience of your product but is vital to be able to monitor, improve, and support it. Logging and monitoring requirements can be neglected, but it's in your own best interests as a tester to ensure they receive sufficient care.

The final section of the book considered non-functional testing. These tests repeated cases that had already been run, but now under extreme conditions: either while the system runs in a degraded state (*Chapter 11, Destructive Testing*), while taken to its loading limits (*Chapter 12, Load Testing*), or pushed beyond them (*Chapter 13, Stress Testing*). These tests need careful checks to measure system resources and performance so that you are ready for the day your product takes off and users flock to use your application.

This is the idealized, gold-plated version of testing. You are unlikely to have time to run all these areas in detail for every feature. Instead, these ideas should be weapons in your armory. Consider them for each project – perhaps a new feature has particular security concerns, adds significant system load, or involves a whole new user interface. Prioritize your tests, and if some areas receive little attention, ensure that is a conscious choice rather than a mistake.

Best of luck running your tests, finding bugs, and releasing great products!

Appendix – Example Feature Specification

This is an example of feature specification for a login feature. It is incomplete because it doesn't include the user interface descriptions, such as the wording of error messages and the appearance of the screens and buttons. All those gaps are noted, and to fully test the feature, you would need all that information from the user experience team.

However, it is complete as a feature specification of the login feature:

ID	Requirement	Notes
Section 1 – Enabling login		
1.1	In version 5.7.1 and later, users can log in to the `example.com` website.	
1.2	By default, when upgrading to a version that supports logging in, logging in is disabled.	
1.3	Logging in can be enabled via a configuration option in version 5.7.1 and later.	Set the `enable_login` option to `True` in the `login_configuration.conf` file.
1.4	Logging in can be disabled via a configuration option in version 5.7.1 and later.	
1.5	When logging in is disabled, the Login button disappears from the web page.	
1.6	When logging in is disabled, all user details are saved.	
1.7	When logging in is re-enabled, users who had previously signed in can log in again.	

Section 2 – Login screen		
2.1	When a user is logged out, the Login button appears in the top right-hand corner of every page in the interface.	You will need to list all those pages.
2.2	The appearance of the Login button is shown in graphic 1.	(Not included here)
2.3	Clicking on the Login button takes users to the login screen.	
2.4	The login screen contains five elements: 1. An email address textbox 2. A password textbox 3. A Submit button 4. A sign-up page link 5. A forgotten password page link	
2.5	The appearance of the login screen is shown in graphic 2.	(Not included here)
2.6	Clicking on the sign-up page link on the login screen takes the user to the Signup page.	(Remember to keep your requirements obvious!)
2.7	Clicking on the forgotten password link on the login screen takes the user to the forgotten password page.	
2.8	The email address textbox on the login screen validates the email.	See the standard requirements for email validity.
2.9	The password box on the login screen does not show the text the user enters.	
2.10	The maximum length of the email address field on the login screen is 320 characters.	
2.11	The maximum length of the password field on the login screen is 50 characters.	
2.12	If the user enters an incorrect email and password combination, an error message appears letting them know.	(Wording not included here)
2.13	If a user enters a valid email address and password combination, they are taken to the home page.	
2.14	When a user is logged in, the account menu is shown at the top right of every page.	Instead of the login button
2.15	The appearance of the account menu is shown in graphic 3.	(Not included here)

2.16	The account menu has a single option to log out.	
2.17	Pressing the Log out button keeps the user on the same page but logs them out.	
2.18	Other than displaying the account menu, logging in has no effect on the web pages.	Actually, doing something with the login is covered in version 2 and is not covered here.
2.19	If a user who has already logged out logs out again, it has no effect.	For instance, if they use a stale webpage having logged out elsewhere
2.20	Pressing the Log out button once logs out every login session for that user.	Even if they were logged in using 10 different browsers, logging 1 out logs them all out.
2.21	A single user can log in up to 20 times using different tabs and browsers.	There's no limit in the code to how many times a user can be logged in; we will test up to 20.
Section 3 – Security		
3.1	If the user enters an incorrect email and password combination, the same error message always appears.	There aren't separate error messages if the email address is correct for privacy.
3.2	If the user enters an incorrect email and password combination, the error message appears for the same length of time regardless of whether the email address is valid.	So, attackers can't use the length of time of response to detect valid email addresses.
3.3	Users are limited to three attempts to log in with the same password per minute (using a rolling window).	
3.4	If a user attempts to log in more than three times in a minute, then an error message appears, letting them know.	(Wording not included here)
3.5	The login, sign-up, and password reset screens are protected against CSRF attacks.	
3.6	Email addresses are stored securely and are only available to employees who require access.	(That needs to be specified; support needs to be able to look people up, the development team shouldn't generally have access to live data, and so on)

3.7	Passwords are hashed and stored securely.	The algorithm should be specified.
3.8	Users are logged out after 10 minutes of inactivity.	If they visit a page after that, they would need to log in again.

Section 4 – Sign-up		
4.1	On the Signup page, there are five elements: 1. An email address field 2. A password field 3. A password confirmation field 4. A Submit button 5. A link back to the login page	
4.2	The maximum length of the email address field on the sign-up screen is 320 characters.	
4.3	The maximum length of the password field on the login screen is 50 characters.	
4.4	Passwords entered on the sign-up screen are validated for complexity.	(Complexity requirements not included here)
4.5	The email address field on the Signup page is validated.	See the standard requirements for email validity.
4.6	The password field does not show the text that the user has entered.	
4.7	If the user enters an invalid email address, then they are shown a warning when they submit the form.	(Wording not included here)
4.8	If the user enters an invalid password, then they are shown a warning when they submit the form.	(Wording not included here)
4.9	If the user enters passwords that don't match, then they are shown a warning when they submit the form.	(Wording not included here)
4.10	If the user enters a new email address that has never been used before, then an email is sent to that address to verify the account.	

4.11	If the user enters an email address that has been entered previously but not verified, then another email is sent to the address to be verified.	
4.12	No feedback should be given to the requester as to whether the email already exists.	To avoid leaking information about email addresses already in use on the system
4.13	If the user enters an email address that has been verified but doesn't have a password set up, then another email is sent to the user with a new link to the password page.	
4.14	If the user enters an email address with a verified email address with a password set, then they are sent another email with a link to the page to reset their password.	
4.15	Verification emails are sent within 1 minute of being requested.	
4.16	The appearance verification emails are shown in graphic 4.	(Not included here)
4.17	When the user clicks a link in the verification email, they are sent to the login screen.	
4.18	When the user clicks a link in the verification email, the system records that that email address has been verified.	(State which database column records that state)
4.19	If a user clicks the link to the Login page on the Signup page, they are taken to the Login page.	
Section 5 – Password reset		
5.1	The password reset page includes three elements: 1. An email address field 2. A Submit button 3. A link to the sign-in page	
5.2	The email address field on the password reset page is validated.	
5.3	If the user enters an invalid email address, then they are shown a warning when they submit the form.	(Wording not included here)

5.4	Whether the email address is on our system or not, the user is shown the same message.	To avoid leaking information about which email addresses have been signed up to the system
5.5	If a user requests to reset the password of an email address that is on the system, then the application sends a password reset email.	
5.6	The appearance of the password reset email is shown in graphic 5.	(Not included here)
5.7	If a user requests to reset the password of an email address that is not on the system, then the application does nothing.	
5.8	The password reset email includes a secure link to let that user reset their password.	
5.9	If a user clicks the link to the Login page on the password reset page, they are taken to the Signup page to enter a new password.	
5.10	If a user enters an existing email address and a new password on the Signup page after following a reset password email link, then the password on their existing account is updated.	
5.11	There are no requirements for new passwords to be different from previous passwords for a user.	
5.12	If an email delivery fails, then no indication is given to a user, but an internal error is raised.	
5.13	Password reset links are valid for 24 hours.	
5.14	If a user clicks an out-of-date password link, then they are redirected to the login page.	
5.15	Users can send a maximum of three password reset emails in a 10-minute rolling window.	
5.16	Password reset emails are sent within 1 minute of being requested.	

Section 6 – Performance		
6.1	The application can support 50 sign-ups per second.	
6.2	The application can support 100 logins per second.	
6.3	The application can support logging in and then out within 1 second.	
6.4	The application can support logging out and then back in within 1 second.	
6.5	All application web pages load within 3 seconds.	
6.6	The application supports 1,000,000 user accounts.	
6.7	The application supports 1,000 users logged in simultaneously.	

Section 7 – Interoperability		
7.1	The login function works on the following web browsers: • Chrome • Firefox • Edge • Safari • Opera	
7.2	The login function works on the last three versions of each web browser.	
7.3	The login function works on the following operating systems: • Windows • macOS • iOS • Android	
7.4	The minimum width of all screens is 512 pixels.	
7.5	The maximum width of all screens is 4,096 pixels.	(Note that this is limited; it's just what we'll test up to)

Section 8 – Documentation		
8.1	All textboxes include tooltips.	(Wording not included here)
8.2	The written documentation describes how to sign up, log in, and reset your password.	
8,3	All existing screenshots in the documentation include the account menu.	
8.4	All existing instructional videos include the account menu.	
Section 9 – Events		
9.1	An event is raised every time a user logs in.	
9.2	An event is raised every time a user signs up.	
9.3	An event is raised every time a user logs out or when their login times out.	
9.4	The system displays how many users have signed up.	On an internal metrics page, which also needs to be specified
9.5	The system displays how many users have signed in during the last 7 days.	

Table A.1 – A functional specification for a simple login page

Index

`Packt.com`

Subscribe to our online digital library for full access to over 7,000 books and videos, as well as industry leading tools to help you plan your personal development and advance your career. For more information, please visit our website.

Why subscribe?

- Spend less time learning and more time coding with practical eBooks and Videos from over 4,000 industry professionals
- Improve your learning with Skill Plans built especially for you
- Get a free eBook or video every month
- Fully searchable for easy access to vital information
- Copy and paste, print, and bookmark content

Did you know that Packt offers eBook versions of every book published, with PDF and ePub files available? You can upgrade to the eBook version at `packt.com` and as a print book customer, you are entitled to a discount on the eBook copy. Get in touch with us at `customercare@packtpub.com` for more details.

At `www.packt.com`, you can also read a collection of free technical articles, sign up for a range of free newsletters, and receive exclusive discounts and offers on Packt books and eBooks.

Other Books You May Enjoy

If you enjoyed this book, you may be interested in these other books by Packt:

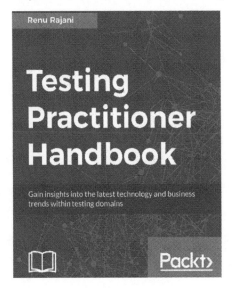

Testing Practitioner Handbook

Renu Rajani

ISBN: 978-1-78829-954-1

- Understand the TCOE model, managed services, the structure of testing in Agile/DevOps engagements, factory models, and crowdsourcing

- Implement testing processes, practices, and automation tools in the Agile/DevOps life cycle

- Adapt to current technologies in social media, mobile, analytics and the Cloud

- Leverage cognitive intelligence/machine-learning, robotics, and the Internet of Things in testing

- How key industries/domains (consumer products and retail, energy and utilities, healthcare, telecom, and automotive) adapt to digital transformation

- Future directions for the QA industry, consulting careers, testing profession, and professionals

API Testing and Development with Postman

Dave Westerveld

ISBN: 978-1-80056-920-1

- Find out what is involved in effective API testing
- Use data-driven testing in Postman to create scalable API tests
- Understand what a well-designed API looks like
- Become well-versed with API terminology, including the different types of APIs
- Get to grips with performing functional and non-functional testing of an API
- Discover how to use industry standards such as OpenAPI and mocking in Postman

Packt is searching for authors like you

If you're interested in becoming an author for Packt, please visit `authors.packtpub.com` and apply today. We have worked with thousands of developers and tech professionals, just like you, to help them share their insight with the global tech community. You can make a general application, apply for a specific hot topic that we are recruiting an author for, or submit your own idea.

Share Your Thoughts

Now you've finished *Software Test Design*, we'd love to hear your thoughts! Scan the QR code below to go straight to the Amazon review page for this book and share your feedback or leave a review on the site that you purchased it from.

`https://packt.link/r/1-804-61256-1`

Your review is important to us and the tech community and will help us make sure we're delivering excellent quality content.

Download a free PDF copy of this book

Thanks for purchasing this book!

Do you like to read on the go but are unable to carry your print books everywhere?

Is your eBook purchase not compatible with the device of your choice?

Don't worry, now with every Packt book you get a DRM-free PDF version of that book at no cost.

Read anywhere, any place, on any device. Search, copy, and paste code from your favorite technical books directly into your application.

The perks don't stop there, you can get exclusive access to discounts, newsletters, and great free content in your inbox daily

Follow these simple steps to get the benefits:

1. Scan the QR code or visit the link below

https://packt.link/free-ebook/9781804612569

2. Submit your proof of purchase
3. That's it! We'll send your free PDF and other benefits to your email directly

Made in United States
Orlando, FL
08 January 2024